D1518260

The Economic Modernization of Spain,
1830–1930

THE ECONOMIC MODERNIZATION OF SPAIN, 1830–1930

Edited by
NICOLÁS SÁNCHEZ-ALBORNOZ

TRANSLATED BY KAREN POWERS AND MANUEL SAÑUDO

NEW YORK UNIVERSITY PRESS
New York and London

Library of Congress Cataloging-in-Publication Data

Modernización económica de España, 1830–1930.
   English.
   The economic modernization of Spain, 1830–1930.

   Translation of: La modernización económica de España,
1830–1930.
   Includes index.
   1. Spain—Economic conditions.   2. Spain—History—
19th century.   3. Spain—History—20th century.
I. Sánchez-Albornoz, Nicolás.   II. Title.
HC385.M62313   1987   330.946'.07   87-5535
ISBN 0-8147-7861-5

CONTENTS

List of Tables and Graphs   *vii*
Preface   *xi*
Contributors   *xiii*

1. Introduction: The Economic Modernization of Spain   *1*
   NICOLÁS SÁNCHEZ-ALBORNOZ

I.   TRANSFORMATIONS IN THE MAIN SECTORS

2. Spain's Demographic Modernization, 1800–1930   *13*
   VICENTE PÉREZ MOREDA

3. Agriculture: A Slow-Moving Sector, 1830–1935   *42*
   GABRIEL TORTELLA

4. A Century of Industrialization in Spain, 1833–1930   *63*
   JORDI NADAL
   with an appendix: An Annual Index of Spanish   *75*
   Industrial Output by ALBERT CARRERAS

5. Transportation and Economic Growth, 1830–1930   *90*
   ANTONIO GÓMEZ MENDOZA

6. Development and Modernization   *107*
   of the Financial System, 1844–1935
   PABLO MARTÍN ACEÑA

7. Foreign Trade and the Spanish Economy   *128*
   during the Nineteenth Century
   LEANDRO PRADOS DE LA ESCOSURA

8. Economic Nationalism and State Intervention,   *151*
   1900–1930
   JOSÉ LUIS GARCÍA DELGADO

v

II. REGIONAL PERSPECTIVES

 9. The Industrial Revolution in Catalonia   *169*
     JORDI MALUQUER DE MOTES

10. The Basque Provinces and the World Market,   *191*
     1900–1930
     PEDRO FRAILE

11. Early Industrialization in Asturias: *213*
     Bounds and Constraints
     RAFAEL ANES

12. Economic Transformations in Galicia in the Nineteenth   *22ɔ*
     and Twentieth Centuries
     JAIME GARCÍA-LOMBARDERO

13. Castile, 1830–1930:   *240*
     The Rise of a Neo-Archaic Agriculture
     NICOLÁS SÁNCHEZ-ALBORNOZ

14. On the Historical Origins   *251*
     of Andalusian Underdevelopment
     PEDRO TEDDE DE LORCA

15. Exports, Internal Demand, and Economic Growth   *268*
     in Valencia
     JORDI PALAFOX

Index   *291*

LIST OF TABLES AND GRAPHS

Tables

	Exchange Rates (1913)	xii
2.1	The Population of Spain, 1787–1930; Annual Average Growth Rates, 1797–1930	14
2.2	Demographic Characteristics of Some European Countries	16
2.3	Average Annual Demographic Growth Rates in the Historical Regions of Spain	18
2.4	Regional Variations in Marital Fertility, 1787–1910	22
2.5	Crude Birth and Death Rates, 1878–1930	24
2.6	Spanish Marriage Patterns, 1787 and 1887–1980	28
2.7	The Urban Population of Spain, 1836–1930	32
2.8	Average Annual Demographic Growth Rates for the Provincial Capitals of Each Region, 1837–1930	33
2.9	Distribution of the Active Population According to Economic Sectors	35
3.1	Sectoral Distribution of Key Indicators, 1900 and 1935	42
3.2	Value of Disentailed Estates, 1798–1900	45
3.3	Crops and Yields of Spanish Agriculture in 1857	48
3.4	Estimated Yearly Cereal Output in Decade Averages, 1800–1929	49
3.5	Agricultural Yields in Several European Countries, 1890–1910	50
3.6	Agricultural Output, Farmland, and Productivity, 1893–1931	53
4.1	Spun Cotton Per Capita	69
4.2	Cast Iron and Steel Per Capita Output	71
4.3	Production of Superphosphated Lime in 1929	73
4.1A	Spanish Industrial Output Indexes (1913 = 100) and Annual Growth Rates	77
4.2A	Five-Year Growth Rates of Spanish Industrial Output, 1831–1935	78
4.3A	Growth Rates of Spanish Industrial Ouput and National Income, 1831–1935	82

4.4A	IPI Growth Rates in Some European Countries, 1831–1935	84
4.5A	Growth Rates of Industrial Output: Spain and "Europe," 1913–1935	86
5.1	Net Trade Flows in Grain, Flour, Wine, and Textiles, 1878 and 1913	101
6.1	Financial Institutions: Total Assets, 1854–1935	113
6.2	Relations between Financial Magnitudes in Nonissuing Private Banks, 1854–1930	114
6.3	Average Annual Growth Rates of Assets of Financial Institutions in Various European Countries	118
6.4	Issue Ratios of Financial Institutions in Various European Countries	119
6.5	Relation of Financial Institutions' Assets to National Product, 1880–1938	120
6.6	The Quantity of Money and Its Components, 1874–1935	122
7.1	Spain's Foreign Trade, 1815–1913	132
7.2	Retained Value of F.O.B. Domestic Exports, 1865–1913	133
7.3	Spanish Foreign Trade: Annual Growth Rates, 1815–1913	134
7.4	Contribution of the Main Commodities to the Increase in Total Exports, 1826–1913	136
7.5	Contribution of the Main Commodities to the Increase in Total Imports, 1826–1913	138
7.6	Ratios of Exports and Imports to National Income: Spain and Europe, 1830–1910	139
7.7	Direct Contribution of Exports to Spain's Economic Growth, 1830–1910	141
7.8	Impact on National Income of Keeping Constant the Net Barter Terms of Trade, 1830–1910	144
9.1	Distribution of the Active Population by Sectors, 1930–1931	170
9.2	Estimates of Added Value, 1914	171
9.3	Per Capita Electricity Output in 1934	171
9.4	Steampower in Industry	172
9.5	The Cotton Industry in 1861	178
9.6	Annual Costs of One Spindle for Cotton Spinning	182
10.1	Trade in Coal and Iron Ore between Great Britain and the Metallurgical Regions of the European and Mediterranean Periphery, 1885–1934	196
10.2	International Iron Ore Market, 1913	197

10.3   F.O.B. Price of "Best" Shipped from Bilbao, 1906–1934   *198*
10.4   British and North American Imports of Iron-and-Steel
        Products, 1900–1935   *201*
10.5   Imports of European Manufactures, 1896–1930   *204*
10.6   Italian and Swedish Exports of Machinery and Capital
        Goods to Great Britain, 1900–1935   *205*
12.1   The Population of Galicia, 1752–1930   *224*
12.2   Cumulative Annual Growth Rates of the Galician
        Population, 1752–1930   *225*
12.3   Cattle Exports to England, 1842–1900   *230*
12.4   Number of Cattle Traded, 1842–1931   *232*
12.5   Land Cultivated for Diverse Crops, 1902–1930   *233*
13.1   Agricultural Gross Product in Old Castile and León,
        1860–1931   *247*
15.1   Average Annual Growth Rates of Orange and Wine Exports,
        1866–1935   *270*
15.2   Prices and Volume of Ordinary Wine Exports, 1874–1898   *271*
15.3   Evolution of Land Area Growing Oranges, 1878–1936   *272*
15.4   Income Distribution for Some Valencian Crops   *273*
15.5   Irrigated Area in Valencia, 1900–1928   *275*
15.6   Crop Distribution on Irrigated Lands, 1922   *283*

Graphs and Map

1.1   Map of Spain—Historical Regions and Main Cities   *12*
4.1A   Indexes of Spanish Industrial Output, 1831–1935   *78*
4.2A   IPIES Annual Growth Rates, 1843–1935   *81*
9.1   Energy Substitution in the Textile Industry: The Case of
        Terrassa   *184*
10.1   British Imports of Iron-and-Steel Products   *202*
10.2   American Imports of Iron-and-Steel Products   *203*
10.3   British Imports of Machinery and Capital Goods   *204*
10.4   British Imports of Italian and Swedish Machinery and
        Capital Goods   *206*
12.1   Number of Heads of Cattle in Galicia, 1859–1935   *232*
15.1   Model of the Impact of Increased Foreign Demand on an
        Economy with Idle Resources   *279*

PREFACE

THIS BOOK is addressed to two different audiences. There are readers who look for books on Spain and its past. Most general works on Spanish history in English focus on major political topics such as its imperial days or its contemporary dramas. Instead, this volume discusses a noteworthy, though neglected, historical issue: the economic development of Spain during the nineteenth and twentieth centuries. The book thus helps the reader comprehend how the present economic conditions—and obliquely Spain's social and political life—were actually shaped.

There are, of course, those who understand how the world economy has radically changed since the Industrial Revolution. Much of what they have learned, however, is how the leading economies performed during this process of change. For comparative purposes, or in order to broaden their scope they may wish to read about less successful nations that completed their transformation later. Spain is among those which long trailed but which has finally reached the end of the road. Its present economy does not rank among the most technologically advanced ones, but by all general standards it belongs to the industrial world.

The book brings together studies by various authors who sum up their most recent research and thoughts on this matter. When I suggested to the Universidad Internacional Menéndez Pelayo that it invite economic historians to discuss Spanish economic modernization, the time seemed ripe for such an endeavor. A group of doctoral dissertations was recently completed and published. Fresh data and an updated methodology provided in these dissertations had extensively renewed this field. Meanwhile, historians from a previous generation had also made important contributions. Presently, modern economic history is a thriving discipline in Spain. To a large extent, this book reflects the state of the art.

During the summer of 1983 historians met in Santander under the auspices of the Universidad Internacional. Suggestions made after the debate concluded that all essays presented there should be published together in one book. These essays are presented here after having been twice completely revised. To the Spanish edition (Madrid: Alianza Editorial, 1985) have been added some updated materials; some redundant arguments and information were omitted, and implications were made explicit for the benefit of an English language readership. With the same purpose in mind, Gabriel Tortella agreed to rewrite his essay, and he presented it in English (Chapter 3). There he recalls basic agricultural developments that previously seemed too obvious to be mentioned for Spanish readers. Albert Carreras, who recently completed an annual estimate of Spanish industrial output up to 1981, kindly agreed to make available and to comment on the 1842–1930 series as a statistical appendix to the general discussion on industrialization by Jordi Nadal (Chapter 4).

The editor wishes to praise the authors for enthusiastically responding to all requests. Special thanks, however, go to Gabriel Tortella and Albert Carreras—as well as to Pablo Martín Aceña who efficiently helped to organize the Santander meeting. Rendering the quite different styles was a hard task that the translators, Karen Powers and Manuel Sañudo, performed effectively. To the new and active Program for Cultural Cooperation between Spain's Ministry of Culture and North American universities, at Minneapolis, recognition is extended for providing funds for the translation of the book. Last but not least, the Universidad Internacional Menéndez Pelayo deserves our gratitude. The most pleasant part of its multiple support was felt when it regally hosted the authors whose contributions are published here in the Magdalena Palace, which overlooks the ocean and the Bay of Santander.

Nicolás Sánchez-Albornoz
New York University

Exchange Rates (1913)

1 British pound	= 25.00 pesetas
1 United States dollar	= 5.14 pesetas
1 German mark	= 1.25 pesetas
1 French or Swiss franc	= 1.00 peseta

NOTE: The exchange rates did not fluctuate greatly prior to 1913.

CONTRIBUTORS

Rafael Anes, formerly at the Historical Research Group of the Banco de España, is now Professor of Economic History at the Universidad de Oviedo. His major contributions are: "Relación entre el ferrocarril y la economía española, 1865–1935," *Los ferrocarriles en España* (Madrid, 1978) and "La industria asturiana en la segunda mitad del siglo XIX," *Revista de Historia Económica* 1, no. 2 (1983).

Albert Carreras teaches economic history at the Universidad de Barcelona. His unpublished dissertation (1983) compares Spanish and Italian industrialization from mid-nineteenth century to the present. He recently contributed "Gasto Nacional Bruto y formación de capital en España, 1849–1958," to *La Nueva Historia Económica en España* (Madrid, 1985), edited by Pablo Martín Aceña and Leandro Prados de la Escosura.

José Luis García Delgado is Professor of Economic Structure at the Universidad Complutense, Madrid, and Deputy Rector of the Universidad Internacional Menéndez Pelayo. He wrote jointly with Santiago Roldán *La formación de la sociedad capitalista en España, 1914–1920,* 2 vols. (Madrid, 1973). His study, "La industrialización española en el primer tercio del siglo XX," has appeared in Ramón Menéndez Pidal, *Historia de España,* vol. 37 (Madrid, 1984).

Pedro Fraile received his Ph.D. from the University of Texas and then joined the Department of Economics of Trinity University (San Antonio). His study, "Crecimiento económico y demanda de acero: España, 1900–1950," has appeared in P. Martin Aceña and L. Prados, *La Nueva Historia Económica en España* (Madrid, 1985).

Jaime García-Lombardero is Professor of Economic History at the Universidad de Santiago and is the author of *La agricultura y el estancamiento económico de Galicia en la España del Antiguo Régimen* (Madrid, 1973).

Antonio Gómez Mendoza received his Ph.D. from Oxford University and is currently at the Department of Economic History of the Universidad Complutense. His major works are: *Ferrocarriles y cambio económico en España (1855–1913)* (Madrid, 1982) and *Ferrocarril y mercado interior en España (1874–1913),* 2 vols. (Madrid, 1984 and 1985).

Jordi Maluquer de Motes, Professor of Economic History at the Universidad Autónoma de Barcelona, is the author of *El socialismo en España, 1833–1868* (Barcelona, 1977). Coauthor of "Un segle d'industrialització catalana, 1833–1936," *Catalunya, la fàbrica d'Espanya* (Barcelona, 1985).

Pablo Martín Aceña studied economics at the Universities of Madrid and Toronto and teaches economic history at the Universidad de Alcalá de Henares. He is also at the Instituto National de Industria. He published *La política monetaria en España, 1919–1935* (Madrid, 1984), *La cantidad de dinero en España, 1900–1935* (Madrid, 1985), and co-edited with L. Prados de la Escosura, *La Nueva Historia Económica en España* (Madrid, 1985).

Jordi Nadal is currently at the Universidad de Barcelona. In 1978 he was visiting at the Institute for Advanced Study at Princeton, New Jersey. His major publications in English are "The Failure of the Industrial Revolution in Spain, 1830–1914," and, with Josep Fontana, "Spain, 1914–1970," both in *The Fontana Economic History of Europe* (Glasgow, 1973 and 1976), vols. 4(2) and 6(2).

Jordi Palafox teaches economic history at the Universidad de Valencia. He is the author of "Estructura de la exportación y distribución de beneficios. La naranja en el País Valenciano (1920–1930)," *Revista de Historia Económica 1,* no. 2 (1983).

Vicente Pérez Moreda teaches historical demography at the Universidad Complutense, Madrid, and has published a book entitled *Las crisis de mortalidad en la España interior, siglos XVI–XIX* (Madrid, 1980).

Leandro Prados de la Escosura studied economics at the Universities of Madrid and Oxford and teaches at Alcalá de Henares. He wrote *Comercio exterior y crecimiento económico en España, 1826–1913* (Madrid, 1982) and "El comercio hispano-británico en los siglos XVIII y XIX," *Revista de Historia Económica 2,* no. 2 (1984). He is also co-editor with P. Martín Aceña of *La Nueva Historia Económica en España* (Madrid, 1985).

Nicolás Sánchez-Albornoz, Professor of History at New York University, is the author of two books of essays—*Jalones en la modernización de España* (Barcelona, 1975) and *España hace un siglo: una economía dual* (Madrid, 1977)—and of three books on nineteenth-century Spanish agricultural prices (Madrid, 1975–1983).

Pedro Tedde de Lorca heads the Historical Research Group of the Banco de España and teaches economic history at the Universidad de Málaga. He is the author of "La banca privada durante la Restauración (1874–1974)," in *La* *banca española en la Restauración,* 2 vols. (Madrid, 1974), and "La Compañía de los Ferrocarriles Andaluces (1878–1920)," *Investigaciones Económicas* 12 (1980).

Gabriel Tortella received his Ph.D. from the University of Wisconsin and taught at the University of Pittsburgh. He is now Professor of Economic History at the Universidad de Alcalá de Henares and editor of *Revista de Historia Económica.* Among his many publications is a book in English: *Banking, Railroads, and Industry in Spain, 1829–1874* (New York, 1977).

1.

INTRODUCTION: THE ECONOMIC MODERNIZATION OF SPAIN

NICOLÁS SÁNCHEZ-ALBORNOZ
New York University

SPAIN played a leading role in the economic growth of the early Modern Age. By incorporating the New World into the world economy, Spain both extended the physical range of the economy and contributed to its overall growth. American precious metals, redistributed through Spain, gave Europe the monetary base on which that economy was able to prosper; in addition, Spain opened up America as a market for Europe. The trade between these continents greatly favored the accumulation of capital and the development of an economic system based on this. Because of its overseas empire, Spain became the world's leading economic power. Its preeminence lasted for over a hundred years, losing ground during the seventeenth century to other, more dynamic economies until the beginning of the nineteenth century, but Spain nevertheless remained powerful enough to keep its overseas possessions and thus to continue to be part of the circle of privileged nations.

Spanish economic history during the early Modern Age is well known, at least in its more conspicuous aspects. Yet, the following period of retrenchment is less well known. It is precisely during this less brilliant time that Spain struggled to become a modern nation. The move from an old to a modern economy has not as yet attracted much attention from historians. For different historical reasons than those given for the early Modern Age, the last one and a half centuries are also important years for the Spanish economy.

Between 1810 and 1824, Spain lost virtually all its overseas empire, retaining only Cuba, Puerto Rico, and the Philippines, which it managed to hold on to until the end of the nineteenth century. These imperial losses compelled the Spanish economy to readjust. Incidentally, in the twentieth century, other European countries have endured an experience similar to Spain's; herein could lie a point for broad comparisons. Spain's setback coincided with the

1

rise of a mercantile and capitalist economy as the country initiated its industrialization. The other nations, however, had already adopted the capitalist system before their major colonial expansion took place. Also, early in the nineteenth century a large part of Spanish production equipment was destroyed during the War for Independence (1808–1814). It took a long time before the level of activity prior to the Napoleonic invasion was again reached. Any actual growth in the Spanish economy was then retarded. Decolonization and destruction, both noneconomic factors, halted the Spanish initial transformation and widened the gap by which emerging industrial nations were overtaking Spain.

The full process of modernization took almost two centuries. The first signs of change can be traced back to the end of the eighteenth century. Jordi Nadal has precisely stated that Catalonia was an "early comer" to industrialization. This region certainly was then among the European regions that initiated change, however, this early start miscarried. Cotton manufacturing was delayed and got under way about 1830.

This book discusses the transition to modernization, most of which took place between 1830 and 1930. It does not cover early steps or the hiatus during the deep and long crisis endured during the first third of the nineteenth century. Nor does it discuss the final stage. Before the process was completed, another dark crisis, the Spanish Civil War, ended a long period of sustained growth and postponed for another quarter of a century the full industrial transformation of the nation. The book deals with the century between those critical periods. These more placid intermediate years afforded the country the chance for a cumulative progress and for a reshaping of its economy. Among the advantages Spain enjoyed at the time was its geographic location near those European economies which first industrialized. Technology, capital, and the demand for goods reached Spain much sooner than the countries situated at the distant periphery from this core. The transitional phase took a substantial period of time, but it was finally completed, and Spain now occupies an intermediate position between the most advanced economies and the developing ones. Spain's economy is therefore comparable to that of those nations of Central Europe and the Mediterranean which did not modernize early but did so during a second wave.

Historians label in various ways the sort of changes which we will be discussing. The term "industrial revolution" is the oldest designation in use. In line with this, Nadal wrote an economic history of Spain in the nineteenth century which he described as "the failure of the industrial revolution in Spain." Industrialization is by now a more common expression. Other historians prefer to speak instead of the formation of a capitalist society. S. Roldán and J. L. García Delgado have used such a term when they studied a brief stage of industrialization in early-twentieth-century Spain, as has M. Gónzalez Portilla when he discusses a similar process in the Basque Provinces. Indeed, the term "capitalism" refers to a broad range of economic changes embracing many fields, such as farming, trade, and finance, but which did not necessarily foster industrialization. For instance, capitalism spread throughout Spain, but industrialization was restricted to a few regions. "Modernization" includes both concepts, industrialization and the rise of capitalism, simultaneously; in addition, it refers to its related social transformations. But this broader expression presents its own problems. Its content is less historically concrete than are the terms "industrialization" and "capitalism." Modernization tends to prompt the opposite concept of tradition, polarizing thought: new versus old. It does clearly suggest, however, a process of change. In addition, modernization is a relative term in that the point of comparison—modern as opposed to old—constantly moves forward in time.

To prevent terminological blurs, economic historians have set down a quantitative basis for modernization criteria. The need for numerical indexes responds to a broad historical trend favoring data measurements. The sporadic building of new industries or the adoption of certain commercial or financial practices, some of which had surfaced in the early Modern Age, do not appear by themselves to be sure signs of modernization. Such a level is only reached when a critical mass of changes is achieved. Hence, finances and demographics are, for instance, considered modern only from the moment changes in both sectors crossed a quantitative threshold, as we shall see later.

The term "modernization" seems best suited to describe the process which this book expects to describe. The book discusses a general process of change and analyzes the transformation of the Spanish economy between 1830 and 1930 from two perspectives. In Part I, seven studies examine national economic performances on a sector-by-sector basis. Following an overview of Spanish demography, the text covers the transformation in agriculture, industry, transportation, finance, and foreign trade. The last chapter of this part deals with the economic role the government played during the first three decades of the twentieth century. Part II examines the disparate experiences of the more significant economic regions of the country—Catalonia, the Basque Provinces, Asturias, Galicia, Castile, Andalusia, and Valencia—and considers what generalizations can be made, since, as will be seen, each region displays a different kind of behavior.

The first chapters suggest Spanish economy did indeed grow. In 1930 the volume of goods and services available was clearly much higher than in 1830. Population, finance, foreign trade, and national income show similar increases. This long-term increase, however, was neither linear nor sustained, as periodic crises in agriculture, industry, and finance interrupted but did not stifle growth. Downturns usually took place when a leading sector lost momentum. This often happened rather early after their start; for example, the cotton textile industry, after an initially successful period, quickly lost its vigor at the end of the nineteenth century. Foreign trade was also subject to bursts. Different items lead exports at different times. This frequent turnover clearly proves that the economy was versatile enough to take advantage of circumstances, but for the same reason the flow of exports appears unpredictable. After 1890 overall exports ceased to grow at as fast a rate as previously. The financial system then took an upward turn and became the most dynamic component of the economy. Between 1890 and 1930 the volume of financial transactions increased precisely when the export sector was contracting, so that the overall effects on the economy canceled each other out. Within most sectors there obviously were discontinuities, and between different sectors there was little correlation. Both types of imbalance were characteristic of growth during this period.

The overall achievements, however, remained modest. On a per capita basis, growth in volume and value appear moderate, and in comparing Spanish agriculture, industry and finance with that of the rest of Europe, the relative backwardness of Spain can be seen to have persisted or to have even increased. In view of this, it is no wonder that Nadal and others stress that the economic performance was a failure.

Economic growth does not lead directly to modernization. As factories, mines, railroads, and some banks began to populate the country, the prominent features of the industrial revolution penetrated into Spain. Agriculture sent its products to local or international markets; commerce put more goods into circulation; capital was amassed; capitalism took root in both the cities and the countryside. All this meant progress, but that qualitative leap which modernization implies did not come until the twentieth century. Then agriculture, finance, and population reached critical levels and generated new relationships, as Gabriel Tortella, Pablo Martín Aceña and Vicente Pérez Moreda show. Various thresholds were then crossed: farming production expanded as agricultural income and productivity grew; the level of banking activities increased in relation to the national income; and the population grew while there was a decrease in the more onerous vital statistics indexes.

The hundred years from 1830 to 1930 should thus be divided into two stages. The first, lasting until the end of the century, corresponds to the time when the economy heated up and underwent irregular, inadequate, yet preparatory changes. The second stage—during the first third of the twentieth century—featured significant transformations, though it lagged some fifty years behind similar transformations in the more advanced European nations. In 1930 the full transformation was still incomplete.

How did these changes occur during this transitional period? According to Nadal, the building of factories does not necessarily lead to industrialization. As already mentioned, Spain ventured into many industrial undertakings, but few of them lasted. Even the more successful ones, like textiles and iron and steel, were successful only in very relative terms. In both these industries, Nadal points out that in 1930 Spain's ranking among European countries had actually gone down. Nadal also discusses the often neglected chemical industry, which had access to many Spanish natural resources. In spite of such obvious comparative advantages, this industry never succeeded. As in other cases, a low internal demand seems to be responsible for such poor performance.

A short demand might be related to a limited purchasing power or to a deficient access to goods. Antonio Gómez Mendoza considers the second part of the alternative by discussing the extent to which the increase in the supply of transportation, principally railroad transportation, fostered economic development in Spain. Around 1850 the country's liberal rulers hoped that building a transportation system quickly would remove a bottleneck from the economy. An extended railroad network was thus constructed in a very short time, though in the long run the production and circulation of goods did not live up to early expectations. Had the system not been constructed, however, the economic development of Spain would have been set back for years and the economic gap in relation to other countries would have widened.

Pablo Martín Aceña analyzes the issue of currency. There were certain parallels between the rapid expansion of the financial system and the railroad system. In both cases, the goal and the means of attaining it, that is, through large foreign investments, were very similar. After establishing the basic banking structures in the nineteenth century, the banks began to exert their role of modern financial middlemen only at the beginning of the twentieth century.

If by increasing internal supply as industry and the railroads did, demand did not increase, producers should have sought to export. On the other hand, internal consumption could have been stimulated by the government, in such ways as in a reduction in the cost of food, but protectionism, which the government introduced, had the opposite effect: it kept the cost of food high. From here on, foreign trade and economic policy become critical points in the discussion. The importance of these issues is attested by the polemical overtones present in Leandro Prados's and José Luis García Delgado's chapters.

Spain exported raw materials and imported manufactured goods and capital. This scenario brings to mind the system that can be now observed in so many nations in the Periphery. In Spain, however, overall growth did not depend as heavily as in these nations on foreign trade. Exports did not contribute much to the growth of national income except during the years from 1860 to 1880, when they accounted for one-third of the growth. Foreign trade reached a limited but positive balance between 1815 and 1930, and according to Leandro Prados, the terms of trade were generally favorable to Spain. The center of the world's economy seems to have had a favorable effect on the Spanish economy. Internal changes, which exports encouraged, were themselves important. Foreign trade stirred otherwise idle land and mining resources, increasing both productivity and income in several regions. This, on the other hand, contrasts sharply with the marginal role colonial trade played then.

The economic model that Spain then developed looked primarily inward; its goal was to capture the large domestic market (the population of Spain in 1860 was half that of the United States), but this market suffered from a very weak consumptive capacity. Both industry and agriculture decided to corner the domestic market, and the weapon they chose to achieve it was the tariff. Protectionism, initially a reactive and short-term measure, became one of the most consistent and lasting policies that Spain pursued over the last century and a half. García Delgado explains in detail the high level which protectionism reached at the beginning of this century. After protectionism severely restricted foreign competition, domestic competition in turn began to be stifled; the old corporative tendencies of the Ancien Régime were revived in a noncompetitive capitalism.

Pérez Moreda's critical analysis of the overall Spanish demography should also be mentioned here. People interact with the economy as both producers and consumers. The population increased slowly along premodern lines and did not even move internally. People were thus not inducing a strong demand. Since, on the other hand, they did not decrease, no pressure was felt to introduce labor-saving technologies.

Slow and irregular advances of the economy over time and by sectors, setbacks in European standards, delayed modernization and inward growth under conditions that afforded little competition—all are conspicuous features of the economic evolution outlined in this book. In addition, there were also special imbalances. Each region undertook its transformation in its own manner. Part II examines these ways, pointing out the common threads.

Industries sprang up in Catalonia and the Basque Provinces under conditions of intense geographical concentration and specialization: the first region specialized in consumer goods; the second, in capital goods. Failed and minor attempts at industrialization are cited here and there, but in no other part of Spain did the process reach the density and continuity that it attained in both of these northern regions.

Were industrial location and success related to local abundance of natural resources? The answer seems to be positive in the case of the Basque Provinces, where rich deposits of iron ore and exports allowed the region to accumulate capital. According to Rafael Anes, however, Asturias, where coal abounded, obtained very meager results. Andalusia, which also had rich and varied mineral deposits, did not industrialize. Catalonia, a region that had to import raw materials like cotton and always fell short in energy resources, did industrialize as Jordi Malquer de Motes points out. The availability of natural resources does not seem to have been a decisive factor in Spanish industrialization.

The Spanish industrial revolution began in Catalonia with the cotton textile industry not much later than in England. After a hiatus (mentioned earlier), the industry became full-fledged in the middle third of the nineteenth century and reached its ceiling by the end of the century. This ceiling was not set by a lack of technology and capital, but by the narrowness of the market. The cotton textile industry sold its merchandise to the domestic market and grew by substituting craft products which previously were widely made throughout the country. In a few chapters we are told how the growth of this Catalonian industry caused the disappearance of linen manufacturing in Galicia and wool in Castile. These chapters also briefly point out to how much income and knowhow were consequently lost by such regions. The rise of one modern industrial center meant, therefore, an increased ruralization for other areas. Thus began an asymmetric relationship between regions of the same nation. In its efforts toward modernization, the cotton industry certainly sought no accommodations with previously existing producers, as opposed to what happened in agriculture. An indication of the cotton textile industry's weakness was, on the other hand, its inability to promote greater consumption. Consequently, lateral expansion into the production of other consumer goods became Catalonia's solution for future industrial growth.

The Basque experience was independent of, and different from, that of Catalonia. High capital investment and large-scale production were its main features; it profited greatly from exports of iron, then a most sought after mineral, and from a close connection with the world market. Pedro Fraile shows that the foreign markets opened up many industrial and trade opportunities similar to those Italy and Sweden had at the beginning of the twentieth century. The Basque iron-and-steel industry, however, did not meet this challenge and, instead, turned toward a domestic market protected by high tariffs. The size of the heavy industry and the expansion of its related metallurgy were hindered. Fraile concludes by denying the frequently stated argument that, between the Center and the Periphery, the second will always lose out. This does not seem to be so in the Spanish case.

If iron-ore exports helped to build the Basque heavy industry, the wine and orange exports did not industrialize Valencia, although they did earn capital for the region. According to Jordi Palafox, Valencia provides an example of modernization without industrialization. The export of citrus fruits and wines freed the region from the bonds of traditional agriculture. Only later, after income and consumption capacity had increased, did light industry begin to arise in the region.

In contrast to the Basque Provinces and Valencia, whose exports helped to revitalize their economies, there are two regional examples where foreign trade did not have the same effect. In the south, Andalusia restrengthened its role as an exporting area by adding minerals to its old staples, wine and oil. From 1820 to 1880 Andalusian exports accounted for roughly half of Spain's total exports, as pointed out by C. E. Nuñez.[1] Such a high volume of exports, however, did not alter the region's overall economy. Pedro Tedde states that the fundamental structure of rural production did not change in the least. Capitalism, but not technology, penetrated into the rural areas, while enclaves of new activities sprang up but did not fuse themselves into the regional economy. Income in Andalusia fell behind in relation to the other regions of Spain. The well-known model of outward growth seems to be applicable here.

In the Northwest, fewer changes occurred. About the middle of the nineteenth century, Galicia exported meat to England and, after that market closed, to Portugal and the rest of the Spanish mainland. Jaime García-Lombardero demonstrates that foreign demand constituted a stimulus, albeit not an overwhelming one, for transformation. Existing agricultural structures in Galicia adapted to this changing market without incorporating any improvements into their production. The regional market became integrated very slowly, as Galicia's only signs of industrial achievement were its coastal canning plants.

In places where there was no foreign demand, there were even fewer changes. When Castile, for example, lost its long-standing export, wool, it had nothing to offer for foreign trade. Encouraged by protectionism, the region fell back on an archaic cereal-production system, which made its economy even more unidimensional. The development of capitalist relations in rural Castile did not bring an accumulation of capital or industrialization. Modernization was delayed there.

Thus it can be seen that each region followed, between 1830 and 1930, its own distinctive path toward modernization. Catalonia stood at the forefront of technological renovation, and it also pioneered in the sort of social change the new technology brought in its wake. Catalonia chose England as a model but sought to sell within the home market. Foreign demand led to the transformation of the Basque country and Valencia at the end of the nineteenth century; the first opted for industrialization; the second, for the export of crops. The coastal regions of Asturias, Galicia, and Andalusia progressed very tentatively, in that their transformation did not take hold. Modernization in continental Spain, as represented by Castile, found no base on which to rejuvenate itself. Castile's economic dependence in all areas increased, not from abroad from which it was isolated, but instead from the more dynamic regions within Spain.

The most advanced industrial technology coexisted then with subsistence agriculture. Large investments of capital coincided with an expanding agriculture based on a high use of manual labor, especially in Galicia, Castile, and Andalusia. Mass production was introduced to an austere market that scarcely had the capacity to consume what it produced. In short, the whole process was unbalanced. In developing inward, some regions at times grew at the expense of others, but the impoverishment of these consumer regions in itself limited the growth of the producing regions. The interdependence among sectors and regions is evident.

The chapters in this book examine individual sectors and regions from different but convergent points of view. In order to develop a full picture of this modernization process, much more research needs to be done. Studies should follow up, for instance, over the subsequent period, when Spain finally became fully modern.

Those who have written on the nineteenth century tend to focus on how successive innovations from the mechanical loom to the orange grove were incorporated into Spanish life. These new activities are assumed to have helped Spain overcome the problems posed by its traditional production system and to have brought it more in line with the more economically advanced nations. The studies in this book seem to conclude that this approach is inadequate in itself and that any increase in output should be analyzed along with a consideration of how that income came to be distributed and used. The imperfect interaction between production and the market seems to offer a telling explanation of Spain's late development.

NOTE

1. "Comercio exterior y desarrollo económico: reflexiones sobre el caso andaluz en la segunda mitad del siglo XIX," *Revista de Historia Económica* 2, no. 2 (1984): 94.

I.
TRANSFORMATIONS
IN THE MAIN SECTORS

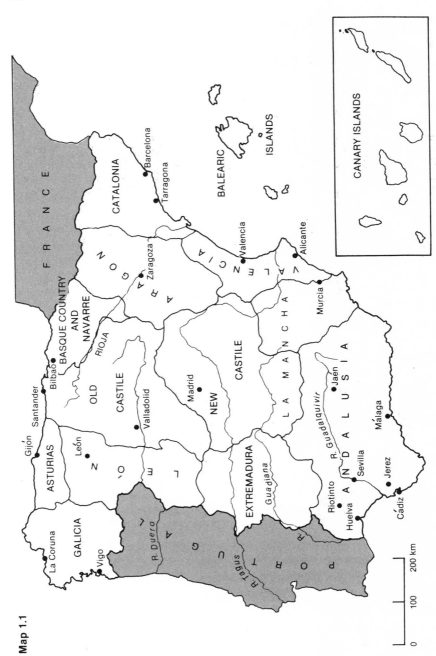

Map 1.1

2.
SPAIN'S DEMOGRAPHIC MODERNIZATION, 1800–1930

VICENTE PÉREZ MOREDA
Universidad Complutense de Madrid

1. SECULAR TRENDS AND DEMOGRAPHIC FLUCTUATIONS (1797–1930)

THE SPANISH POPULATION grew faster between 1800 and 1930 than in any previous historical period of similar length. Even so, this increase was modest when compared to that of other European nations. The term "population explosion"—frequently used to describe modern demography—cannot be applied to the Spanish case prior to 1900. The following study attempts to show that Spain's demographic modernization did not take place until the twentieth century.

If one accepts a Spanish population estimate of 11 million for 1800,[1] then the rise to 18.6 million a century later implies an average annual growth rate of .53%, or .59% if the span is extended up to 1930. Neither figure is much higher than Spain's eighteenth-century growth rate—estimated by M. Livi Bacci[2] as .42%—nor is either on a par with the nineteenth-century rates recorded in neighboring European countries except France. Moreover, Spain's slow demographic pace was by no means uniform. Growth occurred most vigorously in the first half of the century, especially between 1815 and 1860; slackened in the second half; then resurged after 1900 (see Tables 2.1 and 2.2).

Reliable census data are not available from the end of the eighteenth century (1786–1787 and 1797) to the first official censuses of the statistical era (1857 and 1860). There is, however, a general consensus on the relative accuracy of the enumerations carried out during the Liberal Triennium (1821) and during the provincial reorganization of 1833.[3] The figures for these two years fall within an overall period of absolute growth, but they also reveal the stagnation

13

Table 2.1
The Population of Spain, 1787–1930

Year	Population (in thousands)	Year	Population (in thousands)
1787	10,393	1887	17,550
1797	10,536	1897	18,109
1821	11,662	1900	18,594
1833	12,287	1910	19,927
1857	15,455	1920	21,303
1860	15,645	1930	23,564
1877	16,622		

SOURCE: National censuses.
NOTE: Population of the Peninsula, the Canary Islands, and the Balearic Islands; African possessions are not included.

Annual Average Growth Rates,
1797–1930
(between censuses)

Period	Rate	Period	Rate
1797–1860	0.63	1787–1821	0.34
1860–1887	0.43	1821–1860	0.76
1887–1900	0.45	1860–1900	0.43
1900–1910	0.70	1900–1930	0.79

SOURCES: Estimates shown on the left are from M. Livi Bacci, "Fertility and Nuptiality Changes in Spain from the Late Eighteenth to the Early Twentieth Century," *Population Studies* 22, no. 1 (1968): 84. Those on the right are my own from census data.

the Spanish population endured during the early nineteenth century. The latter was marked by serious economic crises, epidemics, and continual warfare, from the war against the French Convention at the end of the eighteenth century until the War for Independence against Napoleon in 1814. Various regional studies agree that a demographic regression, or at least a stagnation, occurred between 1794 and 1815.[4]

A provisional national estimate, based on a sample of two hundred locations spread throughout the Peninsula, shows that the negative effects of these crises—the violent typhoid epidemic in Guipúzcoa and part of Navarre in 1794–1795, the catastrophic harvests of 1803–1805 and 1811–1812, yellow fever in the South and the Southeast, malaria on the interior plateau, and the increased mortality and decreased marriage and birthrates occasioned by the War for Independence (1808–1814)[5] were such that the Spanish population did not recover its late-eighteenth-century size until the 1820s. Because favorable trends of the previous century were interrupted, the nation experienced a loss of potential population as high as 1 million people.[6]

This explains why the average annual growth rate for the years 1787 to 1821 is the lowest rate in Table 2.1. Starting in 1821, however, there was a substantial increase in population, and the second quarter of the nineteenth century exhibited the highest growth rate of the entire period—a rate similar to that recorded for the early twentieth century. What were the reasons for this expansion? Were they related to the first stages of the industrial revolution or to the alleged first "demographic revolution" in Spain?

As Nadal has emphasized, Spanish population growth from the beginning of the eighteenth century to the middle of the nineteenth was unrelated to any industrial modernization. Neither can this growth be called revolutionary, since trends in vital statistics did not substantially change until after 1900. Even during the second quarter of the century, a faster growth rate was not triggered by a real economic modernization, but, rather resulted from administrative improvements, institutional changes, and other exogenous factors— all of which could occur within the context of a traditional economy. According to Nadal, it was the disappearance of the plague; the continued expansion of land put under cultivation; and the increased consumption of new products, such as corn and potatoes, which were responsible for sustained demographic growth until 1860, and not an agrarian or industrial revolution.[7]

The elimination of the plague did not, however, diminish widespread mortality during the eighteenth and nineteenth centuries. Other epidemic diseases such as smallpox, typhoid, yellow fever, and above all cholera were rampant and took their toll on the population. In addition, although increased agricultural production owing to the expansion of land under cultivation and to the massive adoption of American crops—especially the potato—served to feed a growing population more effectively, periodic subsistence crises could not be avoided and escalated throughout the century. As established by Sánchez-Albornoz, food shortages occurred in 1804, 1812, 1817, 1823–1825, 1837, 1847, 1856–1857, 1868, 1879, 1882, 1887, and 1898.[8] Another factor which led to demographic growth between 1820 and 1860 was the almost total interruption of emigration to America, as a result of the Wars of Independence and the loss of the Spanish-American colonies and of the Spanish population policy which remained hostile to emigration until at least 1850. Changes in land tenure and land use introduced by the Liberal Revolution after 1830— church disentailment, elimination of the mesta (a privileged association of transhumant sheep owners and grazers), the final suppression of the tithe, and the like—also contributed substantially to the rise in agricultural production, which in turn fostered a marked increase of population during these decades.[9]

Spain's nineteenth-century demographic growth was of the "traditional" type and was therefore periodically curbed by "traditional" crises, especially in the early years of the century. The declining growth rate after 1860 also indicates that the population was under the constraint of a premodern economy, as witnessed by food shortages, high mortality, and the resumption of emigration abroad.

Such shortcomings already appear when comparing the main characteristics of the Spanish population with those of other European countries during the second half of the century. As evident in Table 2.2, Spain still exhibited high birth and death rates of the premodern type, and had the lowest growth rate in

Table 2.2
Demographic Characteristics of Some European Countries

Country	Annual Growth Rate r (‰) 1801–1900	Birth	Death 1865–1884	Natural Growth (%)	Life Expectancy both sexes (e_0)[1]	Period/ Date	Infant Mortality (0–1) 1900–1902
Sweden	7.9	30.2	18.7	11.5	50.0	1881–90	96
England & Wales	13.1	35.0	21.3	13.7	45.2	1881–90	146
Belgium	6.5[2]	32.0	22.7	9.3	—	—	153
France	3.4	25.5	23.6	1.9	43.5	1889–93	146
Austria	8.1[3]	38.7	31.2	7.5	—	—	219
Russia	13.3	50.3	36.7	13.6	—	—	261
Germany	11.1[4]	38.2	27.1	11.2	49.0	1910–11	206
Italy	6.0[5]	37.2	29.5	7.7	33.5	1872–81	171
	—	—	—	—	41.7	1910	—
Spain	5.3	36.4	31.0	5.4	34.8	1900	200[6]
Europe	7.6	—	—	—	29.0	1860–87	—

SOURCES: Except for items noted, European data are from B. R. Mitchell, *European Historical Statistics, 1750–1970* (London, 1978). The figures for Spain's natural growth between 1865 and 1884 present the unadjusted average for the periods 1865–1870 and 1878–1884 as they appear in Instituto Geográfico y Estadístico, *Reseña Geográfica y Estadística de España* (Madrid, 1888), pp. 13 and 19–20.
1. The European data on life expectancy come from Lorenzo del Panta, "Aspetti dell'evoluzione demografica e del popolamento nell'Italia del XIX secolo," 1983 (draft version), p. 3. German data are from A. Armengaud, "The European Population, 1700–1914," in *The Fontana Economic History of Europe,* Carlo M. Cipolla, ed. (London, 1973), vol. 3. The Spanish estimate for 1865–1884 is from M. Livi Bacci, "Fertility and Nuptiality Changes," p. 91; other data are from the official estimates of the Instituto Nacional de Estadística.
2. Source: Mitchell; period: 1816–1900.
3. Source: Ibid.; period: 1818–1900.
4. Source: Ibid.; period: 1816–1900.
5. Source: Population data are from Lorenzo del Panta, "Italy," in *European Demography and Economic Growth,* W. R. Lee, ed. (London, 1979), p. 219.
6. I have added 5% to the official data because Spanish statistics do not include deaths that occur within the first 24 hours of life. The adjustment was suggested by Livi Bacci, "Fertility," p. 233.

the table (except France). This was due to high general and infant mortality. As a nineteenth-century Spanish writer stated:

> "Today France is the most voluntarily infertile country of Europe, while Spain is the European country with the most inexcusable mortality rate. In the neighboring country, the population barely grows because too few are born. In our country, it barely grows because too many die."[10]

2. ECONOMIC TRANSFORMATIONS AND REGIONAL VARIATIONS IN DEMOGRAPHIC GROWTH

Catalonia was the only Spanish region to undergo genuine demographic modernization during the nineteenth century—a process which was not completed until the early twentieth century. This region's pioneering position can be explained by the high level of economic development that it reached through industrialization. The majority of other Spanish regions did not experience substantial demographic transformations during the nineteenth century. Regional variations in population growth from 1800 to 1930, therefore, reflect either the fluctuations in births and deaths typical of traditional populations or the various migration flows of each region. Given the emphasis on economic motivations in migration theory, it is important to assess, in each case, the "push" and "pull" factors of both overseas migration and internal movements. Only "pull factors" would suggest whether there was a direct relationship between economic modernization and regional variations in demographic growth.

Unless the 1833 figures were underestimated, there was quasi-stagnation in regions, like Old Castile, León, Navarre, and the Basque Provinces during the first three decades of the nineteenth century (see Table 2.3, first column); this contrasts with the annual growth of more than 1 percent recorded in these areas between that date and 1857 in the same table. Such demographic recovery can be explained only by the recuperative mechanisms traditionally set forth after a crisis period—an increase of marriages and births. In any event, this second third of the century, which witnessed the beginning of the important institutional and social changes known as the Liberal Revolution, exhibited the greatest demographic growth, greater even than that of the early twentieth century. Because of the low incidence of external migration during this period, population growth in each region was clearly the result of natural growth and, eventually, of internal migrations. Similarly, at the national level,

Table 2.3
Average Annual Demographic Growth Rates in the Historical Regions of Spain
(per 1,000 inhabitants)

Region	1797–1833	1834–1857	1797–1857	1858–1900	1901–1930
Andalusia	6.5	3.2	7.2	4.5	8.8
Aragón	3.1	7.6	4.9	0.8	4.1
Asturias	4.9	7.9	6.1	4.2	7.8
Balearic Islands	5.7	5.7	5.7	4.0	5.3
Canary Islands	3.9	6.6	5.0	10.0	14.7
New Castile	3.1	3.0	3.1	6.1	13.5
Old Castile	0.1	10.2	4.1	2.4	3.5
Catalonia	5.4	19.4	11.0	4.1	11.7
Extremadura	6.8	10.7	8.4	5.2	8.9
Galicia	7.1	7.9	7.4	2.5	4.0
León	0.8	12.6	5.5	3.1	2.6
Murcia	5.9	8.6	7.0	7.9	6.1
Navarre	1.1	10.6	4.9	0.8	3.9
Valencia	4.1	11.1	6.9	5.6	5.9
Basque Provinces	0.4	15.3	6.3	8.8	13.1
Spain	4.3	9.6	6.4	4.3	7.9

SOURCES: Censuses of 1797, 1857, 1900, and 1930. The data for 1833 are taken from the Royal Decree of November 30, 1833, on the territorial division of the Peninsula and adjacent islands; they are not as accurate as those for later censuses. They also are based on a slightly different territorial organization.

the high annual growth rates then recorded can be attributed only to a strong demographic recovery following the early-nineteenth-century crises. This growth rate was based on a rise in the production staples after the agrarian changes of the 1830s.

There is no evidence of push factors which could have provoked a significant emigration from any Spanish region between 1834 and 1857. Regions that traditionally sent many migrants to Spanish America, like Galicia and Asturias, experienced a notable net increase during the first half of the nineteenth century. This was probably the result of a cumulative positive balance in their vital rates. The lowest growth rate during this period is found in New Castile, where the capital of the nation is located; the early nineteenth century crises— the War for Independence against Napoleon and especially the crisis of 1812— had a devastating impact on the population of Madrid. It lasted until 1850 and delayed the region's demographic recovery.[11]

In contrast, Catalonia experienced a very high growth rate between 1834 and 1857 which cannot be explained solely by natural growth. Moreover, it was the fastest-growing region during the first part of the nineteenth century, in spite of the difficulties it experienced in the late eighteenth century and the first few years of the nineteenth. The bulk of Catalonia's demographic growth took place in the second quarter of the century, obviously reflecting a precocious and striking decline in mortality,[12] as well as immigration from other regions—a phenomenon which coincided with the first stages of Catalan industrialization. Until 1857 this was the only case in which pull factors, related to the early stages of economic modernization, motivated some internal population shifts, even though there were no significant push factors in the majority of other Spanish regions.[13]

Another region that experienced a notable demographic increase, especially after 1833, was Extremadura; between 1797 and 1857 its annual growth rate was second only to that of Catalonia. This seems difficult to believe, considering the region's modest resources, low level of development, and absence of industrial activities. It must be pointed out, however, that in the first half of the nineteenth century Extremadura was probably the region that benefited most from the institutional and social changes related to land tenure and land use, even before the liberal reforms of the 1830s. The transition from a pastoral economy based on the extensive exploitation of the land to an agricultural economy based on intensive cultivation not only permitted but required a higher population density, given the absence of technological improvements and capital in traditional agriculture.[14] In this case, demographic growth was propelled by economic changes but not by the kind of innovations that are usually associated with economic modernization, agrarian transformation, or industrial revolution. Rather, the population increased owing to changes in land use—changes which occurred within the framework of the traditional economy and even reinforced that economy.

During the second half of the nineteenth century, geographic variations in growth rates were determined by regional birth and death trends as well as by the external and internal migrations. These began to gain importance around 1850. The lowest growth rates were found in Navarre, Aragón, Old Castile, Galicia, and León, in that order. These are the same regions that also ranked lowest in 1901–1930, although in different order. This northern fringe of the Peninsula, including Galicia, did not experience substantial economic changes in its traditional agriculture. Instead, a marginal decline in labor productivity and a simultaneous rise of population combined to make these regions the greatest areas of rural exodus during the second half of the nineteenth century and the early twentieth.

From 1850 to 1930 the Canary Islands registered the highest net population increase. It is unclear whether this salient position can be attributed to the islands' outstanding natural growth—seemingly the highest in all of Spain, at least during the last quarter of the nineteenth century—or to migratory pull factors, which attracted not only other Spaniards but foreign immigrants as well. This movement to the islands was motivated by the region's specialization in crops such as bananas, tomatoes, and tobacco as well as by the upgrading of the ports of Las Palmas and Santa Cruz de Tenerife. In any event, once the cochineal cycle of the archipelago came to an end between 1877 and 1887, the Canaries experienced a negative net migration. In the last few years of the century, however, new pull factors appeared, due not to economic modernization, but to the rise of agro-exports and to a dynamic maritime trade.

Aside from this atypical case, those regions that experienced the greatest demographic growth in the last four decades of the nineteenth century were the Basque Provinces, Murcia, and New Castile, in that order. Catalonia ranked low in this period. At the provincial level, however, Barcelona was among those which led in annual demographic growth rates between 1858 and 1900, the other provinces being Vizcaya, Madrid, the Canary Islands, Murcia, Huelva, and Jaén. Leaving the Canary Islands aside again, Madrid's pull factors were more administrative and political in nature than economic, while those of the southern and southeastern provinces were associated with the increased development of mineral resources (lead in Murcia and Jaén and copper in Huelva). Mining required a large labor force and promoted urbanization in these provinces and their surrounding areas; it did not, however, lead to industrialization.[15]

Only in the Basque Provinces and Catalonia, where industrialization had reached an advanced stage by the late nineteenth century, were there significant changes related to a true economic modernization. These changes translated into a strong migratory pull and gave rise to sustained population growth. The correlation between the degree of industrialization and high demographic growth rates was not shared throughout these regions until after 1900; rather, it was limited to the provinces of Vizcaya and Barcelona, the focal points of regional migration. Of the four Spanish provinces that lost population from 1858 to 1900, two—Lérida and Gerona—are in Catalonia, and a third—Alava—is in the Basque region; the last is Huesca, part of whose population probably migrated to both the Basque and Catalan industrial centers.

In short, incipient industrialization attracted internal migrants to Catalonia during the first half of the nineteenth century and contributed to a spectacular rise in the region's population. This increase through migration, however, accompanied a remarkable natural growth due to an early demographic transition. In the last decades of the century, Catalonia and the Basque Provinces or, more specifically, the industrial centers of Barcelona and Vizcaya, were the only areas of Spain where economic modernization generated sustained demographic growth through immigration. Changes in other regions did not modify their traditional economies in any substantial or definitive way; they often fostered population increases that were easily reversible; the cases of Extremadura in the late nineteenth century and Murcia in the early twentieth are instructive.

3. SIGNS OF SPAIN'S DEMOGRAPHIC MODERNIZATION

The following section examines population trends which suggest the degree and chronology of Spain's demographic modernization.

3.1 The Demographic Transition

Catalonia is the only region for which there is conclusive evidence of a substantial fall in the death rate during the first half of the nineteenth century. A similar trend could have occurred, however, in a few other places, such as the Basque Provinces.[16] In the second half of the century, the interior and southern parts of the country stagnated in mortality rates and in this were clearly at a disadvantage vis-à-vis the insular and coastal provinces of the North and East. On the national level, however, Spain barely achieved a minimal reduction in its mortality rate throughout the entire century. Such poor performance is corroborated by trends in life expectancy that stood at 27 years in the late eighteenth century, rose to only 29 years between 1860 and 1887, and finally were close to 35 in 1900. The decline in marital fertility during the nineteenth century was equally small for Spain as a whole, although this trend was already apparent in Catalonia and the Balearic Islands before 1860 and continued unabated there until 1910 (see Table 2.4).

Table 2.4 shows an early decline in the fertility rates of the northeastern Mediterranean regions, especially Catalonia, during the first half of the nineteenth century. A social and economic development in this area, as well as its geographical and cultural proximity to France, led to large-scale adoption of birth control.[17] Instead, the early decline of fertility in some central and northern regions, which stopped after 1860, could not be a veritable one since eighteenth-century birth and fertility rates were probably overestimated. In fact, the high natural growth recorded for these regions between 1820 and 1830 and 1860 is hardly compatible with a significant decline in fertility for the same period.

Table 2.4
Regional Variations in Marital Fertility, 1787–1910

Regions		Δ % 1787–1860	Δ % 1860–1910
East	Catalonia	−22.5	−31.4
	Balearic Islands	−20.2	−21.2
	Valencia	−8.6	−26.4
	Aragón	−5.6	−14.6
South	Andalusia	−5.7	−15.8
	Murcia	1.3	−19.7
Central	New Castile	−0.8	−5.1
	Extremadura	−9.6	−5.0
	León	−15.5	−5.5
North	Old Castile	−11.7	0.9
	Basque Provinces/Navarre	−15.2	−4.1
	Galicia	−12.1	−1.8
	Asturias	−8.4	−1.3
	Canary Islands	−2.0	9.6
	Spain (total)	−10.5	−13.1

SOURCE: Regional marital fertility rates as estimated by M. Livi Bacci, "Fertility and Nuptiality Changes," p. 229.

Industrialization and urbanization must have played an important role in restricting births, since income levels as well as the economic choices of large sectors of the urban population probably influenced fertility patterns early on. Urban fertility rates were apparently very low, as witnessed by the case of Madrid as early as the beginning of the nineteenth century (this could explain the modest decline of fertility in New Castile throughout the century). Fertility rates in provincial capitals were also inferior to those of their rural zones.[18] Although this process was initiated by economic and social pressures, contraceptive practices seem to have spread through geographic and cultural diffusion and through simple spatial contiguity radiating out from Catalonia, its starting point. Consequently, the Balearic Islands, Valencia, Aragón, Murcia, and Andalusia were the regions that experienced the most striking reductions in fertility between 1860 and 1910; with the exception of Aragón, these were also the most urbanized regions of the country, or at least exhibited the highest population densities.

During the second half of the nineteenth century, the Spanish population experienced only a partial and localized move toward demographic transition;

in Catalonia, however, this process took place throughout the nineteenth century and was completed in the first decades of the twentieth. Table 2.5 summarizes the trends in birth and death statistics for the 49 Spanish provinces (50 after the Canary Islands were divided into two provinces in 1927) between 1878 and 1930. In the last quarter of the ninteenth century, 60% of the provinces still showed a crude birthrate of 36 to 42 per 1,000 and a mortality rate of 30 to 37 per 1,000. In the first decade of the present century, however, even the most backward group achieved a mortality rate of under 30 per 1,000, while Catalonia and other Mediterranean regions reached almost "modern" levels with rates of 22, as did the Cantabrian north with 22 to 23. Consequently, the overall national mortality rate fell to 25 per 1,000 during this period. The crude birthrate, however, continued above 36 in two-fifths of the provinces and only fell to 30 per 1,000 in the four Catalonian provinces and the two insular provinces; Madrid and part of the Basque-Navarre region followed closely behind.

The definitive decline of fertility in the rest of the country got under way only slowly in the second decade of the twentieth century, during which time the national birthrate fell by almost 13.5%, a much greater reduction than that of the previous fifty years.[19] Even so, between 1921 and 1930 more than half the provinces still showed a rate higher than 30 per 1,000, and the national rate was still 29.2, just prior to another substantial drop in the 1930s. Therefore, except for Catalonia and adjacent areas, Spain's demographic transition only began in the early twentieth century and proceeded until recent times, when it seems to have ended with the substantial decline in birth and fertility rates of the late 1970s.[20] Modernization of the Spanish population was clearly a twentieth-century phenomenon.

3.2 The Transformation of the Annual Birth and Death Cycle

Traditional populations, like that of Spain, exhibited a specific seasonal distribution of births and deaths throughout the year. Conceptions often took place in the spring with the maximum number of births occurring during the winter, whereas the summer and fall witnessed the greatest number of deaths. Consequently, demographic growth peaked during the first part of the year and contracted steeply during the second part.

This annual cycle went on in Spain unchanged until at least the second half of the nineteenth century; the 1863 cycle, for example, was almost identical to those of the seventeenth and eighteenth centuries.[21] By 1900 the annual cycle of births and deaths became somewhat different: although conceptions and

Table 2.5
Crude Birth and Death Rates, 1878–1930
(quintile values of provincial distribution, B = birth, D = death)

	1878–1900		1901–1910		1921–1930	
	B	D	B	D	B	D
	(Cáceres)	(Palencia)	(Cáceres)	(Palencia)	(Palencia)	(Palencia)
Highest provincial rate	42.3	37.4	41.0	29.8	37.5	24.2
Q1	39.4	34.6	38.3	27.4	34.8	21.5
Q2	37.5	33.2	36.0	26.3	31.9	20.2
Q3	35.9	30.2	33.7	24.0	29.3	18.5
Q4	31.9	27.7	31.3	22.5	26.2	17.5
	(Balearic Is.)	(Balearic Is.)	(Barcelona)	(Balearic Is.)	(Tarragona)	(Balearic Is.)
Lowest provincial rate	29.9	20.9	25.8	19.3	19.5	14.9
Gross national rate	35.7	30.7	34.2	25.0	29.2	19.1

Sources: Instituto Geográfico y Estadístico, *Reseña Geográfica y Estadística de España*, vol. 2 (Madrid, 1912), p. 27, and subsequent *Anuarios Estadísticos de España*.

births continued to rise in the spring and the winter, respectively, the maximum number of deaths shifted to the winter, with the traditional summer months of July and August having the second highest pick. At the beginning of the twentieth century, the seasonal transformation of births had not yet gotten under way, while that of deaths probably did not fully shift to the winter months until lately. Moreover, regional or provincial contrasts show once again that, in 1863 as well as in 1900, the regions of the North (Pontevedra, Guipúzcoa) and the eastern Mediterranean (Gerona, Alicante) led chronologically in this modernization trend over those of the Center (Valladolid, Zaragoza, Ciudad Real) and the South (Málaga).[22]

These changes suggest the following questions: (1) Why would such variations in the seasonal spread of births and deaths be a sign of demographic modernization? (2) In what way was the transformation of the annual cycle of births and deaths related to economic modernization?

Conceptions can obviously stem from individual decisions, while deaths cannot. Thus, the high concentration of conceptions between March and June was perhaps not the result of irrational behavior in the past (some historians have referred to "springtime love" or the "civilization of instinct"[23]) but, rather, was due to a deliberate precaution against exposing newborns to the hazards of the summer and fall. The latter seasons were the most risky, since infant mortality was at its highest. The distribution of conception was also related to the very seasonality of marriage rates; the latter depended on the agricultural calendar, which was highly irregular, as was the monthly flow of peasant income and labor, including the labor of women. For reasons of income, weddings were mostly celebrated in the autumn and the winter. This probably contributed to the observable increase in spring conceptions. Similarly, the slowdown in agricultural labor during the winter and spring also led to the same seasonality of birthrates. The disappearance of this annual cycle of conceptions and births is a reliable indicator of the declining importance of peasant life and of the shrinking role of agriculture within a society's total economy. That this seasonal cycle of births was kept without appreciable changes until 1900, clearly indicates the lasting and foremost role that Spain's agrarian sector and rural population played well into the early twentieth century.

The fact that summer and fall were seasons of highest mortality in 1863 was related to the greater incidence of infectious disease during those months. Even at the beginning of the twentieth century, these diseases, according to official statistics, were the cause of no less than 60% of all deaths. Many, perhaps one-third, were transmitted through the ingestion of contaminated water and food. Infants were especially susceptible, since they frequently contracted fatal cases of diarrhea and gastroenteritis when their nutritional source was changed at the time of weaning. Consequently, infant mortality—including children up to the ages of six or seven—still accounted for almost 50 percent of all deaths in the nineteenth century.

With the exception of smallpox, these digestive disorders were the only contagious diseases for which cures were discovered in the second half of the nineteenth century. As a result, there was a decline in adult deaths related to diseases of the digestive system and a subsequent shift in the maximum adult mortality rate from the summer and fall seasons to the winter. Mortality now became concentrated in the winter months, owing to the high incidence of respiratory illnesses—those which are more difficult to control and which continue to be a major cause of winter deaths among the older population even today.

The slow shift of maximum mortality from summer and fall to winter had not peaked in Spain in 1900; it had not even begun then in many interior and southern provinces. Such a delay highlights the late decline in infant mortality and the continued incidence, though reduced, of adult mortality related to digestive disease, in spite of improvements in sanitary conditions and in the urban environment. The latter included an increase in sanitation and sewer services, the upgrading of the potable water supply, and progress in nutritional hygiene. These improvements occurred simultaneously with industrial growth and urbanization, that is, with the economic modernization of the late nineteenth century. The first stages of industrialization and urban growth, however, also had negative effects on mortality rates owing to the increased incidence of diseases contracted through interpersonal contact—diseases which proliferated in dense populations and crowded living conditions. At the beginning of the twentieth century, respiratory illnesses such as bronchitis, pneumonia, and above all pulmonary tuberculosis (consumption) accounted for one-third to one-half of adult mortality caused by infectious disease. This partial and delayed modification of the annual mortality cycle, as it stood in 1900, is strong evidence of the late economic modernization of Spain, as well as of the huge geographic variations and serious limitations of the process in its early stages.

3.3 The Transformation of Spanish Marriage Patterns

The "European marriage pattern" (as Hajnal calls it) of the Modern Age was characterized both by a significant proportion of people who remained unmarried until old age and by a high average age at first marriage. Given that this pattern reflected economic and social conditions, the increasing alignment of the Spanish marriage pattern with the Western European model provides clues to the chronology and character of the demographic modernization process.

Massimo Livi Bacci showed some time ago that the average age at marriage in Spain rose between 1787 and 1900 and was accompanied by a simultaneous decline in lifelong celibacy; both movements were more intense among men than women. These contrasting trends resulted in a long-term equilibrium of the overall female marriage rate, which remained practically constant during the nineteenth century.[24] In 1786–1787, the percentage of unmarried people between 50 and 60 years of age was 13% to 14% for men and 12% to 13% for women.[25] Godoy's census of 1797 shows that the number of lifelong single people was even greater at the end of the eighteenth century and included more than 17% of both sexes at around 50 years of age (see Table 2.6). Starting in 1797, the percentage of lifelong celibates began to decline until, in 1900, only 6% of the men and 9.5% of the women remained unmarried for life. Data thus point to a considerable increase in the marriage rate during the nineteenth century. Excluding the regions most affected by emigration, where celibacy was more prevalent (especially for women), Spain had a single population of between 4% and 6% by 1900. This rate, according to Hajnal's criteria, was closer to the Eastern European marriage patterns than those of Western Europe, where approximately 15% of the population remained unmarried until old age. The Spanish trend does not concur with that of neighboring countries; rather, it diverges increasingly throughout the nineteenth century and begins to approximate the Western European pattern only at the turn of the century.

The decrease in celibacy was motivated by a striking contraction in the number of clergy and members of religious orders throughout the nineteenth century,[26] as well as in that of the nobility—a reduction which was already under way in the final years of the Ancien Régime. The nobility's matrimonial strategies underwent dramatic changes (still not well researched) when *mayorazgo* (primogeniture) was legally suppressed during the first third of the nineteenth century. Until then, *mayorazgo* had been a prime reason for the celibacy of second-born children who did not inherit property.

A growing propensity to marry may have derived from the greater stability and prosperity of the peasantry after the liberal reforms of the 1840s and during the most important stages of the land disentailment process. It coincided with the almost complete cessation of overseas migration. As mentioned earlier, during this period the population of the interior provinces increased considerably—a trend which can only be explained by a vigorous natural growth prompted in great measure by the rise in marriage rates. Nevertheless, the economic factors associated with the reinforcement of traditional agrarian structures during the first half of the century do not help to explain the decrease in celibacy during the second. The growing demand for labor in the last decades of the nineteenth century in certain areas of the country, together with the availability of rapid, cheap, and comfortable transportation should have expanded the internal labor market, opening up job opportunities for people who previously had no alternative but to migrate to Spanish America or to remain unmarried. Although internal migrations increased slowly in the last quarter of the nineteenth century, this does not fully explain the declining percentage of permanently unmarried people (see Table 2.6), since this is precisely when external migration began to intensify. It appears, then, that

Table 2.6
Spanish Marriage Patterns,
1787 and 1887–1980

	People Who Never Married (% of group 46–50)		Average Age at First Marriage	
Year	Men	Women	Men	Women
1797	17.4[1]	17.2[1]	24.5[2]	23.2[2]
1887	7.3	10.9	27.0	24.2
1900	6.4	10.2	27.4	24.5
1910	6.6	10.2	27.8	25.1
1920	7.5	10.6	27.9	25.7
1930	7.6	11.7	28.2	25.8
1940	9.2	13.7	29.4	26.7
1950	9.6	15.2	29.0	26.4
1960	—	—	29.3	26.4
1970	8.6	12.3	27.5	23.7
1975	9.1	10.9	26.8	23.2
1980	—	—	26.3	23.7

SOURCES: 1797: Censo de la población de España, 1797 (Madrid, 1801). 1887–1975 data are from Benito Cachinero Sánchez, "La evolución de la nupcialidad en España, 1887–1975," *Revista Española de Investigaciones Sociológicas* 20 (1982): 81–99.
1. Arithmetic mean for groups aged 40–49 and 50–59; 2. Arithmetic mean of the estimates for 1786–1787 and 1797.

institutional and legal changes related to progressive secularization and a greater degree of social modernization, rather than the incipient economic modernization of some regions in the late nineteenth century, were the main catalysts that caused the decline of celibacy in nineteenth-century Spain. The reinforcement of traditional agrarian structures in the first half of the century probably also contributed to this trend.

Toward 1800 the average at first marriage in Spain was clearly lower than that of other Western countries. Using Hajnal's methodology,[27] the censuses of 1786–1787 and 1797, as well as those from 1887 on, show a slow and progressive rise in the age at first marriage throughout the nineteenth century—a higher rise in the case of men but also significant in the case of women. At the end of the eighteenth century, men married at an average age of 24.5, while women were barely 23 (although there were interesting regional variations which cannot be elaborated on here). A century later the ages were around 27 for men and 24 for women; this pattern continued into the first decades of the twentieth century and reached its apex around 1940. The age at marriage was tied to peasant access to land and rural employment, as well as to the evolution of nineteenth-century agriculture. Hence, in contrast to the reasons for the decline in celibacy described above, economic conditions had more of an impact on the average age at first marriage than such social and legal factors as regional rights of succession and customary inheritance practices. The latter did not appear to change markedly, except for the abolition of *mayorazgo,* which affected only a limited sector of the population. Livi Bacci has shown the high positive correlation at the end of the eighteenth century between the proportion of landowners and the age at marriage in various regions. In the northern provinces, where there were many landowners, the age at marriage was high. Conversely, there was a high negative correlation between the proportion of landless agricultural workers and marriage age. The many day laborers and farmhands of Andalusia, for example, did not have to wait to inherit land in order to marry and set up their own households.[28]

At the beginning of the present century, the northern Atlantic provinces had a predominance of peasant smallholders and direct cultivators. In this area, the risk of excessive land fragmentation through demographic pressure, combined with the practice of sole or unequal inheritance, gave first sons an advantage over their younger brothers, who were often forced to delay marriage or emigrate. At the other extreme, the high land concentration of *latifundia* (large estates) in Andalusia, for example, meant that large sectors of the population had only tenuous ties to the land. The proportion of landowners there was very low, while that of seasonal wage laborers was very high. In these areas, the subsistence of peasant families did not depend on landowner-ship, and so there were few obstacles to the formation of new marriages at an early age. In large areas of the interior, especially on the northern plateau, small- and medium-sized holdings coexisted with tenant farming and share-cropping, an intermediate situation which was characterized by a certain stability in peasant ties to land and translated into an intermediate age at marriage. It would be helpful, however, to know more about the impact of disentailment on the land tenure system in these areas during the last two-thirds of the nineteenth century; it is quite possible that the net increase of new smallholders and the consolidation of old ones, as well as the stabilization of agricultural labor relations, fostered a progressive delay in the age at mar-riage, especially since equal inheritance was practiced in these regions. Never-theless, the agrarian changes described above are not the main explanation of this trend, since it proceeded throughout the entire period and penetrated nearly every region of the country.[29] On the contrary, the rural crisis of the late nineteenth century, which had a serious impact on Castilian grain cultiva-tion and Andalusian viticulture, was probably an important cause of nuptial changes among the peasantry of both regions. These agrarian circumstances generated a tremendous increase in migration, both internal (rural to urban) and external, and must have had an effect on marriage rates.

In sum, the Spanish marriage pattern never coincided with that of other Western European countries during the nineteenth century. The seculariza-tion of Spanish society during this period increased the propensity to marry and caused Spain to deviate from the norm of high celibacy rates in neighbor-ing countries. In addition, the slow rise of the average age at first marriage—which brought Spain more in line with Western European patterns—was not induced by expectations of social mobility associated with industrial develop-ment and urban growth, as occurred after 1900. Rather, this trend was the result of a possible strengthening of traditional agrarian structures, at least in some regions, and later was accentuated by the inadequacy of those structures as witnessed by the economic and social crises of the late nineteenth century.

3.4 The Rise of Urbanization

At mid-century, Spain's ratio of urban to total population was still not greater than that of previous periods; the seventeenth and eighteenth centuries were marked by a drastic urban decline which affected nearly every Spanish city. In 1750 the average size of Spain's 100 most important cities has been estimated at 13,500 people, practically equal to what it had been in 1530; by

1857 this figure had risen only to 25,000.[30] This means that between the mid-eighteenth and mid-nineteenth centuries the urban population grew at a pace only slightly greater than that of the population as a whole.

Many Spanish regions, however, had inherited a relatively complex urban network from past centuries. Though formed by smaller urban centers, this network gave the nation a head start—similar to Italy and Holland—on other European countries in the urbanization process of the early or mid-nineteenth century. Around 1858 Spain's urbanization level was not inferior to that of France, for instance, where 27% of the population lived in centers of 2,000 inhabitants or more in 1856; by this date 24.6% of the Spanish population resided in centers of 5,600 inhabitants or more.[31] Between 1858 and 1900, the Spanish figure seems to have doubled, since 32% of the population lived in centers of 10,000 or more by 1900, and another 40% resided in centers of 2,000 to 10,000.[32] In less than fifty years, Spain's urban growth rate had risen as much as, or more, than the Italian rate during the entire century.[33]

Even so, the growth of cities in these two Mediterranean nations was clearly slower than in other Western European countries, owing partly to the high urban density that the latter already exhibited at the beginning of the century. Between 1800 and 1910 the urbanization rate—that is, the ratio of urban to total population—probably increased fourfold in Germany and more than threefold in England, Belgium, and even France.[34]

Table 2.7 shows the demographic evolution of the provincial capitals between 1836 and 1930 in relation to the rest of the country and to Spain as a whole. Even though the figures for 1836 are not fully reliable or complete, they do reveal a substantial population growth in the capitals between that date and 1857, even higher than that recorded in the second half of the century. This was a period of demographic expansion for many less prominent centers which were designated as capitals during the provincial reform of 1833 and which experienced growth due to their new administrative functions. Only in a few places, such as Barcelona and Oviedo, can the urban growth of this period be attributed to the effects of industrialization.

Although urban growth proceeded in the second half of the nineteenth century at a rate slightly lower than that of the two previous decades, the contrast with the rest of the country was sharper. This period witnessed the first stages of Spain's modern urbanization process. In comparison with an annual growth rate of 14 per 1,000 in the capitals, the rest of the population experienced a very low growth of only 2.8 per 1,000 annually. The latter rate was the result of a migratory flow which was partly directed abroad and partly directed toward the provincial capitals themselves, especially between 1878

Table 2.7
The Urban Population of Spain, 1836–1930

A. Provincial Capitals Compared with the Rest of Spain

	Absolute Figures			
	1836	*1857*	*1900*	*1930*
Provincial capitals	1,194,000	1,676,689	3,087,658	5,114,223
Rest of Spain	11,450,000	13,777,825	15,506,747	18,449,644
Spain	12,644,000	15,454,514	18,594,405	23,563,867

B. Average Annual Growth Rates (per 1,000 inhabitants)

	1837–1857	*1858–1900*	*1901–1930*
Provincial capitals	16.3	14.3	17.0
Rest of Spain	8.9	2.8	5.8
Spain	9.6	4.3	7.9

Sources: The censuses of 1857, 1900, and 1930; 1836 data are taken from the *Guía del Ministerio de la Gobernación del Reino* (Madrid, 1836).

and 1887. During the first thirty years of the twentieth century, the Spanish population became more urbanized as the demographic growth of the provincial capitals continued. The contrast with the rest of the country lessened as the general population rose in response to the demographic transition and to the drastic reduction in external migration after 1914. At the beginning of the nineteenth century, only Madrid and Barcelona had 100,000 inhabitants, whereas in 1857 Seville and Valencia barely surpassed this figure; Málaga and Murcia reached 100,000 by 1900 and in 1930 there were 11 major Spanish cities including Zaragoza, Bilbao, Granada, Córdoba, and Cartagena. At the same time, the population residing in municipalities of 10,000 inhabitants or more increased from 32% to 43% of the total population, while the proportion of people living in strictly rural municipalities, that is, those with less than 2,000 inhabitants, decreased from 27.5% to 20.5%.

A regional analysis of the urbanization process, presented in Table 2.8, shows that regions which were characterized until 1836 by a low level of urbanization and small cities—Asturias, the Canary Islands, Extremadura, Old Castile, and Galicia, for example—were the regions whose provincial capitals experienced the greatest demographic growth between that date and 1857. In short, the potential growth of the new capitals prompted by the administrative reorganization of 1833 was the dynamic factor in the urbaniza-

Table 2.8
Average Annual Demographic Growth Rates
for the Provincial Capitals of Each Region, 1837–1930

Region	1837–1857	1858–1900	1901–1930
Andalusia	8.9 (12)	7.5 (13)	13.1 (9)
Aragón	15.0 (9)	10.7 (10)	16.8 (6)
Asturias	44.2 (1)	28.9 (4)	15.1 (7)
Balearic Islands	13.5 (10)	9.3 (12)	10.8 (15)
Canary Islands	36.0 (2)	29.9 (2)	17.6 (5)
New Castile	10.6 (11)	14.8 (8)	18.3 (3)
Old Castile	25.2 (5)	11.5 (9)	12.0 (14)
Catalonia	31.8 (3)	17.5 (6)	20.7 (2)
Extremadura	26.1 (4)	6.0 (14)	12.6 (12)
Galicia	24.8 (6)	18.6 (5)	12.5 (13)
León	5.6 (15)	9.9 (11)	17.8 (4)
Murcia	8.8 (13)	29.1 (3)	13.8 (8)
Navarre	8.5 (14)	5.6 (15)	12.8 (11)
Valencia	19.5 (7)	16.4 (7)	12.8 (10)
Basque Provinces	16.7 (8)	29.9 (1)	20.7 (1)
Spain	16.3	14.3	17.0

NOTE: The rates have been estimated from the aggregate population totals of the provincial capitals in each region for each date presented (per 1,000 inhabitants). The figures in parentheses rank, in decreasing order, the regional rates for each period.

tion process of the second third of the nineteenth century. The first stages of industrialization constituted only a secondary factor—a factor which was localized in certain regions, like Asturias and Catalonia. The latter occupied the first and third rank, respectively, in the growth rates of provincial capitals.

Between 1858 and 1900, other factors were important. In the Basque Provinces, Murcia and Asturias, industrial innovations which led to demographic concentration in mining and heavy industry areas triggered urbanization. It is important to emphasize that the exploitation of mineral resources during the second half of the nineteenth century accelerated urbanization there, as well as in some isolated provinces like Huelva and Jaén in Andalusia. Improvements in communications—port facilities in coastal cities and especially railroads—prompted urbanization, particularly when related to mining (railroads and terminal ports of the mining export route); these improvements, however, had little or no effect on the growth of those urban centers whose economies were based on traditional activities. Only the urban growth of the Canary Islands is directly related to improvements in the two large ports of the archipelago and to the subsequent growth of the region's two main cities in the last years of the nineteenth century.

Only after 1900 did industrialization per se—altogether with the political and administrative pull which operated in Madrid—become the main factor in urbanization. This clearly placed the Basque and Catalan capitals at the head of the process, followed by New Castile which benefited from the presence there of the capital of the nation.

3.5 The Transformation of the Occupational Structure

This is the indicator that best illustrates the relationship between Spain's demographic modernization and the nation's economic transformation. A quick review of Table 2.9 will preclude the need for lengthy explanations. In spite of the difficulties of analyzing the occupational statistics of the period 1797–1930, it can be concluded that the percentage of population employed in agriculture did not vary substantially during the nineteenth century and, consequently, neither did the volume employed in industry. An expansion of the industrial work force, a characteristic of the first stages of industrialization, did not occur in Spain as a whole until after 1900, more precisely in the second and third decades of the twentieth century.

From the end of the eighteenth century until 1910, the population employed in agriculture and associated activities stood at 65% of the nation's total labor force, the agricultural labor of women being excluded from Table 2.9. This exclusion, which is also found in international estimates, is due to possible inconsistencies in the reported number of female workers and to the difficulty of assessing their actual labor time, which in most cases was probably seasonal. Nevertheless, nineteenth-century Spanish statistics for the active agrarian population include a group of landowners who were not really part of the labor force and whose incorporation may compensate, in part, for the exclusion of female workers. If women's labor on the land were taken into account, the total work force in the primary sector would increase to approximately 70% and would lower the percentage of industrial workers. Why did the size of the agricultural population stay constant or even grow somewhat while that of the industrial work force remained stationary? This does not seem to fit with the development (though slow and localized) of textile manufacturing, heavy industry, mining, communications projects, transportation, urban construction, and other activities which began in the late eighteenth century and which should have generated a shift in labor demand toward the secondary sector.

The census figures for 1797 require careful interpretation. The substantial size of the tertiary sector should not be surprising, considering the importance

Table 2.9
Distribution of the Active Population
According to Economic Sectors (percentage)

Year	Spain I	II	III	Catalonia (1797 and 1860) Province of Barcelona (1860–1930) I	II	III
1797[1]	65.3	12.8	21.9	52.4	25.1	22.5
1860[2]	63.5	17.3	19.2	53.6[3]	28.1[3]	18.3[3]
				37.5[4]	41.4[4]	21.1[4]
1877	64.1	15.3	20.6	34.3	37.2	28.5
1887	64.7	17.1	18.1	30.1	47.5	22.4
1900	64.8	17.4	17.8	38.6	35.4	25.9
1910	66.0	15.8	18.2	27.5	46.0	26.5
1920	57.3	21.9	20.8	13.5	62.6	23.9
1930	45.5	26.5	28.0	11.2	61.7	27.1

Sources: Censuses of the dates included. The data for Spain between 1910 and 1930 were estimated by the Instituto de Cultura Hispánica, *La población activa española de 1900 a 1957* (Madrid, 1957). The figures for the Province of Barcelona were estimated by Joaquín Arango, "Cambio económico y movimientos migratorios en la España oriental del primer tercio del siglo XX," *Hacienda Pública Española* 38 (1976): 75.
Notes: Sector I = agriculture, forestry, hunting, and fishing; sector II = industry and mining; sector III = other occupations.
1. The male clerical population is included in the figures for this year.
2. From 1860 on the female agricultural population is not included.
3. Catalonia.
4. Province of Barcelona.

of such groups as the military, the clergy, the bureaucracy, and even domestic and institutional servants in late Ancien Régime society. But a portion of these servants also worked part-time in agriculture, as did some of the wage laborers who were classified as industrial workers. If compared with the data for the second half of the nineteenth century, however, the 1797 census shows a relatively high percentage of industrial population vis-à-vis that of the primary sector. This ratio seems especially incongruous in an agrarian economy which had not yet entered the first stages of industrialization, even if one assumes that part of the population included there also engaged in seasonal agricultural labor, a phenomenon for which there is abundant evidence.

　　In a preindustrial society lacking modern communications and exhibiting a high degree of economic self-sufficiency, the specialization of production, whether local or regional, was less prevalent than in modern economies and ensured that a "minimum" percentage of the population would be engaged in craftmanship. On the one hand, internal demand for industrial products and, on the other hand, rudimentary technology and low labor productivity prevented the sector's employment level from falling below this "minimum" threshold. It has been proven for other countries, as distinct from one another as Italy and Norway, that the percentage of the population employed in premodern industry declined during the first stages of modernization, as crafts were replaced by the manufacturing sector; with the building of the railroad, transportation became cheaper, trade increased, and the specialization of production progressed.[35]

Spain's occupational distribution thus remained unchanged throughout the entire nineteenth century and the first half of the twentieth; the rise in the ratio of the population employed in industry to that employed in the primary sector was almost imperceptible. This lack of change was related to the strengthening of traditional agrarian structures—a result of the liberal reforms of the second third of the nineteenth century—which frustrated a true agrarian revolution that would have freed labor for employment in other sectors of the economy. Instead, large segments of the population remained in the countryside, labor productivity declined, and hidden unemployment increased. As a result, rural emigration escalated significantly during the last decades of the century and until World War I was directed abroad more than toward the nation's industrial centers. Around the second decade of the twentieth century, the migratory flow was reoriented toward the industrial regions of Spain. There are two reasons for this radical change: the traditional countries of destination began to raise immigration barriers; and above all, the industrial development of Spain during the war years and the 1920s promoted internal migration. The growing demand for industrial workers in some areas of the country finally reduced the proportion of the active population engaged in agriculture between 1910 and 1920, and most especially between 1920 and 1930.

The occupational distribution also reflects regional and provincial variations in the economic modernization process. Table 2.9 traces the structural evolution of the active population in Barcelona (data for the end of the eighteenth century refer to the entire region of Catalonia), which is predictably different from that of Spain as a whole. Around 1800 the ratio of industrial to agrarian population in Catalonia—and also in the province of Barcelona—was much higher than that of the rest of Spain. Although this difference lasted throughout the second half of the nineteenth century, Catalonia's sectoral distribution of labor did not exhibit either a linear tendency or a substantial transformation until after 1900. Variations between the Catalan and overall Spanish cases were appreciable at the beginning of the period and were accentuated throughout the nineteenth century, but the definitive transformation of the occupational distribution did not take place in Catalonia or in all Spain until the first third of the twentieth century.

4. A SLOW AND LATE DEMOGRAPHIC MODERNIZATION

As a whole, the Spanish population did not experience a deep transforma- tion until the first third of the twentieth century. At that time, the majority of Spanish provinces—following the lead of Catalonia and adjacent Mediterra- nean areas—began the transition toward modern behavior as far as fertility and mortality is concerned. Only after 1900 was there a partial and localized modification in the seasonal mortality cycle, although there were still no noticeable changes in the cycle of conceptions and births. The year 1900 also witnessed an important turn in the Spanish marriage pattern, which during the nineteenth century had diverged considerably from the "European model." The urbanization rate increased in the first decades of the twentieth century, continuing a process of population concentration that had begun in the last two-thirds of the nineteenth century, especially in the provincial capitals. The relative size of the agrarian population declined significantly only after 1910, when the industrial labor force began to expand considerably. This trend was followed by a rise in the tertiary sector in the 1920s. Although the sheer growth of the Spanish population from the end of the eighteenth century to 1930 is a "misleading sign" of the nation's economic progress, the indicators of demographic modernization after 1900 seem to be an accurate reflection of the chronology and characteristics of Spain's economic modernization.

NOTES

1. Francisco Bustelo, "Algunas reflexiones sobre la población española del siglo XVIII," *Anales de Economía* 15 (1972): 97; Miguel Artola, *La burguesía revolucionaria (1808–1869), Historia de España Alfaguara,* vol. 5 (Madrid, 1973), p. 63.

2. Massimo Livi Bacci, "Fertility and Nuptiality Changes in Spain from the Late Eighteenth to the Early Twentieth Century," *Population Studies* 22 (1968) 1: 84, 90.

3. The former was published at the beginning of 1822 and has been commonly cited since then. The latter was included in the *Real Decreto* of November 30, 1833, and established the new territorial division of the Peninsula and adjacent islands. It was also cited by Pascual Madoz in the Spanish version of A. Moreau de Jonnès's work, *Es- tadística de España* (Barcelona, 1835), pp. 39–40.

38 Vicente Pérez Moreda

4. Jordi Nadal, "Les grandes mortalités des années 1793–1812: effets à long terme sur la démographie catalane," *Problèmes de mortalité* (Paris, 1965), pp. 409–421; Pablo Fernández Albaladejo, *La crisis del Antiguo Régimen en Guipúzcoa, 1766–1833: cambio económico e historia* (Madrid, 1975), pp. 208–228; Ángel García Sanz, *Desarrollo y crisis del Antiguo Régimen en Castilla la Vieja: Economía y Sociedad en tierras de Segovia, 1500–1814* (Madrid, 1977), pp. 88–89; A. G. Sanz Marcotegui, "Demografía y Sociedad de la Barranca de Navarra, 1768–1860" (Ph.D. diss., Universidad Complutense de Madrid, 1982).

5. Many references to this can be found in Ángel García Sanz, *Desarrollo y crisis*, p. 88 and A. G. Sanz Marcotegui and M. A. Zabalza, "Consecuencias demográficas de la Guerra de la Convención en Navarra: La crisis de mortalidad de 1794–1795," *Príncipe de Viana* 44 (1983): 63–87. See also, among others, Vicente Pérez Moreda, *Las crisis de mortalidad en la España interior, siglos XVI–XIX* (Madrid, 1980), pp. 375ff.; David-Sven Reher, "La crisis de 1804 y sus repercusiones demográfricas: Cuenca, 1775–1825," *Moneda y Crédito* 154 (1980): 43; María Carbajo Isla, "Primeros resultados cuantitativos de un estudio sobre la población de Madrid, 1742–1836," *Moneda y Crédito* 107 (1968): 71–91.

6. Details of the estimate are found in Vicente Pérez Moreda, "La evolución demográfica española en el siglo XIX: tendencias generales y contrastes regionales," in *L'evoluzione demografica dell'Italia nel secolo XIX: Continuità e mutamenti, 1796–1914* (forthcoming).

7. Jordi Nadal, "The Failure of the Industrial Revolution in Spain 1830–1913," in C. M. Cipolla, ed., *The Fontana Economic History of Europe*, vol. 4, pt. 2 (London, 1973), pp. 532–539.

8. Nicolás Sánchez-Albornoz, *Las crisis de subsistencias de España en el siglo XIX* (Rosario, 1963), pp. 8–9.

9. This is suggested by Gonzalo Anes, "La agricultura española desde comienzos del siglo XIX hasta 1868: algunos problemas," in *Ensayos sobre la economía española a mediados del siglor XIX* (Madrid, 1970), pp. 259ff.; Josep Fontana, *La crisis del Antiguo Régimen, 1808–1833* (Barcelona, 1979), pp. 46–47, 253–256. Jordi Nadal posits a direct relationship between the disentailment and the increase in agricultural production in Nadal, "The Failure," p. 24. See also the recent article by Enrique Llopis, "Algunas consideraciones acerca de la producción agraria castellana en los veinticinco últimos años del Antiguo Régimen," *Investigaciones Económicas* 21 (1983): 135–151.

10. César Silió y Cortés, *Los que nacen y los que mueren* (Valladolid, 1897), p. 11.

11. David Ringrose, *Madrid and the Spanish Economy, 1560–1850* (Berkeley and Los Angeles, 1983), pp. 27–28.

12. Jordi Nadal, "Demografía y economía en el origen de la Cataluña moderna: un ejemplo local, Palamós (1705–1839)," *Estudios de Historia Moderna* 6 (1956–1959): 290.

13. Nadal has also pointed out the possibility of a labor shortage in Catalonia during this period as a consequence of the "ripple effects" of the region's demographic crisis at the beginning of the century. See his *La población española, siglos XVI a XX* (Barcelona, 1973), pp. 140–142.

14. The conversion of pastureland into farming land in Extremadura was attempted even before the height of the disentailment period (see Llopis *supra*) and continued in

later years. See Juan García Pérez, *Las desamortizaciones eclesiástica y civil en la provincia de Cáceres, 1836–1870: Cambios en la estructura agraria y nuevos propietarios* (Cáceres, 1982). The relationship between the area's low population density in the eighteenth century and its pastoral economy was evident among contemporaries, as the following excerpt from a 1771 memoir indicates: "If Extremadura could rid itself of the shepherds of the *Mesta* and their 3.5 million sheep, the population would rise from one-half million to more than 2 million inhabitants" (Nadal, "The Failure," p. 19).

15. Nadal, "The Failure," pp. 99ff.

16. For a discussion of infant mortality see Nadal, "Demografía y economía." For the Basque case see the evidence presented by Emiliano Fernández de Pinedo in *Crecimiento económico y transformaciones sociales del País Vasco, 1100–1850* (Madrid, 1974), p. 116, and by Albaladejo, *La Crisis,* p. 225.

17. The post-1820 decline of Catalan fertility has been proven by Jordi Nadal and Armand Sáez in "La fecondité à Saint Joan de Palamós (Catalogne) de 1700 à 1859," *Annales de Démographie Historique* (1972): 109–110, and more recently by Jaime Benavente, "Social Change and Early Fertility Decline in Catalonia," paper presented at the annual meeting of the Population Association of America, Minneapolis, 1984, and published in *Jornades de Població* (January 1985).

18. Livi Bacci, "Fertility and Nuptiality Changes," pp. 99–100; see also Joaquín Arango, "La teoría de la transición demográfica y la experiencia histórica," *Revista Española de Investigaciones Sociológicas* 10 (1980): 190–191.

19. Nadal, *La población española,* p. 234.

20. Isabel Agüero and Alberto Olano, "La evolución reciente de la fecundidad en España," *Revista Española de Investigaciones Sociológicas* 10 (1980): 121–150; I. Agüero, J. Leguina, and A. Olano, "La gran caída de la natalidad," *El País,* 2 December 1981, p. 32.

21. Compare, for example, the graphs included in V. Pérez Moreda, *Las crisis de mortalidad,* pp. 206–213, with those of that Nicolás Sánchez-Albornoz presents for 1863 in "La modernización demográfica: La transformación del ciclo vital anual, 1863–1960," in *Jalones en la modernización de España* (Barcelona, 1975), pp. 156ff.

22. Sánchez-Albornoz, "La modernización demográfica," pp. 162–167.

23. Philippe Ariès, *Histoire des populations françaises et de leurs attitudes devant la vie depuis le XVIIIe siècle* (Paris, 1971), p. 402.

24. Livi Bacci, "Fertility and Nuptiality," pp. 216–220.

25. Livi Bacci, in D. V. Glass and R. Revelle, eds., *Population and Social Change* (London, 1972), and "Fertility and Nuptiality," p. 220, n. 56.

26. Although the ratio of clergy to total population had already begun to decrease in the second half of the eighteenth century. See Felipe Ruíz Martín, "Demografía eclesiástica hasta el siglo XIX," *Diccionario de historia eclesiástica de España,* vol. 2 (Madrid, 1972), pp. 682–733.

27. John Hajnal, "Age at Marriage and Proportions Marrying," *Population Studies* 7 (1953) 2: 111–136.

28. Livi Bacci, "Fertility and Nuptiality," pp. 221–223.

29. From various studies on the consequences of disentailment in different areas of the northern plateau, one can deduce that small- and medium-sized holdings increased among the peasantry. See, for example, Germán Rueda Hernánz, "La desamortización

de Mendizábal en la provincia de Valladolid, 1836–1853," *Investigaciones Históricas* 2 (1980): 93–251, and "Estudio comparativo de las consecuencias de la desamortización de tierras en tres zonas de Europa: Departamento del Norte (Francia), Nápoles (Italia) and Valladolid (España)," *Hacienda Pública Española* 69 (1981): 107–123; and Rosa Ortega Candell, *Las desamortizaciones de Mendizábal y Madoz en Soria* (Soria, 1982), esp. pp. 108 and 162–177.

30. Ignacio Lozón Ureña, "Evolución histórica de la población urbana española," *Revista Internacional de Sociología* 26 (1978): 251.

31. Artola, *La burguesía,* p. 67.

32. Salustiano del Campo, *Análisis de la población de España* (Barcelona, 1972), p. 18.

33. Lorenzo del Panta, "Aspetti dell'evoluzione demografica e del popolamento nell'Italia del XIX secolo," *Convegno su l'evoluzione demografica dell'Italia nel secolo XIX* (Assisi, 1983), draft version, p. 16.

34. Paul Bairoch, "Population urbaine et taille des villes en Europe de 1600 à 1970: présentation de series statistiques," in *Démographie urbaine, XV–XX siècles* (Lyon, 1977), p. 11.

35. References to these cases can be found in Colin Clark, *The Conditions of Economic Progress* (London, 1960), pp. 502–503.

FURTHER READINGS

Arango, Joaquín. "Cambio económico y movimientos migratorios en la España oriental del primer tercio del siglo XX: algunas hipótesis sobre determinantes y consecuencias." *Hacienda Pública Española* 38 (1976): 51–80.

———. "La teoría de la transición demográfica y la experiencia histórica." *Revista Española de Investigaciones Sociológicas* 10 (1980): 169–198.

Cachinero Sánchez, Benito. "La evolución de la nupcialidad en España, 1887–1975." *Revista Española de Investigaciones Sociológicas* 20 (1982): 81–99.

De Miguel, Amando. *Diez errores sobre la población española.* Madrid, 1982.

Díez Nicolás, Juan. "La transición demográfica en España, 1900–1960." *Revista de Estudios Sociales* 1 (1971): 1–71.

García Barbancho, Alfonso. *Las migraciones interiores españolas: Estudio cuantitativo desde 1900.* Madrid, 1967.

Livi Bacci, Massimo. "Fertility and Nuptiality Changes in Spain from the Late Eighteenth to the Early Twentieth Century." *Population Studies* 22 (1968) 1: 83–102 and 2: 211–234.

———. "Fertility and Demographic Growth in Spain in the Eighteenth and Nineteenth Century." In D. V. Glass and R. Revelle, eds., *Population and Social Change,* London, 1972, pp. 176–187.

Melón, Amando. "Los censos de la población en España, 1857–1940." *Estudios Geográficos* 43 (1951): 203–281.

Nadal, Jordi. "The Failure of the Industrial Revolution in Spain, 1830–1913." In C. M. Cipolla, ed., *The Fontana Economic History of Europe*, vol. 4, pt. 2, London, 1973, pp. 532–626.

———. *La población española, siglos XVI a XX.* 3d. ed. Barcelona, 1973.

Pérez Moreda, Vicente. *Las crisis de mortalidad en la España interior, siglos XVI–XIX.* Madrid, 1980.

Reher, David-Sven. "Desarrollo urbano y evolución de la población: España 1787–1930," *Revista de Historia Económica* 4, no. 1 (1986): 39–66.

Sánchez-Albornoz, Nicolás. "La crisis de subsistencias de 1857" and "Crisis alimenticia y recesión demográfica." In *España hace un siglo: una economía dual.* Barcelona, 1968.

———. "La modernización demográfrica: La transformación del ciclo vital anual, 1863–1960." In *Jalones en la modernización de España,* Barcelona, 1975, pp. 147–180.

Tortella, Gabriel. "La economía española, 1830–1900." In Manuel Tuñón de Lara, ed., *Historia de España*, vol. 8, Madrid, 1981, pp. 17–27.

3.
AGRICULTURE: A SLOW-MOVING SECTOR, 1830–1935

GABRIEL TORTELLA
Universidad de Alcalá de Henares

DURING THE nineteenth and the early twentieth century, agriculture was the most important economic activity in Spain, at least from a purely quantitative standpoint. This can be readily appreciated by glancing at Table 3.1, which shows that by 1900 two of every three Spanish workers were farmers; while this proportion had decreased by the end of our period, still nearly one in every two Spanish workers was a farmer in 1935. Agricultural productivity, however, remained very low, as panel C in Table 3.1 shows, especially in 1900, when it stood at only two-thirds of the national average and at about one-half of industrial productivity. Taking into account the fact that overall Spanish productivity was already very low by European standards even in 1935, this is clear evidence of the serious retardation of Spanish agriculture, especially until around 1900. Other corroborating facts, such as

Table 3.1
Sectoral Distribution of Key Indicators, 1900 and 1935
(Manpower, National Income, and Productivity)

	A Manpower		B National Income		C Productivity	
	1900	*1935*	*1900*	*1935*	*1900*	*1935*
1. Agriculture	67	45	46	35	0.69	0.78
2. Industry	15	33	20	32	1.33	0.97
3. Services	18	23	34	34	1.89	1.48
4. Total	100	100	100	100	1.00	1.00

SOURCE: Panels A and B, Alcaide Inchausti (1976), table 2; Panel C, estimated from A and B.

42

the appallingly poor diet of the average Spaniard, confirm the impression gathered from the figures. This stagnating sector weighed heavily on the economy as a whole: agriculture was also the largest exporting sector, in spite of the crisis of wine exports and the boom in mineral exports at the end of the nineteenth century. Due to its sheer size, the agrarian sector's evolution had to have an overwhelming influence on the evolution of the rest of the economy and the country in general.

Agricultural backwardness was therefore one of the most salient causes of the slowness with which the Spanish economy underwent its process of modernization during the period under study. In turn, agricultural retardation can be explained by the interplay of two sets of factors—physical and geographical as well as institutional and political. This chapter is concerned with both factors while attempting to assess the performance of the agricultural sector and its impact on the rest of the economy. It is devided into three sections: in the first, the changes in the structure of landownership and land tenure, loosely designed in Spanish with the term *desamortización* (disentailment roughly being the English equivalent) is examined; in the second, the main contours of the evolution of output and productivity is described; in the concluding section an attempt is made to gauge the contribution of the agricultural sector to the development and modernization of the Spanish economy and society.

I

Unequal distribution of landownership seems to have existed in Spain since time immemorial, but the most recent formation of very large estates (*latifundia*) is generally considered to be a consequence of the medieval reconquest (*Reconquista*) of land from the Moors by the Christians, a process whereby a small number of aristocratic families and monasteries emerged as the proprietors of most of the land in the southern half of the Iberian Peninsula. The consequence was the extreme poverty of the great majority of peasants and the great wealth and power of these *latifundistas*. One should not forget, however, that even though the Spanish case might have been extreme, most other European countries had very uneven land distribution, and many feudal landowners in preindustrial times, so that, in one way or another (one thinks of the "dissolution of the monasteries" and the "enclosure movement" in England), practically all of them ended up decreeing some sort of land reform which changed the system of land tenure and permitted the introduction of technical improvements and growth of output.

In its broad outlines, the Spanish disentailment followed the model of the French Revolution. It consisted essentially in the expropriation (with compensation) of a large fraction of the lands and buildings belonging to the church, the municipalities, and the state and in the auction of these "nationalized" lands, the proceeds of which constituted a sizable share of the budget revenues during the middle decades of the nineteenth century. In a milder version, nonetheless, disentailment had started prior to the French Revolution. Most of the properties of the church and the towns were held in mortmain; that is, they could not be sold by their owners, as they were entailed. Entailment was viewed as an obstacle to economic progress by eighteenth-century enlightened thinkers and rulers (Herr [1958]), and under Charles III in the mid-eighteenth century, moderate steps toward the disentailment of some church lands had been undertaken without much success. Considerable extensions were disentailed in the late eighteenth and early nineteenth centuries: by then disentailment had become one of the bases of the liberal program; as such, it was put into effect when the liberals (*progresistas*) were in power and was suspended when the conservatives (*moderados*) held sway.

The disentailment of church lands was carried out in two stages. The properties of the religious orders were nationalized and sold in auction by a decree of 1836, under the liberal prime minister J. A. Mendizábal, who conceived the measure as the keystone of his economic program to finance the liberal side in the Carlist civil war and to create, in Mendizábal's own words, "a copious family of landowners" economically interested in the triumph of the liberal cause. Sales proceeded actively in the following years, and by 1841 some 425 million pesetas worth of land (about 13% of the total value of land disentailed) had been acquired.

In 1841, under the regency of Gen. B. Espartero, a law was issued which included the properties of the "secular" (nonmonastic) church among those subject to nationalization, that is, expropriation. By this law, therefore, all church estates were considered susceptible to disentailment, and sales proceeded apace until, in 1844, the conservatives came to power. Total sales during the 1836–1844 period amounted to 862 million pesetas (see Table 3.2), roughly three-fifths of total church wealth in 1836.

In 1855, with the liberals again in power, the Madoz law (named after its main sponsor, P. Madoz, finance minister) was issued. It was also called the "general disentailment law" because it redefined those properties subject to disentailment, the new definition encompassing state and municipal lands. Its main aim was, therefore, to sell all real estate which did not belong to private individual owners. With amendments and occasional suspensions, the Madoz

Table 3.2
Value of Disentailed Estates, 1798–1900
(in millions of pesetas)

	(1) Church and Charities	(2) Municipal	(3) Other	(4) Total
1798–1814	376	0	0	376
1836–1844	862	0	0	862
1855–1856	123	40	29	192
1858–1867	428	499	110	1,037
1868–1900	304	354	77	735
Total	2,093	893	216	3,202

SOURCE: Tortella (1981), with modifications.

law nevertheless remained vigorous for the remainder of the century, and under its aegis large portions of church and public lands were sold to private citizens. In fact, by 1875 the bulk of "national" lands (over 90%) were sold. From then on disentailment was, comparatively speaking, a mere trickle.

How did disentailment affect the structure and distribution of landownership? The most widely accepted opinion is that it increased the holdings of the great landowners and thereby aggravated the unequal distribution of property. This thesis, however, is quite difficult to test empirically, for we lack the data which would allow us to measure the unevenness of landownership before and after disentailment: at present, for instance, we cannot compare the concentration of landownership around 1800 with the same variable around 1900. Lacking objective proof for their hypothesis, historians have turned to the *mechanism* whereby disentailment was carried out as evidence of its perverse effects on distribution. Disentailed lands were not disposed of according to principles of equity but, rather, with the purpose of maximizing receipts in a short time: they were sold in auction to the highest bidder. This means that the buyers had to be people of means so as to be able to outbid the others. As a consequence, one might infer, poor peasants, who needed the land most, did not receive any. This frequently made viewpoint, although difficult to support with figures, appears unassailable. To conclude from this, however, that ownership became more unevenly distributed is to take an unwarranted step. To say that only the rich bought land is one thing; to say that the rich were so few in number as the former owners is quite another, very unlikely, proposition.

The research done so far appears to support the statement that buyers of disentailed land were well-to-do: aristocrats, clergymen, landowners, merchants, businessmen. Even here the evidence is not conclusive, for the profession of the buyer is often omitted in the documents. The most solid work on the effects of disentailment on ownership is being done by Richard Herr who, given the fragmentary character of the sources, has chosen to deal with local cases rather than with the whole country or even large regions. Herr's work on local townships in the provinces of Salamanca and Jaén (Herr [1974a, 1974b]) fully supports his thesis that disentailment did not introduce a fundamental modification in the structure of ownership; or, in other words, that land changed hands—by and large from the church and the municipalities to lay private owners—but in general there was neither increased concentration nor significant dispersion of holdings. In those villages where large absentee landowners predominated, disentailed estates were bought by holders of a similar type; in those villages where ownership was more evenly distributed land sales were more widely scattered. In spite of the smallness of Herr's samples, both in space and in time (so far he has limited himself to the 1798–1808 period), his painstaking analyses appear convincing.

In an article surveying the disentailment issue in general (Herr [1974a]), Herr states that the most important effect of disentailment was neither political nor social but economic. In his opinion, the main significance of disentailment lay in the fact that it brought into cultivation large tracts which had been idle or underutilized before. This increase in tilled acreage was required to feed a population whose numbers had been increasing steadily since the beginning of the eighteenth century. Population pressure had brought about a steady increase in the prices of food, and of land itself, which became a desirable means to solving the country's fiscal problems. Disentailment was thus the single stone which could kill two birds: high food prices and a state of chronic financial crisis. Herr finds proof that disentailment was more an economic solution than an ideological issue in the fact that it was implemented by conservative governments at the end of the eighteenth century and by liberals such as Mendizábal and Madoz later on.

Disentailment undoubtedly was good business for the wealthy, who could buy and wait for prices to rise. But it probably was the landowning nobility who benefited most, since they often obtained full title to lands they did not previously own and over which they had only held mostly symbolic seigneurial rights. In fact, they exchanged feudal vestiges for actual bourgeois ownership. The church appears as the obvious loser: it lost its landed wealth. On closer examination, however, the church may not have done all that badly: Spanish budget figures show that the government transferred more in compensations and subsidies to the church than it received from the sale of church estates. How the municipalities fared is almost impossible to determine from budget figures. The only clear losers from disentailment were poor farmers and peasants, who had long benefited by encroaching upon church and public lands and had a more difficult time after these lands became private. Historians see in the plight of peasants, especially those in the South, the cause of the frequent rural rebellions of the second half of the nineteenth century. It is a reasonable hypothesis.

II

How did this gigantic real estate operation affect agriculture and its product? The massive import of the operation is undeniable: although very rough, the best estimates calculate that disentailment caused some 10 million hectares to change hands, approximately 40% of all Spanish arable land (Simón Segura [1973], p. 282). Herr puts the value of this land at between one-quarter and one-third of total value of Spanish real estate. Even admitting that not all disentailed land was arable, a transfer of land of such magnitude is generally assumed to have allowed for a considerable expansion of cultivation and growth of output. The most commonly held explanation of this expansion is as follows: church, states, and townships were not supposed to be very efficient entrepreneurs. According to this view, large extensions lay untilled due to lack of enterprising spirit on the part of the church and the public bodies. Private owners, on the contrary, considering their land as a productive asset and trying to obtain maximum profit from it, would exploit it more rationally and effectively.

This reasoning, however, is not totally convincing. If the private owner is a large holder who considers land a prestige asset, he may also undercultivate it. The situation could be even worse if the new buyer were a mere speculator or lacked the necessary capital or technical knowledge for cultivation. On the other hand, public owners could (and in fact they did, although to what extent is not known) rent out their land to farmers and tenants who, if the leases were stable enough, would normally behave very much like private owners. The presumption, therefore, that disentailment brought about an expansion of tilled acreage, although plausible, should not be taken for granted. Other factors such as the abolition of the tithe, the dissolution of the Mesta (the powerful organization of transhumant sheep owners and grazers, whose flocks had customarily been trampling and encroaching on farmers' lands for centuries), the improvements in transportation and communications, the decidedly protectionist policies in favor of grain cultivation after 1820, and the slow but steady increase in total population may all have exercised a more powerful pressure to extend cultivation than did disentailment per se.

In fact, we only have a rough idea of what happened during most of the nineteenth century. The tithe was definitively abolished in the 1830s, and this deprives historians of a reliable source to estimate the output of the main agricultural products. Until a reliable statistical body was organized for agriculture at the end of the century, knowledge of cultivated land and of output was a matter of guesswork. We know, however, of an attempt by the government to make an estimate of agricultural output and acreage for the year 1857 (Table 3.3). Even its authors dismissed this estimate as too low. In fact, however, it might have been closer to reality than they thought, given the fact that 1857 was a bad agricultural year. The yields per hectare, the productivity, and the consumption per capita that this estimate implies are certainly on the low side, but when compared with the more reliable figures we have for the late nineteenth and early twentieth centuries they reveal a not unacceptable order of magnitude.

Recourse must be made to indirect methods of estimation so we can have an idea, however approximate, of the evolution of Spanish agriculture during the nineteenth century. A recent, as yet unpublished, and very interesting attempt has been made by James Simpson to estimate the output of the main cereals by making some assumptions about consumption per capita. (It should be kept

Table 3.3
Crops and Yields of Spanish Agriculture in 1857

	(1) Acreage (1,000 hectares)	(2) Harvest (1,000 hectoliters)	(3) Hectoliters/ hectare	(4) Metric cwt./ hectare
			Yields	
1. Wheat	2,925	17,192	5.87	4.57
2. Barley	1,273	10,086	7.92	4.51
3. Rye	1,185	5,995	5.05	3.64
4. Maize	368	3,448	9.36	7.02
5. Chickpeas	218	520	2.38	
6. Rice	29	268	9.17	
7. Wine	1,143	5,405	4.72	
8. Olive oil	800	998	1.24	
9. Potatoes	204	467[a]	2.29[b]	22.90

Source: Moreno Villena (1882), pp. 118–119, reproducing data of the Junta General de Estadística.
a. metric tons; b. metric tons/hectare.

in mind that, although their relative importance was slowly decreasing, cereals and legumes, of which cereals were by far paramount, constituted over three-fourths of all agricultural land and amounted to well above one-half of agricultural output by 1900.) From an early census (the *Censo de Frutos y Manufacturas*) Simpson has estimated per capita consumption at the beginning of the nineteenth century: by relating these estimates to those obtained from official statistical sources for the early twentieth century, and by making some assumptions about the way in which consumption evolved, Simpson has been able to arrive at the tentative figures shown in Table 3.4. What these figures reveal is a modest growth in the output of wheat (the main staple); an even more modest growth in rye output (definitely considered as an inferior good by Spaniards); a remarkably fast growth in a relatively new crop, maize (which to a certain extent replaced rye in the diet of northern Spaniards), and a most impressive growth in a minor crop, rice, which is characteristic of the Mediterranean coast and an indicator of the agricultural development of this area. All in all, the evolution of the major crop, wheat, epitomizes the evolution of Spanish agriculture during the period considered: it expanded slowly and steadily, more slowly than Italian or French wheat during those periods of the nineteenth century when comparison is possible (the mid and late century). Although the tentative nature of the data does not allow for very subtle

Table 3.4
Estimated Yearly Cereal Output
in Decade Averages, 1800–1929
(1,000 metric tons)

	(1) Wheat	(2) Rye	(3) Maize	(4) Rice
1800–1809	1,643	376	208	25
1810–1819	1,722	383	229	34
1820–1829	1,801	390	252	43
1830–1839	1,938	408	282	54
1840–1849	2,165	444	328	71
1850–1859	2,404	481	379	93
1860–1869	2,584	504	421	111
1870–1879	2,778	514	457	124
1880–1889	2,712	533	502	139
1890–1899	2,816	550	547	166
1900–1909	2,892	578	607	193
1910–1919	3,330	615	678	232
1920–1929	3,747	660	767	298

SOURCE: Simpson (1985).

inferences, it seems quite clear that growth in output accelerated in the early
twentieth century, and not only in wheat or cereals, as we shall see later.

The growth of output which the figures in Table 3.4 reveal did not at all
constitute an "agricultural revolution"—far from it. As Table 3.5 shows, Spanish cereal yields were very low at the beginning of the twentieth century; this
implies that growth in output had only been possible because of a parallel
expansion in cultivated land. The similarity between Spanish and Italian yields
suggests a clue as to the causes of Spanish agricultural retardation. Given the
physical and institutional similarities between the two countries (Portugal
could be added, but we lack data) there is little doubt that this lack of progress
was caused by a mixture of geographical and cultural factors which are hard to
separate. In my view, however, the weight of climatic and soil conditions is
very heavy in Spain, possibly more so than in Italy or Portugal. In the words of
a classic in historical geography (Pounds [1947], 217):

Table 3.5
Agricultural Yields in Several European Countries,
1890–1910

	(1) Wheat	(2) Barley	(3) Rye	(4) Oats	(5) Potatoes
Spain					
1891–1900	7.6	9.2	6.9	7.9	n.d.
1901–1910	9.0	11.5	7.9	7.7	n.d.
Italy					
1890–1896	7.9[a]	6.5[b]	7.8[b]	7.1[b]	61.1[b]
1901–1910	9.5	9.0[c]	14.1[c]	9.3[c]	95.0[c]
France					
1892	12.7	11.9	11.0	10.8	105.0
1902	13.6	13.7	8.7	12.8	76.7
Britain					
1891–1900	25.3	20.9[d]	n.d.	17.4[d]	146.2[d]
1901–1910	22.1	21.1[e]	n.d.	19.0[e]	141.1[e]
Germany					
1892	17.1	17.0	14.2	14.4	111.7
1902	19.7	18.9	15.4	18.0	134.1
Upper Silesia					
1891–1900	15.5	16.6	13.3	15.0	110.0
1901–1910	17.6	18.7	15.3	17.6	125.5

SOURCES: Spain: Sotilla (1981); Italy: Mitchell (1976); France: O'Brien and Keyder
(1978); Britain: Mitchell (1976) and O'Brien and Keyder (1978); Germany: Mitchell
(1976); Upper Silesia: Haines (1982).
NOTE: Measures are in metric cwt./hectare.
a. 1890–1896;   b. 1890–1895;   c. 1909–1910;   d. 1892;   e. 1902.

Large areas, particularly on the Meseta, are almost bare of soil, and elsewhere the rainfall is so low that the land is barren steppe. The agrarian problem turns on the rainfall and the fertility of the soil. In the North, where rainfall is adequate—and often more than adequate—the land is hilly and the soil is thin and leached.

Both technology and physical conditions militated against Spain's agriculture. During the Middle Ages and Early Modern period the technological innovations in civilization were in large part best adapted to the lands of Northern Europe: this is the case with practically every single agricultural innovation mentioned in textbooks, from the "heavy plow" to the many varieties of "convertible agriculture and farming." With only a few minor exceptions, Spanish agriculture (and Southern European as a whole) remained tied to the two-field rotation of cereal cultivation, with the "light plow" scratching the sandy soils, much as in the time of the Roman Empire (when this technique, by the way, had been the best available). In my view, this accumulation of agricultural innovations adapted to the moist, heavy, rich soils of Northern Europe, which culminated in the "Agricultural Revolution" of the Early Modern Era—first in the Netherlands and then in England—is the main explanation of the gap in incomes and living standards between Northern and Southern Europe which became increasingly apparent during the nineteenth century. But it was not only that Spain, together with the Mediterranean basin in general, experienced physical conditions ill-suited to the techniques which were the basis of the Agricultural Revolution. Even within the Mediterranean context, Spain's agricultural conditions were generally poor. Neither in Italy nor in Portugal, its closest neighbors, did thin and rocky soils combine with lack of rainfall to make such a high proportion of land unsuitable for cultivation as was the case in Spain.

There was a brighter side, however. On the Mediterranean coast the nineteenth century, and even earlier periods, witnessed the start of the fruit and market gardening which fills with terror the hearts of farmers of the European Common Market in the 1980s. Wines, raisins, figs, almonds, hazel nuts, olive oil, and (above all) citrus fruits appear on the export side of the Spanish trade balance beginning in the middle of the nineteenth century. There lay the future of Spanish agriculture, but this future did not develop fully until well into the twentieth century. At the end of the nineteenth century, traditional crops used up three-fourths of arable land and produced about one-half of the total agricultural value, while orchard cultivation, using about one-eighth (12%) of arable land produced one-fourth of the total value.

Why was the transition from traditional to modern agriculture so slow? There is a simple answer: protectionism. As Sánchez-Albornoz showed a long time ago, Spanish tariff duties on wheat have been high at least since 1820 (Sánchez-Albornoz [1963]). Tariff protection became more and more vital to wheat farmers as transportation methods improved, and the competition of more efficient agricultural systems became keener. If freer trade had been allowed, foreign wheat exports would undoubtedly have caused a reduction in the number of Spanish wheat farmers, normally the less efficient ones. This would have entailed a redeployment of resources toward more productive crops and techniques (potatoes, maize, livestock; more fertilizers, better rotations, irrigation schemes) and, most important in this reallocation of resources, a process of outmigration from the Meseta to cities and abroad. Of course, all these processes did take place but at a slower pace than freer trade would have allowed. In fact, by opting for tariff protection, Spanish policymakers consciously or unconsciously made a choice for social stability and against rapid economic and social change. Free trade and the social dislocation it would have entailed could have brought about fast economic growth by allowing a better reallocation of resources; but this involved a high-risk operation: rapid migration—its social causes and consequences—could have provoked a political explosion. After disentailment the social and political atmosphere was very strained, especially in the southern countryside. Tariff protection, while slowing down growth, helped preserve social peace and the status quo.

Protection also hurt Mediterranean products in that those Spanish exports often faced protected markets (in other Mediterranean countries generally; sherry wine faced protection in England; raisins, in the United States; etc.).

A group of scholars who have been devoting their efforts to recent Spanish agrarian history have lately published an excellent work in which, based upon official figures, they estimate the Spanish agrarian product and its main components for a few key dates including the end of the nineteenth century and the beginning of the twentieth (Table 3.6). This pioneering work evinces a growing agricultural sector, whose total product increased 55% during the first three decades of the twentieth century, implying an average yearly growth of 1.4%. According to Table 3.1, agricultural productivity grew faster than average during this period, although it still remained below average at the end.

The average growth rate of 1.4% stands clearly above the rate of population growth for the same period, which was about 0.8%; by implication, agrarian per capita income increased at an approximate average rate of 0.6%. Although respectable, and probably unprecedented in Spain, this per capita rate is undoubtedly lower than the growth rate for all income per capita. According to the available estimates, national income per capita grew at a rate of 1.3%,

Table 3.6
Agricultural Output, Farmland, and Productivity, 1893–1931

	1893	1900	1910	1922	1931
(A) Output (millions of pesetas of 1910)					
1. Grains and legumes	2,027	1,992	2,045	2,567	2,376
2. Vineyards	568	424	385	451	416
3. Olive fields	257	227	233	369	397
4. Other[a]	777	800	1,121	1,471	2,109
5. TOTAL (1 + 2 + 3 + 4)	3,629	3,443	3,789	4,868	5,298
6. Woods and pastures	423	422	316	367	286
7. Livestock	736	810	1,132	1,482	1,657
8. GRAND TOTAL (5 + 6 + 7)	4,788	4,675	5,232	6,707	7,241
(B) Farmland (1,000 hectares)					
1. Grains and legumes	11,777	13,706	14,182	15,511	16,172
2. Vineyards	1,460	1,429	1,347	1,334	1,540
3. Olive fields	1,123	1,197	1,379	1,622	1,911
4. Other[a]	1,464	1,490	1,976	1,810	2,341
5. TOTAL (1 + 2 + 3 + 4)	15,829	17,822	18,884	20,277	21,964
6. Woods and pastures	28,046	27,367	26,044	25,281	23,602
7. GRAND TOTAL (5 + 6)	43,875	45,189	44,928	45,558	45,566
(C) Productivity (pesetas of 1910 per hectare)					
1. Grains and legumes	172	145	144	165	147
2. Vineyards	389	297	286	338	270
3. Olive fields	229	190	169	227	208
4. Other[a]	529	537	567	813	901
5. TOTAL AGRICULTURE	229	193	200	240	241
6. Woods and pastures	15	15	12	15	12
7. TOTAL LAND PRODUCTIVITY[b]	109	103	116	147	159
8. TOTAL LAND PRODUCTIVITY[c]	92	86	91	115	123
9. LABOR PRODUCTIVITY[d]	1,188	1,087	1,127	1,554	1,918

Source: Grupo de Estudios de Historia Rural (1983).
a. mainly fruits and orchards; b. includes livestock; c. excludes livestock; d. pesetas of 1910 per male agricultural worker.

about double that for agriculture. Therefore, although agriculture developed enough to allow a clear improvement in the diet of the average Spaniard, the other two major sectors (industry and services) developed considerably faster.

The increase in agricultural output was made possible by an increase in the productivity of land and labor and an expansion of acreage. Land productivity, however, did not grow by much (Table 3.6, Line C-5) because grains and legumes, the least productive of its subsectors, remained overwhelmingly the most important in terms of acreage: it occupied about three-quarters of all cultivated land by 1931. This, in turn, was made possible by tariff protection.

Owing to very steep tariff duties, this inefficient subsector actually expanded its acreage during those years (see Table 3.6, Line B-1). Among the consequences of such decided state protection to wheat growers stand, naturally, high bread and food prices: relative peace and quiet in the countryside was thus obtained at the expense of a dismal standard of living of urban workers.

Fortunately, however, the amount of land devoted to high productivity crops, such as fruit orchards, potatoes, beets, and fresh vegetables generally, increased as well. The acreage devoted to orange groves, although very small in relative terms, doubled. The real value of its output nearly quadrupled. The productivity of each acre devoted to orange cultivation was over 10 times the average productivity of Spanish agriculture, and nearly 17 times the productivity of land devoted to cereal. Although maybe not so large, similar proportions applied in the cases of crops such as almonds, potatoes, and beets. The transfer of resources—basically land and labor—toward these products was one of the chief mechanisms that brought about higher productivity.

The productivity of traditional Mediterranean products such as vines and olive trees measured in pesetas per hectare increased very little or, as in the case of the vine, they in fact diminished. Yields per hectare, however, improved. Vine acreage went down during the first decades of the twentieth century and recovered later on; the decline was due to the spread of phylloxera, a plague which had affected French vines some fifteen years earlier. At first Spain had benefited: its wine exports soared as French production fell. Later on, as French production recovered and phylloxera ravaged Spanish vineyards, the acreage shrank and, though it recovered somewhat, never reached the level of the late nineteenth century.

Agrarian labor productivity increased faster than land productivity (Table 3.6, Line C-9). More than to the introduction of novel technology, which took place to a very limited extent, this increase was due to outmigration. The number of agricultural workers slowly but steadily went down during the first third of the twentieth century, from 5 million in 1900 to 4 million in 1935. The average number of hectares cultivated per worker went up from 2.4 in 1900 to 5.3 in 1931. This more than doubling of the acreage tilled by one worker offers a clear indication of the increase in labor productivity and the reduction of the so-called disguised unemployment, so characteristic of backward economies, whereby a fraction of apparently employed agricultural workers in reality contribute nothing to output. In Spain, the fall in the number of agricultural workers did not bring about a decrease in output even though cultivation techniques were not substantially improved.

III

Agricultural change is a vital part of economic development. First of all, because all developing economies are largely agrarian and, therefore, without agricultural change, there can hardly be social and economic change. Furthermore, a series of concrete tasks must be performed by the agricultural sector as economic modernization proceeds. These tasks are the following: (1) Food surpluses must be produced to feed the growing nonagrarian, largely urban population. (2) Agriculture must provide a strong market for industrial goods, typically clothing and other consumer goods, implements, fertilizers, and other equipment. In fact, economic growth consists to a vast extent in this exchange of agricultural for industrial surpluses. (3) Savings accumulated in the agrarian sector must be transferred through capital markets or through taxes and contribute to industrial capital formation. (4) The increase in agricultural productivity plus the growth in population due in part to better diets should generate a labor surplus whose outmigration would contribute to the growth of the industrial labor force. (5) A growing economy must import equipment and technology; agricultural exports typically help to finance these imports.

How did Spanish agriculture perform with regard to the requirements sketched above during the period under consideration? That, aside from the expansion of cultivated land, it underwent little change is suggested by a fact which Pérez Moreda (1983) has recently underscored: the proportion of labor in agriculture remained unchanged from the beginning to the end of the nineteenth century. Growth appears to have been extremely slow during the nineteenth century, as suggested by the low levels of productivity (Table 3.6), per capita consumption, and the estimated wheat output (Table 3.4). If this had not been the case, then productivity and consumption levels around 1800 should necessarily have been nearly zero.

Let me conclude this chapter by examining how Spanish agriculture performed the five tasks mentioned above. As we already know, the task of improving and expanding the output of food so as to sustain a growing urban population and to upgrade the average diet was not very satisfactorily accomplished. Of course, there was some increase in cereal output but not enough to surpass by much the growth of population in the long run. Although official figures are lacking, the estimates in Table 3.4, plus other indirect evidence, support this assessment. The rate of urbanization remained low throughout the nineteenth century: only 9% of the population lived in towns of more than

100,000 in 1900. The proportion was 15% by 1930. The percentage of non-agricultural labor remained about constant throughout the nineteenth century: it stood at 33% in 1900 and went up to 55% by 1935. All this points in the same direction as our output figures and guesses: near stagnation in the nineteenth century, beginnings of change in the twentieth. More hints in the same sense are supplied by what we know about diets. On this topic we have scattered evidence for different times and places: on the one hand, we know that periodic widespread famines occurred at least as late as the mid-1860s; on the other, numerous testimonies reflect very low average calorie and protein intakes in cities (especially large cities) at the end of the nineteenth and well into the twentieth centuries. (See, for instance, *Comisión para el estudio* [1909], Dirección General de Aduanas [1896], Luis y Yagüe [1903], Membiela y Salgado [1885], Pérez Moreda [1980], Ringrose [1983], Sáenz Díaz [1878], Sánchez-Albornoz [1977], Simpson [1985], Tortella [1983].) Exports of grain during the mid-nineteenth century have been adduced to prove that cereal output expanded during the nineteenth century (Anes [1970]); we must keep in mind, however, that the amounts exported were usually very small. According to official figures published by Leandro Prados (1982b), average net yearly exports of wheat and wheat flour for the 1826–1849 period were about 20,000 metric tons, something slightly below 1% of the average yearly crop. In time, however, net exports diminished and eventually became negative: the yearly average for 1850–1875 was 180,000 metric tons, and after 1875 Spain became a net importer of wheat and flour. These figures suggest not only long-term stagnation in output per capita but also technological stagnation, since the exporting period coincided with the height of the practice of disentailment: growth of output was possible through increased acreage, not through better yields.

Possibly the worst failure of Spanish agriculture in the nineteenth century was as a market for industrial products. The role of peasant consumption as a factor in the growth of the mostly Catalan textile cotton industry is frequently mentioned; it is clear, however, that the low level of consumption created a continuous threat of overproduction after the mid-nineteenth century, as Nadal (1973) and Sudriá (1983) have shown, and that the development of the textile industry during the years 1830 to 1855 was due more to the substitution of Catalan cotton textiles for English (thanks to tariff protection) and for more traditional fibers, such as wool and linen. A recent paper (Prados [1983]) has established that Spanish textile consumption was below that of England or France and, furthermore, that it increased at a slower rate. Since the majority of

Spaniards at that time were peasants and farmers, this is one more proof of the shallowness of that sector as a market.

Agriculture was even shallower a market for equipment. As a whole, the sector simply did not acquire modern implements, and it remained wedded to the ancestral so-called Roman plow, made of wood entirely except for a small plowshare, the primitive wood-and-stone thresher drawn by a mule or a donkey, and the like. There are innumerable statements by contemporaries and evidence from modern scholars about the technological stagnation of Spanish agriculture in the nineteenth century (*Comisión para el estudio* [1909], Dopico [1982], Garrabou [1978], Maluquer [1983]). This means that the market for such industries as iron and steel, other metals, mechanical manufacture, and heavy chemicals (which made a timid appearance in Spain during the nineteenth century) had to wait until the twentieth to grow; agriculture, which was a key market for these industries in Britain, Germany, and the United States, played no such role in Spain. As a concrete example, I have found in my research that, when the Spanish Nobel Dynamite Company erected a superphosphate factory around 1890 to take advantage of the surplus sulphuric acid which was a byproduct of manufacturing nitroglycerin, it soon found its sales so low that the company decided to close the plant after a few years (Tortella [1983a]). As in Portugal, only a few steam threshers were introduced in Spain at the end of the nineteenth century, especially in large wheat farms with considerable economies of scale (Reis [1982]).

It is difficult to establish with any precision to what extent agriculture performed its task of supplier of capital to other sectors; for the time being, it can be said that it transferred a certain amount of capital, although clearly insufficient and poorly allocated. One of the channels for the transfer is taxes. Although tax evasion by large landowners was an undisputed fact, the agricultural sector as a whole shouldered more than its proportional share of taxes (Fuentes [1961], Comín [1984]). A large part of the taxes extracted from agriculture, nonetheless, were not productively invested; as I have argued elsewhere (Tortella [1978]), a large part of state expenditure was squandered in military and other unproductive employments.

The amount of private savings and their channeling are more difficult to trace. Indirect evidence would suggest that only a very small fraction of agricultural savings was productively invested in other sectors. In the first place, if farmers hardly invested in their own farms, which they knew well, why should they have invested in industrial or commercial activities which were alien to them? We have several portrayals of farmers' mistrust, not only of industry and trade, but also of banks (not an unjustified mistrust, at least at that time), which made them hoard precious metals rather than deposit them and gain interest. In the second place, several banking history studies have shown that the number of landowning individuals among bank founders in the mid-nineteenth century was disproportionately exiguous (Sánchez-Albornoz [1968], Tortella [1973]). When the main banks and savings banks appeared at the end of the nineteenth and beginning of the twentieth centuries, they did so in industrial and commercial areas, not in agrarian provinces or towns.

The transfer of manpower from agriculture to industry was very limited during the nineteenth century (nil in relative terms), and it took place, though moderately, in the first third of the twentieth. The relatively slow growth of Spanish population prior to 1900 is probably the main explanation of this phenomenon; high death rates, the main cause of slow population growth. Illiteracy and general ignorance, together with poor diets, low standards of living, and government negligence, in turn are the main explanations for the high death rates. Agriculture, therefore, is only partly to blame for the limited population transfer. It must be noted, moreover, that when outmigration from the countryside started in earnest from the 1880s onward, the cities were unable to absorb it, and a large part of the emigrants went abroad. International outmigration, however, was common in most Western European countries during that period.

Some reference has already been made to grain exports in the mid-nineteenth century. On this point, agriculture certainly contributed to economic development; unfortunately, it took place at the wrong time. Indeed, when the first stirrings of industrialization made themselves felt in the 1880s Spanish grains (like those of most of Europe) not only were not exported but were met with strong competition in Russian and American cereals.

Nonetheless, this was also the time when Spanish agriculture started to show its export potential, which derived from those products in which it had absolute and comparative advantages, such as those typical of Mediterranean agriculture, plus others not necessarily Mediterranean such as wool, skins and leather, livestock, and forestry products such as cork. In spite of the small percentage of soil and resources these products absorbed, they represented about 35% of total—agricultural and nonagricultural—exports. Although its expansion proceeded slowly even after 1900, this was the portion of Spanish agriculture which performed the task of exporting for development. Due to the phylloxera plague, however, wine lost its top export rank in the mid-1890s to ores and minerals.

To conclude, agricultural stagnation explains to a large extent the relative retardation of the Spanish economy during the period under study. Agricultural stagnation, in turn, was determined by physical and institutional factors that, in large part, Spain shared with the countries of the Western Mediterranean basin.

FURTHER READINGS

Alcaide Inchausti, Julio (1976). "Una revisión urgente de la serie de Renta Nacional española en el siglo XX." In Instituto de Estudios Fiscales (1976), pp. 1127–1150.

Anes Alvarez, Gonzalo (1970). "La agricultura española desde comienzos del siglo XIX hasta 1868: algunos problemas." In Banco de España (1970), pp. 253–263.

———— Luis Angel Rojo, and Pedro Tedde, eds. (1983). *Historia económica y pensamiento social,* Madrid.

Bairoch, Paul (1963). *Révolution industrielle et sous-développement,* Paris.

———— (1973). "Agriculture and the Industrial Revolution, 1700–1914." In Cipolla (1973), pp. 452–506.

Banco de España (1970). *Ensayos sobre la economía española a mediados del siglo XIX,* Madrid.

———— (1982). *La economía española al final del Antiguo Régimen. III. Comercio y colonias,* Madrid.

Bona, Francisco Javier de (1877). "Producción de los cereales." *Gaceta Agrícola del Ministerio de Fomento,* II, pp. 257–264.

Cipolla, Carlo M. (1973), ed. *Fontana Economic History of Europe,* vols. 3 and 4(2) (London, 1972–1973).

———— (1970). *The Economic History of World Population,* Baltimore.

Comín, Francisco (1984). "Algunos resultados de la Reforma Tributaria Mon-Santillán." In Miguel Artola and Luis María Bilbao, eds., *Estudios de Hacienda de Ensenada a Mon,* Madrid, pp. 85–104.

Comisión para el estudio de la producción y consumo de trigo. Su nombramiento. Actas de sus sesiones. Dictamen y apéndices (1909). Madrid.

Dirección General de Aduanas (1896). *Informe acerca de la producción comercio y consumo de trigo en España,* Madrid.

Dopico Gutiérrez del Arroyo, Fausto (1982). "Productividade, rendementos e tecnoloxía na agricultura galega de fins do seculo XIX." *Grial Anexo Historia,* 1, pp. 66–81.

Fuentes Quintana, Enrique (1961). "Los principios del reparto de la carga tributaria en España." *Revista de Derecho Financiero y Hacienda Pública,* 41, pp. 161–298.

García-Lombardero y Viñas, Jaime (1985). "Los efectos de la protección arancelaria sobre la producción de cereales en España, 1890–1910." In P. Martín Aceña and L. Prados de la Escosura (1985), pp. 192–203.

Garrabou, R. (1978). "Cultius, collites i rendiments a la Segarra i Alt Anoia: el comptes d'unes finques de Guissona, Sant Martí i Castellfollit de Riubregós." *Estudis d'Història Agrària,* 1, pp. 241–280.

Grupo de Estudios de Historia Rural (1983). "Notas sobre la producción agraria española, 1891–1931." *Revista de Historia Económica,* I, 2, pp. 185–252.

Haines, Michael R. (1982). "Agriculture and Development in Prussian Upper Silesia, 1846–1913." *Journal of Economic History,* 42, no. 2, pp. 355–384.

Herr, Richard (1958). *The Eighteenth-Century Revolution in Spain,* Princeton.

——— (1974a). "El significado de la desamortización en España." *Moneda y Crédito,* 131, pp. 55–94.

——— (1974b). "La vente des propriétés de mainmorte en Espagne, 1798–1808." *Annales Economie, Société, Civilisation* (1974), pp. 215–228.

Institució Alfóns el Magnànim (1983). *I Colloqui d'Història Agrària,* Valencia.

Instituto de Estudios Fiscales (1976). *Datos básicos para la historia financiera de España (1850–1975),* 2 vols., Madrid.

Llopis Agelán, Enrique (1983). "Algunas consideraciones acerca de la producción agraria castellana en los veinticinco últimos años del Antiguo Régimen." *Investigaciones Económicas,* 21, pp. 135–151.

Luis y Yagüe, R. (1903). *Bromatología popular urbana,* Madrid.

Maluquer de Motes, Jordi (1983). "Las relacions entre agricultura i indústria en el desenvolupament capitalista catalá del vuit-cents. Algunes hipótesis." Institució Alfóns el Magnànim (1983), pp. 199–212.

Martín Aceña, Pablo, and Leandro Prados de la Escosura (1985), eds. *La Nueva Historia económica en España,* Madrid.

Membiela y Salgado, Roque (1885). *Higiene popular. La cuestión obrera en España o estado de nuestras clases necesitadas y medios para mejorar su situación,* Santiago.

Mitchell, B. R. (1976). *European Historical Statistics 1750–1970,* New York.

Moreno Villena, Pedro (1882). *Geografía-estadística astronómica, física, fabril y comercial de Europa con especialidad de España,* Valencia.

Nadal, Jordi (1973). "The Failure of the Industrial Revolution in Spain, 1814–1913." In C. M. Cipolla, ed., 4(2), London, pp. 533–626.

O'Brien, P., and C. Keyder (1978). *Economic Growth in Britain and France, 1870–1914,* London.

Pérez Moreda, Vicente (1980). *Las crisis de mortalidad en la España interior (siglos XVI–XIX),* Madrid.

———— (1983). "En defensa del Censo de Godoy: observaciones previas al estudio de la población activa española de finales del siglo XVIII." In Anes, Rojo, and Tedde (1983), pp. 283–299.

Pounds, Norman (1947). *An Historical and Political Geography of Europe.* London.

Prados de la Escosura, Leandro (1982a). *Comercio exterior y crecimiento económico en España 1826–1913: tendencias a largo plazo.* Estudios de Historia Económica, no. 7, Madrid.

———— (1982b). "Comerico exterior y cambio económico en España (1792–1849)." In Banco de España (1982), pp. 173–249.

———— (1983). "Producción y consumo de tejidos en España, 1800–1913: Primeros resultados." In Anes, Rojo, and Tedde (1983), pp. 455–471.

Reis, Jaime (1982). "Latifúndio e progresso técnico: a difusão da debulha mecânica no Alentejo, 1860–1930." *Análise Social,* XVIII (71), 2, pp. 371–433.

Ringrose, David R. (1983). *Madrid and the Spanish Economy, 1560–1850,* Berkeley and Los Angeles.

Sáenz Díaz, Manuel (1878). "Estudio de los alimentos que consume la clase labradora y los braceros de algunas provincias de España." *Memorias de la Real Academia de Ciencias Exactas, Físicas y Naturales.* Vol. 8, Madrid.

Sánchez-Albornoz, Nicolás (1963). *Las crisis de subsistencias de España en el siglo XIX,* Rosario, Argentina.

———— (1968). "Los bancos y las sociedades de crédito en provincias: 1856–1868." *Moneda y Crédito,* 104, pp. 39–68.

———— (1975). *Los precios argícolas durante la segunda mitad del siglo XIX. Volumen I. Trigo y Cebada,* Madrid.

———— (1977). *España hace un siglo: una economía dual,* 2d ed., Madrid.

Simón Segura, Francisco (1973). *La desamortización española en el siglo XIX,* Madrid.

———— (1984). "La desamortización española del siglo XIX." *Papeles de Economía Española,* 20, pp. 74–107.

Simpson, James (1985). "El consumo y la producción de cereales panificables en el siglo XIX" (typescript).

Sotilla, Eduardo de la (1981). "Producción y riqueza agrícola de España en el último decenio del siglo XIX y primero del XX." *Agricultura y Sociedad*, 18 (originally published in 1911), pp. 303–409.

Sudriá, Carles (1983). "La exportación en el desarrollo de la industria algodonera española, 1875–1920." *Revista de Historia Económica*, I, 2, pp. 369–386.

Tortella, Gabriel (1973). *Los orígenes del capitalismo en España. Banca, industria y ferrocarriles en el siglo XIX*, Madrid.

———— (1978). "La formación de capital en España, 1874–1914: reflexiones para un planteamiento de la cuestión." *Hacienda Pública Española*, 55, pp. 399–415.

———— (1981). "La economía española, 1830–1900." In Manuel Tuñón de Lara, ed., *Historia de España*, VIII (Barcelona), pp. 11–167.

———— (1983a). "La primera gran empresa química española: la Sociedad Española de la Dinamita (1872–1896)." In Anes, Rojo, and Tedde (1983), pp. 431–453.

———— (1983b). "El consumo y la producción de trigo en España a finales del siglo XIX" (typescript).

4.
A CENTURY OF INDUSTRIALIZATION IN SPAIN, 1833–1930

JORDI NADAL
Universidad de Barcelona

THE ultimate purpose of this book is to analyze Spain's transition from an Ancien Régime society to a capitalist one. A "society of Ancien Régime" means a society based on subsistence agriculture, a privileged aristocracy, and the control of ideas. The transition to a capitalist society should produce what is generally known as an industrial, liberal, and bourgeois society. The term "should produce" is used instead of "produces" because in 1930 the transition process in Spain was far from complete.

Therein lies the uniqueness of the Spanish experience. Even in the course of a century from 1833 to 1930, the transformations related to industralization in Spain do not reach the significance and depth that they reach in other places. During this period there certainly are changes: the population doubles in size; the production of grain barely keeps pace with the population; most sectors of modern industry are introduced into the country; and the passé monarchy, which is out of touch with constitutional ideas, is pushed to the edge of extinction. The agricultural sector in 1930, however, continues as the dominant force within the economy, and the privileged classes remain as resistant to change as ever.

Therefore, the subject of this chapter refers, not only to a process of development, but also to the constraints that impede the overall process. The first part of this chapter deals with the period between the death of Ferdinand VII (1833) and the end of the First Republic (1874) and corresponds to what has been called the "bourgeois revolution." The second part deals with the period from 1875 to 1930 and corresponds to the "bourgeois reaction."

During the first period, the most relevant socioeconomic occurrence was the consolidation of power of a landed oligarchy (composed of the old manorial aristocracy and a nucleus of new bourgeois landowners created by land disen-tailment). This consolidation of power took place at the expense of peasant farmers and concentrated the wealth in the hands of relatively few; it also blocked the formation of an internal market which would have had enough consumption capacity to spur a true industrialization. After several initial spurts, which in some cases go back to the eighteenth century, Spanish industry ended up stifled by the inelasticity of demand. Even the construction of the railroad network, erroneously conceived by some as a providential remedy to the country's stagnation, did little to allow Spain to escape from its economic morass. In sum, the shortcomings of the bourgeois revolution resulted in the weakness of Spain's first stage of industrial development.

There is no need to elaborate on the textile industry's stagnation at the end of this period (both Nicolás Sánchez-Albornoz and Leandro Prados have traced downward trends in textile consumption beginning in 1860),[1] nor on the insignificance of the iron-and-steel industry during its Andalusian (1832–1864) and Asturian (1865–1879) phases. Instead, it will be more useful to examine what caused the cotton industry's unexpected rise during the second third of the nineteenth century and to include an analysis of the chemical industry—an industrial sector whose meaning has been largely overlooked by historians.

Catalan cotton manufacturing reached the factory stage after 1830, when the mule-jenny and the mechanical loom replaced the *bergadana* and the hand loom. The immediate result was an increase in productivity and a decrease in prices. The domestic market opened up to printed calicoes and other native products. As import substitution took place, cotton products absorbed an increasingly larger share of the home market at the expense of other fabrics. Catalan textile manufacturing not only closed the door to imports; it also displaced the Galician linen industry. Xan Carmona brings out this point in his excellent study on the collapse of domestic industry in rural Galicia.[2] Around 1750 the operation of about 15,000 linen looms provided income for some 50,000 families (one-fourth of the total census count) in the already declining Galician agrarian sector. A century later the lack of mechanization; the loss of colonies; contraband; the duty-free status granted to foreign yarns; and, above all, the competition from Catalan producers had crushed the Galician linen industry before any modern industrialization could be intro-duced in the region. The dimensions of the market aside, there was no other part of Europe where cotton dominated linen as it did in Spain. In a sharp analysis of the Catalan formula for business success, Carmona pointed out that less emphasis was placed on the traveling salesman and much more on the silent partnerships between wholesalers from La Coruña and Vigo (or Madrid, Valladolid, Granada, and others when researchers decide to investigate these notarial registries) and the producers from Catalonia. These associations assured the continuity of both supply and demand at the expense of other suppliers, especially household industry, which was limited to peasant consumption. Furthermore, Catalan capital played a decisive part in financing the *Compañía de los Ferrocarriles de Medina a Zamora y de Orense a Vigo* (Railroad from Medina to Zamora and from Orense to Vigo); this company provided one of the two links between Galicia and the rest of Spain, and during the last quarter of the nineteenth century it allowed the abandonment of coastal navigation as a means of transporting goods.

In addition to the rise of the cotton industry and the decline of the iron-and-steel industry, this era also produced a downturn in the chemical industry. At the end of the eighteenth century, Spain was a major exporter of saltwort and an incipient importer of lyes and mordants, which were supplied by the English and the French. After the War for Independence (1808–1819), the rapid recovery of the Catalan textile industry encouraged François Cros of Montpellier (France) to establish in Sants, on the outskirts of Barcelona, the first Spanish factory to produce vitriol, or sulfuric acid. From 1820, Cros and many imitators freed Catalonia from its long-standing dependence on materials for mordants. In 1830–1831 a series of investigations done by the regional Board of Trade and the central Council of Tariffs showed that Catalan production of copperas, or iron sulfate, already supplied the region with half of its needs. This development, however, was cut short. As the new domestic producers were able to replace foreign mordants, their French and British competitors promoted artificial soda, which held great promise for the chemical industry. This Leblanc soda was produced at a much lower cost and with a higher grade of alkali than that obtained from glasswort ashes; the Leblanc soda not only stimulated the growth of the glass, paper, and hard soap industries; it also expanded its own uses through the sale of a chemical byproduct, hydrochloric or muriatic acid which, when transformed into chloride of lime, constituted the best bleaching agent for fabrics and paper. Before artificial soda, the chemical industry had its major outlet in the textile industry, but after the introduction of artificial soda it became multidimensional, serving a wide ranging and ever increasing number of other manufacturers. Although the Spanish chemical industry started out well, it could not keep up with foreign competition and suffered a forty-year stagnation (1830–1872) until the Sociedad Española de la Dinamita factory opened up in Galdácano.

In 1880 Spain produced 860,000 square meters of window panes, one-twentieth of what was produced in Belgium and one-tenth of what was produced in only one region of France. In 1885 the Spanish consumption of paper was estimated at an annual 1.5 pounds per person, as compared with 3.5 pounds in Italy, 7.5 pounds in France, and 11.5 pounds in Great Britain. The slow pace of urban development, the cultural backwardness, and the low level of hygiene all combined to limit the use of glass, books, newspapers, and soap in nineteenth-century Spain. In spite of an abundant array of raw materials (salt, sulfur, pyrites, and manganese), the manufacture of Leblanc soda and its derivatives did not take hold in Spain. In the case of soda, there was little demand and an inherent lack of economies of scale, and in the case of its derivative, hydrochloric acid, which was produced abundantly as a highly toxic chemical by-product, foreign alkali manufacturers were willing to sell it at any price just to rid themselves of it. Because of these conditions several attempts (including those of François Cros's son and Manuel Agustín Heredia in Málaga) to produce these materials did not succeed until the first decade of the twentieth century, when the German-financed company Electroquímica de Flix, the United States-financed Electra del Besaya, and the Belgian-financed Solvay et Cie established the first alkali- and chlorine-producing factories. Since the Leblanc method had already become obsolete, the factory in Tarragona employed an electrolytic-processing procedure, while the ones in Bárcena and Barreda located in the province of Santander used an ammoniacal processing method.[3]

From 1875 on, the "bourgeois reaction" prevailed, and the first stage of Spanish industrialization came to a close. Because of the weakness of industrialization, the agricultural crisis which broke out in 1880 could not be prevented and became an endemic problem later. In Europe the formation of a world market for grains, brought about by a revolution in transportation, precipitated a restructuring of the rural economy based on new crops and increased productivity. In Spain industrial demand was not sizable enough to stimulate an increase in agricultural production and productivity, nor to create jobs in urban centers, which would have absorbed the surplus of day laborers from the South and small property owners from the Northeast, who cultivated unprofitable farms.

Instead of looking for radical changes, the bourgeoisie reverted to old expedients. Sharing the same problems, landowners and industrial managers joined forces demanding protection not only from the foreign wheat and industrial products but also from the domestic threat of a rising workers' movement, which pressed to have the effects of economic underdevelopment more equally spread within Spanish society. Cánovas answered these demands passing protectionist laws also reinforcing the colonial pact. On the other hand, repression hindered the normal development of trade unions and out-lawed strikes and workers' demands as though they were real revolutionary menaces.

The tariff policies of the Restoration, which were the core of its economic policy, simply reinstated all the painstaking regulations set forth during the previous fifty years. The following review of legislation concerning grain imports is quite revealing: in August 1820 the importation of wheat, barley, other grains, and foreign flours was prohibited while the price of a *fanega* (about 1.6 bushels) of wheat, whose price was taken as a bench mark, was not to exceed 80 reales and a quintal of flour 120 reales in peninsular markets. This utter closing of the Spanish market lasted until August 1869. Then the Figuerola tariff, enacted at the time of the "Glorious Revolution," substituted this prohibitionist system for a protectionist one. A duty of just three pesetas on each metric quintal was imposed on foreign wheat. The purpose was to make a dent and then gradually widen it. Instead, the Restoration cut short the process and reinstated the old policy. Foreign wheat cost 5.82 pesetas from August 1877 to December 1890, 8 pesetas from December 1890 to February 1895, 10.5 pesetas from February 1895 to 1906, and so on. This uninterrupted series of increases culminated in the law of July 16, 1922—a law which remained in force until 1928—prohibiting imports of foreign wheat as long as the price of domestic wheat did not go over 52 pesetas per metric quintal for a month in the markets of Castile. In 1922 this situation had reverted exactly to where it had been in 1820!

Such a policy explains the surprising course of Spanish cereal agriculture. Wheat alone occupied more than one-third of the cultivated land, and the total acreage for cereals and legumes combined was 80%. This agricultural system was very inefficient, as the average yields of wheat per seeded hectare barely reached 7 to 8 metric quintals (from 4 to 5 metric quintals per cultivated hectare). This led to a situation of impending bankruptcy as soon as Russian and American grains began to overrun the foreign markets. Ignoring all warnings and firmly entrenched behind a barrier of protective tariffs, the peasant farmers of the interior and small- and medium-sized landowners reacted to their precarious state by increasing production on lands that increasingly yielded less. The result was a paradox; this backward agricultural system with low productivity defied all logic by increasing, instead of decreasing, the acreage given over to cereal cultivation. According to estimates provided by the Grupo de Estudios de Historia Rural, the cereal system (acreage in cereals and legumes, fallow fields, and temporarily untilled lands) increased by 2.5 million hectares between 1900 and 1931.[4] This enormous amount of added acreage hindered any possible gains in productvity that might have been attained through improved fertilizers, machinery, and so on. Wheat yields in 1931 were the same as they had been in both 1900 and 1874; in addition, this pattern shows up in other cereal crops and in the other two components of the Mediterranean agricultural trilogy—the olive and the vineyard. Naturally this agricultural stagnation impaired associated activities like flour processing. In 1900 there were more than 17,000 traditional water mills on rivers, and they accounted for 55% of all flour-processing transactions. The modern flour mills, using the so-called Austro-Hungarian method, were located mostly in Catalonia where, in spite of the tariff, Russian grain imports were shipped into Spain.

The social costs of the Spanish agricultural system also took their toll: completely outdated rental contracts, relics of the Ancien Régime, were kept in force in Galicia and Catalonia by means of a *rabassa morta* (a contractual agreement in Catalonia dealing with profits from vineyard cultivation); wretched salaries and seasonal unemployment in the areas of large landed estates (Andalusia, Extremadura, and La Mancha); the unbelievably high incidence of subsistence farming in smallholder regions like Old Castile and León; and the control of power by dominant economic groups which guaranteed an efficient repressive apparatus. Migration to South America was the most effective safety valve of the time, and in many locations entire populations took advantage of this remedy. Foreign migration added up to 1.5 million emigrants during the years 1904–1913, that is, 8% of the entire population. During and after World War I, when this migratory outlet was closed off social tensions rose to such a level that some authentic revolutionary attempts occurred.

The large sectors of the economy were certainly interdependent. The cotton industry provides the best example. During the last two decades of the nineteenth century, until 1898, Catalan textiles had found in the Antilles a solution to the inelasticity of internal demand. After the Treaty of Paris, which stripped Spain of the last vestiges of its colonial empire, "excess production with no market" was the continual bane of businessmen and their backers. The devaluation of the peseta; the repatriation of migrants and soldiers (177,168 military personnel returned from Cuba and Puerto Rico between the end of the war and March 1899 on ships owned by the Cía Transatlántica; and the attempt to open new markets, especially in Argentina even at ruinous prices, mitigated in part the effects of the disaster. In the long run, however, overproduction became chronic and irremediable, except under unusual circumstances (e.g., as in World War I). Eusebio Bertrand y Serra, president of the

Regulatory Board for the Cotton Industry, stated in 1931, "the loss of export markets marked the beginning of the textile crisis which, with very few reprieves, has continued throughout the last thirty years." One obvious reprieve occurred in 1914, when "Divine Providence in the form of the horrors of World War I allowed the industry to get back on its feet."[5]

The problem of surpluses and the narrowness of the market caused the textile industry to lose all its dynamism during the Restoration period. A comparison of the figures for 1882–1883 and those for 1925–1929 in Table 4.1 clearly reveals why the Spanish textile industry had one of the lowest growth rates in Europe.

At the beginning of the Restoration, on a per capita basis the Spanish cotton industry was sixth among European countries; at the end of Primo de Rivera's dictatorship, it had plummeted to tenth place. At that time, the cotton industry, measured according to volume of employment and, more importantly, by added value, was still the main industry of Spain. It was, however, an industry with obsolete equipment, lacking vigor and outreach. It was on the defensive. After achieving through protection full control over the home market (based on constant pesetas, the duties charged on foreign yarns and textiles— whether unfinished, bleached or dyed—were in 1925 three times higher than what they had been in 1913), it demanded in 1926 the creation of the already mentioned Regulatory Board. In July of that year the industry obtained by

Table 4.1
Spun Cotton Per Capita
(annual averages in kilograms)

1882–1883		1925–1929	
1. United Kingdom	18.96	1. United Kingdom	13.74
2. Switzerland	7.87	2. Belgium	11.60
3. Belgium	5.05	3. Switzerland	7.50
4. Germany	3.23	4. France	7.33
5. France	3.00	5. Germany	5.90
6. Spain	1.90	6. Netherlands	5.51
7. Netherlands	2.27	7. Italy	5.16
8. Austria	2.05	8. Austria	4.03
9. Sweden and Norway	1.90	9. Sweden	3.44
10. Italy	1.50	10. Spain	3.23
11. Portugal	0.73	11. Portugal	2.09

SOURCES: Thomas Ellison's (1886) *The Cotton Trade of Great Britain*, 2d. ed. (London, 1968), pp. 147–148; my calculations are based on B. R. Mitchell's data in *European Historical Statistics, 1750–1970*, New York, 1975.

decree a *numerus clausus,* that is, a prohibition against opening up new factories as well as expanding old ones.

The evolution of the capital goods industry was certainly different from that of the consumer goods industry but ultimately was no better off. The Restoration had witnessed the rise and fall of the mining industry. Spanish output of lead bars had totaled 20% of world production and 38% of European production from 1881 to 1910; the output of pure copper extracted from Spanish mines accounted for 10% of world production and 51% of European production—and iron ore made up 13.3% of Europe's production. Mining reached its apex during the first decade of the twentieth century, when the export of its products made up more than one-third of the value of all combined exports. After that decade, these figures fell gradually, not only because of transportation hardship caused by World War I, but also because of more in-depth structural factors. Mining yields not renewable materials; veins become, therefore, exhausted, and production costs increase while profits decrease.

Spain was only a pawn in a process that allowed the great industrial powers of Europe—Great Britain, France, and Belgium—to dominate a part of the world's mineral resources. They were especially attracted to Spain by the "general" laws of December 1868, which by doing away with "arraignments" in effect transferred to the concessionaires all subsoil property rights. Foreign capital eagerly invested in the exploitation of a mining industry that was either totally undeveloped or only partially developed along precapitalist lines, like the lead-mining operation in the southern *sierras* from Alpujarra to Cartagena. Checkland, Avery, and Harvey have shown the huge profits generated by the large Tharsis and Riotinto companies.[6] This author has brought to light the income earned in the form of dividends from the Peñarroya company, and Albert Broder's thesis does the same for other large mining companies. (The thesis also mentions the many failures that occurred during this time of feverish speculation.) Foreign companies exploited Spanish mining interests on a massive scale while keeping their options flexible enough so that they could switch to other regions in the event of a financial downturn. During the 1920s, for example, the Cie. d'Aguilas acquired iron mines in Algeria and manganese mines in Morocco; Peñarroya opened a lead smeltery in Megrine and Tunisia and, together with the Asturienne, opened a zinc smeltery in Indochina; Río Tinto bought diverse mineral deposits in Rhodesia; and so on. In the case of Río Tinto, it must be mentioned that pyrites—a raw material used almost exclusively to produce sulfuric acid from the last third of the nineteenth century until 1913, when pyrites from Huelva provided the world with more than half of its sulfuric acid—had to endure from this date on the competition of natural sulfur from North America.

During the Restoration, the mining industry became "an enclave of importing countries" that generated huge sums of money, very little of which filtered down to Spanish society.[7] The only exception was the iron mining industry. In Vizcaya, the participation of local businessmen in the establishment of hematite projects for the production of Bessemer steel generated enough financial resources to open, starting in 1882 with the formation of Altos Hornos and La Vizcaya, the modern Spanish iron-and-steel industry. From 1882 to 1929 (the year of maximum production before the Great Depression), Spanish output of cast iron went up sixfold; Biscayan, which represented 57% of the total, sevenfold. These increases seem quite substantial when compared with figures from cotton textile industry, which gained only 70% during the same forty-seven-year period. Overall, the growth of the iron-and-steel industry seems almost four times larger than that of the cotton industry. However, looking at it from the perspective of international industrial development, this growth looks less impressive.

During the period 1880–1884 (see Table 4.2), Spain produced an annual average of 8 kilograms of cast iron per inhabitant, a low figure compared with the 274 kilograms produced in the United Kingdom and the 132 in Belgium. Spain ranked eighth among the ten countries considered (which are not the same countries used to compare cotton production in Table 4.1) with only

Table 4.2
Cast Iron (1880–1884) and Steel (1925–1929)
Per Capita Output (five-year averages in kilograms)

Cast Iron (1880–1884)		Steel (1925–1929)	
1. United Kingdom	279	1. Belgium	432
2. Belgium	132	2. Germany	250
3. Sweden	91	3. France	213
4. Germany	64	4. United Kingdom	171
5. France	51	5. Sweden	98
6. Austria	20	6. Austria	90
7. Hungary	10	7. Hungary	47
8. Spain	8	8. Italy	44
9. Russia	5	9. Spain	30
10. Italy	0.8	10. USSR	24

SOURCE: My calculations are based on B. R. Mitchell's information in *European Historical Statistics, 1750–1970*, New York, 1975.

Russia at 5 kilograms per person and Italy at less than 1. During the 1925 to 1929 period, Spanish production of steel (steel was now produced instead of cast iron) increased to 30 kilograms per inhabitant, but the increase in other countries was so much faster that Spain dropped from eighth place to ninth, ahead of only the USSR. Italy, which at first lagged, surpassed Spain as it had already done with regard to the cotton industry. With a per capita production of 44 kilograms it went over the 30 turned out by Spain. At the end of the Restoration, the iron-and-steel and capital goods industries seem dynamic compared with the consumer goods industry (represented by the cotton industry) only because the latter was holding off.

The chemical industry also presented many similarities to the others. Beginning in 1872, the success of the mining industry spurred the parallel growth of explosives. Some thirty years later, when agricultural fertilizers became the most important branch of the chemical industry, the appearance of natural phosphates from Magreb offered Spain an exceptional opportunity. Mixed with an equal amount of sulfuric acid, phosphates become superphosphated lime, the most effective fertilizer. Pyrites from Huelva accounted for half of the world's sulfur; North African phosphate rocks were proving to be the most economical and thus undercut the French sources from Somme and the American from Florida. The entire coast between Huelva and Barcelona took advantage of this income-producing opportunity as superphosphate factories dotted the landscape. The production of fertilizers was doubly profitable: first, there was a huge demand; second, there was direct production, without the problems caused by residues and by-products, such as was the case with soda. At the end of the Restoration period, fertilizers were the bastion of the Spanish chemical industry.

In 1929 Spain produced 1 million tons of superphosphates; in Europe this figure was surpassed only by France, which produced 2.3 million tons, and by Italy, with 1.3 million. In relative terms, however, these Spanish figures are not as impressive. The production of fertilizer per hectare of grain did not exceed 127 kilograms, an amount which placed Spain, not in third place, but eleventh among the sixteen countries listed in Table 4.3. The extraordinarily high income produced by fertilizers was offset by the backwardness of cereal agriculture. On the other hand, citrus crops, beets, and tomatoes (in the Canary Islands) required substantial amounts of British ammonium sulfate, and this had a decisive effect on the balance of trade. In this particular case the problem was not demand but, rather, supply; the ammonia water which was produced by gas factories and batteries of coke did not have, in the majority of

Table 4.3
Production of Superphosphated Lime in 1929
(kilograms/hectare used for cereals)

1.	Netherlands	1,896
2.	Belgium	421
3.	Switzerland	268
4.	United Kingdom	244
5.	France	213
6.	Denmark	206
7.	Italy	179
8.	Portugal	168
9.	Sweden	159
10.	Norway	140
11.	Spain	127
12.	Greece	75
13.	Germany	66
14.	Austria	49
15.	Hungary	37
16.	USSR	2.5

SOURCES: My calculations are based on A. N. Gray's information in *Phosphates and Superphosphate* (New York, 1947), p. 262, for the production of fertilizer, and on B. R. Mitchell, *European Historical Statistics, 1750–1970* (New York, 1975), pp. 210–226, for the acreage cultivated.

NOTE: In countries where the iron-and-steel industry was important, the need to produce superphosphates was limited by the large-scale use of "industrial wastes" or the residues of the steel furnaces, which provided a large share of the phosphoric acid required for cereal production. In the case of Germany, the waste products, popularly called *Thomasmehl,* made up three-quarters of the phosphorus used for agriculture in 1929.

cases, enough substance to be of chemical value. Moreover, the high cost of electricity prohibited the production of calcic cyanamide from carbide.

In 1930 as the Restoration period drew to a close, Spain certainly had more industry than in 1874 and 1833, but it was also more backward than at either of the two nineteenth-century dates. In comparison to France and the United Kingdom (all problems of backwardness and underdevelopment must be measured in relative terms), Spain's international ranking was very low. In this sense, the century of Spanish industrialization from 1833 to 1930 can undoubtedly be considered a failure.

NOTES

1. Nicolás Sánchez-Albornoz, "El consumo de textiles en España, 1860–1890: Primera aproximación," *Hacienda Pública Española* 68 (1981): 229–35; Leandro Prados de

la Escosura, "Producción y consumo de tejidos en España (1792–1913): Primeros resultados," in *Historia económica y pensamiento social,* ed. Gonzalo Anes et al., Madrid, 1983, 455–71.

2. Xan Carmona, "Producción textil rural e actividades maritimo-pesqueiras na Galicia, 1750–1905" (Ph.D. diss., Universidad de Santiago, 1983).

3. Jordi Nadal, "La debilidad de la industria química española en el siglo XIX: Un problema de demanda," *Moneda y Crédito,* 176 (1986): 33–70. On the rise of the gas industry, see Carles Sudriá, "Notas sobre la implantación y el desarrollo de la industria del gas en España, 1840–1901," *Revista de Historia Económica* 1, no. 2 (1986): 97–118.

4. Grupo de Estudios de Historia Rural, "Notas sobre la producción agraria española, 1891–1913," *Revista de Historia Económica* 1, no. 2 (1983): 243.

5. Eusebio Bertrand y Serra, "Un estudio sobre la industria textil algodonera," *Boletín del Comité Regulador de la Industria Algodonera* 4, no. 33 (1931).

6. J. G. Checkland, *The Mines of Tharsis: Roman, French, and British Enterprises in Spain,* London, 1967; D. Avery, *Not on Queen Victoria's Birthday: The Story of the Rio Tinto Mines,* London, 1974; Charles E. Harvey, *The Rio Tinto Company: An Economic History of a Leading International Mining Concern, 1873–1954,* London, 1981.

7. Nicolás Sánchez-Albornoz, *España hace un siglo: una economía dual,* 2d ed., 1975, Madrid, p. 22. A case in point was the English company Riotinto, which for the period 1910–1914 earned, after it paid its investment costs and generously purveyed its reserve fund, the annual average of 1,214,500 pounds in dividends. This was equivalent to a day's wages at 3 shillings per day for more than 8 million pit miners who made up the category of best-paid workers. These workers supported some 27,000 families and, based on the figure of 5 people per family, would have accounted for two-fifths of the provincial census count of 310,000 inhabitants in 1910.

APPENDIX
AN ANNUAL INDEX OF SPANISH INDUSTRIAL OUTPUT*

ALBERT CARRERAS
Universidad de Barcelona

1. INTRODUCTION AND METHOD

STUDY of the industrialization process requires quantification. Indexes that measure industrial output attempt to fulfill that need. In Spain the first index available was published by the *Consejo de Economía Nacional* (CEN), and it only started in 1906.[1] For the previous period, María Teresa Costa's 1861–1899 "index of industrial growth" is totally inadequate. It contains serious flaws with respect to how data were aggregated from the eight series upon which it was based. The result is an inadmissible 7 percent annual growth rate for all thirty-nine years under consideration.[2] Highlights of the new index (IPIES) I am offering here are the following:

(1) Greater time range: The period 1842–1935 is covered on an annual basis; and the period 1831–1841, on an irregular basis.
(2) Greater coverage: Eighty-four series are made up. (CEN used eighteen series for the period 1906 to 1929 and thirty-eight starting in 1929.) They represent over 40% of the industrial production. In fact, since many estimates for the years between 1913 and 1929 are often unreliable, this percentage varies between 40% and 80%.

---

*The results, and the methods I use to obtain them, are amply discussed in the introduction and the first part of my unpublished doctoral dissertation, "La producció industrial espanyola i italiana desde mitjan segle XIX fins a l'actualitat" (Universidad Autónoma de Barcelona, 1983). A summary of it is offered in Albert Carreras, "La producción industrial española, 1842–1981: construcción de un índice anual." *Revista de Historia Económica* 2, no. 1 (1984): 127–157, from which I have taken some excerpts. IPIES, which is used throughout this chapter, stands for *Indice de la Producción Industrial Española* (Spanish Industrial Output Index).

(3) Better weighting: Added values per output unit in 1913 and esti-
    mates for 1929 are utilized. Unfortunately, indirect methods were
    employed in these estimates, since there were no industrial cen-
    suses before 1958.
(4) More probable fluctuations: For the period 1906 to 1935, when
    comparisons are possible, fluctuations in the IPIES index with re-
    spect to the CEN index are less abrupt. The formula I used in es-
    timating the annual indexes is:

$$I_i = \frac{\sum\limits_{i,\,j}^{n,\,m} p_{t,j}\, q_{i,j}}{\sum\limits_{i,\,j}^{n,\,m} p_{t,j}\, q_{t,j}} \cdot 100$$

Note: q = quantities produced; p = prices (in this case, the added values per
output unit); $j = 1, \ldots, m$ is the number of products; $i = 1, \ldots, t, \ldots, n$ is
the number of years; $t \cong n$.

One set of IPI (Industrial Production Index) "prices" was calculated for
1913 and another for 1929, and then both sets were combined in 1913
(1831–1913: IPI with the weight of 1913; 1913–1935: IPI with the weight of
1929). The results can be seen in Table 4.1A and Graph 4.1A.

2. LONG-TERM TRENDS

The cumulative annual IPIES growth rate for the period 1831–1935 was
2.85%. As the population growth between 1833 and 1930—two years during
which census counts were taken—was 0.67%,[3] the per capita IPIES increase
was therefore 2.17% for this century. Table 4.2A shows this growth in five-
year averages. Some basic yet important conclusions can be drawn from this
table: (1) Over a century, the trend of the industrial output was positive,
except during the last five-year period, 1931–1935; (2) the greatest growth
occurred during the period 1840–1860; (3) other periods of rapid growth
were 1871–1875 and 1926–1930; and (4) the main crises, aside from the
1931–1935 period, which really ushered in a completely different era, were
those of 1866–1870 and 1886–1890.

During the period 1800–1985,[4] Spanish industry appears to have grown
steadily, in spite of the stagnation that was suffered during the initial three

Table 4.1A
Spanish Industrial Output Indexes (1913 = 100) and Annual Growth Rates (in percentages)

Year	IPIES	Δ	Year	IPIES	Δ	Year	IPIES	IPI-CEN	IPIES	IPI-CEN
1831	8.3	—	1871	38.7	10.9	1906	87.1	80.0	6.7	—
. . .			1872	41.5	7.2	1907	92.2	88.5	5.9	10.6
1835	10.3	—	1873	46.9	12.9	1908	95.3	90.6	3.4	2.4
1842	11.9	—	1874	44.0	−6.2	1909	90.0	87.5	−5.6	−3.5
1843	12.7	7.1	1875	45.9	4.4	1910	93.0	86.6	3.3	−1.0
1844	15.3	20.3	1876	47.1	2.7	1911	95.2	87.5	2.4	1.0
1845	16.5	7.5	1877	49.7	5.5	1912	104.7	98.2	9.9	12.3
1846	16.7	1.5	1878	48.6	−2.3	1913	100.0	100.0	−4.5	1.8
1847	15.6	−6.9	1879	47.7	−1.7	1914	99.8	93.1	−0.3	−6.9
1848	16.6	6.3	1880	49.1	2.9	1915	104.2	82.1	4.4	−11.9
1849	19.0	14.5	1881	53.9	9.7	1916	109.0	93.4	4.7	13.8
1850	20.7	9.0	1882	55.3	2.7	1917	106.9	96.4	−1.9	3.2
1851	23.0	11.4	1883	59.3	7.3	1918	109.0	96.7	1.9	0.3
1852	23.8	3.2	1884	59.1	−0.3	1919	101.0	86.1	−7.3	−11.0
1853	23.6	−0.6	1885	60.2	1.9	1920	105.8	93.4	4.7	8.5
1854	23.3	−1.5	1886	55.5	−7.8	1921	106.9	97.5	1.1	4.3
1855	24.9	7.0	1887	53.8	−3.1	1922	108.7	89.1	1.7	−8.6
1856	27.0	8.3	1888	56.3	4.7	1923	122.1	107.8	12.3	20.9
1857	27.8	3.2	1889	60.5	7.5	1924	128.2	124.0	5.1	15.1
1858	28.7	3.2	1890	62.5	3.2	1925	133.5	127.3	4.1	2.7
1859	29.7	3.5	1891	62.6	0.1	1926	140.9	140.6	5.6	10.4
1860	31.2	5.2	1892	65.8	5.3	1927	145.0	139.7	2.9	−0.6
1861	32.5	4.0	1893	71.9	9.2	1928	158.7	142.7	9.5	2.1
1862	31.1	−4.3	1894	69.2	−3.8	1929	159.3	149.3	−0.3	4.6
1863	32.0	3.1	1895	68.9	−0.4	1930	166.7	151.0	5.3	1.2
1864	32.1	0.3	1896	70.7	2.5	1931	149.5	147.3	−10.3	−2.5
1865	33.2	3.3	1897	66.8	−5.4	1932	148.2	141.3	−0.9	−4.1
1866	32.6	−1.8	1898	74.0	10.7	1933	146.6	135.8	−1.1	−3.9
1867	35.0	7.2	1899	78.5	6.2	1934	149.9	147.2	2.3	8.4
1868	31.7	−9.4	1900	80.8	2.9	1935	154.9	154.2	3.3	4.8
1869	32.7	3.3	1901	81.3	0.6					
1870	34.9	6.8	1902	85.7	5.5					
			1903	84.9	−0.9					
			1904	81.0	−4.6					
			1905	81.6	0.7					

SOURCE: A. Carreras, *La producció industrial espanyola i italiana desde mitjan segle XIX fins a l'actualitat* (Ph.D. diss., Universidad Autónoma de Barcelona, 1983), pp. 149–151, and my own estimates.

Graph 4.1A   Indexes of Spanish Industrial Output, 1831–1935
IPIES and IPI-CEN
(1913 = 100)

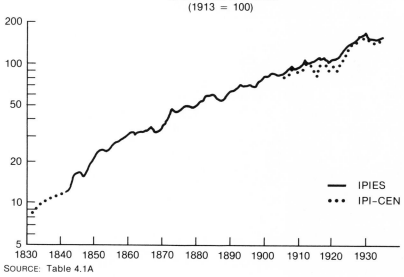

SOURCE: Table 4.1A

Table 4.2A
Five-Year Growth Rates of Spanish Industrial Output,
1831–1935 (in percentages)

1831–1885			*1881–1935*	
1831–35/1836–40	(a) ⎤	4.3	1881–85/1886–90	0.1
1836–40/1841–45	(a) ⎦		1886–90/1891–95	3.2
1841–45/1846–50		4.6	1891–95/1896–1900	1.8
1846–50/1851–55		6.0	1896–1900/1901–05	2.3
1851–55/1856–60		4.0	1901–05/1906–10	2.0
1856–60/1861–65		2.2	1906–10/1911–15	1.9
1861–65/1866–70		0.7	1911–15/1916–20	1.1
1866–70/1871–75		5.4	1916–20/1921–25	2.4
1871–75/1876–80		2.2	1921–25/1926–30	5.1
1876–80/1881–85		3.5	1926–30/1931–35	−1.0

SOURCE: Calculations are based on Table 4.1A.
NOTE: (a) Based on only two observations for 1831–35 and on four for 1841–45; data are lacking for the five-year period 1836–1840.

decades of the nineteenth century and during the 1930–1950 depression. It also experienced a sharp growth from 1950 to 1974. These exceptions underscore, by contrast, the underlying continuity of industrial development that took place during the one hundred years examined in this book.

3. LEADING SECTORS AND STRUCTURAL CHANGE

Available data do not confirm the existence of anything like a big spurt, since the highest rates are only mediocre. Consequently, no leading sectors can be identified. The one time which comes closer to a takeoff is the period 1831–1860, when annual growth rates of 4.7% were experienced. Although one may suspect that figures for this period were overestimated (see discussion further on[5]), this was presumptively the fastest growth period. Previously Spain suffered through a long depression, various foreign wars, an invasion, and many revolutions, as well as the loss of its continental American empire. Such a 1831–1860 takeoff was clearly led by the cotton textile industry while all consumer goods industries were also booming, except, of course, those depleted by industrialization, as were hemp and linen spinning and weaving.

When the growth capacity of the cotton textile industry weakened for various reasons that would take too long and that are too controversial to enumerate here, other sectors took up the slack. Between 1870 and 1890 it was mainly the mining sector: iron and pyrites and, to a lesser extent, coal, lead, and mercury. A decade later, around 1880, the iron-and-steel industry took off, continuing to expand until the beginning of the twentieth century. But neither mining nor the iron-and-steel industry were able to attain the high overall growth rates of the previous period. Nevertheless, various consumer goods industries (canned goods, wool and hard-fiber textiles, the manufacturing of cork and gum elastic, and sugar refining) reached higher-than-average growth rates during the 1880s.

The first third of the twentieth century witnessed overall dynamic growth. Electricity became the most rapidly and regularly growing industry. On its coattails the industries that heavily consumed this energy (inorganic chemicals; artificial fibers; cement; and, in the 1920s, iron and steel) or those that were particularly affected by the productive flexibility electricity afforded (mechanical construction) also grew considerably.

A closer look at the structural changes in industry provides solid evidence of this broad dynamism of the consumer goods industry; this dynamism lasted from the middle of the nineteenth century until the beginning of the twentieth—up to World War I. Also evident is a lag in the capital-goods industry, which was still in its infancy around 1860, because it took no advantage of the opportunity the construction of the railroad network had offered. This industry would not raise substantially until the 1920s, when a strong increase in the gross domestic formation of fixed capital would spur it along. It was precisely during these years that Spain passed from the first to the second level of industrialization, according to Walter Hoffman's typology.[6]

4. REGIONAL VARIATIONS

The aggregate data presented here hide strong regional variations that are analyzed in detail in the second part of this book. It should, however, be mentioned that, according to Jordi Nadal's estimates, based on financial sources, on the regional distribution of industrial output in 1856 and 1900, Catalonian growth in the second third of the nineteenth century and Basque growth in the last third seem to be higher than average for Spain.[7] Catalonia's growth was based on the consumer goods industry, and the Basque Provinces' on the mining and the iron-and-steel industries. Meanwhile, Andalusia, which was probably the first manufacturing region around 1820, and the two Castiles stood much lower than the average. Valencia and Asturias maintained and slightly improved their positions. Galicia, on the other hand, regressed, particularly in the first half of the nineteenth century. Although there is a lack of data for the first decades of this century, it is quite likely that the process of regional differentiation intensified, as can be deduced from an increase in migrations.

5. FLUCTUATIONS

Two sources of instability are discernible: the first and most frequent is related to irregular agricultural outputs, causing domestic fluctuations in the food supply. This type of instability tended to decrease with time. As late as 1857, Spain still suffered from "subsistence crises" that sharply increased both the price of wheat and the mortality rate. During the rest of the century, there were additional agricultural crises (1868, 1878, 1882, 1887, 1893, and 1898) that greatly affected prices, rural income, and private consumption, but they no longer had devastating effects on the population.[8] After 1905 these crises faded out until the post–Civil War period (1945–1949), a time of regression in gross domestic output.

The second source was cyclical, and it was produced by investments that generated demand on the capital goods industries. Deviations from the century-long trend of investment and industrial production thus appear to be conspicuously correlated.[9] In Table 4.1A and Graph 4.2A, the annual variations in the IPIES can be seen clearly. There, the combined effects of the cyclical process of industrial growth and of the fluctuations in agricultural output transmitted through the consumer goods industries can also be observed. The years of negative growth are still quite frequent (26 out of 93 years), reflecting a very fragile industrial base.

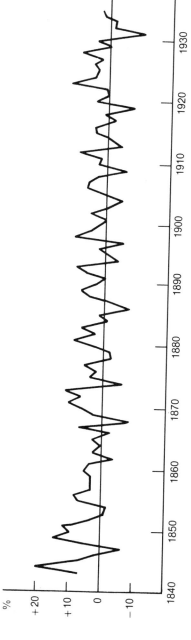

Graph 4.2A   IPIES Annual Growth Rates, 1843–1935
(in percentages)

SOURCE: Table 4.1A

6. INDUSTRIAL PRODUCTION AND ECONOMIC GROWTH

The purpose of this appendix is to present a new index to measure industrial output. However, a comparison with other economic indicators is needed if only as contrast to the validity and reliability of the results arrived at herein. With this in mind, the following question becomes essential: What contribution did industry make to the economic growth of Spain? To answer this basic question, two sources that deal with the evolution of national income in Spain must be consulted: (1) Julio Alcaide's annual series for the twentieth century;[10] (2) for the nineteenth Leandro Prados's reelaboration of Mulhall's estimates linking them to Alcaide's annual series.[11] Here, the resulting series is called MPA (Mulhall-Prados-Alcaide). Another recent estimate is that of the national income from the viewpoint of gross national expenditure (GNB).[12] Table 4.3A presents a comparison of the MPA, GNB, and IPIES growth rates.

A comparison of the three columns in Table 4.3A reveals some interesting results. Assuming that the three are perfectly compatible, it is possible to confirm that industry's contribution to the economic growth of Spain was positive for the entire period under consideration, particularly for the years 1831–1860. Only between 1913 and 1935 was the contribution zero or perhaps slightly negative; however, estimates of national income vary so much that it is impossible to state it forcefully. If, on the other hand, we assume that

Table 4.3A
Growth Rates of Spanish Industrial
Output and National Income, 1831–1935
(in percentages)

	Industrial Output	National Income	
	IPIES	MPA	GNB
1831–1860	4.67	0.92	. . .
1860–1890	2.34	1.42	1.14
1890–1913	2.06	1.61	1.64
1913–1935	2.01	2.04	1.22
. . .			
1831–1935	2.85	1.46	. . .
. . .			
1860–1935	2.16	1.66	1.32
. . .			
1890–1935	2.04	1.82	1.44

Source: See Table 4.1A.

the three series are not fully compatible, the question arises whether the industrial growth was overestimated during the first period or whether the national income was underestimated or both.

7. SPANISH AND EUROPEAN INDUSTRIALIZATION

Any comparison of different industrial production indexes, estimated through nonhomogenous methods, has a limited value; it will nevertheless help to point out broad similarities and differences in the evolution of Spanish industry within the context of European industrialization. Table 4.4A suggests historical periods within the industrialization process of Spain.

1831–1861: The beginning of the industrial revolution in Spain

IPIES figures start in 1831, but until 1842 there are wide gaps, so that the series cannot be presented annually. In spite of this, there is enough evidence to prove that between approximately 1831 and 1861 Spanish industrial production increased at a high (although fluctuating) rate compared with both the growth of national income and the development of the more advanced industrial nations, such as Great Britain and France, or with nations on a level with Spain, such as Austria and Hungary. The chronological limits of the period can vary slightly. It could be validly argued, for instance, that this period started in 1842 or terminated in 1873. Whatever the case, economic growth during the 1840s and 1850s in Spain was exceptional.

This conclusion is in total agreement with current research, particularly with the work of Nicolás Sánchez-Albornoz, Jordi Nadal, Gabriel Tortella, Josep Fontana, and Jordi Maluquer de Motes.[13] Around 1861 Spain had progressed significantly, so much so that it was making up for the time it lost during the first third of the century, when industrial production became stagnant because of the Napoleonic wars and the loss of the American colonies. In spite of the political instability that characterized the times, the magnitude of the advance cannot and should not be underestimated. In 1863 French statistician Maurice Block wrote an article on the Spanish society and economy, based on the data available up to 1861. It carried a forceful title: "The Material Resurrection of Spain."[14]

1861–1913: The failure of the industrial revolution in Spain

Jordi Nadal's phrase, "the failure of the industrial revolution in Spain," describes Spanish industrialization during this crucial period. Before having had an opportunity to consolidate its industrial progress, Spain lapsed into a

Table 4.4A
IPI Growth Rates in Some European Countries, 1831–1935
(in percentages)

	Spain	Great Britain	France	Germany	Italy	Russia	Sweden	Austria	Hungary
1831–1861	4.66	2.53	2.16	...	...	...	...	3.13	2.18
1861–1890	2.28	2.41	1.34	3.95	1.62	4.68	3.44	2.86	2.90
1890–1913	2.06	2.01	2.45	4.06	2.97	5.08	4.06	2.78	3.44
1913–1935	2.01	1.28	0.25	0.46	1.94	...	2.81	...	...

SOURCES: Spain: IPIES (Table 4.1A), Austria and Hungary (the two parts of the Austro-Hungarian Empire before 1918): J. Komlos, "Economic Growth and Industrialization in Hungary, 1830–1913," *Journal of European Economic History* (1981) 1, pp. 5–46 (Table 17, "manufacturing, mining, and construction"). For the other countries from 1831 to 1913: B. R. Mitchell, *European Historical Statistics, 1750–1970* (New York, 1975), table E1; from 1913 to 1935: V. Paretti and G. Bloch, "Industrial Production in Western Europe and the United States, 1901 to 1955," *Banca Nazionale del Lavoro Quarterly Review* 39 (1956): 3–51 (Table 2).

NOTE: No figures are given for Austria, Hungary or the USSR after 1913, for two reasons: these countries underwent great territorial changes as a consequence of World War I and of the Russian Revolution of 1917, and the series ending in 1913 does not easily fit those beginning after the war.

long period of slow growth, following a typical pattern set by Victorian England. This comparison between the two countries must not be understood in a literal sense. Although the form and the chronology, generally speaking, were similar, the basic causes were completely different. Spanish industrial production lost ground in relation to the majority of the other eight countries under consideration. Until 1890 the Spanish growth rate surpassed even those of France and Italy, but from 1890 to 1913 it was, along with the British growth rate, the lowest. The slow-down began during the long stagnation in period 1861–1868 and was clearly visible after 1873. From then until the Dictatorship (1923), no cycles of expansion comparable to those experienced between 1842 and 1873 occurred.[15] The causes for this premature lessening in industrial growth are extensively analyzed by the aforementioned authors, and do not need repeating here. It should be added, however, that the close relationship of the Spanish economy with "mature" economies, such as those of the British and the French, may also explain the slowdown in Spanish industrial growth.[16] In contrast, in those countries which industrialized later, in closer association to new economic powers such as Germany and the United States, the two leaders in the "Second Industrial Revolution," displayed higher rates of industrial growth.[17]

Notwithstanding, as Jordi Nadal has emphasized, the failure was mostly relative. Industrial growth was not interrupted. From 1861 until 1913 the long-term growth rates were unequivocally positive. During the Bourbon Restoration, industry grew at a fairly stable rate.

1914–1935: Growth and fluctuations

The Spanish IPI maintained a similar rate of growth as in the period 1890–1913, except that during this period the rate of increase was relatively higher; only Sweden had a higher rate. Yet it would be incorrect to assume that these were years of linear and regular growth in Spain and in Europe. From 1914 to 1935 Spanish and European industries passed through three very clearly defined stages (see Table 4.5A).

The first stage (until 1922) is characterized by a production stagnation that existed both during the expansion period of World War I and during the postwar depression. Production levels varied relatively little. Industrial output grew a total of 9% until 1916, and it stayed more or less at that level except for the crisis of 1919. What really changed was the international distribution of production: weak Spanish growth contrasted with the collapse of European industry, and the result looks like a strong Spanish recovery. The distribution of national income also shifted in favor of profits, to the detriment of wages.[18]

Table 4.5A
Growth Rates of Industrial Output:
Spain and "Europe," 1913–1935
(in percentages)

	(1) *Spain*	(2) *"Europe"*	(3) = (1) − (2)
1913–1922	0.93	−1.72	2.65
1922–1929	5.61	5.53	0.08
1929–1935	−0.47	−0.19	−0.28

SOURCES: Spain: IPIES (see Table 4.1A); V. Paretti and G. Bloch, "Industrial Production in Western Europe and the United States, 1901 to 1955," *Banca Nazionale del Lavoro Quarterly Review* 39 (1956): 3–51.
NOTE: Here "Europe" means: West Germany, Austria, Belgium, Denmark, France, Great Britain, Greece, Holland, Ireland, Italy, Luxembourg, Norway, Sweden, and Turkey.

The second stage, from 1922 to 1929 (in Spain until 1930), seems to have generated a strong expansion in industrial production in Spain as much as it did in the rest of Europe. The annual growth rate reached 5.6% over eight years, a situation unprecedented since 1869–1873.

The third stage (1929–1935) covers the early phase of the depression. The slump does not seem to have been too steep in Spain. The various IPIs, however, paint a contradictory picture of the period and of the intensity of the crisis. In terms of 1913 prices, industrial production from 1929 to 1933 remained stable; in terms of 1929 prices the IPIES for these years fell 8%, and in 1958 prices the drop was 18%. This could be the key in understanding the period: there existed enormous changes in relative prices and, consequently, in the intraindustrial structure. Whatever the case, Spain seems to have taken this transformation in stride (see Table 4.5A).

NOTES

1. Consejo de Economía Nacional, *La renta nacional de España* (Madrid, 1945).

2. María Teresa Costa Campi, *La financiación exterior del capitalismo español en el siglo XIX* (Barcelona, 1983).

3. See Vicente Pérez Moreda, chapter 2 in this book.

4. Carreras, *La producció industrial*, pp. 146–147.

5. See the second paragraph of section 6. Leandro Prados is convinced that the growth rate must be reduced by half. Since this period presents a weaker statistical base

of information, there is certainly much room for revision. I do not believe, however, that the results should be reduced as much. In any case, they will always be greater than those for subsequent periods.

6. Carreras, *La producció industrial,* Part 3.

7. See also Albert Carreras, "La producción industrial catalana y vasca, 1844–1935. Elementos para una comparación," in Manuel González Portilla, Jordi Maluquer de Motes, and Borja de Riquer, eds., *Industrialización y nacionalismo: análisis comparativos* (Barcelona, 1984).

8. Nicolás Sánchez-Albornoz, *España hace un siglo: una economía dual* (Madrid, 1977), and Grupo de Estudios de Historia Rural, *Los precios del trigo y la cebada en España, 1891–1907* (Madrid, 1980).

9. I have estimated the investments given in Albert Carreras, "Gasto Nacional Bruto y Formación de Capital en España, 1849–1958: primer ensayo de estimación," in Pablo Martín Aceña and Leandro Prados de la Escosura, eds., *La Nueva Historia Económica en España* (Madrid, 1985), pp. 17–51.

10. Julio Alcaide, "Una revisión urgente de la serie de renta nacional española en el siglo XX," in *Datos básicos para la historia financiera de España, 1850–1975,* vol. 1 (Madrid, 1976), pp. 1127–1150.

11. Leandro Prados de la Escosura, *Comercio exterior y crecimiento económico en España, 1826–1913: tendencias a largo plazo* (Madrid, 1982), pp. 66–69. Also available are recent estimates done with indirect methods by foreign researchers (P. Bairoch and N. F. R. Crafts). This set of evaluations is discussed in more detail in Carreras, "La producció industrial," pp. 19–22.

12. Carreras, "La producció industrial," pp. 40–41. GNB stands for Gasto Nacional Bruto.

13. Sánchez-Albornoz, Introduction, *España hace un siglo*; Jordi Nadal, "The Failure of the Industrial Revolution in Spain, 1830–1930," in C. M. Cipolla, ed., *The Fontana Economic History of Europe,* vol. 4(2) (London, 1973), pp. 533–626; Gabriel Tortella, *Banking, Railroads, and Industry in Spain, 1829–1874* (New York, 1977); Josep Fontana, *Cambio económico y actitudes políticas en la España del siglo XIX* (Barcelona, 1973), chap. 3; Jordi Maluquer de Motes, *El socialismo en España, 1833–1868* (Barcelona, 1977), chap. 1.

14. Maurice Block, "Resurrección material en España." *Revista General de Estadística* (1863) 11: 6–40.

15. The periods 1842–1846, 1847–1852, and 1868–1873. In each of these periods of expansion industrial output grew between 40% and 53% at annual rates that varied between 5% and 9%.

16. Regarding commercial connections, see Leandro Prados de la Escosura, *Comercio exterior,* chap. 3. In regard to the flow of capital see Albert Broder's unpublished thesis, "Le rôle des intérêts économiques étrangers dans la croissance de l'Espagne au XIXème siècle" (1981).

17. I use the expression popularized by David S. Landes, *The Unbound Prometheus. Technological Change and Industrial Development in Western Europe from 1750 to the Present* (Cambridge, 1969). Table 4.4A emphasizes the difference in Spanish industrial development at the end of the nineteenth century and the beginning of the twentieth in comparison to the principal European countries, except Great Britain. The explanation

that most resembles what I am suggesting here is Pablo Martín Aceña, "España y el patrón oro, 1880–1913," *Hacienda Pública Española* (1981) 69: 267–290; this article takes exception to Spain's not adopting the gold standard, thus cutting itself off from the international economy. This choice was critical at a time of economic expansion.

18. For the period 1914–1922 and, in general, until 1936, see Josep Fontana and Jordi Nadal, "Spain, 1914–1970," in Cipolla, ed., *The Fontana Economic History of Europe*, vol. 6, pt. 2 (Glasgow, 1975), pp. 460–529.

FURTHER READINGS

The first modern summary is Jaime Vicens Vives's "La industrialización y el desarrollo económico de España de 1800 a 1936," in *Première Conférence Internationale d'Histoire Économique. Contributions. Communications. Stockholm. 1960* (Paris—The Hague, 1960), pp. 129–136, reproduced in J. Vicens Vives, *Coyuntura económica y reformismo burgués* (Barcelona, 1968), pp. 145–156. There he summarized several previous works, including the prominent *An Economic History of Spain,* jointly written with Jordi Nadal (Princeton, 1969), whose first Spanish edition came out in 1959.

In 1970, Jordi Nadal published an important essay where he reviewed the agricultural constraints and the development of the cotton-textile and the iron-and-steel industries, "La economía española, 1829–1931," in *El Banco de España. Una historia económica* (Madrid, 1970), pp. 317–417. Three years later he published "The Failure of the Industrial Revolution in Spain, 1830–1913," in C. M. Cipolla, ed., *The Fontana Economic History of Europe* (London, 1973), vol. 4, pt. 2, pp. 553–626, expanded in to *El fracaso de la revolución industrial en España* (Barcelona, 1975). In 1981 Nadal wrote "El fracaso de la revolución industrial en España. Un balance historiográfico," in *Papeles de Economía Española* 20 (1984): 108–125. Ten years after the publication of *El fracaso, Información Comercial Española* (*ICE*) devoted its July 1985 issue, no. 623, to a review of Nadal's summaries and contributions. Gabriel Tortella's, José Luis García Delgado's, and Pedro Fraile's contributions should also be read.

In the same issue of *ICE*, there are two bibliographic overviews: one by Sebastián Coll on mining; the other by Albert Carreras on the consumer goods industry. For the iron-and-steel industry, see "Further Readings" of Pedro Fraile at the end of Chapter 10 in this book. The work compiled by Manuel González Portilla, Jordi Maluquer de Motes, and Borja de Riquer, *Industrialización y nacionalismo: análisis comparativos* (Barcelona, 1984), includes, among other interesting essays, one on the iron-and-steel industry by Luis María

Bilbao, "Renovación tecnológica y estructura del sector siderúrgico en el País Vasco durante la primera etapa de la industrialización (1849–1880). Aproximación compartiva con la industria algodonera de Cataluña," and another important essay by Jordi Maluquer de Motes, "Cataluña y el País Vasco en la industria eléctrica española, 1901–1935," and, in addition, Albert Carreras's work also cited in note 7 of this chapter.

Jordi Nadal has published several studies of regional industrial change: "Industrialización y desindustrialización del Sureste español, 1817–1913," *Moneda y Crédito,* no. 120 (1972): 3–80; "Notas sobre la industria asturiana de 1850 a 1935," *Historia de Asturias,* vol. 8 (Oviedo, 1981), pp. 111–117; "Los dos abortos de la revolución industrial en Andalucía," *Historia de Andalucía,* vol. 6 (Madrid, 1984), pp. 399–433, and jointly with Jordi Maluquer de Motes, "Catalunya, la fàbrica d'Espanya. Un segle d'industrialització catalana, 1833–1936," in *Catalunya, la fàbrica de Espanya,* a catalogue of the industrial exhibition under the same name (Barcelona, 1985), pp. 19–159.

5.
TRANSPORTATION AND ECONOMIC GROWTH, 1830–1930

ANTONIO GÓMEZ MENDOZA
Universidad Complutense de Madrid

THE RUGGED TOPOGRAPHY and climate of the Iberian Peninsula hindered the improvement of the Spanish transportation system during the Ancien Régime. By mid-eighteenth century, however, other European nations had already begun to upgrade their systems, a process which resulted in a considerable expansion of transport services during the course of the nineteenth century. These countries gradually adopted a series of technological innovations, including the construction of sturdier roads, the opening of inland canals, the use of steel rails, and the substitution of animal traction for steampower. As a result, productivity increased, which in turn permitted a reduction in transportation costs. These changes were especially beneficial for bulky cargoes that had a high weight-to-value ratio, like minerals and coal, products which played a crucial role in nineteenth-century industrialization.

Historians have examined the degree to which transportation contributed to economic growth from three perspectives. First, they have established that advances in the transportation sector led to the formation of larger markets, an essential requirement for the greater division and specialization of labor. Indeed, the volume of cargo moved by the various modes of transportation, especially by the railroads, grew faster than did the national products of several European nations.[1] In the case of Belgium, France, and England, the growth rate of railroad output was twice that of the gross national product; in countries with less developed transportation systems, like Spain the demand for railroad services was even more elastic as the national product increased. Why did the volume of transport cargoes increase in relation to GNP? The explanation is twofold: first, the modernization of transport generated "income effects" which derived, in large part, from the high income elasticity of

90

demand for railroad services; second, it produced "price effects" which derived from the greater efficiency and productivity of the new modes of transport. These advances permitted a decrease in the volume of resources needed to provide a particular volume of transportation. The result was a reduction in transport charges which benefited customers by lowering the price of goods and services and benefited producers by lowering the price of intermediate goods.

Second, economic historians have analyzed the backward linkages of the new modes of transport by studying the demand generated for certain products. They have estimated the proportion of pit coal, processed steel, and building materials, for example, that producers delivered to the transportation sector. Moreover, the construction of railroads and, to a lesser degree, the opening of canal networks led to the mobilization of thousands of men and to the expansion and restructuring of financial markets.[2]

In like manner, they have studied the forward linkages of the new transportation sector, that is, linkages or effects which generated rapid growth rates in other sectors of the economy. The railroads, for example, generated demand for steel products, which in turn fostered technological innovations such as the Bessemer process. The latter resulted in drastic reductions in the cost of steel and in subsequent price cuts in other sectors of high steel usage. Another focus of study has been the railroad's contribution to upgrading the skills of the work force. It is undeniable that there was a cause-and-effect relationship between the installation of Compañía de los Caminos de Hierro del Norte de España's repair facilities in Valladolid and the subsequent development of the mechanical repair industry in that city.[3]

In this chapter, several issues will be examined. Section 1 assesses the state of transportation facilities at the beginning of the nineteenth century. It will be shown that the road system was insufficient to meet the needs of the Spanish economy. The traditional transportation system was organized in a manner which might have been suitable for the needs of the Ancien Régime but was totally inadequate for an economy in the midst of development. The expansion of transportation facilities was clearly required for further growth.

In light of modern development theory, Section 2 analyzes the pros and cons of the economic policy choices of mid-nineteenth century governments. In short, there were two options: development via either "excess capacity" or "shortage." The liberal government of the so-called Progressive Biennium (1854–1856) chose the first option and backed the construction of a railroad system.

Finally, Section 3 deals with the effects of nineteenth-century innovations in the transportation industry. First, the railroad succeeded in reducing the volume of productive resources necessary to obtain a determined volume of transportation services. In order to calculate these savings, an estimate is made of the railroads' "social savings." Second, the reduction of transportation costs affected the decisions of the consumers of railroad services. Agriculture was the sector that benefited most. In order to analyze changes in the internal market, I have attempted to identify the principal trade flows and changes in the balance of trade for a series of products in various Spanish regions for two different periods.

1. TRANSPORTATION AT THE BEGINNING OF THE NINETEENTH CENTURY

At the end of the eighteenth century, complaints regarding the poor state of the roads often appeared in the works of famous authors and in the accounts of foreign travelers. Both groups concurred that the means of communication were insufficient, that the roads were impassable—even recently constructed roads turned into quagmires after a few days of rain—and that, above all, transportation was expensive.

The infrastructure was inadequate; in 1856, for example, France's road system was eight times more extensive than Spain's. In addition, France had more than 11,000 kilometers of inland canals, while Spain had only a few hundred.[4] Nevertheless, it should be recalled that some major improvements had been made since the mid-eighteenth century. Public works projects had received the support of important politicians and the construction of major roads like the Guadarrama, Reinosa to Santander or the Peña de Orduña were undertaken. In the second half of the eighteenth century, an average of 37 kilometers of roads were constructed annually. In the first third of the nineteenth century, that pace increased to an annual average of 85 kilometers. In general, the accomplishments of the period did not always contribute to the country's real needs. In some places, there was very little construction, and travel routes followed dried-up riverbeds or paths, suitable only for horses. According to the accounts of foreign travelers, however, some roads were actually wide and luxurious and could be considered among the finest in Europe. But time would prove that the new roads were poorly built and even more poorly maintained.

The quality of construction was an accurate reflection of Spain's sad financial state. Construction was financed by tolls, which according to some authors were collected haphazardly at the end of the eighteenth century. Whether the collection of tolls was spotty because the roads were bad or whether the roads were bad because the collection of tolls was spotty has been the subject of frequent debate. Whatever the case, resources for highway improvement were indeed scarce.

Roads were impassable except by foot or on horseback. The worst roads were in Catalonia and Valencia. In Castile, where it rained less, the roads were dusty and heavily traveled by large herds of animals and two-wheeled carts in groups of "one or two hundred, together in rows . . . presenting the traveler with the image of a Chinese caravan."[5]

The difficult course of the roads and the poor quality of the roadbeds combined with the organization of transportation itself, as will be seen later, required that cargoes be carried by pack animals, and the best pack animals undoubtedly were mules.[6] The following quotation is instructive: "The strength of mules and their sure-footedness on rough terrain (whether hauling freight on their backs or pulling it in wagons), the simplicity of their diets, their endurance, and their greater capacity for hard work are the reasons mules are better-suited than horses for work as pack animals, especially in regions that are geographically rugged."[7]

Overland transport in Spain was expensive, slow, and risky. Contemporary reports blamed the cost of transportation for the poor state of inland trade, for the wide variations in the prices of goods, and for the relative absence of regional specialization. Using prices from 1884 (a date subsequent to the period under investigation) as a bench mark, it is clear that freight transportation was cheaper by cart than by mule.[8] For a distance of 170 kilometers, it cost 16.6 pesetas to transport one hectoliter of wine by pack mule; by cart, it cost 9.6 pesetas, a difference of 42%. In short, transportation costs represented about 40% of the average price of wine in that year. Transport costs for raw materials were naturally much higher. The cost of a 190-kilometer haul would quadruple the price of a cartload of English coal, while the same journey by pack mule would raise the price sevenfold.[9]

The organization of overland transportation can be grouped into three categories.[10] The first group was composed of muleteers, who not only transported merchandise that usually consisted of expensive imports but also functioned as small traders. Another group was made up of professional carters, whose services were employed by the government agencies of Madrid. The third and most important group consisted of farmers who transported bulky items of little value during the agricultural dead season.

The majority of services were provided, as David Ringrose has stated, by these farmer-carriers.[11] Their dual occupation in agriculture and transportation explains their preference for mules. "The convenience of having animals that could both cart and perform agricultural work faster than oxen is the reason why they chose horses and mules."[12] When the dead season began in the countryside, the farmers would employ their animals and carts in transportation services. This work represented an additional source of income during a time of the year when their opportunity costs were low, and the most they had to lose was some free time.

It is clear that there was a very close relationship between agriculture and transportation—so close, in fact, that Spanish transportation in the first half of the nineteenth century was actually a seasonal industry. This situation, however, did have its advantages in that the farmers who worked in both agriculture and transportation received less than the market rate for their services, since their fixed costs were already subsumed in their agricultural endeavors. This system assured the regular sale of raw materials which were high in bulk and low in price; under normal circumstances, transportation costs for such materials would have fluctuated considerably and caused dramatic price changes.

The transportation system described above was quite sufficient for an unchanging subsistence economy. After the mid-eighteenth century, however, a demographic increase and a probable rise in per capita income exposed the deficiencies of the system. As the population increased, the demand curve for transportation shifted without a corresponding shift in the supply curve. Moreover, the increase in population required the breaking up and plowing of more land for cultivation, and this in turn reduced the acreage available for pasture. The reduction of pastureland halted the possible expansion of overland transport. In addition, the public works projects undertaken during the first third of the nineteenth century were very modest. The construction of canals was insignificant, and coastal trading had its difficulties, owing to inadequate port facilities which permitted only vessels with small draughts to dock.

In sum, the transportation system of the first half of the nineteenth century was distinguished by its high cost and seasonal nature; both can be traced to a lack of technological innovations in the sector. The transport problems confronting the Spanish economy created conditions that would hinder future development. While horses and mules were needed for farm work in increasing numbers, the transportation industry's demand for the services of these animals also continued to grow. The result was a transportation system that became even more expensive.

2. MID-NINETEENTH-CENTURY TRANSPORTATION POLICIES AND ECONOMIC DEVELOPMENT

With regard to the formulation of economic policy, the governments of the Progressive Biennium had two options: they could direct the human and financial resources of the country either toward the modernization of transport or toward the expansion of the manufacturing sector. In essence, the decision hinged on what modern development theorists call investment in social overhead capital (SOC), as in the first option, or investment in directly productive activities (DPA), as in the second option.[13] The following paragraphs briefly outline Hirschman's theory of unbalanced growth.

The theory states that in developing countries the simultaneous expansion of SOC and DPA is improbable. With this in mind, the theory of unbalanced growth attempts to establish an optimal investment sequence for economies whose resources are scarce or inferior to the total sum of investment possibilities. In Hirschman's opinion, the major problem confronting undeveloped countries stems less from a lack of resources than from a lack of the means and capacity to mobilize them.

Logically, the goal is to increase activities that are directly productive by making a minimal investment in them, as well as in social overhead capital. To accomplish this, two methods can be employed. According to the first method, investments in SOC should precede those in DPA. This sequence is called development via excess capacity. An initial expansion in SOC investments will lower the cost of DPA investments or generate greater investments in DPA.

According to the second strategy, priority should be given to DPA investments. This is known as development via shortage and is based on the assumption that a rise in costs will generate a series of pressures that will, in turn, favor an expansion of SOC.

The selection of the most appropriate investment sequence at each particular stage of development is crucial. According to Hirschman, both sequences produce economic incentives and pressures, so that the ultimate selection of a sequence will depend on the motivations of entrepreneurs and on their response to government SOC initiatives.

Considering this theoretical framework, it is evident that the mid-nineteenth-century officials responsible for Spain's economy favored the strategy of "excess capacity" and gave state backing to the construction of the railroad network. They were convinced that a minimum investment in the transport sector was a necessary prerequisite to the introduction of directly productive activities and to the subsequent development of the Spanish economy. As demonstrated previously, poor transportation was an obstruction to Spain's economic development, and it can, therefore, be concluded a priori that Spanish officials selected the most beneficial strategy.

Hirschman himself, however, has reservations about this method, even though he believes that a minimum of social overhead capital is always necessary. He reasoned that an excess SOC would be transformed into an essentially permissive economic policy which would invite but not compel investments in DPA. A policy of this type serves to reinforce motivations that already exist in the economy rather than to generate new ones. For this reason, Hirschman feels that in developing countries a policy of "excess capacity" could lead to a squandering of resources.

Hirschman's reservations influenced Gabriel Tortella, who argued that the construction of the Spanish railroad "ahead of demand" not only failed to promote industrialization but also impeded development by diverting scarce resources.[14] Tortella blamed state policy, in particular the promulgation of the Railroad Law of 1855 for the nation's delayed industrialization. After the passage of this law, a period of feverish construction succeeded in opening up almost 5,000 kilometers of railroad lines, placing the Spanish system ahead of the Italian by 1865. During these ten years, the principal lines were laid out and the familiar radial pattern was established. These lines would become the framework for the two major railroad companies, the Caminos de Hierro del Norte de España and the Compañía de Madrid, Zaragoza y Alicante, both of which were heavily financed by the French.

How did the law of 1855 promote such a rapid response? First, it allowed the provisional chartering of railroad joint-stock companies before state grants were awarded for the lines; this facilitated access to financial markets. Second, the Spanish government pledged support for the construction either by guaranteeing a minimal return on investment or by subsidizing each kilometer of track that was laid. Third, the railroad companies were granted tax-exempt status for the import of all the materials needed to build the lines for a period of ten years. Fourth, the government guaranteed foreign investments against any confiscations or seizures caused by war.[15]

What reasons can be cited in defense of the strategy adopted by the progressive government? As previously mentioned, a minimum SOC investment was essential for the expansion of DPA investments. In Spain the SOC investment took the form of a railroad network as opposed to a canal system. Transportation had been a bottleneck for Spanish development since the end of the eighteenth century. Among economic historians there is a consensus on this general point, but a fair amount of disagreement exists about the manner and intensity with which the problem was addressed.

Tortella is of the opinion that too many railroads were constructed to meet the real needs of the Spanish economy at mid-nineteenth century and that it would have been wiser to advance more evenly. Nadal, on the other hand, states that the physical organization of the network was inadequate.[16]

It makes little sense to go over the advantages and disadvantages of developing manufactures, since this was not the option chosen by Spain's ministers. Later on, this study focuses on the economic effects generated by technological innovations in the field of transportation. In any event, given that the majority of railroad investments was foreign, it is questionable whether that same capital could have been channeled into alternative investments in industry.

3. THE RAILROAD'S CONTRIBUTION TO THE DEVELOPMENT OF THE SPANISH ECONOMY

In order to measure the contribution of the railroads to the economic development of Spain, two issues will be examined: (1) An attempt will be made to measure the direct benefits of the railroad in relation to its capacity to save productive resources. (2) The connections or, in Hirschman's terminology, the linkages between the railroad and the rest of the economy will be analyzed. Backward linkages refer to the final products of other sectors which are used as inputs in railroad operations. Forward linkages measure the response of consumers of railroad services vis-à-vis the reduction of transportation prices.

The backward linkages, in this case, refer to a wide gamut of indispensable items needed for the construction and operation of the railroads, such as iron and steel products; fuel, wood, and other construction materials; and, above all, labor and capital. Tedde's study of railroad investments has demonstrated that investments were made in the transportation sector in proportions unprecedented for that era.[17] His estimates have also confirmed that the Spanish contribution was substantial and, of course, much more important than what was previously thought; 40% of the capital invested in the railroads in 1890 derived from Spanish resources. In a recently published article, Platt states that this figure reached 60% when Spanish government subsidies were taken into account.[18] The estimate of the director of the Compañía de Madrid, Zaragoza y Alicante, Eduardo de Maristany, lays in between. Referring to the beginning of the twentieth century, he writes: "Four billion *pesetas* are invested in the railroad industry, half of which is from Spanish sources."[19] The railroad not only succeeded in mobilizing these massive financial resources; it also helped to create a new class of small investors who channeled their savings into financial markets.

The construction of roadbeds and the laying of rails employed thousands of workers and undoubtedly helped to minimize the adverse effects of agricultural unemployment during the dead season. During the first four months of 1863, an average of almost 56,000 laborers, assisted by more than 2,600 horses and mules, was employed daily to construct 500 kilometers of rail lines.[20] Although a systematic study on the relationship between the railroad and the labor market has yet to be done, the preceding figures and Stefano Fenoaltea's suspicions with regard to the Italian case lead to the conclusion that the major effects of railroad construction were rooted in the sector's demand for manual laborers.[21]

The impact on the national iron-and-steel industry was minimized by the tariff policy regarding imports for railroad construction. This has been brought out by authors such as Tortella, Nadal, and Sánchez-Albornoz, among others.[22] Conversely, the railroad contributed substantially to the expansion of the coal industry; by my own estimates, the demand for fuel during the period 1865 to 1913 rose to one-quarter of national output.[23]

In the absence of studies on the backward linkages of the railroads, on one hand, and sectoral analyses of industries that could have benefited from government support, on the other, it is difficult to reach a conclusion on the effectiveness of the Progressive Biennium's economic policy. The recent experience of developing countries can shed some light on the question. Sectoral interdependency is weak in these economies, and in spite of the importance of the primary sector, the consumption of manufactured goods is insignificant. The case of the Spanish iron-and-steel industry is instructive; its backward linkages with other sectors and services were limited and remained circumscribed to the area in which the industry was located.[24]

In the following pages, the other two effects of the railroad will be examined in greater detail. First, the railroad's capacity to be a "saver" of productive resources is analyzed.

3.1 Direct Benefits

The construction of the railroad generated savings in productive resources which, when reallocated to other economic sectors, facilitated a rise in production. These effects can be analyzed by measuring social savings, that is, by estimating the additional costs which would have been paid for transportation over a period of one year had the railroad not existed and had the most economical alternative means of transportation been used.[25] If certain assumptions can also be made—for example, a totally inelastic demand for transportation, perfect competition, and full employment—then the social savings is a measure of the loss of gross national product necessary for the constant maintenance of the level of activity achieved by means of the railroad.

My estimates are for the years 1878 and 1912 and exclude all passenger service and all shipments of "express" items (luggage, fish, and currency), livestock, and goods used by the railroad companies themselves. If, hypothetically, the railroad network had been closed down in either of the two years under consideration, the freight would have been shipped through alternate means, that is, via a combination of overland transportation, coastal trading, and inland canals. The bulk of the cargo, however, would be transported overland.

My estimates show that the social savings of Spanish railroads reached 536 million pesetas in 1878 and 2,425 million in 1912.[26] The first figure represents between 10.5% and 11.9% of the national income in 1878, as calculated by the English statistician Mulhall. The social savings for 1912 fall between 19.2% and 23.7%, according to the Consejo de Economía's estimates (1945), and the same figures apply for Alcaide's more recent estimates (1976). Assuming that Spain's economic growth rate was approximately 1.6%, the savings for 1878 confirms that closing the railroad network would have set the economy back by seven years.

A 10% contribution to the national income is by any estimate quite substantial. Although Mulhall's estimates of the Spanish national income are internally coherent, they have not yet been confirmed and should be supplemented by another means of measuring social savings. For example, an estimate can be made of the arable land that became available on construction of the railroad, owing to the reduction of land devoted to forage crops which were previously needed to feed pack animals. According to my estimates, 520,000 mounts would have been required in order to substitute for the railroad, and it would have taken more than 1 million tons of barley to feed them. The land needed to produce this quantity of feed would have constituted 37% of the total of the land devoted to cereal production in 1891. The availability of such an extensive area of land for the production of grains was especially significant at a time of substantial demographic growth.

3.2 Some Observations on the Structure of the Internal Market

Since the railroad is a service industry, its final product represents an input for all its users. In order to assess the magnitude of the industry's forward linkages, one would have to consider the aggregate of all the transformations that occurred in the sectors which availed themselves of railroad services. Economists know how difficult it is to gather these figures; therefore, the following analysis is limited to the changes in internal trade for major products.

Who were the railroad's principal clients? The works of Anes[27] and Tedde[28] have demonstrated that the primary sector was the railroad's chief client. Cereals and their derivatives, wines and brandies, were the principal cargoes. The railroad statistics analyzed by Rafael Anes show that minerals and industrial products ranked lowest in railroad usage. Both Anes and Tedde put an end to speculation that tied the expansion of mining during the last third of the nineteenth century to the construction of the railroad network. The reason is quite simple: the cost of transporting raw materials represented only a small proportion of the price of exporting ores, since the principal mining districts were located near the ports of embarkation.

In other words, the railroads did not find a client in industry. The reason was not, however, that railroad expansion impeded industrial development, as Tortella postulates. The lack of balanced growth with simultaneous advances in SOC and DPA was, according to Tortella, the cause of the crisis at the end of the 1860s.[29] Anes and Tedde have shown, on the contrary, that the origin of the crisis was agricultural and was caused by the food shortages of 1866 to 1868.[30]

The reduction of overland transportation prices accelerated the integration of the national market: Nicolás Sánchez-Albornoz, in writing about agricultural prices in the second half of the nineteenth century, states that this process culminated at the end of the century.[31] It seems clear that the integration of the national market was linked to the development of the railroads. The railroads ended the departmentalization of the Spanish economy, and as markets expanded, economies of scale were achieved. The attainment of a uniform price helped both consumers and producers alike, since monopolistic situations were eliminated as distance became less of an obstacle. The railroads altered the terms of trade among different producing regions, favoring those most distant from markets by means of a rise in real income.

The change in relative prices brought about by the reduction in transport costs altered the commercial relations between regions. A more definitive study of this change would require data on the structure of trade prior to the railroad's construction. Unfortunately, an analysis of interregional toll collections would indicate neither routes nor the origin nor destination of products.[32] Similar difficulties occur with the data for coastal trading and preclude a reconstruction of trade patterns between Spanish ports. The statistics for coastal trading, however, are somewhat richer in that they include a record of the cargo's origin or destination. The researcher is also faced with an uphill battle when trying to gather railroad data. The main companies generally just published the tonnage of shipments. Only Norte; Madrid, Zaragoza y Alicante; Almansa, Valencia y Tarragona; Tarragona, Barcelona y Francia; and Andaluces (only for some years) published the totals by types of cargo. Only Norte's figures are broken down to include stations of origin and destination—data that permit a study of the trade of all merchandise carried and the movements of passengers for each year between 1874 and 1930, except for the period 1887 to 1900.

The figures shown in Table 5.1 present a comparison of net trade flows—defined as the difference between the merchandise shipped and received from the stations of one province—for five regions served by the Norte railroad and for four types of cargo in 1874 and 1913.

Table 5.1
Net Trade Flows in Grain, Flour, Wine, and Textiles, 1878 and 1913
(metric tons in thousands)

	Textiles		Grains		Flour		Wine	
	1878	1913	1878	1913	1878	1913	1878	1913
Castile	−4.5	−3.8	+81.0	+81.0	+92.4	+96.8	+8.0	−29.5
Basque Provs. and Santander	+0.3	−2.3	−60.4	−40.2	−68.9	−28.8	−38.5	−71.3
Rioja	−0.7	−4.3	11.3	32.3	+0.3	+11.8	+49.3	+7.0
Aragón	−1.8	−2.2	−4.8	−8.9	+25.0	+12.5	+25.9	+7.8
Catalonia	+12.4	+14.4	−50.6	−83.8	−16.5	+1.6	+2.4	+16.3

Sources: Caminos de Hierro del Norte de España, *Datos estadísticos, 1878 y 1913*; A. Gómez Mendoza, *Ferrocarril y mercado interior en España (1874–1913)*, Madrid, vol. 1, 1984 and vol. 3, 1985.
Notes: A plus or minus sign indicates the existence of a surplus or of a deficit. Shifting cargoes to other national railroads or to foreign railroads are not included.
Castile includes the stations in the provinces of Madrid, Segovia, Ávila, Valladolid, Palencia, and Burgos; the Basque Provinces and Santander include the three Basque Provinces and Santander; Rioja includes Navarre and Logroño; Aragón excludes Teruel; Catalonia includes only Lérida and Barcelona.

The comparison between 1878 and 1913 brings to light a series of transformations in the trading positions of the regions under consideration. Castile maintained great stability in its grain and flour exports but went from exporting to importing wine. Surprisingly, the region's deficit in textiles was appreciably reduced during this period. The contraction in textile consumption was more apparent than real, however, since it reflected a large surplus in the province of Madrid in 1913. If Madrid is excluded, the Castilian deficit in textiles increased from 2.950 metric tons in 1878 to 5.830 metric tons in 1913; that is, it doubled. The deficit in wine was a reflection of the phylloxera crisis in Castilian vineyards. Because of the railroads, surplus wine also became available from the wine-producing regions of Southern Spain.

As far as the Basque Provinces and Santander are concerned, the most outstanding feature is the striking reduction in their deficits in grain and flour. With the loss of Cuba and Puerto Rico, Santander ceased to operate as a port for transatlantic trade. The shortage of wine, which almost doubled between the two years, must have been resolved by bringing wine from the southern subplateau, since supplies were also limited in neighboring areas. A surprising surplus in textiles was indicated for 1878; this reflected a movement of goods into the Peninsula's interior from the maritime provinces of Santander and Guipúzcoa. Since the coastal trade of 1878 did not provide textiles in sufficient volume to explain this traffic, it is likely that they were imported.

The most striking trend in the Rioja was the sharp decline in wine shipments, owing undoubtedly to agricultural pests and an increasing specialization in the production of cereals. In spite of the wine crisis, the deficit in textiles increased more than sixfold, a rise which is not attributable only to increased consumption but also to the gradual substitution of the railroad as a vehicle for the commercialization of textiles.

The two Catalan provinces experienced a significant improvement in their trading positions (within the limitations imposed by statistics on volume). There was an increase in textile exports and a conversion of the deficit in flour and wine into a surplus. Some explanations should be provided. First, the province of Barcelona specialized increasingly in the milling of grain brought from interior provinces, as indicated by a 67% increase in the cereal deficit. Second, in spite of a 16% rise in the sale of textiles to other provinces between 1878 and 1913, it is important to point out that these were also years of the growing commercialization of textile production within the province of Barcelona. The proof is that, in 1878, 43% of textile shipments were destined for stations within the province, while in 1913 this percentage rose to 69%.

4. FINAL CONSIDERATIONS

With the General Railroad Law, the progressives displayed their conviction that economic modernization of the nation required the transformation of the transportation system. To ensure the success of this policy, the government passed laws which made railroad investments attractive to both Spanish savers, still unfamiliar with stock-exchange transactions, and to foreign investors, who generally shunned Spanish investments because of their high financial risk. The law was overwhelmingly successful, and the foundation for the future railroad system was firmly established in the ensuing ten years. By 1864, the railroad companies' actual assets totaled 1,313 million pesetas.[33]

This volume of capital was fifteen or sixteen times higher than that available to the industrial sector, a ratio which has led Tortella to conclude that the railroad was constructed at the expense of industry.[34] In accordance with this theory, the lack of industrial initiatives would be explained by the absence of a suitable legal code, by the lack of status subsidies, and by the shortage of money in financial markets. In contrast to the Spanish case, Tortella uses the English experience as an example of a more balanced investment policy. In 1865 English railroad capital represented two-thirds of the capital invested in industry.[35] In 1865, however, the pace of railroad construction was not as rapid as in the initial phases. If one examines the decade 1831–1840, during which the English railroad network tripled in size, it becomes clear that the formation of fixed capital in the railroad sector surpassed the formation of industrial capital by 23%.[36]

Those who have studied the Spanish case have agreed that the Railroad Law facilitated a considerable influx of foreign capital which otherwise would not have been invested in Spain. Instead, it is the participation of Spanish capital in railroad investments that has become the subject of debate. The estimates of Tortella and Broder led Nadal to conclude that "Spanish investment was too small to be blamed for the lack of industrialization."[37] Tedde's more recent estimates, however, have placed overall Spanish investment for the nineteenth century at about 1 billion pesetas, "a substantial amount, which could, of course, have constituted an investment source for alternative activities."[38] This information has generated a renewed interest in Tortella's theory, making further research into the topic an imperative. In particular, estimates are needed of the social rate of return of the railroads as well as of other economic sectors, especially industry.

In the absence of these studies, the topic has been developed around the question of the railroad's "indispensability" for Spain's economic growth. Was the railroad indispensable, and if so, can this indispensability be measured? Transportation was rudimentary, primitive, costly, and subject to the seasonal availability of the farmer-carriers, causing a situation in which products had to be stored for months in order to meet consumption needs. More important, there was a lack of technical innovation in the traditional transport sector. All these factors combined to make the railroad indispensable; of this, there is little doubt. But was it indispensable enough to temporarily sacrifice Spain's industrial development, in particular the development of the iron-and-steel industry? In my opinion, it was. The computation of social savings for 1878 reveals that the lack of railroad construction would have set the Spanish economy back by a minimum of seven years.

NOTES

1. P. K. O'Brien, "Transport and Economic Growth in Western Europe, 1830–1914," *Journal of European Economic History* 11 (1982): 336–37.
2. Ibid.
3. J. García Fernández, *Crecimiento y estructura urbana de Valladolid* (Barcelona, 1974), pp. 29–30.
4. A. Gómez Mendoza, *Ferrocarriles y cambio económico en España (1855–1913): Un enfoque de Nueva Historia Económica* (Madrid, 1982), p. 24.
5. J. Canga Argüelles, *Diccionario de Hacienda* (Madrid, 1833), p. 391.
6. See my "The Role of Horses in Transport in a Backward Economy: Spain in the Nineteenth Century, Some Preliminary Findings," in *Horses in European Economic History: A Preliminary Canter,* M. Thompson, ed. (Reading, Mass., 1983), chap. 9.
7. Junta Consultiva Agronómica, *La Ganadería en España: Avance de 1891,* vol. 1 (Madrid, 1892), p. 144.
8. Gómez Mendoza, *Ferrocarriles,* p. 89.
9. Ibid.
10. D. Ringrose, *Transportation and Economic Stagnation in Spain, 1750–1850* (Durham, 1970).
11. Ibid.
12. Junta Consultiva Agronómica, *La Ganadería,* p. 143.
13. The following analysis is based on A. O. Hirschman, *The Strategy of Economic Development* (New Haven, 1958), chap. 5. For an excellent synthesis of this work consult A. P. Thirlwall, *Growth and Development,* 2d ed. (London, 1978), pp. 177–186.
14. G. Tortella, *Los orígenes del capitalismo en España* (Madrid, 1982), pp. 11–12 and chap. 5.
15. Ibid., pp. 168–169.

16. J. Nadal, "The Failure of Industrialization in Spain, 1830–1913," in *The Fontana Economic History of Europe*, vol. 4, pt. 2, C. M. Cipolla, ed. (London, 1973), pp. 533–626.

17. P. Tedde, "Las compañías ferroviarias en España, 1844–1913, in *Los ferrocarriles en España, 1844–1913*, M. Artola, ed. (Madrid, 1978), p. 47 and passim.

18. D. C. M. Platt, "Las finanzas extranjeras en España, 1820–1870," *Revista de Historia Económica* 1 (1983): 148.

19. E. Maristany, "Notas sobre la Conferencia de 1905," Archive of the MZA, box 88–130.

20. Dirección General de Obras Públicas, *Boletín de Fomento* 3 (1864).

21. S. Fenoaltea, "Italy," in *Railways and the Economic Development of Europe, 1830–1914*, P. K. O'Brien, ed. (London, 1983) p. 72 and passim.

22. N. Sánchez-Albornoz, *España hace un siglo: una economía dual* (Madrid, 1977), p. 21.

23. Gómez Mendoza, *Ferrocarriles*, p. 170.

24. V. J. Shaw, "Exportaciones y despegue económico: el mineral de hierro de Vizcaya, la región de la ría de Bilbao y algunas de sus implicaciones para España," *Moneda y Crédito* 142 (1977): 87–114.

25. Gómez Mendoza, *Ferrocarriles*, chap. 2.

26. Ibid, pp. 93–97.

27. R. Anes, "Relación entre el ferrocaril y la economía española, 1865–1935," in *Los ferrocarrilles en España, 1844–1943*, M. Artola, ed. (Madrid, 1978), pp. 355–512.

28. Tedde, "Las compañías."

29. Tortella, *Los orígenes*, p. 186.

30. Tedde, "Las compañías," pp. 124–129.

31. N. Sánchez-Albornoz, *Los precios agrícolas durante la segunda mitad del siglo XIX*, vol. 1, *Trigo y cebada* (Madrid, 1975).

32. S. Madrazo Madrazo, "Portazgos y tráfico en la España de finales del antiguo régimen," *Moneda y Crédito* 160 (1982): 58.

33. Nadal, *The Failure*, pp. 40–41.

34. Tortella, "*Los orígenes*," pp. 177–183.

35. Ibid., pp. 178–179.

36. C. H. Feinstein, "Capital Formation in Great Britain," in *The Cambridge Economic History of Europe*, vol. 7, pt. 1, P. Mathias and M. M. Postan, eds. (London, 1978), pp. 40–41.

37. Nadal, *The Failure*, p. 39.

38. Tedde, "*Las compañías*," p. 114.

FURTHER READINGS

Anes, R. "Relación entre el ferrocarril y la economía española, 1865–1935." In M. Artola, ed., *Los ferrocarriles en España, 1844–1943*. Madrid, 1978, pp. 355–512.

Casares, A. *Estudio histórico económico de las construcciones ferroviarias en el siglo XIX.* Madrid, 1973.

Gómez Mendoza, A. *Ferrocarriles y cambio económico en España (1855–1913): Un enfoque de Nueva Historia Económica.* Madrid, 1982.

Nadal, J. "The Failure of Industrialization in Spain 1830–1913." In C. M. Cipolla, ed., *The Fontana Economic History of Europe,* vol. 4, pt. 2. London, 1973, pp. 533–626.

Ringrose, D. *Transportation and Economic Stagnation in Spain, 1750–1850.* Durham, 1970.

Tedde, P. "Las compañías ferroviarias en España, 1844–1913." In M. Artola, ed., *Los ferrocarriles en España, 1844–1943.* Madrid, 1978, pp. 13–354.

Tortella, G. *Los orígenes del capitalismo en España.* Madrid, 1982.

Wais, F. *Historia de los ferrocarriles españoles.* Madrid, 1974.

6.
DEVELOPMENT AND MODERNIZATION OF THE FINANCIAL SYSTEM, 1844–1935

PABLO MARTÍN ACEÑA
Universidad de Alcalá de Henares

1. INTRODUCTION

THE TERM "financial system" refers to the complex of economic institutions that specialize in mediating between main borrowers and lenders, that is, commercial banks, savings banks, insurance companies, investment trusts, finance companies, and credit unions.

The three functions that, according to Rondo Cameron, can or should be carried out by these institutions are serving as intermediaries between savers and investors; supplying part or all of the means of payment, that is, generating money; and monitoring entrepreneurial undertakings—a role to which Cameron attributes great importance, especially in view of the close relationship between banking and industry in nineteenth-century Europe.[1] Moreover, these financial institutions, themselves, expand and multiply because of the important economic advantages that they derive from their activities.[2]

A financial structure is characterized by the nature and diversity of the financial institutions of which it is composed. Raymond Goldsmith distinguishes three basic types of structure, taking into account their different historical experiences. The first type exhibits a low share of financial institutions in all financial assets outstanding, a low financial interrelations ratio (below 0.5), and a clear predominance of commercial banks over other institutions; this structure is usually prevalent in the first stages of economic growth. The second structure is similar to the first except that public credit institutions and state intervention play a role equal or superior to that of the

107

private sector. The third type, which coincides with the financial structure of developed countries, is characterized by a higher share of financial institutions in total financial assets; a less important role for banking, accompanied by greater diversification of financial institutions and instruments; and a higher financial interrelations ratio, generally in the order of unity.[3]

The transition from a structure of the first or second type to one of the third type is called financial development and modernization. Signs of modernization and development, therefore, will be: (1) the diversification of financial institutions and a trend toward specialization; (2) the expansion of the number and types of financial instruments; (3) an increase in the share of assets issued by financial institutions in the total assets of the economy; and (4) a high financial interrelations ratio. The higher the latter the more pronounced will be the separation between the processes of saving and investment and the greater will be the economies of scale.

Between 1844—the year in which Spain entered the era of modern banking with the creation of the Banco de Isabel II and the Banco de Barcelona—and 1935, the banking system underwent a radical change. In 1856, the year in which two important banking laws were passed, there were 13 banks and credit associations with 170 million pesetas in paid-up capital.[4] In 1892 the number of private banks (excluding the Banco de España) increased to 35, with 210 million pesetas in paid-up capital.[5] At the beginning of 1921, the number of banks reached 150, with approximately 850 million pesetas in paid-up capital; finally, in 1935 the total number of Spanish banks was over 200, with 1.6 billion pesetas in paid-up capital.[6] This continuous rise in the number of financial institutions was accompanied by a slow but gradual modernization of the system, as will be seen later.

Fortunately, there are many studies that deal with this process. The seminal works of Ramón Canosa and Tallada Paulí[7] have been followed by more recent and analytical research. Nicolás Sánchez-Albornoz has studied the formation of the banking system as well as the history of individual institutions,[8] and Gabriel Tortella has produced a detailed historical analysis of Spanish banking for the years 1856 to 1868.[9] Pedro Tedde has carried out a thorough investigation of the inner workings and contributions of banking to economic development from 1874 to 1914.[10] And both Tortella and Rafael Anes have examined the role and evolution of the Banco de España between the mid-nineteenth century and 1930.[11] To the above-mentioned works one must also add the research on the twentieth century that has been carried out by Santiago Roldán, García Delgado, and Juan Muñoz, and more recently by Gabriel Tortella and Jordi Palafox.[12] In addition, there are numerous regional studies both of banks and of other financial institutions that are cited in "Una historia de la banca privada en España."[13]

In spite of this extensive bibliography, there are two important topics that, until now, have been barely touched upon: a comparison with the financial structures of other countries and a quantitative analysis of long-term changes— that is, a study that attempts to trace the evolution of the financial interrelations ratio in different periods and to analyze the changes in both the composition of financial assets and the quantity of money. This chapter focuses on these two topics. The period under investigation is 1844 to 1935.

2. THE MODERNIZATION OF THE FINANCIAL SYSTEM

The Legal Framework

The role of banking laws in the evolution of the financial system is difficult to overestimate. Official criteria create the legal framework which bounds the behavior of credit institutions and conditions their development. Laws also determine the levels of competitiveness or degrees of freedom within which the sector operates. The more restrictive the banking legislation, the less competitive the system will be in general, and the less efficient will be its intermediate functions. What follows is a review of the four most important legislative bench marks.[14]

(1) The Ley de Sociedades por Acciones of 1848 (Joint Stock Company Law of 1848) imposed stringent restrictions on the founding of banks of issue and prohibited the creation, without government authorization, of joint-stock companies. This prohibition also acted to restrict the establishment of credit institutions that operated as joint-stock companies. The 1848 law marked the closing of a relatively liberal period throughout which the Commercial Code of 1829 had permitted fairly unrestricted banking activities. The code placed very few obstacles in the way of founding financial institutions and required only the approval of the Tribunal of Commerce. The detrimental effects of the law of 1848 have been studied by Tortella. After substantiating that the Commercial Code contributed to the rapid multiplication of credit institutions in the 1840s, he concludes that the law of 1848 retarded the development of Spanish banking for several years.[15] In those years, the issue of notes and the credit market were monopolized by three institutions: the Banco Español de San Fernando, the Banco de Barcelona, and the Banco de Cádiz. Alongside them were numerous private bankers who were grouped, for tax purposes,

into an official guild called "Capitalist Merchants" and who attended to local credit needs.[16]

(2) In 1856 two important laws favored the development of banking: the Ley de Bancos de Emisión (Banks of Issue Law) and the Ley de Sociedades de Crédito (Credit Company Law). This new legislation faciliated the consolidation of capital and the creation of joint-stock companies and also contributed to a tremendous expansion of the number of credit institutions. Although government authorization was required for the establishment of new banks, these two laws were, in large part, fairly liberal, especially in relation to the kinds of commercial transactions that were permitted and with respect to the supervision of institutions.

The Banks of Issue Law allowed only one Bank of Issue in each commercial district and required that all capital be paid up at the time of constitution. It did not, however, impose a limit on the volume of currency issued.[17] In addition, it authorized banks "to discount, to draw checks, to lend, to keep current accounts, to carry out collections, to receive deposits, and to contract with the government." The only prohibition was that they could not use their own assets as collateral when making loans, nor could they be overdrawn or deal in public securities.[18]

The Credit Company Law was even more liberal and authorized all kinds of banking transactions, which are listed in its fourth article.[19] Aside from this, it did not establish a minimum reserve fund; more important, it did not set a cash ratio or any sort of liquidity coefficient. The officials of credit institutions were, therefore, free to adopt whatever measures of liquidity and investment seemed most beneficial. Finally, the Ley de Sociedades por Acciones of 1869 (Joint Stock Company of 1869) lifted all restrictions on "the creation of regional and agricultural banks, banks of issue and discount, and credit companies."[20] The system, therefore, was transformed from being extremely restrictive in 1848 to a moderately interventionist in 1856, and to absolute freedom in 1869.

(3) The third legislative bench mark consisted of the decree of March 19, 1874, that granted a monopoly of issue throughout the whole national territory to the Banco de España. This represented one more step in what Tortella and Anes have called the slow formation of the Spanish central bank.[21] In view of the pattern that evolved in other countries, the creation of a single issuing institution is a sign of modernization, though from a theoretical point of view, the advantages of monopoly vis-à-vis freedom of issue are yet to be demonstrated.[22] In any case, the decree of 1874 reduced the financial system's level of competitiveness and placed control of the credit market in the hands

of a single institution—an institution that did not always function in a manner conducive to the economy's growth.[23]

(4) Last, mention should be made of the Ley de Ordenación Bancaria (Banking Ordinance) of 1921. With regard to the rules governing private banks, the finance minister stated when submitting the bill to the National Assembly that "The banking industry, because of its nature, cannot be an absolutely free industry."[24] By means of this law, the Ministry of Finance tried to regulate banking activities precisely to put an end to the relative freedom of the industry.

The most meaningful provisions of the Banking Ordinance are those of article 2, which restricts or regulates banking operations. This article created the Consejo Superior Bancario (Supreme Banking Council) which was granted extensive powers, the most important of which are:

- the fixing of minimum amounts of capital for credit institutions
- the setting of a minimum ratio between said capital and the reserve fund on the one hand, and the volume of deposit accounts on the other
- determination of the minimum interest credited to current accounts, certificates, time deposits, and similar transactions
- the setting of a ratio between real assets and demand liabilities
- the fixing of minimum rates of interest and other conditions for banking operations

In addition, the Consejo Superior Bancario had other prerogatives such as imposing sanctions and inspecting institutions. Although these regulations may seem abusive, it is important to bear in mind that the law of 1921 represented a significant shift in the attitude of the state, which from then on became increasingly interventionist.

In conclusion, the evolution of the financial system from 1844 to 1935 can be divided into five periods. The first was a period of almost absolute freedom and lasted from 1829 to 1848. This stage was followed by a more restrictive period that lasted until 1856, during which the development of the banking industry was stymied. In the third phase, the system was once again characterized by extensive freedom, and the relative absence of restrictions gave way to high levels of competitiveness. These are the years that Sánchez-Albornoz calls the "formative" period of the Spanish banking sector.[25] In 1874, with the concession to the Banco de España of a monopoly of issue, the system's level of competitiveness was reduced, but ample financial freedom and a minimum level of official intervention were maintained. Last, the Banking Ordinance of

1921 opened a new stage that lasted until very recently, in which the competitiveness and freedom of the system were curtailed. If the years 1854 to 1930 are considered together, they can be characterized as a period of moderate financial liberalism.

Growth and Structural Changes

In this section a survey will be made of the structure and growth of the financial sector and of the changing composition of banking assets and liabilities from 1854—the earliest date for which minimally acceptable aggregate data are available—to 1935.

Table 6.1 presents the evolution, by subsectors, of the financial institutions' total assets. Most evident is the predominance of the banking subsector (Banco de España, private banks), whose assets in 1935 still represented almost 80% of the total. Within this subsector, the central bank occupied a salient position. In 1900, after almost half a century of banking development, the Banco de España still retained 68% of the financial system's total assets—a situation that indicates the system's high degree of concentration and the importance and power of the issuing institution. But, since private commercial banking experienced spectacular growth during World War I and the 1920s, these positions shifted in the twentieth century. In 1929 the central bank ranked second, and the nonissuing banks controlled almost 50% of the assets generated by the financial sector.

The system was additionally characterized by insufficient financial specialization (shown by the limited variety and number of institutions listed in Table 6.1). Savings banks and savings associations did not acquire true importance until the 1920s and 1930s. In 1935 they issued approximately 11% of the total assets, a relative limited proportion. The table also indicates that the public credit institutions—to use current terminology—experienced only minimal growth. Until 1913, this group's assets were represented solely by those of the Banco Hipotecario, which in that year controlled 5.5% of the total. In the 1920s new institutions appeared, such as the Banco de Crédito Local, the Banco de Crédito Industrial, and the Banco Exterior, all of which specialized in financing single sectors or activities. In all, the participation of public credit institutions in 1935 rose to approximately 10.5%.

In short, until 1900 the financial structure was marked by a relative lack of diversification, a predominance of the banking sector, and an excessive weight of the Bank of Issue—traits that are generally typical of the first stage of financial development. By 1930 the structure had begun to vary; the private

Table 6.1
Financial Institutions: Total Assets, 1854–1935
(in millions of pesetas)

	1854	1873	1880	1900	1913	1929	1935
1. Banco de España	128	234	1,067	2,706	2,846	6,304	7,005
2. Private banks	48	337	431	984	848	11,702	13,296
3. Savings banks and credit companies	n.a.	17	59	131	349	1,998	2,886
4. Public credit institutions	—	19	59	63	236	2,075	2,720
5. Total	176	607	1,616	3,984	4,279	22,079	25,907

SOURCES: R. Anes, "El Banco de España"; *Anuario(s) Financiero y de Sociedades Anónimas*; Banco de España, *Memoria(s) Anual(es)*; Consejo Superior Bancario, *Boletines*; P. Martín Aceña, *La política monetaria*; P. Tedde, "La banca privada"; G. Tortella, *Los orígenes del capitalismo*; Tortella, "La evolución del sistema."
NOTE: Line 1 excludes available credit; in line 3 the figures correspond to the balances of savings accounts; n.a. = not available.

commercial banks gained prominence, and the central bank was no longer the institution with the highest concentration of assets. Other substantial institutions arose that specialized in financing particular sectors or in issuing new liabilities, such as saving accounts. Still, it could not be said that the system had reached an advanced stage of development. At the end of the 1920s and the beginning of the 1930s, the Spanish financial system was at the crossroads, that is, it was in the process of transition from an underdeveloped to a modern financial structure.

Table 6.2 provides the statistical material needed to study the changes in the composition of banking assets and liabilities that, in turn, reflect changes in the intermediation functions of the credit institutions and their degree of connection with the real economy. The relations between certain financial indicators were selected to indicate the banking industry's behavior. These indicators reveal how the banking system performed its credit functions, changes in financial sources, and variations in the demand for banking assets by the public.

(1) The first characteristic that should be pointed out is a marked change in the relations between IR/TR and ER/TR (see columns 9 and 10)—relations that express the ratio between internal resources (paid-up capital and reserve funds) and total resources on one hand, and external resources (deposits) and total resources on the other. In the formative period, internal resources represented a large proportion of the system's total assets, almost 70% according to the data presented in Table 6.2. This high percentage declined between 1854

Pablo Martín Aceña

Table 6.2
Relations between Financial Magnitudes in Nonissuing Private Banks,
1854–1930 (in percentages)

	National Income	Bank Deposits	$\dfrac{D}{NI}$	$\dfrac{CA}{D}$	$\dfrac{C}{D}$	$\dfrac{C}{TBA}$	$\dfrac{I}{TBA}$	$\dfrac{L}{TBA}$	$\dfrac{IR}{TR}$	$\dfrac{ER}{TR}$
					(millions of pesetas)					
Years	1	2	3	4	5	6	7	8	9	10
1854	n.a.	37	n.a.	n.a.	75.0	16.7	45.9	23.1	68.4	31.6
1874	4,497	63	1.4	98.9	75.9	20.6	42.7	16.3	60.5	39.5
1880	5,210	179	3.4	97.7	47.4	16.8	44.3	24.3	49.9	50.1
1900	10,152	334	3.3	78.6	63.9	19.0	21.4	26.0	30.0	70.0
1913	13,086	515	3.9	59.0	17.9	10.2	32.0	37.9	23.7	76.3
1920	32,863	3,223	9.8	78.5	17.1	7.0	23.7	19.9	23.4	76.6
1930	31,503	6,740	21.4	66.6	15.2	8.3	46.4	19.6	17.5	82.5

SOURCES: See sources for Table 6.1 and also Alcaide, "Una revisión urgente de la serie de Renta Nacional," Instituto de Estudios Fiscales, *Datos básicos para la historia financiera de España (1850–1975)*, vol. 2 (Madrid: 1976).
NOTE: The figures for national income for 1874 and 1880 correspond respectively to the estimates for 1870 and 1879 made by Prados de la Escosura using Mulhall's calculations; see L. Prados, *Comercio exterior y crecimiento económico en España, 1826–1913: Tendencias a largo plazo* (Madrid, 1982).
  The letter symbols represent the following terms: D = total deposits; NI = national income; CA = current accounts; C = bank cash; I = investment portfolio; L = loans; TBA = total banking assets; IR = internal resources (capital and reserve funds); ER = external resources (total deposits); TR = total resources (capital, reserve funds and deposits); n.a. = not available.

and 1900 at a time when the private banking sector was undergoing a process of development and consolidation. By 1900 the situation had been reversed, and external sources were now in the majority, while internal resources had declined to about 30%. As the century advanced, this decline continued until it reached below 20% by the 1930s.

So, while the banking sector depended on internal resources at the middle of the nineteenth century, in the twentieth century it operated largely with external resources. The transition from a traditional to a modern banking system began in the last decades of the nineteenth century at the height of the Restoration. According to Pedro Tedde, this was a period during which the banking sector experienced a tremendous expansion. The change can be attributed to various factors. On the one hand, there was a rise in public confidence in the financial system, paralleled by an increased preference on the part of the nonbanking private sector for financial assets as opposed to real assets. On the other hand, there was a striking intensification of banking intermediation that led to a much greater volume of deposits.

(2) The second inference that can be made from Table 6.2 is that bank deposits grew tremendously in absolute terms, as well as in terms of the

national income. In absolute figures, the increase was spectacular. The volume of deposits practically doubled from one period to the next. The years of greatest growth occurred between 1913 and 1920, when bank deposits increased to 2.5 billion pesetas, and in the 1920s, when they increased to more than 3.5 billion pesetas. Between 1854 and 1900 bank deposits multiplied nine times and, in the following thirty years, twenty times. On the other hand, the growth of the banking sector's monetary liabilities was much greater than that of the national income. This is confirmed upon examining the D/NI ratio in column 3. This ratio rose from 1.4 in 1874 to 21.4 in 1930, indicating that deposits grew fifteen times more than the national income for the same period. It is also evident that the deposits/national income ratio underwent a much steeper increase in the twentieth century than in the nineteenth, although the net product of the Spanish economy grew more between 1900 and 1930 than it did between 1874 and 1900. The remarkable change in this ratio arises from two factors: (a) that the financial system developed at a much greater rate than the general economy and (b) that the growth of financial assets was far superior to that of real assets.

(3) The rapid growth in the total volume of deposits was accompanied by a change in their structure or composition. While in 1874 current accounts or demand deposits represented almost 80% of the total monetary liabilities, by 1930 this percentage had been reduced to 67%, and it declined to 59% in 1913 (see column 4). This gradual decrease in the CA/D ratio can be explained by a possible trend in public preference away from demand deposits and toward time deposits, which were less liquid but more profitable. Another important development was the appearance and growth of nonbanking financial institutions that permitted the nonfinancial private sector to substitute part of its portfolio of certificates for savings accounts generated by the new financial intermediaries. This argument might be especially valid for the first third of the twentieth century that saw the growth of nonbanking savings institutions. The growth of deposits—in particular of time deposits and savings accounts—suggests that the public chose to increase its proportion of assets in the form of bank money. This facilitated the banking system's ability to increase its portfolio of nonfinancial assets, that is, to finance a greater volume of real investments and to expand its portfolio of loans and credits.

(4) The C/D ratio (column 5), which can be obtained by dividing the total bank cash reserves by the volume of deposits, expresses what is known in current terminology as the cash ratio and reflects the sector's measure of liquidity. A marked change can be observed in this ratio as well. Between 1854 and 1930 the cash ratio plummeted from 75% to 15%. At mid-nineteenth

century, credit institutions had a large liquid reserve, since the balance of current accounts and time deposits was 75% backed by cash and deposits at the Bank of Issue. In 1930, however, this backing was much weaker. In seventy-five years the volume of bank reserves, or what can be called liquidity of the first degree, had been reduced by 80%.

Another way to look at this change would be to focus on the evolution of the ratio of bank reserves to total banking assets (column 6). In the nineteenth century cash assets absorbed about 20% of all banking investments, but early in the twentieth century that percentage shrank until it reached between 7% (1920) and 8% (1930). The meaning of these changes in both the cash ratio (C/D) and the C/TBA relation is fairly simple. As each individual institution (and the system as a whole) became consolidated and deepened in experience, it tried to maximize the yield of its resources. This was logically accomplished by bringing down the volume of idle cash balances, thereby decreasing the cash ratio. This decrease was also abetted by the banking sector's access to new forms of liquidity, especially after 1917 with the issue of government securities that could be pledged automatically at the central bank.

The transition from a high cash ratio to a much lower one took place, as in other cases, at the end of the nineteenth century and the beginning of the twentieth. Between 1900 and 1920 the cash ratio was reduced by not less than twelve points. The importance of this cut for the overall economy may be better understood if one takes into account that the C/D ratio is one of the "proximate determinants" of the quantity of money and that its decrease contributed to the growth of the money supply.

(5) Last, let us examine columns 7 and 8 that, together with column 6, reflect the structure of banking assets, that is, how resources were employed. The I/TBA and L/TBA ratios indicate, respectively, the proportion of total assets represented by the investment portfolio on one hand and loans and credits on the other. Tedde shows that both coefficients reveal how intensively the banking industry fulfilled its financial role. He also stresses that "a high ratio (in the first coefficient) indicates that resources were increasingly appropriated to finance the productive sectors of the economy."[26] According to Table 6.2, the investment portfolio and loans and credits absorbed nearly 60% of the total banking assets. Between 1854 and 1880, and again in 1930, investments generally represented a larger proportion than in the intervening years, 1900–1920. Because resources are found in investment portfolios, this does not mean, however, that Spanish banks focused on promoting enterprises subscribing the original capital or later acquiring stocks and bonds. Rather, it was the banks' purchases of government securities that accounted

for a large part of these investments. In 1930 more than 40% of the banking sector's portfolio was in government debt. This argument does not hold, however, for the earlier period when banks and railroad companies, as well as banks and industrial enterprises, were interlocked. Before 1900 the investment portfolio reflected the banks' contribution to the development of the real sector. Loans and credits represented an average of 24% of total assets in the nineteenth century; the twentieth century figure is only slightly higher, 26%. In all cases, however, the volume of resources that the banking sector devoted to this type of income-producing asset remained very stable.

3. FINANCIAL GROWTH AND INTERMEDIATION LEVELS: A COMPARATIVE ANALYSIS

In this section a comparative analysis will be conducted of both the growth of the assets of Spanish financial institutions and of intermediate levels for different periods. Tables 6.3, 6.4, and 6.5 include the information necessary for such a comparison. Spanish data derive from Spanish sources; data for other countries were taken from Raymond Goldsmith.[27]

Table 6.3 presents the average annual growth rates of the assets of financial institutions in various European countries. In column a the rates have been estimated in monetary terms; in column b in real terms. Except during the years 1913–1929, when World War I caused inflationary effects, real and nominal increases remained practically equivalent. On the other hand, the average European growth rate was slightly higher in the nineteenth century than in the twentieth—a logical development, considering that the former century saw the creation and consolidation of Europe's modern financial system.

The most interesting observation about Spain is that the growth rate of the assets of its credit institutions was not very different from the rates recorded for other European countries. This claim is especially valid for the system's formative period, 1854–1873; for the years of its consolidation, 1880–1900; and for the period 1929–1935 in spite of the difference between the Spanish crisis and the world crisis of those years. Conversely, the Spanish experience of the first three decades of the twentieth century contrasted markedly with that of the rest of Europe. From 1900 to 1913, Spanish growth rates were clearly inferior to those of other countries. In nominal terms, the Spanish rate of 0.6% is quite below the overall European rate of over 5%. These years can be called the golden age of the gold standard in which the Spanish economy

Table 6.3
**Average Annual Growth Rates of Assets of Financial Institutions
in Various European Countries (in percentages)**

	1854–1873		1880–1900		1900–1913		1913–1929		1929–1938[1]	
	a	b	a	b	a	b	a	b	a	b
Spain	7.4	n.a.	4.6	4.2	0.6	0.3	10.8	7.3	2.7	3.1
Belgium	8.7	n.a.	5.6	5.4	6.4	5.5	261.6	−3.6	3.6	6.0
Britain	10.0	n.a.	4.2	4.8	5.7	3.3	14.8	1.8	3.4	1.4
Denmark	n.a.	n.a.	5.1	5.5	5.9	5.4	5.7	2.6	3.3	3.4
France	6.2	n.a.	4.4	5.4	3.8	3.3	12.8	1.1	4.4	4.5
Germany	n.a.	n.a.	2.5	3.1	2.7	2.2	5.7	1.9	3.6	5.1
Holland	n.a.	n.a.	3.3	4.5	5.8	4.7	7.3	5.3	3.6	5.1
Italy	n.a.	n.a.	3.6	3.7	8.0	6.3	12.1	1.9	4.2	5.2
Norway	n.a.	n.a.	4.2	4.8	5.7	4.3	7.9	5.2	0.5	0.3
Sweden	n.a.	n.a.	4.5	4.6	5.5	4.5	5.8	3.2	4.6	2.6
Switzerland	n.a.	n.a.	4.7	4.5	6.8	7.4	5.3	0.6	1.1	3.5
U.S.A.	n.a.	n.a.	6.4	7.3	6.5	4.5	8.4	5.4	2.3	3.9
Europe[2]	8.1	n.a.	4.2	4.6	5.2	4.3	8.8	3.1	3.2	3.5

Source: Goldsmith, *Financial Structure,* Tables 4.4 and 4.5. For Spain, see Table 1.
Notes: a = current prices; b = constant prices; n.a. = not available.
1. For Spain, 1929–1935.   2. The average for 1913–1929 excludes Germany.

did not participate. These were also years of economic restraint brought on by the monetary and fiscal stabilization program of Villaverde, the minister of finance in 1900. Another but opposite difference appears in the following period, 1913–1929. During these sixteen years the Spanish financial system grew at a rate of 7%, whereas the European rate was only 3%, that is, less than half. The European lag may reflect the problems and tensions that accompanied the restoration of the gold standard, while Spain's rapidly rising rate may be explained by the financial expansion of the war years and the dynamism experienced by the whole system between 1926 and 1929, the last four years of the Primo de Rivera dictatorship.

The Issue Ratio of Financial Institutions

The issue ratio of financial institutions is one of the most important indicators for determining the role played by financial institutions and their level of development. Goldsmith defines this ratio as the relation between the net variations of the assets generated by financial institutions during a particular period and the net variation of the gross national product or national income during the same period.[28] Because the true financial flow is usually unknown, the numerator is calculated by taking the first difference between the stocks of existing assets at the beginning and closing dates of the period for which the issue ratio is being estimated. Financial development is reflected in a growing value of the issue ratio and in the fact that the greater the degree of development, the higher the ratio will be.

According to the data in Table 6.4, all countries experienced growth of the issue ratio until the third decade of the twentieth century, when it fell as a result of the Great Depression. Spain also moved toward growth, as indicated in the leap from a ratio of 0.5 for 1880–1900 to 1.5 for 1929–1935.

On the other hand, Table 6.4 also reveals some notable differences between countries as a result of variations in their levels of financial development. In the period 1880–1900, only Germany, Switzerland, and the Scandinavian nations had ratios above the European average (the Scandinavian phenomenon has been explained by Sandberg in various works).[29] The rest of the countries had attained an intermediate level of financial development, with the exception of Italy and Spain, which remained at an inferior level. From 1913 to 1929 and from 1929 to 1935 the Spanish ratio, in spite of having increased, continued to be lower than the European average. Compared with 6.0 for Italy, 5.5 for France, and 5.6 for Great Britain, the Spanish financial system's

Table 6.4
Issue Ratios of Financial Institutions (∅)
in Various European Countries

	1880–1900	1900–1913	1913–1929	1929–1938[1]
Spain	0.5	0.1	0.9	1.5
Belgium	5.3	8.5	−2.9	4.2
Britain	3.3	5.4	6.5	3.7
Denmark	6.5	9.9	7.4	6.7
France	3.0	3.6	8.5	5.5
Germany	2.4	2.8	5.2	5.6
Holland	1.7	4.2	5.9	5.9
Italy	1.9	6.2	7.2	6.0
Norway	6.5	9.4	9.8	1.3
Sweden	5.4	7.0	6.0	7.5
Switzerland	7.1	15.1	12.2	3.4
U.S.A.	4.3	5.3	7.8	4.4
Europe	4.0	6.6	6.6	4.7

Source: Goldsmith, *Financial Structure*, Table 4.7. For Spain see Tables 6.1 and 6.2.
Note: $\emptyset = \dfrac{\Delta \text{ Total Assets of Financial Institutions}}{\Delta \text{ Gross National Product}}$

1. for Spain, 1929–1935.

issue ratio did not even reach 2.0. This is a clear indication of the degree to which the Spanish financial sector was underdeveloped and of the low level of intermediation to which the Spanish economy was subject, even as late as 1930.

Last, an estimation will be made of what Goldsmith calls the "Financial Interrelations Ratio" (FIR). In a strict sense, this is defined as the ratio between the total assets issued by financial institutions and the market value of national wealth.[30] What is being calculated, then, is a ratio between stock magnitudes. Because estimates of national wealth are not available in the majority of cases, researchers usually use the gross national product or national income as alternative macromagnitudes. This is exemplified in Table 6.5. The statistical data in this table confirm the arguments presented above and also illustrate the Spanish economy's low intermediation level in absolute terms as well as in comparison with other European countries. In the five periods selected, the Spanish coefficient is markedly below that of the European average. It is interesting that 1900 and 1913 are the years of greatest lag, since the 1880 coefficient of 31% is practically less than half the European average, while the coefficients of 39% and 31% for those years are 2.5, four times lower, respectively, than the figure for Europe as a whole. The turn of the century, then, saw a slackening of Spain's financial development at precisely the time when

Table 6.5
Relation of Financial Institutions' Assets
to National Product, 1880–1938
(in percentages)

	1880	1900	1913	1929	1938[1]
Spain	31	39	33	69	75
Belgium	73	114	158	89	99
Britain	71	94	109	85	140
Denmark	95	147	184	186	198
France	50	96	104	90	130
Germany	95	93	103	131	158
Holland	46	62	83	110	187
Italy	36	61	97	95	137
Norway	107	136	166	241	187
Sweden	89	123	136	138	161
Switzerland	153	184	287	261	325
U.S.A.	49	86	91	129	185
Europe	77	104	133	136	163

SOURCE: Goldsmith, *Financial Structure*, Table 4.7. For Spain see Tables 6.1 and 6.2.
1. for Spain, 1935.

the rest of the European economies were developing at an accelerated pace. In my opinion, this phenomenon is yet another of the negative economic effects that resulted from the failure to integrate the Spanish monetary system into the gold standard.[31] After 1913 Spain recovered somewhat and achieved financial intermediation levels in 1929 and 1935 of 69% and 75%, respectively, half of that of developed Europe.

Even in absolute terms, Spain's financial underdevelopment is obvious. If Goldsmith is correct in his theory that an intermediation ratio of 100 is indicative that a country has a developed financial sector and has reached a satisfactory, though not optimal intermediation level, then Spain in 1935 had not yet crossed the threshold leading to financial development. Europe as a whole can be said to have crossed it by 1900. Moreover, in 1929 all the countries listed in Table 6.5 were close or over the 100 level; in 1935, all except Spain. In conclusion, in spite of the rapid growth of Spanish credit institutions between 1850 and 1930, on the eve of the Civil War, Spain had the lowest financial intermediation level and the most underdeveloped financial system in Western Europe.

4. THE QUANTITY OF MONEY AND ITS COMPOSITION

Another unmistakable sign of the financial system's modernization was the deep change that took place between 1855 and 1935 in the composition of the money supply. As is well known, "money is a financial instrument that, as such, constitutes a credit and represents, therefore, a liability for the institutions (central bank and commercial banks) that issue it and an asset or a means of maintaining wealth for those who possess it."[32] In a modern economy, the money supply includes two components: currency held by the public (coins and notes in circulation) and bank money, which includes current accounts or demand deposits, time deposits, and savings accounts in banks and other financial institutions.

In Table 6.6 one can observe the evolution of two different definitions of the money supply, M1 and M2—the former being a narrow definition and the latter a broader category that includes time deposits and all savings accounts. The table also indicates the basic components of both definitions of money and their changes over time. From 1874 to 1913, the quantity of money, however defined, increased slowly. Narrowly defined, the money supply multiplied by 1.8; broadly defined (column 6), by 2.2, resulting in an average annual growth rate of 1.6% and 2.1%, respectively. These rates were inferior

Table 6.6
The Quantity of Money and Its Components, 1874–1935
(in millions of pesetas)

Years	Currency Held by the Public (1)	Current Accounts at the Banco de España (2)	Demand Deposits (3)	Money Supply (M1) (4)	Time Deposits and Savings Accounts (5)	Money Supply (M2) (6)
1874	1,605	71	62	1,738	31	1,769
1880	1,513	192	175	1,880	97	1,977
1900	2,261	697	262	3,220	271	3,491
1913	2,418	486	304	3,208	641	3,849
1920	4,793	1,139	2,273	8,205	1,759	9,964
1930	4,971	825	3,470	9,266	5,438	14,704
1935	4,940	769	3,588	9,297	6,560	15,857

SOURCES: G. Tortella, "La oferta monetaria"; P. Tedde, "La banca privada"; P. Martín Aceña, *La cantidad de dinero en España*.
NOTES: Column (1): specie and notes from the Bank of Issue; column (2): the figure for 1856 corresponds to the sum of notes from all issuing banks; column (3): includes current accounts of non-issuing private commercial banks and of banking credit companies; column (4): column (1) + column (2) + column (3); column (5): includes time deposits and savings accounts in banks, savings banks, and nonbanking credit companies; column (6): column (4) + column (5).

to those recorded for other countries during the same years.[33] The period from 1913 to 1935, however, was one of higher growth rates for both magnitudes. The money supply, M1, multiplied by 3; M2 by 4. The contrast is even more striking if one takes the average annual growth rates and compares them with those calculated for the years 1874 to 1913. Considering the data in Table 6.6, then, it is evident that between 1913 and 1935 the money supply (M1) grew by about 5%, the total quantity of money (M2), by more than 6%. In real terms, however, the increase was less. Subtracting inflation, the rates were down to 2.4% for the narrow definition of the money supply and 4% for the broader definition—percentages which, although nominally lower, are still higher than those recorded forty years earlier.

For the purposes of this analysis, it is more important to examine the evolution of the principal components of the monetary magnitudes and the modifications that occurred from the earliest year for which data are available to 1935. The major structural characteristics and changes of the quantity of money are discussed in the following paragraphs.

(1) The proportion of currency in circulation within the category of money continually declined. The data in Table 6.6 make it clear that until 1920 currency in circulation was the most significant component but that after 1874

it was beginning to lose ground. In quantitative terms, its proportion within the total quantity of money was 91% in 1874, the year in which a monopoly of issue was granted to the Banco de España; 63% in 1913 at the end of the first stage of the Restoration; and 48% in 1920, that is, below 50% two years after World War I. These percentages continued to shrink in the 1920s and 1930s, when in 1930 currency represented only 34% of the quantity of money and only 31% five years later. Moreover, although the data do not appear disaggregated in Table 6.6, specie—gold and silver until 1880 and only silver thereafter—was the form of currency most used during the nineteenth century.[34] Specie, however, lost this position in the twentieth century when bank notes came to represent 90% of all cash.

(2) In contrast to the decline in currency circulation was the newly acquired importance of bank deposits. In 1874 the latter represented a sheer 9% of all liquid assets; in 1935, the last year of this period, it represented 70%. The transition to a system in which money issued by financial institutions prevailed came rather late (early in the 1920s). This change in the composition of money is perhaps a sure sign of the monetary system's modernization.[35] The twentieth century saw the transformation from a system dominated by legal tender to one dominated by bank money: the nineteenth century had seen a transition from a system based on specie to one based on fiduciary money. In more technical terms, it can be stated that between 1874 and 1935 there was an increase in the ratio of deposits to currency that, according to the data presented in Table 6.6, went from 0.1 in 1874 to 0.5 in 1900 to 2.2 in 1935. In addition, two other important changes that are related to bank money are evident in this table. The first was the declining importance of the Banco de España's current accounts within the total demand deposits as well as within the complex of time deposits and savings accounts. While in 1874 the Banco de España's current liabilities represented 53% of total monetary liabilities (current and term), a little more than a half-century later (1931) the proportion had been reduced to 8%.

The other meaningful change was the rapid increase in time deposits and savings accounts, which grew at a much higher rate than the demand deposits of nonissuing banks. Taking 1874 and 1935 as the beginning and closing dates of the period, the average annual growth rate was 9.2% for the first date and 6.9% for the second. This difference indicates that the money supply, broadly defined, grew at a higher rate than the money supply, narrowly defined. While in 1874 the two magnitudes barely differed, by 1935 the former had multiplied by 9 and the latter by only 5.

5. CONCLUSION

The foregoing analysis leads to the conclusion that the Spanish financial system underwent a conspicuous process of development and modernization between 1844 and 1935. The statistical information presented leaves no doubt that, in the near-century under investigation, Spain's financial structure approximated the third type defined by Goldsmith—that is, a financial structure characterized by a high share of financial institutions in total financial assets, a diversification of credit institutions and instruments, and a high ratio of financial intermediation. At the same time, the structure of financial assets and liabilities experienced a profound change, which means that the banking system achieved great efficiency in performing its basic functions. In addition, the monetary system experienced a radical transformation. It went from being based on specie at the middle of the nineteenth century to being based on fiduciary money by 1900; afterward, it was converted into a system in which bank money predominated—a characteristic of modern monetary systems.

All these obvious changes reflect signs of the financial sector's level of development and modernization. The rise in levels of financial intermediation contributed in a decisive way to the increased economic well-being experienced in Spain between 1830 and 1930. In addition, these changes took place within a legal framework characterized by a high level of financial liberalism and a limited degree of state intervention. This study has confirmed that the point of transition from a traditional to a modern financial system was fixed at the turn of the century, the year 1900 being a key date in which signs of the modernization of the Spanish credit structure can be clearly discerned. The first two decades of the twentieth century were also a period of tremendous growth of financial institutions and of a rapid transformation of the entire system.

In spite of deep changes in the Spanish financial system, the process of modernization was not concluded in 1935. This can be observed especially by looking at Spain's ratio of financial intermediation, which was still under 100 in that year. Second, the data show that the changes that took place in the Spanish credit structure, while important, had not been sufficiently intense to eliminate the gap between the Spanish and European financial structures. At the end of the period under investigation, the Spanish financial system continued to lag behind that of the other countries of Western Europe—the latter being characterized by a higher level of financial intermediation and by a greater degree of diversification and specialization.

Finally, in view of the statistical information presented and taking into account what is known about the economic growth of the Spanish economy during these hundred years, it can be concluded that Spain's financial development outpaced the development of the real sector of the economy. In other words, with the exception of clearly defined periods, the supply of banking services increased more rapidly than did the demand for financing. All in all, the financial system did not limit or obstruct the growth of the Spanish economy between 1844 and 1935.

NOTES

1. R. Cameron, *Banking in the Early Stages of Industrialization* (New York, 1970), pp. 10ff.

2. L. A. Rojo, *Renta, precios y balanza de pagos* (Madrid, 1974), pp. 61–62. "Financial intermediaries can reap economies derived from large-scale financial investment by lowering the costs of research, study and administration of loans, by reducing risks through the diversification of their allocations, by programming their maturity dates, etc.; and at the same time, financial intermediaries, acting as lenders, can generate financial instruments that offer savers relatively homogeneous and low-risk financial assets which, in turn, provide those mediating institutions with abundant resources with which to finance the real sector of the economy."

3. R. W. Goldsmith, *Financial Structure and Development* (New Haven, 1969), pp. 33–35.

4. G. Tortella, "La evolución del sistema financiero español de 1856 a 1868," in *Ensayos sobre la economía española de mediados del siglo XIX* (Madrid, 1970), p. 19.

5. P. Tedde de Lorca, "La banca privada española durante la Restauración (1874–1914)," in *La banca española en la Restauración,* vol. 1, P. Schwartz and G. Tortella, eds. (Madrid, 1974), p. 330.

6. Consejo Superior Bancario, *Boletines* (Balances de la banca privada), nos. 1–5.

7. R. Canosa, *Un siglo de banca privada (1845–1945): Apuntes para la historia de las finanzas españolas* (Madrid, 1945); J. M. Tallada Paulí, *Historia de las finanzas españolas en el siglo XIX* (Madrid, 1946).

8. N. Sánchez-Albornoz, "De los orígenes del capital financiero: La Sociedad General de Crédito Mobiliario Español, 1856–1902," *Moneda y Crédito* 97 (1966): 29–67; "La crisis de 1866 en Madrid: La Caja de Depósitos, las sociedades de crédito y la Bolsa," *Moneda y Crédito* 100 (1967): 3–40; "Los bancos y las sociedades de crédito en provincias: 1856–1868," *Moneda y Crédito* 104 (1968): 39–68; "La formación del sistema bancario español, 1856–1868," *International Review of the History of Banking* 10 (1975): 1–40.

9. G. Tortella, "La evolución del sistema," and *Los orígenes del capitalismo en España* (Madrid, 1973).

10. P. Tedde, "La banca privada," pp. 217–455.

11. G. Tortella, "El Banco de España entre 1829 y 1929: La formación de un banco central," in *El Banco de España: Una historia económica* (Madrid, 1970); R. Anes, "El Banco de España (1874–1914): Un banco nacional," in P. Schwartz and G. Tortella, eds., *La Banca española en la Restauración,* vol. 1 (Madrid, 1974).

12. S. Roldán and J. L. García Delgado, *La formación de la sociedad capitalista en España, 1914–1920* (Madrid, 1973); J. Muñoz, "La expansión bancaria entre 1919 y 1926: La formación de una banca nacional," *Cuadernos de Información Comercial Española* 6 (1978): 98–162; G. Tortella and J. Palafox, "Banking and Industry in Spain, 1918–1936," *Journal of European Economic History* 13 (1984)2: 81–111.

13. "Una historia de la banca privada en España," *Situación,* 1982–1983.

14. For a panoramic view of the historical evolution of Spanish banking regulation see G. Pérez de Armiñan, *Legislación bancaria españoia,* 6th ed. (Madrid, 1983), esp. chap. 2.

15. G. Tortella, "El principio de responsabilidad limitada y el desarrollo industrial de España, 1829–1868," *Moneda y Crédito* 104 (1968): 69–84.

16. R. Canosa, *Un Siglo de banca,* pp. 40–41.

17. Article 20 of the Banks of Issue Law of 1856 indicated only that banking officials should be careful to maintain sufficient cash and liquid assets—whose term does not exceed ninety days—to cover their debts in bank notes, current accounts, and deposits.

18. Ley de Bancos de Emisión, 1856, articles 14 and 15.

19. Article 4 of the "Ley para el establecimiento de sociedades anónimas de crédito," *Colección Legislativa de España,* vol. 67, (1856), p. 77.

20. Ley de Sociedades por Acciones, 1869, article 1.

21. G. Tortella, "El Banco de España"; Anes, "El Banco de España."

22. P. Schwartz, *Central Bank Monopoly in the History of Economic Thought: A Century of Myopia in England* (Madrid, 1983).

23. G. Tortella, "Las magnitudes monetarias y sus determinantes," in *La Banca española en la Restauración,* vol. 1 (Madrid, 1974), p. 519; Anes, "El Banco de España," 1974.

24. Ministerio de Economía y Hacienda, "Discurso del Excmo. Sr. D. Francisco de A. Cambó," in *Ordenación Bancaria de España* (1921), p. 29.

25. N. Sánchez-Albornoz, "La formación del sistema," pp. 2, 3.

26. P. Tedde, "Agregación regional de las principales magnitudes bancarias (1874–1914)," in *La Banca española en la Restauración,* vol. 2 (Madrid, 1974), p. 500.

27. R. W. Goldsmith, *Financial Structure,* chap. 4.

28. Ibid, pp. 178–183.

29. L. G. Sandberg, "Banking and Economic Growth in Sweden before World War I," *Journal of Economic History* 38 (1978): 650–680.

30. R. W. Goldsmith, *Financial Structure,* pp. 26–27. For a theoretical study of the significance, construction, and limitations of the FIR (Financial Interrelations Ratios) see chap. 2 of this work.

31. P. Martín Aceña, "España y el patrón oro, 1880–1913," *Hacienda Pública Española* 69 (1981): 267–290.

32. L. A. Rojo, *Renta,* p. 59.

33. G. Tortella, "Las magnitudes monetarias," pp. 468–469.
34. Ibid., pp. 473–481.
35. Pablo Martín Aceña, *La cantidad de dinero en España, 1900–1935* (Madrid, 1985), pt. I.

FURTHER READINGS

Anes, Rafael. "El Banco de España (1874–1914): un banco nacional," in P. Schwartz and G. Tortella, eds., *La Banca Española en la Restauración,* vol. 1. Madrid, 1974, pp. 107–215.

Canosa, Ramón. *Un siglo de banca privada (1845–1945): Apuntes para la historia de las finanzas españolas.* Madrid, 1945.

Martín Aceña, Pablo. *La cantidad de dinero en España, 1900–1935.* Estudios de Historia Económica, no. 12. Madrid, 1985.

——. *La política monetaria en España, 1919–1935.* Madrid, 1984.

Sánchez-Albornoz, Nicolás. "De los orígenes del capital financiero: La Sociedad General de Crédito Mobiliario Español, 1856–1902." *Moneda y Crédito* 97 (1966): 29–67.

——. "La crisis de 1866 en Madrid: la Caja de Depósitos, las sociedades de crédito y la Bolsa." *Moneda y Crédito* 100 (1967): 3–40.

——. "Los bancos y las sociedades de crédito en provincias 1856–1868." *Moneda y Crédito* 104 (1968): 39–68.

——. "La formación del sistema bancario español, 1856–1868." *Review of the History of Banking* 10 (1975): 1–40 (reprinted in *Jalones de la modernización de España,* [Barcelona, 1975]), pp. 17–29.

Tallada Paulí, J. M. *Historia de las finanzas españolas en el siglo XIX.* Madrid, 1946.

Tedde, Pedro. "La banca española en la Restauración," in P. Schwartz and G. Tortella, eds., *La banca española en la Restauración,* vol. 1. Madrid, 1974, pp. 217–455.

Tortella, Gabriel. "La evolución del sistema financiero español de 1856 a 1868." in *Ensayos sobre la economía española de mediados del siglo XIX.* Madrid, 1970.

——. *Los orígenes del capitalismo en España.* Madrid, 1973.

Tortella, Gabriel, and Jordi Palafox. "Banking and Industry in Spain, 1918–1936." *Journal of European Economic History* 13 (1984)2: 81–111.

7.
FOREIGN TRADE AND THE SPANISH ECONOMY DURING THE NINETEENTH CENTURY

LEANDRO PRADOS DE LA ESCOSURA
Universidad de Alcalá de Henares

THIS CHAPTER attempts to offer a long-term view of the evolution of foreign trade and its impact on the process of economic change in Spain from the end of the Napoleonic War to World War I. The study is rooted in the debate on the connections between trade and growth in the European Periphery.

1. HISTORIOGRAPHICAL INTRODUCTION

The interaction between external demand and changes in internal supply is an important factor in the development process. Interest in this relationship has transcended the field of economic history and has raised questions about whether the nineteenth-century experiences of today's developed nations are analogous to the present experiences of less developed countries. Contrasting perceptions of the past and present—the "stylized economic facts," in the words of Kaldor—have influenced the economic policies recommended for developing nations. Nurkse's theory of trade as the engine of nineteenth-century growth, as opposed to the external sector's less dynamic role in Third World economies of the first half of the twentieth century, has given rise to policies of "balanced growth," where the role of foreign trade has been deliberately reduced.[1] Similarly, Myrdal, Singer, and Prebisch's interpretation of export specialization in primary products as a vicious circle of underdevelopment have led to policies of import substitution and the promotion of national industry.[2]

In the last three decades the emphasis economists have placed on the history of the development process has on the other hand stimulated economic historians to study trade and growth. Adherents of the current theories of "dependency" and "unequal exchange," as well as their critics, have based their arguments on historical evidence. A lack of quantitative data and the difficulties inherent in this type of investigation, however, have led historians to supplement their traditional sources (the opinions of contemporaries) with the interpretations of development economists. The latter are frequently founded on an empirical base of "overstylized facts" that is both weak and fragmentary; yet historians have adopted these interpretations with the same facility with which they used to accept contemporary accounts.

The historiography of the relationship between trade and growth in the European Periphery, especially the Spanish case, is not an exception to this practice. The interpretations of contemporaries are complemented by the opinions of modern development economists, the latter being casually applied to the nineteenth-century Spanish experience. The cases of Vicens Vives and Nadal are instructive. Vives suggests that the tariff of 1869 put the "mineral wealth of Spain at the disposal of England and France" with the result that Spain was divested of that wealth by foreign enterprises,[3] whereas Nadal links railroad construction to the expansion of export-oriented mining and concludes that it was an "instrument of colonization and exploitation."[4] The same can be said of the interpretation of Berend and Ránki when they state that:

> On the Iberian Peninsula, though there was a substantial increase of foreign trade, and foreign investments did introduce new elements in the economy, there was no real economic growth or transformation of the economy.[5]

Harrison, in turn, has suggested a parallel between the type of capitalist development described by Gunder Frank for nineteenth-century Latin America and the Spanish case:

> As the outward-oriented exporting lobby of landlords, mine owners and merchants gained strength and found expression for their interests in the liberalising of trade, so Spain (like Latin America) was converted into a satellite of the industrial metropolis of north-west Europe, which extracted often irreplaceable supplies of raw materials for its own use, sending back large quantities of manufactured goods and surplus capital.[6]

In addition, the potential forward linkages of mineral exports were, in the opinion of Sánchez-Albornoz, appropriated by the purchaser countries, while the profits were funneled back to the investor countries. The result was that "the mines were converted into foreign enclaves, linked only territorially to Spain, and lacked articulation with the rest of the Spanish economy."[7] Sánchez-Albornoz synthesizes the theoretic bases of this interpretation by placing the Spanish case within the wider context of Center-Periphery relations in nineteenth-century Europe. He suggests that "it is natural that the inequality between industrialized and non-industrialized nations should begin with regions that are in close proximity to one another."[8]

The inability of southern Europe to initiate a process of modern economic growth in spite of the stimulus provided by the industrialization of northwestern Europe—an inability emphasized by Arthur Lewis—has led economic historians to adopt a negative view of the role of foreign trade in the nineteenth-century modernization of the European Periphery.[9] Most unfavorable interpretations of the export sector's role in the evolution of the peripheral European economies—and the Spanish case is no exception—rest on the baseless hypothesis that, in the absence of foreign trade, an alternate, more beneficial route to development would have been attempted. The implicit alternative model is founded on the following economic reasoning: the export of raw materials implied a substantial opportunity cost for the Spanish economy. This cost consisted of nonexporting activities embodied in the productive resources exported, which would otherwise have been used to contribute to greater, long-term development. Nevertheless, these hypothetically alternative activities were sacrificed in the interests of assuring a permanent supply, at decreasing prices, of primary products to the countries of the Center and in the interests of providing a market for these countries' manufactured goods. The hypothesis of autarchic development rests, then, on certain assumptions: (1) that alternative uses existed for the factors of production employed in the export sector and (2) that, in order for the autarchic development model to be more successful than development in an open economy, it would be required that the economy obtain significant gains in productivity in the internal sector and that this be achieved independently of growth in the export sector.[10]

2. TRENDS IN FOREIGN TRADE

Tables 7.1 and 7.3 illustrate the long-term trends in foreign trade from 1815 to 1913. Data are presented in overlapping ten-year averages.[11] Two long swings can be distinguished in exports: the first covers the years 1815 to 1850, during which growth proceeded slowly; the second encompasses the period from the 1850s to the 1880s, the apogee of nineteenth-century exports.

After this period, there was a gradual decline in export expansion until World War I. Imports followed similar patterns, with only slight differences. The decades of the mid-nineteenth century did not exhibit the same linear evolution for imports as for exports. From 1850 to 1880, three distinct phases can be discerned: (1) during the second half of the 1850s and first years of the 1860s, there was a tremendous acceleration of imports that was tied to the beginning of the industrialization process and to the importation of railroad materials; (2) in the second half of the 1860s and throughout most of the 1870s, there was relative stagnation; (3) in the final years of the 1870s and throughout the 1880s, there was a renewed acceleration.

When the returns to foreign factors used in the production of exportable goods is subtracted from the total value of exports, the result is the "retained" exports or net export earnings.[12] Until the liberalization of foreign investment in 1869, substantial differences did not exist between total and retained exports. It is interesting to note that, during the last four decades of the period, there were no notable discrepancies between the expansion of total and retained exports. This fact sheds doubt on the hypothesis that total export statistics are deceptive and do not reflect long-term trends in nineteenth-century Spain's net export earnings.[13]

The slower long-term growth of imports in comparison with exports explains the reduction in the Spanish trade deficit during the nineteenth century. There are two distinct phases in the evolution of the balance of trade (see Table 7.1, column 8). The first was characterized by the deficit and encompassed the years 1815 to 1870. During this time Spain's debtor position was slowly reduced until the 1840s but rose again during the 1850s and 1860s. The second phase was one of progressive improvement in the Spanish position and culminated in the 1890s. This creditor position, however, deteriorated after Cuba's emancipation in 1898. Considering the difference between retained exports and imports, the surplus phase included only the 1880s, 1890s, and the decade prior to World War I (see Table 7.2).[14]

The terms of trade (the prices of exports in relation to those of imports) determine the import capacity by unit of exports and are an indicator of the static gains from trade. In other words, the terms of trade determine whether the country in question derives a greater or lesser value from trade than that of the resources it sacrifices to the production of exportable commodities. Two stages can be distinguished in the evolution of the terms of trade: the first stage was one of notable progress and spanned the years between the end of the Napoleonic Wars and the 1880s; the second stage (1890–1913) was a period of deterioration. During the years when the terms of trade were favorable, the

Table 7.1
Spain's Foreign Trade, 1815–1913
(10⁶ current pesetas)

	F.O.B. Domestic Exports				C.I.F. Net Imports				
	(1)	(2)	(3)	(4)	(5)	(6)	(7)	(8)	(9)
	Value at Current Prices	Value at 1854 Prices	Purchasing Power (in Terms of Imports) 1854 Prices	Fisher Price Index 1854 = 100	Value at Current Prices	Value at 1854 Prices	Fisher Price Index 1854 = 100	Commodity Trade Balance (1):(5)	Net Barter Terms of Trade 1854 = 100 (4):(7)
1815–1824	107.3	73.6	52.6	145.7	156.8	76.9	204.0	−49.5	71.4
1820–1829	105.0	85.2	67.6	123.3	131.6	84.7	155.3	−26.6	79.4
1825–1834	110.2	99.3	90.3	111.0	121.4	99.5	122.0	−11.2	91.0
1830–1839	121.5	107.9	99.4	112.6	127.8	104.6	122.2	−6.3	92.1
1835–1844	134.7	115.8	112.7	116.3	146.2	122.3	119.5	−11.5	97.3
1840–1849	146.6	130.2	143.7	112.6	153.4	150.4	102.0	−6.8	110.4
1845–1854	163.9	158.4	167.6	103.5	173.6	177.5	97.8	−9.7	105.8
1850–1859	229.8	219.3	239.1	104.8	259.7	270.2	96.1	−29.9	109.1
1855–1864	287.2	258.0	283.0	111.3	408.8	402.8	101.5	−121.6	109.7
1860–1869	320.1	293.4	290.7	109.1	451.6	410.2	110.1	−131.5	99.0
1865–1874	412.7	372.1	360.4	110.9	448.5	391.7	114.5	−35.8	96.9
1870–1879	500.5	438.7	487.8	114.1	490.0	477.6	102.6	10.5	111.2
1875–1884	646.4	592.5	757.8	109.1	595.0	697.5	85.3	51.4	127.9
1880–1889	784.2	802.7	1000.3	97.7	705.9	900.4	78.4	78.3	124.6
1885–1894	866.5	920.8	1051.6	94.1	721.4	875.5	82.4	145.1	114.2
1890–1899	1055.8	1054.8	1134.1	100.1	786.7	845.0	93.1	269.1	107.5
1895–1904	1187.5	1080.5	1044.4	109.9	994.0	874.2	113.7	193.5	96.7
1900–1909	1222.5	1103.3	1017.9	110.8	1093.7	910.7	120.1	128.8	92.2
1905–1913	1330.4	1274.3	1280.5	104.4	1167.2	1123.4	103.9	163.2	100.5

SOURCES: Export and import values at current prices, L. Prados de la Escosura (1986), "Una serie anual del comercio exterior español (1784–1913)," Revista de Historia Económica, IV, 1. Export and import price indices, L. Prados de la Escosura. "Las relaciones reales de intercambio entre España y Gran Bretaña, 1714–1913," in P. Martín Aceña and L. Prados de la Escosura, eds. (1985), La Nueva Historia Económica en España, pp. 119–165. Prices in pounds sterling have been converted into current pesetas with an annual exchange rate series.

NOTE: Decade average figures overlap.

Table 7.2
Retained Value of F.O.B. Domestic Exports, 1865–1913
(10^6 current pesetas)

	(1)	(2)	(3)	(4)
	Value at Current Prices	Value at 1854 Prices	Purchasing Power (in Terms of Imports) 1854 Prices	Trade Balance
1865–1876	396.9	357.9	346.6	−51.6
1870–1879	459.7	402.9	448.1	−30.3
1875–1884	587.2	538.2	688.4	−7.8
1880–1889	719.3	736.2	917.5	13.4
1885–1894	797.4	847.4	967.7	76.0
1890–1899	964.7	963.7	1036.2	178.0
1895–1904	1054.1	959.1	927.1	60.1
1900–1909	1059.8	956.5	882.4	−33.9
1905–1913	1172.6	1123.2	1128.6	5.4

SOURCES: Table 7.1 for export and import total values. Retained value estimates for mineral products come from L. Prados de la Escosura, "El comercio hispano-británico en los siglos XVIII y XIX. (II) Tendencias y estructura," *Revista de Historia Económica* (forthcoming).
NOTE: Decade average figures overlap.

import capacity by unit of exports grew at an annual rate of 1%, whereas the following period (1880–1913) saw an annual deterioration rate of 0.8%. On the whole, however, the terms of trade improved for Spain between 1815 and 1913 (see Table 7.1).[15] The principal underlying reasons for the sustained improvement in the relative prices of exports were the rising demand for raw materials in the industrialized countries (especially Great Britain) and a relatively inelastic Spanish supply on the one hand, and an increased efficiency in industrial production in the advanced nations that led to a fall in the prices of manufactures on the other. In the decades preceding World War I, the reduced growth of British productivity, the tremendous demand for manufactures in the countries of immigration, the shortage of coal, and the devaluation of the peseta produced a rise in the prices of Spanish imports and brought about a deterioration in the terms of trade.[16]

One of the most important indicators for a developing country is the purchasing power of its exports in terms of imports or the import capacity of its export volume (also known as the income terms-of-trade index). This index is formulated by dividing the value of exports at current prices by the index of import prices (or by multiplying the terms of trade by the export volume). The evolution of purchasing power is similar to that of exports at current and constant prices, characterized as it is by sustained growth during the years 1815 to 1880 and by a slackening in the three decades prior to World War I (see Table 7.3). The contrast between the growth rates of purchasing power

Table 7.3
Spanish Foreign Trade: Annual Growth Rates, 1815–1913 (%)

	Total Domestic Exports			Retained Domestic Exports			Net Imports	
	(1) Current Prices	(2) 1854 Prices	(3) Purchasing Power	(4) Current Prices	(5) 1854 Prices	(6) Purchasing Power	(7) Current Prices	(8) 1854 Prices
1815/24–1845/54	1.4	2.6	3.9	1.4	2.6	3.9	0.3	2.8
1820/29–1850/59	2.6	3.2	8.1	2.6	3.2	5.1	2.3	3.9
1825/34–1855/64	3.2	3.2	3.8	3.2	3.2	3.8	4.1	4.7
1830/39–1860/69	3.2	3.3	3.6	3.2	3.3	3.6	4.2	4.6
1835/44–1865/74	3.7	3.9	3.9	3.6	3.8	3.7	3.7	3.9
1840/49–1870/79	4.1	4.1	4.1	3.8	3.8	3.8	3.9	3.9
1845/54–1875/84	4.6	4.4	5.0	4.3	4.1	4.7	4.1	4.6
1850/59–1880/89	4.1	4.3	4.8	3.8	4.0	4.5	3.3	4.0
1855/64–1885/94	3.7	4.2	4.4	3.4	4.0	4.1	1.9	2.6
1860/69–1890/99	4.0	4.3	4.5	3.7	4.0	4.2	1.9	2.4
1865/74–1895/04	3.5	3.6	3.6	3.1	3.2	3.2	2.7	2.7
1870/79–1900/09	3.0	3.1	2.5	2.5	2.6	2.0	2.7	2.2
1875/84–1905/13	2.4	2.6	1.8	2.0	2.1	1.3	2.3	1.6
1815/24–1875/84	3.0	3.5	4.5	2.8	3.3	4.3	2.2	3.7
1820/29–1880/89	3.4	3.7	4.5	3.2	3.6	4.4	2.8	3.9
1820/29–1900/09	3.1	3.2	3.4	2.9	3.0	3.2	2.7	3.0
1815/24–1905/13	2.8	3.2	3.6	2.7	3.0	3.4	2.2	3.0

SOURCES: Tables 7.1 and 7.2.

and export volume sheds some light on the role played by the terms of trade in the expansion of the import capacity of Spanish exports. In this manner, the differences between the growth rates of the purchasing power of exports and the volume of exports demonstrate (other things being equal) the influence of relative prices. In Table 7.3 it can be observed that up to the 1880s the growth of exports at constant prices was less than that of the purchasing power of exports. The difference between the two is about 20% in favor of the latter—a situation that illuminates the contribution made by the terms of trade to the growth of Spain's import capacity. In the last decades of the period under investigation, the ratio was reversed, and the volume of exports grew more rapidly than did the purchasing power of exports. When one takes the whole period from 1815 to 1913 into account, there is a slight difference of about 5% in favor of the latter.

It can be inferred from this discussion, that the maintenance of favorable relative prices during most of the nineteenth century was exceedingly important for Spain. The leading role played by the expansion of import capacity, however, can be attributed to the volume of exports.

3. PATTERNS OF TRADE

The expansion rates of the aggregate value of foreign trade are determined by variations in both the commodity composition and geographic distribution of that trade. Tables 7.4 and 7.5 express the changes in the total value of exports and imports as a result of variations in the leading products. In Table 7.4 one can discern an export structure based on agrarian and mineral products that exhibited, nevertheless, a certain degree of flexibility, as demonstrated by the frequency with which some products replaced others as the leading exports throughout the nineteenth century. The differences between this structure and that of the currently underdeveloped countries, whose economies are based on monoculture, are manifest. During the first half of the nineteenth century, a readjustment in the commodity composition of exports took place, raw materials becoming the basis of trade. This pattern differs widely from the previous balance between manufactured goods and raw materials.[17] The export expansion of the first half of the century was based primarily on products such as wine, especially sherry; flour and lead; and followed by olive oil, raisins, and cork.

Between mid-century and the 1880s, the export base expanded. Next to sherry, which reached its apogee in the 1870s, common wine was the leading product, especially during the years of phylloxera in France. Minerals and metals constituted the second most important items, while olive oil, raisins, cork, cattle, esparto, and quicksilver rounded out the core group of exports. From 1890 to World War I, wine declined owing to the recuperation of the French vineyards and the spread of phylloxera to Spain, while minerals, especially iron ore, experienced sustained growth. During these years, exports also became diversified: in addition to the agrarian and mineral products (almonds, oil, oranges, lead, copper), light industrial products, such as cotton cloth, shoes, and leather goods were added to the export base—products that were practically absent from Spanish exports since the colonial era.

During the period 1815–1880, the geographic distribution of exports reveals an association between their growth and their concentration. France and Great Britain purchased more than 50% of Spanish exports, with Cuba accounting for as much as an additional 25%. In contrast, the years from 1880–1913 saw a slackening of growth rates accompanied by a diversification of

Table 7.4
Contribution of the Main Commodities to the Increase in Total Exports, 1826–1913 (%)
(current values)

	from 1826-35a to 1840-49b	from 1840-49b to 1850-59	from 1845-54c to 1855-64	from 1850-59 to 1860-69	from 1855-64 to 1865-74	from 1860-69 to 1870-79	from 1865-74 to 1875-84	from 1870-79 to 1880-90	from 1875-84 to 1885-94	from 1880-89 to 1890-99	from 1885-94 to 1895-1904	from 1890-99 to 1900-09	from 1895-1904 to 1905-13
Common wine	19.9	10.7	14.1	20.3	9.5	10.7	43.9	61.0	28.7	—	—	—	—
Sherry		22.6	11.5	5.1	25.5	18.9	—	—	—	—	—	—	—
Olive oil	3.5	4.1	5.5	6.6	2.9	—	—	1.7	1.6	0.4	7.0	7.8	—
Almonds	—	1.0	1.4	1.2	0.4	0.6	0.4	0.3	1.4	2.5	3.0	4.1	3.2
Oranges	0.1	0.9	2.0	3.2	2.4	2.0	3.7	3.3	1.1	5.2	14.0	14.4	5.9
Raisins	5.7	4.7	4.3	1.3	5.3	7.3	1.6	—	—	—	—	0.7	—
Wheat	2.6	6.4	2.8	—	3.5	3.2	—	—	—	—	—	—	—
Flour	7.3	12.3	9.5	—	—	—	—	—	—	—	—	—	—
Grapes	n.a.	n.a.	0.3	1.1	0.5	0.3	1.1	1.6	2.2	1.2	0.9	2.0	2.1
Livestock	0.1	n.a.	2.1	4.3	5.1	3.0	1.7	1.8	1.3	1.3	4.1	2.9	—
Wool	1.2	1.7	—	—	—	—	0.3	1.3	1.8	0.9	1.5	2.0	1.8
Cork	2.6	2.6	1.9	3.1	3.2	2.2	0.6	1.1	3.8	—	6.6	8.0	4.3
Esparto	n.a.	n.a.	0.9	4.0	5.8	2.9	0.1	—	—	—	—	—	—
Shoes	n.a.	n.a.	1.3	1.4	3.2	2.7	0.9	0.9	4.2	4.9	0.3	—	—
Skins & hides	n.a.	n.a.	n.a.	—	1.2	2.2	1.2	0.1	0.7	2.6	4.6	2.2	2.1
Cotton manufactures	n.a.	n.a.	n.a.	n.a.	n.a.	n.a.	n.a.	n.a.	n.a.	n.a.	n.a.	0.2	6.0
Quicksilver	n.a.	n.a.	—	—	3.0	4.8	1.3	—	—	1.3	0.4	—	—
Lead, bars	3.4	9.7	8.5	7.8	7.2	11.2	8.0	—	—	5.0	5.6	10.4	8.3
Copper, metals	n.a.	n.a.	n.a.	n.a.	n.a.	n.a.	n.a.	n.a.	n.a.	1.4	3.6	8.0	6.9
Minerals:													
copper ore	—	—	—	—	—	—	—	3.0	—	—	—	6.0	—
iron ore	—	1.4	3.6	5.7	14.0	20.3	20.8	12.0	7.7	7.1	20.4	27.5	6.4
others	—	—	—	—	—	—	—	—	0.9	3.7	4.7	3.8	7.8
Other goods	53.4	21.9	30.3	34.9	7.3	7.7	14.4	14.6	44.6	62.5	19.6	—	43.6
Total Exports (% Δ)d	33.0	56.8	75.2	39.3	43.7	56.4	56.6	56.7	34.1	34.6	37.1	15.8	12.0

SOURCE: L. Prados de la Escosura (1982), *Comercio exterior y crecimiento económico en España, 1826–1913: tendencias a largo plazo* (Madrid), p. 40, and Table 7.1.
NOTES: The symbol — indicates that no actual increase took place in the value of these items between these years. Contributions are estimated as the percentage of the increase in each commodity over the sum of all increases in exported commodities. n.a.: not available; a: 1826, 1827, 1830, 1831, and 1835; b: 1841, 1842, 1846, and 1849; c: 1846, 1849, 1850, 1851, 1852, 1853, and 1854; d: all years included in the averages.

exports. In the last three decades of this period, Germany, Holland, Italy, the United States, and Argentina accounted for a substantial part of the rise in Spanish exports.

Imports demonstrated an even greater degree of diversification than exports. Quantitative data on imports are less reliable, however, since the contraband trade was considerable until the 1870s, especially in cotton manufactures and tobacco. Reconstructed import series, therefore, do not accurately reflect the actual trade that took place.[18]

The first half of the nineteenth century witnessed the expansion of food imports such as sugar, codfish, and cacao—characteristic of the import structure of the colonial period—as well as the importation of raw materials such as cotton, coal, and timber; unfinished products such as linen yarn; and capital goods such as iron and steel products and machinery. The decades from 1850 to 1880 can be divided into two subphases with regard to tariff policies: the years 1850 to 1860 were years of protectionism whereas the years 1870 to 1880 were a time of moderate trade liberalization. The rapid growth of imports in the second half of the 1850s and the first half of the 1860s is related to railroad construction.[19] During the 1870s and 1880s, a gradual but consistent modification took place in the composition of imports. Industrial raw materials and capital goods—cotton, coal, and machinery, for example— replaced foodstuffs and consumer goods, with the exception of wheat, which became a permanent element of the import structure after 1882 (see Table 7.5).

Between 1891 and 1913 the growth of imports slackened owing to the extreme protectionist policies introduced in 1891, policies that were reinforced by the devaluation of the peseta and the subsequent abandonment of the gold standard. These tariff barriers, the effective protection of which is still unknown, must have limited the foreign supply of capital goods. This, in turn, leads to the question of how seriously the industrialization process, which depended on these goods, was affected. The protectionist argument about infant industries would require an analysis of the costs or the net benefits of the radical protectionist policy of 1891. In these final decades of the period, industrial raw materials and capital goods represented 50% of the increase in Spanish imports.

The geographic distribution of imports followed the same patterns as those of exports. Until 1870, Great Britain, France, Cuba, and later Germany and the United States shared the task of supplying the bulk of Spain's external demand. High growth rates proceeded in tandem with a striking degree of geographic concentration until the end of the 1880s. After 1890 the gradual diversification of imports occurred parallel to a fall in growth rates.

Table 7.5
Contribution of the Main Commodities to the Increase in Total Imports, 1826–1913 (%)
(current values)

	from 1826-35a *to* 1840-49b	*from* 1840-49b *to* 1850-59	*from* 1845-54c *to* 1855-64	*from* 1850-59 *to* 1860-69	*from* 1855-64 *to* 1865-74	*from* 1860-69 *to* 1870-79	*from* 1865-74 *to* 1875-84	*from* 1870-79 *to* 1880-89	*from* 1875-84 *to* 1885-94	*from* 1880-89 *to* 1890-99	*from* 1885-94 *to* 1895-1904	*from* 1890-99 *to* 1900-09	*from* 1895-1904 *to* 1905-13
Railrds. mats.	—	—	2.1	17.9	3.8	—	7.3	1.6	2.6	4.7	13.0	2.4	9.4
Chemical products	n.a.	n.a.	n.a.	2.7	2.5	0.2	1.3	2.2	3.7	3.0	10.5	17.1	12.5
Machinery	3.6	2.8	1.9	2.6	2.4	2.8	8.1	6.6	1.9	0.4	1.8	15.4	3.8
Iron & steel manufactures	6.4	—	1.3	0.6	6.4	3.1	4.6	3.5	0.7	5.0	8.6	3.9	—
Ships	n.a.	n.a.	n.a.	2.9	2.2	4.8	—	6.2	5.6	3.7	6.1	5.0	—
Lumber	2.2	3.4	3.0	2.2	6.0	4.3	7.0	3.5	8.9	13.5	14.3	12.7	5.3
Coal	4.0	2.2	1.6	0.6	21.9	6.0	4.0	0.6	—	4.2	9.9	17.8	16.0
Cotton, raw	12.2	10.6	3.6	0.6	1.9	29.2	11.9	1.3	1.8	2.4	2.0	—	—
Wool, raw	0.3	0.2	0.3	0.6	—	2.5	2.1	—	—	—	—	—	—
Linen yarn	9.8	2.7	4.0	9.4	10.4	—	5.1	4.8	—	—	—	—	1.4
Wool manufactures	10.5	3.9	2.7	2.2	3.7	5.3	2.6	0.7	0.6	0.2	4.8	5.1	—
Skins & hides	8.6	—	0.7	1.7	1.9	2.5	2.5	0.7	2.9	1.3	—	—	—
Manure (nitrate)	n.a.	n.a.	1.4	1.0	—	—	2.0	4.0	—	1.4	8.8	10.1	3.8
Livestock	1.1	2.4	1.2	0.1	14.0	—	11.4	10.1	8.7	4.7	—	6.9	8.1
Wheat	—	8.7	5.2	5.9	0.2	3.2	—	12.8	2.6	—	—	—	—
Brandy	0.4	1.5	2.3	1.6	—	—	—	0.8	3.6	—	—	—	—
Sugar	12.9	7.0	4.5	2.6	1.6	2.5	2.7	3.7	1.3	—	0.2	3.6	3.7
Codfish	13.0	—	1.4	1.6	—	—	0.3	1.9	—	—	—	—	0.2
Cocoa	15.0	—	—	1.5	—	—	—	—	—	—	—	—	—
Other goods	—	54.6	62.8	42.3	21.1	33.6	27.1	35.0	55.1	44.5	20.0	39.0	35.4
Total Imports (% Δ)d	26.4	69.3	135.5	73.9	9.7	8.5	32.7	44.1	21.2	11.5	37.8	21.2	17.4

SOURCE: L. Prados de la Escosura (1982), *Comercio exterior y crecimiento económico en España, 1826-1913: tendencias a largo plazo* (Madrid), p. 41, and Table 7.1.
NOTES: The symbol — indicates that no actual increase took place in the value of these items between these years. Contributions are estimated as the percentage of the increase in each commodity over the sum of all increases in exported commodities. n.a.: not available; a: 1826, 1827, 1830, 1831, and 1835. b. average of 1842 and 1843 with 1849 (in the cases of machinery and lumber, values for 1846 and 1848 are included—for wool manufactures, value for 1846 is included); c: average of 1849 and 1850–1854—exceptions for machinery, lumber, and wool manufactures as in b; d: all years included in the averages.

4. FOREIGN TRADE AND ECONOMIC CHANGE

In a revision of Nurkse's theory of foreign trade as the engine of nineteenth-century economic growth, Kravis hinted at some of the prerequisites that would have had to exist in order for export-led development to occur.[20] Kravis's list of prerequisites can also function as a test for defining the role of the export sector in a particular economy over time. Given that Spain does not seem to represent a case of export-led growth, it is in this second sense that an examination of Kravis's propositions is pertinent to this study.

(1) Structural economic changes could be attributed to external demand whenever the proportion of exports in the national income was high or at least growing in relation to the national product—that is, whenever export rates increased substantially.[21] Table 7.6 lists the export and import rates for Spain and for Europe as a whole between the years 1830 and 1913. The rise of foreign trade during the mid-nineteenth century was noteworthy in both cases. In the second quarter of the nineteenth century, European import and export rates doubled; in the third quarter, they increased by only one-third and one-half, respectively. In the Spanish case, rates rose less rapidly from 1830 to 1860 and then increased precipitously during the years 1860 to 1880—especially the export rate, which increased more than one and a half

Table 7.6
Ratios of Exports and Imports to National Income:
Spain and Europe, 1830–1910 (%)

| | (Current Prices) Exports | | | (Centered Three-Year Averages) Imports | |
	Spain	Europe	Continental Europe	Spain	Europe
1830	2.9	4.4	3.9	2.9	4.8
1860	4.6	9.4	8.1	7.0	10.6
1880	12.4	12.5	11.5	11.2	15.6
1890	13.4	12.6	11.7	11.1	15.2
1900	11.4	11.4	10.8	10.9	14.3
1910	10.7	13.2	12.3	9.1	16.0

SOURCES: Europe: P. Bairoch (1976), pp. 78–79; Spain: Five-year average exports and imports, L. Prados de la Escosura (1986), "Una serie anual del comercio exterior español (1784–1913)," *Revista de Historia Económica*, IV(1), pp. 103–150. National income, L. Prados de la Escosura (1982), *Comercio exterior y crecimiento económico en España, 1826–1913: tendencias a largo plazo* (Madrid), p. 69, for 1832, 1860, 1882, and 1890; J. Alcaide (1976), "La renta nacional de España (1901–1970): una revisión urgente," in Instituto de Estudios Fiscales, *Datos para la historia financiera de España, 1850–1970*, 2 vols. (Madrid), for 1901 and 1910.

times. The parallels described for the mid-nineteenth century between the evolution of European and Spanish export and import ratios in relation to income can be extended to the beginning of the twentieth century, especially in the case of exports, even though the importance of foreign trade in the economy was reduced during this period. A broadening gap between the European and Spanish rates occurred during the decade that preceded World War I—a gap in which Spain began to lag behind. In conclusion, the prerequisite that exports should grow proportionately more than the national income was fulfilled during the period 1830 to 1890.

(2) An increase in exports could have had a multiplier effect on the economy if that increase was concentrated in a sector which played a leading role in economic growth for any of the following reasons: (a) the leading export sector grew faster than the rest of the economy; (b) it exhibited greater productivity than the economy as a whole; (c) it was capable of triggering growth in other sectors.

In spite of recent and valuable historiographical contributions, it is still not possible to offer concrete responses to questions regarding Spain. Exports were, of course, concentrated in particular economic sectors. External demand played a dominant role in the development of mining and associated industries.[22] An analogous situation occurred in the commercial agriculture of the peninsular periphery with products such as almonds, oranges, grapes, raisins, and esparto. Between 1850 and 1880 wine exports accounted for 70% of the increase in viticultural production. Other products, such as cork and cotton goods, also carried greater weight in the export sector than could be discerned from the percentage of total exports in relation to national income. Moreover, in spite of the little data available, evidence suggests that the export sector grew at a higher rate than the economy as a whole (see Table 7.7). In specific cases, such as mineral and metal outputs, this hypothesis was confirmed; iron ore production, for example, grew at an annual cumulative rate of 8.5% from 1860 to 1913, while lead production grew 2.3% annually during the same period.

Second, it is also difficult to determine the extent to which the total factor productivity in the production of exports was greater than the average productivity of the economy as a whole. At first appearance, however, this ratio would seem logical, since the stimulus of external demand would have led to the introduction of technological changes and to a greater and more efficient use of the factors of production. In mining, for example, evidence points to an increase in productivity between 1870 and 1900.[23] It would be difficult to claim the same increased efficiency for commercial agriculture. In Spanish

Table 7.7
Direct Contribution of Exports to Spain's Economic Growth, 1830–1910 (%)

	Annual Growth of National Income		Annual Growth of Exports		Direct Contribution of Exports to the Growth of National Income	
	Current Prices	Constant Prices	Current Prices	Constant Prices	Current Prices	Constant Prices
1830–1860	1.4	0.9	3.0	3.0	6.2	8.3
1860–1890	0.6	1.4	4.1	4.5	31.4	14.1
1890–1910	2.9	1.5	1.8	1.5	8.3	11.1
1830–1890	1.0	1.2	3.5	3.8	10.2	7.9
1860–1910	1.5	1.4	3.2	3.3	9.8	10.4
1830–1910	1.5	1.2	3.1	3.2	6.0	6.7

SOURCES: National Income, L. Prados de la Escosura (1982), *Comercio exterior y crecimiento económico en España, 1826–1913: tendencias a largo plazo* (Madrid), p. 69; current values of exports, L. Prados de la Escosura (1986), "Una serie anual del comercio exterior español (1784–1913)," *Revista de Historia Económica* 4(1); export price indices, L. Prados de la Escosura (1985), "Las relaciones reales de intercambio entre España y Gran Bretaña," in P. Martín Aceña and L. Prados de la Escosura, eds., *La Nueva Historia Económica en España* (Madrid).
NOTE: Direct contribution of exports to economic growth $[\Delta Y/Y]$ has been estimated by multiplying the growth rate of exports $[\dot{x}]$ times the share of exports in national income $[x/y]$ at the beginning of the period and dividing the result by the growth rate of national income $[\dot{y}]$.

$$\frac{\Delta Y}{Y} = \left(\dot{x} \cdot \frac{X}{Y} \right) : \dot{y}$$

agriculture as a whole, the permanent retention of nearly 70% of the active population in the agrarian sector throughout the nineteenth century suggests the absence of substantial changes in productivity.[24] This consistency, however, might obfuscate the labor transfers that took place from the subsistence sector to commercial agriculture—transfers that appear to have generated a rise in productivity in the primary sector.

Third, the export sector created externalities for the rest of the economy, the quantification of which is an extremely arduous task. Some of the ways of exploring this issue are as follows:

(1) One possible externality would have favored the formation of social overhead capital. The railroad is an appropriate example. Although, as pointed out by Anes and Gómez Mendoza, goods transported by railroad in Spain were generally directed toward internal consumption, this mode of transport was nevertheless tied to export activities in mining and commercial agriculture.[25] The apogee of the Basque shipbuilding industry in the last years of the nineteenth century constitutes yet another case of the formation of social overhead capital derived from the stimulus of foreign trade.[26]

(2) A second type of externality involves those export commodities which undergo a considerable loss of weight during their manufacture for final consumption and that tend to foster local transforming industries. This is a common characteristic of mineral products (iron, copper, mercury, and lead), where the export of crude minerals was replaced by that of metal in different degrees of manufacture. In the cases of mercury and lead, metal was the product which was exported from the inception of trade. The intensity of the forward linkages of this process is still in need of detailed study, though it is generally assumed that these linkages were not strong except in the Basque iron industry.[27] One indicator of the externalities derived from the export of iron ore is the large capital investment in Basque commercial enterprises—an investment that, during the late nineteenth century, grew ten times more than in the rest of Spain.[28] In addition, the iron-and-steel industry was the principal recipient of investment derived from the profits of iron-ore exports. The apogee of Basque heavy industry is reflected in statistics that show that the Basque Provinces were responsible for three-quarters of the increase of cast iron in Spain between 1876 and 1913.[29]

(3) The export of a raw material can contribute to the growth of a region if it generates an income distribution—associated with the use and return of the productive factors—that tends to increase the propensity to save. Tortella and Tedde de Lorca have examined this proposition for the years of the Restoration. In export areas like the Basque Provinces and Valencia, external demand represented a clear stimulus for a rise in savings. Between 1874 and 1913 there was a remarkable rise in the volume of Spanish savings accounts, with the Basque Provinces and Navarre accounting for 54% and Valencia for 9%.[30] Tedde de Lorca has demonstrated, in turn, that the first branches of the large banks were established in the mining regions of Andalusia during the first five years of the twentieth century.[31]

(4) Last, the expansion of an export product raises the productivity of the economy if it leads to a greater use of factors of production that were previously underutilized. In nineteenth-century Spain, for example, a situation of hidden unemployment existed in agriculture.[32] At the same time, mineral resources had no alternative uses to exports. If demand were hypothetically limited to the national market, the marginal utility of mineral products would approximate zero. Consequently, the export of national resources that were not used in the home market and the rise of employment in mines and commercial agriculture affected the economy in the form of an increase in the real income of Spain.

In addition, economic growth was stimulated by foreign investments if the latter were induced by the demand for primary products in the industrialized countries. That foreign capital flooded into the export sectors is undeniable proof of this. It was exports that were the dynamic element, then, and not internal demand in the country receiving the investments.

The railroad, followed by mining, were the sectors in which international investment had the greatest importance. The recent studies of Anes, Tedde de Lorca, and Gómez Mendoza prove that internal demand was the critical factor in the development of the Spanish railroad.[33] Nevertheless, the expectations of the export sector certainly influenced the decision of foreign financiers to invest in Spain. This idea seems to be implicit in the words of Nadal, when he points out that "from its origins, the bulk of the railroad system was intended as an instrument of colonization and exploitation."[34]

In mining, it was external demand that fostered foreign investment. Similarly, it was also external demand that attracted foreign capital to the agro-export sector for the provision of such products as raisins, sherry, and the like.

In short, although it is still not possible to venture the exact dimensions of its contribution, it can be implied that foreign investment, in global terms, played an important role in Spain's process of capital formation during the second half of the nineteenth century.[35]

So far, it is impossible to estimate the contribution of exports to the growth of the Spanish economy during the nineteenth century, since data needed to estimate the foreign-trade multiplier are not available. It is feasible, however, to uncover the direct contribution of exports to the economy's expansion rate. For three distinct phases of the nineteenth century, Table 7.7 shows the extent to which the growth rates of the Spanish economy depended on the export sector. Note that the estimates of national income prior to 1900 are derived from a revision of the figures calculated by the British statistician Mulhall, and for this reason the resultant growth rates constitute only orders of magnitude of the Spanish economy's long-term trends.[36] The contribution of exports to the expansion rate of national income was striking from 1860 to 1890, especially during the 1860s and 1870s, while its contribution during the first half and last years of the nineteenth century was less important, although not negligible by any means.

On the whole, exports increased at a rate more than twice as great as that of national income between 1830 and 1913, thereby characterizing the export sector as one of the most dynamic sectors of the Spanish economy. There is no exact correlation, however, between the phases of acceleration in export growth and in national income. Until 1890 the expansion of national income was accompanied by an acceleration of exports. In contrast, after the last decade of the century, a gradual loss of synchronism took place between the evolution of the export sector and the general economy. The isolation of Spain in the international economy—brought on by the Spanish repeal of the gold standard—the erection of strong tariff barriers, growing competition on the world market, combined with the revolution in transatlantic transportation—all are hypotheses that attempt to explain the slackening of Spain's export expansion.[37]

An indicator of the static gains of foreign trade can be obtained by examining the terms of trade. Table 7.8 presents a hypothetical exercise in which the rates of increase and decrease of the national income are estimated had the terms of trade remained unchanged. In column 1, the terms of trade appear constant for the years 1815 to 1824; in column 2, the terms of trade are assumed to remain constant for the years 1880 to 1889. The negative symbols indicate that the national income should have been inferior to what it actually was, owing to the constant relative prices of exports. These estimations presuppose a situation in which all other things are equal, that is, that the rest of the variables that usually operate in an economy remain unaltered. The positive symbols, in contrast, indicate that the national income should have been superior in a situation where the terms of trade remain constant.[38] It can be observed that the evolution of the terms of trade during the greater part of the

Table 7.8
Impact on National Income
of Keeping Constant the Net Barter
Terms of Trade, 1830–1910 (%)

	(1) *1815–24* *Net Barter* *Terms of Trade*	*(2)* *1880–89* *Net Barter* *Terms of Trade*
1830	−0.6	—
1860	−1.6	—
1880	−5.5	—
1890	−5.0	1.2
1900	−3.0	3.3
1910	−3.1	2.6

Sources: Tables 7.1 and 7.6.
Note: The formula used is

$$\frac{\Delta Yi}{Yi} = \frac{Xi}{Yi}\left(\frac{\text{TOTo}}{\text{TOTi}} - 1\right)$$

where Xi is exports in year i; Yi, national income in year i; and TOTo and TOTi are the net barter of trade in the base year and year i, respectively.

nineteenth century had a positive effect on the national income, with a certain deterioration in the final decades of the period. Nevertheless, when the relative prices of exports declined—that is, the late nineteenth and early twentieth centuries—the national income was higher than what would have existed had the terms of trade remained constant since the beginning of the nineteenth century.

5. FINAL CONSIDERATIONS

This chapter has presented an overview of the export sector and its relationship to the economy. From this view it is possible to extract the main traits of the contribution of trade to Spain's economic growth:

(1) During the nineteenth century, exports grew at a greater rate than the national income and made a significant contribution to its growth, especially between the 1860s and the 1890s. Given the limited importance of foreign trade in the economy, however, the static gains suggested by the favorable terms of trade did not have a great impact on national income in quantitative terms.

(2) During the first half of the nineteenth century, Spain was compensated for the loss of its colonies by the rising demand for primary products by the industrializing countries, especially France and Great Britain, and by these countries' provision of manufactured goods at prices that were relatively favorable to Spain.

(3) The expansion of exports meant that idle resources could find an outlet in foreign markets, thereby increasing Spain's international purchasing power. The stimulus of external demand also contributed to a better distribution of resources upon promoting the development of sectors that possessed comparative advantages. Evidence exists in this respect that demonstrates that exports proceeded from sectors that had greater productivity than that of the general economy.

(4) Increased import capacity led to the acquisition, not only of basic foodstuffs and consumer durables, but also of industrial inputs and capital goods, which were not available in the internal market and that helped to remove some of the obstacles to economic development.

(5) The agro-export expansion fostered the development of the agrarian sector, since the rise in income and the substitution of subsistence crops for commercial crops increased the size of the market for foodstuffs. In a parallel manner, greater agrarian income tended to generate a demand for industrial

products that was satisfied, in large part, by national industry. At the same time, the railroad, which was associated to a certain degree with the export boom, reduced transportation costs in the interior and contributed to the formation of an internal market for manufactures and primary products.

It is quite clear that the Center's contribution to the Periphery—a large supply of resources and technology and a demand for raw materials—did not foster modern economic growth in Mediterranean Europe during the nineteenth century. Accepting this fact does not mean, however, that the export sector was responsible for Spain's relative backwardness. On the contrary, it should be noted that, in spite of the stimulus that exports provided for the expansion of the market economy, for the creation of infrastructure, and for a certain degree of structural change, trade—because of its limited dimensions—was not vigorous enough to exercise a strong influence on the Spanish economy. In a hypothetical absence of foreign trade, the economic performance of export regions would probably be similar to that of the most backward regions of Spain's interior.[39] Nevertheless, this does not constitute a complete explanation for Spain's lack of modern economic development in the nineteenth century. As Kravis has skillfully stated: "Export expansion did not serve in the nineteenth century to differentiate successful from unsuccessful countries. Growth where it occurred was mainly the consequence of favorable internal factors, and external demand represented an added stimulus which varied in importance from country to country and period to period."[40] The unequal response to the stimulus of external demand in the various export regions of Spain verifies this assertion. The Spanish economy's inability to attain complete modernization is related to the agrarian sector's failure to achieve an appreciable rise in productivity and to the limited size of the internal market for manufactured products—a consequence of the low levels of per capita income.

NOTES

1. See R. Nurkse, "Contrasting Trends in Nineteenth and Twentieth Century World Trade," in R. Nurske, ed., *Patterns of Trade and Development* (London, 1962).

2. G. Myrdal, *An International Economy* (New York, 1956); R. Prebisch, *The Economic Development of Latin America and Its Principal Problems* (New York, 1950), and *Towards a Dynamic Development Policy for Latin America* (New York, 1963); H. W. Singer, "The Distribution of Gains between Investing and Borrowing Countries," *American Economic Review* (Papers and Proceedings) 60 (1950): 473–485.

3. J. Vicens Vives, *Manual de historia económica de España,* 9th ed. (Barcelona, 1972), pp. 597–598.

4. J. Nadal, "The Failure of the Industrial Revolution in Spain, 1814–1913," in C. M. Cipolla, ed., *The Fontana Economic History of Europe,* vol. 4, pt. 2 (London, 1973), p.552. A substantially expanded version of this study is *El fracaso de la Revolución industrial en España, 1814–1913* (Barcelona, 1975).

5. I. T. Berend and G. Ránki, *The European Periphery and Industrialization, 1780–1914* (Cambridge, 1982), p. 135.

6. J. Harrison, *An Economic History of Modern Spain* (Manchester, 1978), p. 54.

7. N. Sánchez-Albornoz, *España hace un siglo: una economía dual,* 2d ed. (Madrid, 1977), p. 21.

8. Ibid., p. 22.

9. W. Arthur Lewis, *Growth and Fluctuations, 1870–1913* (London, 1978), pp. 164–167.

10. A similar approach can be found in N. H. Leff, *Underdevelopment and Development in Brazil,* 2 vols. (London, 1982).

11. These figures are taken from L. Prados de la Escosura, "Una serie anual del comercio exterior español, 1784–1913," *Revista de Historia Económica* 4 (1986)1: 103–150.

12. The net profits are arrived at by subtracting the returns to foreign factors of production employed in mining. The calculation has been formulated by considering several historians' estimates of the retained value for the leading mineral products. See L. Prados de la Escosura, "Long-run Trends in the Purchasing Power of Spain's Exports to Great Britain, 1714–1913" (unpublished).

13. This position is defended by A. Broder, "Le rôle des interêts étrangers dans la croissance de l'Espagne, 1767–1923" (Ph.D. diss., Université de Paris IV–Sorbonne, 1981).

14. The difference between retained exports and imports does not solely reflect the balance of trade, since, upon subtracting the returns to foreign factors employed in the production of exportable goods, elements of the balance of services are taken into consideration. Nor does the difference reflect the balance of payments on current account.

15. I am using the Spanish-British terms of trade as an indicator of Spain's terms of trade. The provisional estimates formulated for the latter begin during the mid-1820s and are much less reliable than the Spanish-British estimates. The considerable importance of Great Britain with respect to Spain's commerce justifies the use of the Spanish-British figures as a proxy for the Spanish terms of trade. For an estimate of Spain's terms of trade see L. Prados de la Escosura, *Comercio exterior y crecimiento económico en España, 1826–1913: tendencias a largo plazo* (Madrid, 1982), pp. 82 and 111. The Spanish-British terms of trade are taken from L. Prados de la Escosura, "Las relaciones reales de intercambio entre España y Gran Bretaña en los siglos XVIII y XIX," in P. Martín Aceña and L. Prados de la Escosura, eds., *La Nueva Historia Económica en España* (Madrid, 1985), pp. 119–165.

16. See the discussion in Prados de la Escosura, "Relaciones reales de intercambio."

17. See L. Prados de la Escosura, "Comercio exterior y cambio económico en Es-

paña, 1792–1849," in J. Fontana, ed., *La economía española al final del Antiguo Régimen, III: Comercio y colonias* (Madrid, 1982), pp. 171–249.

18. An estimate of contraband trade is included in Prados de la Escosura, "Una serie anual del comercio."

19. See A. Gómez Mendoza, *Ferrocarriles y cambio económico en España, 1855–1913* (Madrid, 1982), chap. 4.

20. Nurkse, "Contrasting Trends"; I. B. Kravis, "Trade as a Handmaiden of Growth: Similarities between the Nineteenth and Twentieth Centuries," *Economic Journal* 80 (1970), pp. 850–872.

21. I. B. Kravis, "The Role of Exports in Nineteenth-Century United States Growth," *Economic Development and Cultural Change* 20 (1972): 387–405.

22. Prados de la Escosura, *Comercio exterior*, pp. 72–73.

23. There was an evolution of the productivity of labor during this period. See Prados de la Escosura, "Relaciones reales de intercambio."

24. See V. Pérez Moreda, Chap. 2, in this work.

25. See R. Anes, "Relaciones entre el ferrocarril y la economía española, 1855–1935," and P. Tedde de Lorca, "Las compañías ferroviarias en España, 1855–1935," both in M. Artola, ed., *Los ferrocarriles en España, 1844–1943,* vol. 2 (Madrid, 1978); Gómez Mendoza, *Ferrocarriles.*

26. British Parliamentary Papers, 84 (1901): 11–14, Report of the British Consul, Bennett. See also M. Gónzalez Portilla, *La formación of de la sociedad capitalista en el País Vasco, 1876–1913,* 2 vols. (San Sebastián, 1981), esp. vol. 1, chap. 6.

27. See J. Nadal, "The Failure," pp. 583–584; Sánchez-Albornoz, *España hace un siglo,* pp. 21–22. The links between mineral exports and the creation of employment are treated in Valerie J. Shaw, "Exportaciones y despegue económico: el mineral de hierro de Vizcaya, la ría de Bilbao y algunas de sus implicaciones para España," *Moneda y Crédito* 142 (1972): 87–114. A revisionist interpretation can be found in G. Tortella, "La economía española, 1830–1900," in M. Tuñón de Lara, ed., *Historia de España,* vol. 8 (Barcelona, 1981), pp. 11–167.

28. Calculated using Nadal, "El fracaso," p. 120, table 7.

29. Estimated from ibid., appendix 6.

30. Calculations taken from G. Tortella, "Las magnitudes monetarias y sus determinantes," in P. Schwartz and G. Tortella, eds., *La banca española en la Restauración,* vol. 1 (Madrid, 1974), pp. 451–522, tables V-11 and V-12 (pp. 499–500).

31. P. Tedde de Lorca, "Una lectura de El fracaso de la Revolución industrial en España, 1814–1913 de Jordi Nadal," *Moneda y Crédito* 146 (1976): 105–121.

32. See Gómez Mendoza, *Ferrocarriles,* pp. 98–104; G. Toniolo, "Railways and Economic Growth in Mediterranean Countries: Some Methodological Remarks," in P. O'Brien, ed. *Railways and the Economic Development of Western Europe, 1830–1914* (London, 1983), pp. 227–236, 229–230.

33. P. Anes, "Relaciones entre el ferrocarril y la economía"; Tedde de Lorca, "Las compañías ferroviarias"; Gómez Mendoza, *Ferrocarriles.*

34. J. Nadal, "El fracaso," p. 50.

35. G. Tortella, "La formación de capital en España, 1874–1914: Reflexiones para un planteamiento de la cuestión," *Hacienda Pública Española* 55 (1978): 408 and 415.

36. For a discussion of these figures, see Prados de la Escosura, *Comercio exterior,* pp. 66–68.

37. The impact on the Spanish economy of the repeal of the gold standard is analyzed in P. Martín Aceña, "España y el patrón-oro, 1880–1913," *Hacienda Pública Española* 69 (1981): 267–290.

38. The method for arriving at these estimates has been taken from C. Goldin and F. Lewis, "The Role of Exports in American Economic Growth during the Napoleonic Wars, 1793–1807," *Explorations in Economic History* 17 (1980): 6–25. Similar estimates have been carried out by J. Williamson, *Late Nineteenth Century American Economic Development: A General Equilibrium History* (Cambridge, Mass., 1974), chap. 10.

39. This is a hypothesis suggested by Leff for the Brazilian case that should be contrasted to the Spanish case. See Leff, *Underdevelopment and Development,* vol. 1, chap. 5, and vol. 2, chap. 4.

40. Kravis, "Trade as a Handmaiden of Growth," p. 850.

FURTHER READINGS

Bairoch, P. *Commerce extérieur et développement de l'Europe au XIXe siècle.* Paris, 1976.

Berend, I. T., and G. Ránki. *The European Periphery and Industrialization, 1780–1914.* Cambridge, Mass., 1982.

Fontana, J., ed. *La economía española al final del Antiguo Régimen, III. Comercio y colonias.* Madrid, 1982.

García Sanz, A. "El comercio exterior de exportación en la economía española, 1850–1914." *Anales del C.U.N.E.F.,* pp. 110–149.

Maluquer de Motes, J. "El mercado colonial antillano en el siglo XIX." In J. Nadal and G. Tortella, eds., *Agricultura, comercio colonial y crecimiento económico en la España contemporánea,* pp. 322–357. Barcelona, 1974.

Martín Aceña, P., and L. Prados de la Escosura, eds. *La Nueva historia económica en España.* Pt. II. "La integración en la economía internacional." Madrid, 1985.

Nadal Farreras, J. *Comercio exterior y subdesarrollo.* Madrid, 1978.

Prados de la Escosura, L. *Comercio exterior y crecimiento económico en España, 1826–1913: tendencias a largo plazo.* Madrid, 1982.

———. "Las relaciones reales de intercambio entre España y Gran Bretaña en los siglos XVIII y XIX." In P. Martín Aceña and L. Prados de la Escosura, eds., *La Nueva Historia Económica en España,* pp. 119–165. Madrid, 1985.

Tortella, G. "La economía española, 1830–1900." In M. Tuñón de Lara, ed., *Revolución burguesa, oligarquía y constitucionalismo, 1834–1923*, pp. 9–167, chap. 6. Madrid, 1981.

Tortella, G., P. Martín Aceña, J. Morilla Critz, and L. Prados de la Escosura. "Agricultura, energía y comercio en la España contemporánea." *Revista de Historia Económica*. Vol. I (1983), 2, "Comercio exterior," pp. 291–386.

8.
ECONOMIC NATIONALISM AND STATE INTERVENTION, 1900–1930

JOSÉ LUIS GARCÍA DELGADO
Universidad Complutense de Madrid

THE PURPOSE of this chapter is to examine the relationship between economic nationalism and state intervention in Spain during the first third of the twentieth century. Criteria will also be proposed for evaluating the effects of economic policies on the modernization of the Spanish production system. The chapter is divided into three sections.

The first section discusses the spiraling economic nationalism of the first three decades of the 1900s—a time during which government policy, having completed the transition toward protectionism, resorted to additional instruments and methods that can clearly be designated as those of state intervention.

Section 2 defines, describes, and in some sense categorizes the main components of the nationalist and protectionist policy that was carried out in Spain between the end of the nineteenth century and the demise of Primo de Rivera's regime (1929).

The last section evaluates the results of that policy—a policy that increasingly dealt with national self-sufficiency and administrative control over both production and the market. Specifically, it focuses on the industrial policy of the dictatorship (1923–1929). This limited scope aims to stress how Primo de Rivera's interventionism just reinforced and broadened previous policies of protecting and regulating the national market. This section relates to the central issue of this book in that it addresses—although not for the entire period—whether state interventionism acted as a catalyst or an obstacle in the modernization process.[1]

1. THE TREND TOWARD ECONOMIC NATIONALISM

The nationalist orientation of Spain's economic policy was elicited during the last decade of the nineteenth century.[2] An earlier European depression and the invasion of European grain markets by distant continental and overseas producers brought about crises in Spanish agriculture, cotton textiles, Basque iron and steel, and Asturian coal. The financial sector was similarly affected because of the peseta's foreign exchange crisis in the last years of the nineteenth century. Spanish economic nationalism reacted by fostering the consolidation of a major group of entrepreneurs who were interested in cornering the home market. It also led to the proliferation of regenerationist or pseudo-regenerationist literature that saw protectionism as a panacea both for the country's economic difficulties and for its colonial crisis. Businessmen and doctrinaire writers succeeded in pushing both the Conservative and Liberal parties, as well as the nascent bourgeois political organizations of Catalonia and the Basque Provinces, toward strong protectionist strategies.[3]

The first quarter of the new century witnessed the creation of a motley and encumbered, though not yet solid, system of protectionism. New developments, renewed pressure from industrial interest groups, more advanced doctrines of national self-sufficiency, and new political platforms all reinforced nationalist attitudes during the first decades of the twentieth century.

The most important determinants of this new trend were rooted in two outstanding historical events: the loss of Spain's last colonies and World War I. The first prompted a significant influx of overseas capital, improperly called repatriation. The second generated exceptional profits for the Spanish business community because of Spain's neutrality in the war. Both events explain the continuity and intensification of nationalist attitudes in both theory and practice. The huge remittances of capital from emigrants to the New World, as Vicens Vives has accurately emphasized, provided "a substantial explanation for the resistance of the Spanish economy after 1898."[4] It is also important to ask, along with Sardá, "What would have happened to Spain after 1913 if World War I had not occurred?"; perhaps the extraordinary wealth accumulated during the war was the only thing that kept the Spanish economy afloat in the postwar period."[5]

The formation of owners' associations also accelerated during this time. In 1900 the powerful Liga Marítima Española (Spanish Maritime League) was created to "represent the aspirations of its membership before public opinion and official policy groups and to use all legitimate means of propaganda and influence to promote national maritime affairs." An affiliated group, the Hullera

Nacional (National Coal Association), came into existence in 1906 and proposed to "promote and develop the Spanish coal industry by bringing before government officials numerous resolutions and measures that would benefit the industry."[6] The ensuing scenario was enacted by those groups that explicitly supported protection from foreign and domestic competition. The Central Siderúrgica de Ventas (Iron Cartel), founded in 1907—thirteen years after the very powerful and effective Liga Vizcaína de Productores (Biscayn Producers League)—and the Asociación Patronal de Mineros Asturianos (Asturian Mine Owners Association), founded in 1913, became the most dynamic industrial owners' associations of the early twentieth century. During World War I these entrepreneurial groups had many opportunities to flex their muscles. Their 1916 campaign against Santiago Alba, who intended to tax the windfall profits generated by the war, is instructive. The entrepreneurs staged an authentic, well-orchestrated offensive—led by Francisco Cambó—against "the hateful crime of intending to legislate a bill that would have allowed the Treasury to participate in the industrialists' wartime profits."[7] This case clearly demonstrates the effective coordination of Catalan, Basque, and Asturian industrialists around 1920. With Primo de Rivera's dictatorship, the proliferation of these economic interest groups reached an apex.[8]

Doctrinal formulations also attained new heights. From the beginning of the twentieth century, the echoes of the "vibrant and vehement" regenerationist literature, as described by Ramón y Cajal,[9] continued to reverberate even more loudly. In 1905 Flores de Lemus wrote that, long before the outbreak of the European conflict, the cultural ambience was dominated by a "protectionist reaction," the irresistible advance of which—not only in Spain, of course—succeeded in "replacing cosmopolitanism with exclusive nationalism."[10] But, as Marvaud[11] has pointed out, the exacerbation in Spain of doctrinal nationalist positions was indeed spectacular during World War I and has already been the subject of a detailed study.[12] A few examples of this trend should suffice. The fundamental platforms from which the thesis of economic nationalism developed and expanded were the *Revista Nacional de Economía* (*National Economic Journal*) and the two National Economic Congresses that took place between 1914 and 1918. The periodical contributed, during the first years of its publication (1916 to the early 1920s), to put the doctrine of Spanish economic nationalism together.[13] The first editorial, entitled "Nuestro Programa" (Our Program), left no doubt that the periodical's purpose was:

> to awaken dormant energies, to revive the patriotism of capitalists, politicians, and businessmen, so that they can contribute to the creation of a strong and

robust national economy and free us from the tutelage of other economies that export capital in advance of their armies . . . with this periodical we have created an organ for the study and publication of economic doctrines.[14]

The index of the first issue of the *Revista Nacional de Economía* fully confirms this initial programatic declaration. Along with various articles describing some of Spain's economic problems—most related to the war—three articles approached the nationalist question in doctrinal terms: Guillermo Graell, secretary of the Catalan major industrialists' association, writing on the "Concept of the National Economy," stated that "the current outcry is to nationalize at all costs and to nationalize everything in unison"; the director of the periodical, Emilio Ríu, wrote an essay entitled "Can and Should Spain Become an Independent Nation?" This essay commented on the fundamental thesis of contemporary nationalist thought; finally Durán y Ventosa was the author of an article called "How Nations Become Powerful."

The National Economic Congresses were equally important, especially the Second Congress, held in Madrid in 1917. These congresses served as forums where spokesmen of powerful economic groups met with government representatives for the purpose of planning strategies to achieve "our economic nationalization" (the opening motto for the congress).

One unifying element can be extracted from the multitude of doctrines put forth during the war. The ideal of national self-sufficiency or economic autarchy was the common ground for all the various recovery plans, whether they were directed against "denationalization" (Carr states that "the roots of economic nationalism lie in this hey-day of foreign control of mineral resources,"[15]) or were recapitulations of protests against "national decadence."

Quantity does not imply quality. The majority of these doctrines were not original; their authoritative arguments were frequently based on references from Wagner, List, Wolf, Schmid, Röder, and Oldenberg, which did not always apply to the Spanish case. Also browsing through tens of thousands of pages of the *Revista Nacional de Economía* and the works of such prolific writers as Emilio and Daniel Ríu, Joaquín Sánchez de Toca, Vicente Gay, Guillermo Graell, Durán y Ventosa, Gregorio Fernández Díez, Cristóbal Massó, Leandro Cubillo, and Eloy Luis André, one seldom finds deep or rigorous analyses. Román Perpiñá best illustrates the weakness and affectation of these doctrines in his reproduction of the following text from Eloy Luis André—a text he considers "vulgar and petulant":

> The base of a country's economic autonomy is rooted in its ability to produce, through its own efforts, all its needs. That is to say that without this economic

postulate, independence is not possible. As Kant said, in order for a nation to be a moral entity in its own right, one goal is paramount—that it provide, in itself and for itself, the means of subsistence in a practical and natural way.[16]

Hence, long before Miguel Primo de Rivera's rhetoric and the rise of corporative economic thought, enthusiastic yet theoretically poor expressions of economic nationalism were already prevalent.[17]

In the words of Madariaga, the "nationalist ferment"[18] was also reflected in new attitudes and political alliances. The Spanish economy's growing introversion had a perceptible echo in the programatic declarations and campaigns of polic.cal parties in one region or another. If in the 1890s the "Bilbao-Barcelona-Valladolid axis" controlled the economic decisions of Spain, at the turn of the century this axis was bolstered by the Liga Regionalista (Regionalist League) and the Partido Nacionalista Vasco (Basque Nationalist Party) and was further strengthened through an alliance with the Asturian coal entrepreneurs. These entrepreneurs were represented by the Partido Reformista (Reform Party), headed by Melquíades Alvarez, who at times became their joint spokesman.[19]

2. THE CORNERSTONES OF INTERVENTION:
TARIFF PROTECTION, ADMINISTRATIVE PROTECTIONISM,
AND CORPORATIVISM

Economic nationalism was embodied in the specific measures of protection, development, and organization of production. These three elements formed an intricate and complex web whose internal boundaries were difficult to define. For clarification, three basic types of mechanisms can be distinguished:

First, there were protective measures that blocked or impeded foreign competition, thereby reserving the home market for national firms and products. These included increasingly higher duties (especially the tariffs of 1906 and 1922) as well as various measures that tended to restrict foreign capital in selected economic branches and to pay off the external debt while at the same time encouraging foreign participation in some industrial and tertiary enterprises.

Second, there were supportive and incentive measures for national production, whose purpose was the nationalization of raw materials and import substitution. These measures were grouped under the so-called policy of national industrial development that was enacted in the laws of February 14, 1907, and March 2, 1917, as well as in the law decree of April 30, 1924.

Finally, there were stricter measures of state intervention in production and commercialization, the goal of which was to encourage general or sectoral regulation and organization. This process culminated in the avowedly corporative organization of production and of the market under the dictatorial regime.

When viewed from a certain historical perspective, Spain's nationalist economic policy featured various measures that were inextricably intertwined in, and responded to, dialectic stages, with each stage warranting more intense and farther-reaching protection. First, protection was solicited to assist infant industries or industries that were technologically inferior to their counterparts in other countries; the goal was to compensate for initial disadvantages. Later, these same industries would demand an increase in the content, coverage, or application of earlier concessions, either to maintain newly achieved positions or to combat renewed international competition. Tariff barriers were thus erected; a resort to direct, fiscal, administrative, and credit incentives was attempted; when the former measures were thought to be insufficient, consumption was restricted to national products; and the ultimate step was that national industry was forced to adhere to an officially prescribed course of business. Tariff protection, administrative protectionism, and the corporative organization of production were superimposed on a process that led more and more to markedly nationalist goals.

This economic policy also evolved in a particular sequence. The tariff protection measures were passed gradually, but from the turn of the century they intersected with administrative intervention. The corporative organization, which became part of the dictator's anticrisis policy, brought to a high point the previous interventionist array established by the many councils, committees, and associations created after World War I. The end of the war, however, saw the elimination of much of the "spontaneous or automatic protection" afforded to Spanish producers by the exceptional wartime conditions of both maritime traffic and the international market.

Spain was not alone in its use of staunch protectionism; rather, it was this policy's pervasiveness at all levels of the economy that makes the Spanish case unique. From the end of the nineteenth century, "the ideal of national self-sufficiency was pursued with such intensity that by 1906, Spain had the highest tariff barriers in Europe."[20] Twenty years later, the League of Nations denounced the average level of Spanish tariffs as the most protectionist in the world, offering mathematical proofs which may have erred in detail, but not in their overall meaning.[21]

Another characteristic of Spanish protectionism was its nearly complete lack of coordination. The latter was the result of "concessions made to one interest group at the expense of another," giving rise to a "discordant and often contradictory" policy that was formulated through "long and laborious" negotiations. The resulting inconsistencies, as well as occasional difficulties in attaining effective levels of protection, were compounded as time went on. In the 1920s, when Bernis proposed to protect the Spanish Merchant Marine, he first pointed out the need to get rid of the "existing protectionism" that obstructed his purpose—that is, the protection of basic industrial products, of shipbuilding, and of shipping.[22] Ten years later, Román Perpiñá expressed the same caveat, though in a more general vein:

> Spain's economic policy clearly leans toward complete autarchy. First, the policy requires protection for foodstuffs and raw materials with the aim that as many of these goods as possible be produced and consumed in Spain; second, it requires protection for industry and for the purpose of eliminating foreign competition from the internal market and of ensuring that all Spanish consumption should be tied to Spanish production. This system . . . has been created by the constant influence of pressure groups. . . . Only in this manner could such a simplistic system as autarchy have come into existence.[23]

The system was simplistic because it disregarded its limitations and costs. The former were tied to the small size of the Spanish market during the first third of the twentieth century. Spain's population density was well below the European average and resulted in limited purchasing power in vast areas of the country. As noted by Perpiñá:

> [Spanish economic policy] has had one and only one preoccupation—production; one and only one method—the nationalization of production; and one great error—the belief that Spanish consumption was unlimited and that the entire nation possessed adequate purchasing power. In other words, policy has been more concerned with production than with problems of the market.[24]

One might wonder if there was a viable alternative to protection in turn-of-the-century Spain. Carr, for example, states that "it is difficult to conceive of any other way in which Spanish politicians could have behaved,"[25] but protection at all costs already had its shortcomings in terms of material growth and economic progress. The benefits of protectionism seem to have run their course by the last years of Primo de Rivera's dictatorship, when the "buffer" of Spanish war profits was deflated at the same time that the international prosperity of the 1920s vanished.[26] The simplicity of the protectionist system is also apparent when its allegedly "integral" nature is examined. A system that purported to assist all sectors ignored the fact that "the protection of one sector was always achieved at the expense of another." Thus, when Gual Villalbí defended the concept of "integral protectionism" in the National Assembly in January 1928, Flores de Lemus replied that the latter was "a reckless term which was better suited to advertisements for apothecary shops and grocery stores."[27] In fact, the production of textiles, steel and iron products, and coal and grain in Castile, Extremadura, and Andalusia was achieved at the expense of other sectors with higher export potential. These latter included export mining, viticulture, and fruit-growing. It is no wonder that those groups that were tied to the few remaining export sectors were often among the most open opponents of protectionism. Román Perpiñá, one of the most vocal critics of economic autarchy, began his earliest and most vehement attacks against the protectionist policy around 1935, when he was director of the Centro de Estudios Económicos Valencianos (The Valencian Center for Economic Studies). This organization was associated, through its leadership, with the region's export-oriented agricultural and mercantile interests.[28] In addition, protectionism set industrialists against producers of domestic agricultural goods. Protectionist policy often led to harsh confrontations, such as the 1916 incident in which Alba, the leader of the agriculturalists from Castile, opposed Cambó who represented the main industrial groups of the northern and Catalan periphery. Alba had tried to tax the windfall profits of the war and was thwarted by the second group. In short, such incoherent system of protection assisted or hindered various sectors according to their relative positions of economic and political power at any given moment.

3. INTERVENTIONISM VERSUS MODERNIZATION: THE DEFENSIVE ECONOMIC POLICY OF PRIMO DE RIVERA

Two precautions should be taken when analyzing the relationship between interventionism and modernization: (1) implicit values should be spelled out, and (2) the temporal and sectoral scope of the problem under investigation should also be carefully set. In the following pages, I have attempted to take these precautions into account, trying to spell out value judgments and being careful to refer to interventionism only where it pertains to the "defensive" economic policies of the Primo de Rivera dictatorship.

The main components of this policy can be easily enumerated. It was an economic policy designed to confront the consequences of the industrial crisis that occurred at the close of World War I—consequences that were still keenly felt and that set in motion a series of actions. It should not be forgotten that in Barcelona Miguel Primo de Rivera witnessed the Catalan banking crisis and the problems of overproduction in certain branches of the manufacturing sector, both of which occurred in a rarefied climate of social violence. Not surprisingly, one of his first projects was to impose a severe policy of public order aimed at curbing the labor movement; the number of strikes was reduced drastically in the first few months after the coup d'état of September 13, 1923. Another major component of the anticrisis policy was the neutralization of postwar competition, both foreign and internal.[29]

To fight foreign competition, import duties were raised across the board by means of article 19 of the Royal Decree of March 8, 1924, which created the Consejo de Economía Nacional (The National Economic Council). Additional duties were also imposed on specific items at particular times. Although the tariff revision that should have been carried out in 1927 under the precepts of the 1906 Ley de Bases (Basic Law) was indefinitely postponed, the Royal Decree of July 20, 1927, revoked the Ley de Autorizaciones (Law of Authorizations) that had permitted certain reductions of conventional tariff rates during the negotiation of commercial treaties and agreements.

Soon, however, tariff protection was not enough. In order to overcome the crisis, national production was encouraged. An extensive network of fiscal, credit, and general administrative measures was added to the tariff structure. Hundreds of resolutions were enacted. The preamble of the Royal Decree Law of April 30, 1924, which promulgated the New Plan of Assistance to foster the Creation and Development of Industrial Enterprises, spelled out the many ways in which protectionist state intervention could be put at the service of the nation's economy.

This "fear of the market" was the very definition of the dictator's industrial policy—a policy that was designed to confront the threat of overproduction in the internal market. The restriction of competition was made into a harsh and lasting policy with the enactment of the Royal Order of November 4, 1926, and the creation of the Regulatory Commission of Industrial Production. The commission decreed that, henceforth, no company or industrial enterprise could be established, expand, or move its existing facilities without the commission's authorization. It would be reasonable to conclude that this decree was equivalent to a legal prohibition of technological innovation.[30]

All these measures finally coalesced in a complicated corporative structure, the apex and base of which were the Consejo de Economía Nacional and the sectoral committees. In this "copious and dense set of agencies," wrote Velarde, appearances were not deceiving; "in general, those which represented economic pressure groups went on to become either part of the Consejo de Economía Nacional or part of one of the corporative agencies created by the Dictatorship." The institutionalization of pressure groups was extended into the political arena, that is, into the corporative National Assembly.[31] In September 1929 the same occurred in the administration, as these pressure groups became part of the newly created Ministerio de la Economía Nacional (Ministry of the National Economy), which assumed the responsibilities of the former Regulatory Commission.

This depiction of the dictatorship's defensive policy leads us to examine its intricate mesh of provisions that included tariff protection; direct development of production; and the sectoral organization and regulation enacted during World War I, when essential products were scarce and costly. Four points should be considered in this regard.

First, interventionism, as well as tariff protection, was extensive, preventive, and generalized. In Carr's words, "it was an exaggeration of the faith that nineteenth century protectionists had in the national market."[32] This move was no part of the rise of a public sector as found then in many modern economies, but part of the traditional "paternalistic" approach of the Spanish state.[33] The dictatorship did not promote a public sector aiming to rationalize the economic system; rather, it functioned to blur the boundaries between the public and private sectors, to the detriment of both. If Primo de Rivera's determination to institutionalize and give continuity to the policies of his dictatorship were criticized as "illegitimate constitutionalism,"[34] his brand of interventionism can furthermore be considered only a caricature of what state intervention should be in a contemporary capitalist economy.

Second, the system was highly inefficient. The immediate effect of the dictator's intervention was the generation of a "more rigid production system."[35] The "corporative corset," as it has often been called, was not an unwarranted metaphor; an ambience of asphyxiation prevailed. A few months after the end of the dictatorship, Calvo Sotelo himself recognized this:

> It is dangerous to provide a system with general preventive powers. Previous consent from a committee to set up a small industry, to update a machine or to finish a project caused great delays and sometimes irreparable damage.[36]

"A deficient doctrinal and statistical base" and an "underprepared bureaucracy"[37] have been offered as extenuating circumstances, but the real cause of the inefficiency was the magnitude and preventive character of the regime's brand of economic interventionism. This was the source of the bureaucratic anomalies and irregularities that were frequently denounced as corruption after the fall of Primo de Rivera and during the Second Republic. A system, however, that allowed personal and group pressure to sway its decisions and, in addition, was run by a "code of silence," could not help but produce corruption. Under these circumstances, corruption was a spontaneous, predictable, and natural outgrowth of the system.

Third, the ultimate consequence of the dictator's policy of protectionism and industrial development must be emphasized: "the final result, according to Velarde, was an increase in the monopolistic tendencies of the system."[38] The incorporation of owners' groups into corporative organizations and their participation in the shaping of economic policy could lead only to a rise in the degree of economic concentration and the proliferation of monopolistic practices. This situation favored the erection of "entrance barriers" for new competitors, since established business interests determined the conditions for opening new enterprises. What resulted was a sectoral status quo that led to entrepreneurial laxity. There was no need to worry about reducing costs in a weak industry, since under conditions of monopolistic control and a reserved market, profits could be increased simply by raising prices. As expressed by Palafox, "the legitimization of this oligopoly, together with a low technological level," evolved into a form of "defensive capitalism"[39] that could never have led to the development of competitive industry.

Fourth, the defensive economic policy of the dictatorship manifested a nationalism that was both capricious and contradictory. It tried to block foreign companies from controlling important Spanish economic sectors at the same time that it relinquished control of some fundamental activities. It was an ambitious policy, yet many nationalization projects and public monopolies yielded poor results. The creation of the petroleum monopoly in June 1927 is instructive. This was the most ambitious nationalist undertaking of Primo de Rivera's regime; it was a "shining light" in an otherwise ill-conceived industrial policy, and some considered it to be the only "sure bet of the Dictatorship."[40] Calvo Sotelo, the project's chief advocate, envisioned a totally integrated economic and administrative organization that would control the supply, transportation, refinement, and distribution of oil products to the entire market. From the very beginning the viability of the original project was jeopardized by the strategy of the Spanish banks in selecting an administration for the monopoly (CAMPSA), by enormous pressure from large international companies, and by diplomatic tensions caused by the nationalization of petroleum.[41] The fragmentation of what was conceived as a total project, the dependence on foreign companies for transportation and refinement, and CAMPSA's relegation to tasks of distribution all became institutionalized as oil became a crucial product for the Spanish energy sector. The profits and advantages reaped from the petroleum monopoly ended up justifying its existence.

The contradictory nature of the dictatorship's economic nationalism is otherwise well illustrated. In spite of the pompous declarations of "creating a sense of national economy" and "achieving a genuinely Spanish economy,"[42] the regime granted a monopoly to the powerful International Telephone and Telegraph Company for the development of Spanish communication services in August 1924. The concession gave the company almost absolute control over the sector on a long-term basis and included not only proprietary rights—IT&T was the majority stockholder—but rights over the acquisition and distribution of equipment. Spain became thus exclusively dependent on supplies from that company.

If these four main traits of Primo de Rivera's defensive economic policy are correctly appraised, one cannot but conclude that interventionism hindered the process of growth and structural change in the Spanish economy during the 1920s; although a fully negative evaluation of each and every interventionist practice of the period under investigation would be rash, indeed. Perhaps the only statement that can be now made is that there are signs that the economic interventionism in the first third of the twentieth century was not well planned or attuned to the needs of the Spanish industrialization process.[43]

NOTES

1. This chapter expands a paper entitled "From Tariff Protection to Corporativism," which was delivered at the Colloquium on Contemporary Spain at the Universidad Complutense (Madrid, April 1983). The first two parts follow the text of the paper closely with the exception of some changes of style and content—the latter owing to the incorporation of a new bibliography. The proceedings of the colloquium were published in *España 1898–1936: estructuras y cambio,* and edited by José Luis García Delgado (Madrid, 1984). A more in-depth study of the topic can be found in "La industrialización española en el primer tercio del siglo XX," *Historia de España,* vol. 22: *Los comienzos del siglo XX,* R. Menéndez Pidal, ed. (Madrid, 1984).

2. For interesting data on the events leading up to the "forced turn" toward protectionism see José M. Serrano Sanz, "La política de comercio exterior en la Restauración (1875–1895): el viraje hacia el proteccionismo" (Ph.D. diss., Universidad de Barcelona, 1982). A partial account of some of his conclusions can be found in Serrano Sanz, "La política de comercio exterior en los inicios de la Restauración (1875–1881)," *Investigaciones Económicas* 21 (1983): 209–226.

3. From among recent proprotectionist studies on the strategy of owners' associations and political parties at the end of the nineteenth century, Joseph Harrison's works on the Basque Provinces stand out: "El coste de oportunidad del Programa naval español de 1907: ¿pantanos o acorazados?" *Hacienda Pública Española* 38 (1976): 111–122; "Los orígenes del industrialismo moderno en el País Vasco," *Hacienda Pública Española* 55 (1978): 209–222; and "La industria pesada, el Estado y el desarrollo económico en el País Vasco, 1876–1936," *Información Comercial Española* 598 (1983): 21–32.

4. J. Vicens Vives with J. Nadal, *Manual de historia económica de España*, 9th ed. (Barcelona, 1979), p. 655.

5. Juan Sardá, *La política monetaria y las fluctuaciones de la economía española en el siglo XIX* (Madrid, 1948), p. 296.

6. *Manual de la Liga Marítima Española: cinco años de labor, 1900–1905*, Prologue by Antonio Maura (Madrid, 1906), pp. 8 and 261.

7. Salvador de Madariaga, *España: ensayo de historia contemporánea*, 13th ed. (Madrid, 1979), p. 252.

8. Raymond Carr, *Spain, 1808–1939* (Oxford, 1966), p. 580.

9. S. Ramón y Cajal, *Recuerdos de mi vida* (Madrid, 1923), p. 294.

10. "Cartes de Flores de Lemus al Ministro de Hacienda García Alix," *Hacienda Pública Española* 42–43 (1976): 394.

11. Angel Marvaud, "L'évolution économique de L'Espagne au cours de la guerre mondiale," *Revue des Sciences Politiques* (1920): 35.

12. Santiago Roldán and José Luis García Delgado with Juan Muñoz, *La formación de la sociedad capitalista en España, 1914–1920*, 2 vols. (Madrid, 1973), esp. vol. 1, pp. 255–323.

13. J. Velarde Fuertes, "El nacionalismo económico español y la Institución Libre de Enseñanza: El caso de Leopoldo Alas Argüelles," *Información Comercial Española* 517 (1976): 100.

14. "Nuestro Programa," editorial signed by La Redacción, *Revista Nacional de Economía* 1 (1916): 4.

15. Carr, *Spain*, p. 391.

16. Román Perpiñá, *Memorandum sobre la política del carbón* (Valencia, 1935), p. 48. Eloy Luis André's text corresponds to "El problema de la crisis del carbón en España," *Revista de Economía y Hacienda* 8 (1916): 163.

17. Carlos Velasco, "Concentración e intervención en la Dictadura: hechos e ideas," *Cuadernos Económicos de ICE* 10 (1979): 181.

18. Madariaga, *España*, p. 276.

19. J. Velarde Fuertes, "Problemas de la realidad económica española en la época de Alfonso XIII," in *Historia social de España. Siglo XX* (Madrid, 1976), p. 27.

20. Carr, *Spain*, p. 394.

21. "El arancel en nuestra historia económica," *Información Comercial Española* 322 (1960): 43.

22. Carr, *Spain*, p. 395; J. Varela Ortega, *Los amigos políticos: partidos, elecciones y caciquismo en la Restauración, 1875–1900* (Madrid, 1977), p. 204; Francisco Bernis, *La capacidad de desarrollo de la economía española* (Madrid, 1925), p. 44.

23. Román Perpiñá, "De Economía Hispana," in *De Economía Hispana, Infraestructura, Historia* (Barcelona, 1972), pp. 88–89.

24. R. Perpiñá, "De Economía Hispana," pp. 64–65.

25. Carr, *Spain*, p. 396.

26. Vicens Vives, *Manual*, pp. 695–696.

27. "El arancel," pp. 42–43.

28. Recently, another focus of protest against extreme protectionism was highlighted: that of the cattle exporters in Galicia. See J. A. Alonso Rodríguez, "La banca y la economía gallega en el primer tercio de siglo XX," in *España, 1898–1936* (Madrid, 1984), pp. 189–236. A few years ago Teresa Carnero also pointed out the tactically free-trade positions that "the agrarian groups of the Levantine periphery" adopted in the last third of the nineteenth century and, in particular, the grape growers who in the 1870s and 1880s experienced an unprecedented high point in the rise of foreign demand for wine. See her *Expansión vinícola y atraso agrario, 1870–1900* (Madrid, 1980), p. 31.

29. J. Velarde Fuertes, *Política económica de la Dictadura,* 2d ed. (Madrid, 1973), p. 151.

30. Jordi Palafox, "La crisis de los años 30: sus orígenes," *Papeles de Economía Española* 1 (1980): 40.

31. Velarde, *Política económica,* pp. 145 and 159.

32. Carr, *Spain*, p. 580.

33. Madariaga, *España*, p. 277. On the formation of corporate capitalism in Europe between the two world wars, see Luis Angel Rojo, *Keynes: su tiempo y el nuestro* (Madrid, 1984), pp. 297ff.

34. Carr, *Spain*, p. 586.

35. Velarde, *Política económica,* p. 159.

36. José Calvo Sotelo, *Mis servicios al Estado: seis años de gestión, apuntes para la historia* (Madrid, 1930), p. 260.

37. Velarde, *Política económica,* p. 38.

38. Velarde, *Política económica,* p. 159.

39. Jordi Palafox, "La gran depresión de los años treinta y la crisis industrial española," *Investigaciones Económicas* 11 (1980): 27; Josep Fontana and Jordi Nadal, "Spain, 1914–1970," in Carlo M. Cipolla, ed., *The Fontana History of Europe: Contemporary Economies,* vol. 6, pt. 2 (London, 1976), pp. 473–479.

40. Velarde, *Política económica,* p. 173; A. Ramos Oliveira, *El capitalismo español al desnudo* (Madrid, 1935), p. 166.

41. Robert H. Whealey, "La diplomacia española del petróleo: de junio de 1927 a abril de 1931," *Cuadernos Económicos de ICE* 10 (1979): 511 and 533.

42. As stated in the Decree Law of February 16, 1927, cited by Velarde, *La política económica,* p. 148.

43. Pablo Martín Aceña and Francisco Comín, "La industrialización en el primer tercio del siglo XX," *Revista de Historia Económica,* vol. 3, 2 (1985): 335–340.

FURTHER READINGS

In addition to the works cited in the Notes, the following titles would be useful for further study of this topic:

An excellent general summary of state intervention during the first stages of European industrialization can be found in B. Supple's "The State and the Industrial Revolution, 1700–1914," in *The Fontana Economic History of Europe: The Industrial Revolution,* vol. 3 (London, 1973), pp. 301–357. This essay comments on A. Gerschenkron's *Economic Backwardness in Historical Perspective* (Cambridge, Mass., 1962), as well as on other works. Supple's essay also includes a comprehensive bibliography on the industrialization of France, Germany, Great Britain, Italy, and Russia.

As for Spain, in addition to the works of Pugés, Blas Vives, Elli Lindner et al. on protectionism, numerous essays on economic nationalism have been compiled in the five issues of *Cuadernos Económicos de ICE,* published in 1978 and 1979 in *Información Comercial Española*; nos. 5, 6, and 7–8 deal with the so-called nationalist way of Spanish capitalism, and no. 10 deals with the dictatorship of Primo de Rivera. See also *España, 1898–1936: estructuras y cambios,* cited. There are four additional articles of interest on economic nationalism. The authors are J. Vázquez García, J. Antonio Biescas Ferrer, J. Muñoz García, and A. Elorza. A. Elorza has recently written a very informative interpretation of Ortega y Gasset's political philosophy as it relates to economic nationalism, entitled *La razón y la sombra: Una lectura política de Ortega y Gasset* (Barcelona, 1974).

II.
REGIONAL PERSPECTIVES

9.
THE INDUSTRIAL REVOLUTION IN CATALONIA*

JORDI MALUQUER DE MOTES
Universidad Autónoma de Barcelona

IN RECENT DECADES, sustained economic growth and widespread concern with problems of underdevelopment have pressured economic historians into directing their efforts toward development studies. Their main project has been to measure the developmental levels and growth rates of national economies by estimating data sets for their major macromagnitudes. This type of analysis is quite relevant, especially for countries like Spain where basic statistical data for historical research are still missing.[1] Large aggregate figures, whether totals or averages, however, ignore regional diversity and obscure the relations between economic sectors.

Regional and sectoral analysis should, therefore, receive more attention from scholars; time seems ripe to fill part of this historiographical void. Since the general concern with economic growth—in any form and at any price— has shifted to a new emphasis on reconversion and reindustrialization, economic historians now have the chance to focus instead on what triggers development and on what spatial and sectoral structures evolve.[2] For several national economies, this approach is particularly fitting because of their high regional and sectoral concentration of industry. A historical analysis of Italian industrialization, for example, implies an examination of the successes and

---

*The title of this work needs some clarification, since I agree with such scholars as P. Mathias and G. Mori that the term "industrial revolution" should be reserved for the British case. Inasmuch as this term reflects a whole complex of changes that occurred first in Great Britain and then spread to other countries, another term (i.e., "industrialization process") seems to be more appropriate to characterize the experience of the rest of the world. This is the term that I use throughout in this chapter; "industrial revolution" appears in the title to underscore the global nature of my explanation, even at the risk of blurring nuances.

169

failures of the region that Luciano Cafagna calls the "little country"—a region formed by the nation's three northwestern provinces.[3] Similarly, to study the process in Spain leads to an almost exclusive study of the Basque and Catalan regions.

1. A BASICALLY INDUSTRIAL ECONOMY

When the Great Depression occurred, the Catalan economy was already basically industrial. In 1930 twice as many people were employed in industry as in agriculture; the active population in Catalonia's secondary sector was almost identical to that of Britain and much higher than that of France, Italy, or Spain as a whole (see Table 9.1).[4]

The ratio between the added value of the secondary sector and that of the primary sector probably favored the former, since industrial productivity is higher than agricultural productivity. Lack of a detailed calculation of Catalonia's net product precludes any precise estimate of sectoral incomes. Available data, however, suggest that there was a superiority of industry over agriculture as early as 1914 (see Table 9.2). Although these data have not been sufficiently pondered, they can be considered a provisional indicator of each sector's added value.

Prior to 1930, the use of electrical energy both in industry and at home had become quite generalized; electricity consumption, then, can be used to measure the disparity between Catalonia and the rest of Spain. In per capita terms, Catalonia and the Basque Provinces (the other Spanish industrial area of the period) consumed more than twice the Spanish average and four times more

Table 9.1
**Distribution of the Active Population
by Sectors, 1930–1931**

	Primary	Secondary	Tertiary
Great Britain	6.0	54.0	39.5
Catalonia	27.5	53.5	19.0
France	35.5	38.5	26.0
Italy	47.0	35.5	17.5
Spain	48.0	34.0	18.0

Source: Santo Luis Gil Ibáñez, "La población activa en España, 1860–1930" (Ph.D. diss., Universidad Complutense de Madrid, 1979), pp. 309 and 325.

Table 9.2
Estimates of Added Value,[a] 1914
(in millions of pesetas)

	Sedo	Vicens	Vandellos
Catalonia (agriculture)	350	341	—
Catalonia (industry)	1,700	—	—
Spain (agriculture)	4,000	—	4,130[a]
Spain (industry)	2,300	—	2,250

SOURCE: J. Maluquer de Motes, "Les relaciones entre agri-cultura i indústria en el desenvolupament capitalista catalá del vuit-cents." 1er Col.loqui d'Història Agraria, Barcelona (Valencia, 1983), pp. 199–200.
a: Includes the added value of livestock.

than any other region (see Table 9.3). In absolute terms, the Catalan market absorbed approximately one-third of Spain's total electricity output, though the region had only a little over one-sixth of the nation's population.

Moreover, the Catalan industrialization process was unique. Around 1930, Catalonia, along with the Basque Provinces, constituted an anomaly within the predominantly agricultural society of Spain and even within the entire Medi-terranean area, with the sole exception of the Italian "industrial triangle." In

Table 9.3
Per Capita Electricity Output in 1934

	Kilowatts/Hour/Inhabitants
Belgium	490
Germany	460
Great Britain	445
Catalonia	410
Basque Provinces	405
Northern Italy (1932)	395
France	365
Italy	285
Spain	146

SOURCE: J. Maluquer de Motes, "Cataluña y el País Vasco en la industria eléctrica española, 1901–1935," Industrializa-ción y nacionalismo: análisis comparativos (Barcelona, 1984). The figure for northern Italy was derived from G. Mortara, Caratteri e sviluppo dell'industria elettrica nell'economia ital-iana (Milan, 1984), p. 262.
NOTE: Figures rather refer to the energy demand (produc-tion + imports) in each of the respective electrical systems; the volume of each country then becomes an indication of consumption.

terms of per capita electricity usage, Catalonia, the Basque Provinces, and northern Italy shared similar consumption levels. In addition, these areas exhibited levels above those of France and not far below those of highly industrialized countries such as Great Britain, Germany, and Belgium. The gap between the industrialized centers of the Mediterranean and the most developed European economies was not significant; however, when the rest of the Italian and Iberian peninsulas and the other nonindustrialized Mediterranean regions are considered, the gap becomes abysmal.

Within the context of these few industrial regions of the Mediterranean, Catalonia exhibited one distinctive and important feature: precociousness. By 1860 Catalonia was the only one of these regions to reach a relatively advanced level of industrialization. The set of data needed to prove this assertion is still lacking, but anyone familiar with the contemporary economic history of Europe would agree that the other economies in question did not reach the "take-off stage" until the last third of the nineteenth century.

Consequently, the Catalan economy was the only one in the Mediterranean area that aligned itself successfully with the "first-comers" of industrialization. At mid-nineteenth century, Catalonia's mechanization level compared favorably with that of the most advanced Western countries. In Table 9.4, the two economies ranking highest in per capita for motor power, Belgium and Germany, applied a very high percentage of their steam engines to extract raw materials from the subsoil (almost 65% in Belgium in 1845)—Catalonia, ranking third, lacked mineral resources.

Catalan industrialization was carried out in the absence of local iron and

Table 9.4
Steampower in Industry

	Horsepower	Hp/1,000 Inhabitants
Belgium, 1860	98,757	20.8
Germany, 1861	365,000	9.6
Catalonia, 1861	9,960	5.8
France, 1861	191,000	5.1
Czechoslovakia, 1863	31,765	4.2
Austria, 1863	43,387	2.4
Russia, 1860	60,000	1.0

SOURCE: A. Van Neck, *Les débuts de la machine à vapeur dans l'industrie belge, 1800–1850* (Brussels, 1979); the figure for Catalonia is from Fernando Garrido, *La España contemporánea* (Barcelona, 1867), p. 408.

coal deposits. The lack of these materials, in contrast to Belgium, Germany, and the Spanish Basque Provinces, makes Catalan development a complex process, so that simple explicative models are not applicable. While Basque industrialization benefited from strategic raw materials, Catalan industrialization was accomplished in spite of a lack of these materials. It goes without saying that this deficiency would cause serious limitations and notorious shortages.

2. A CASE OF INDUSTRIALIZATION
WITHOUT NATURAL RESOURCES

The availability of natural resources does not, by itself, explain modern economic growth. In spite of its rich subsoil, Southern Spain has remained a relatively underdeveloped region. Nevertheless, abundant resources can provide a tremendous advantage, in terms of costs, over potential competitors. The export of such resources can, in turn, increase the capacity to import other raw materials and capital goods. Since Catalonia did not enjoy any of these advantages, its industrial evolution must be explained in other terms. The development of Catalonia in the nineteenth century was rooted in the fertile ground created by the preceding historical era; in other words, in the series of transformations that occurred before the onset of industrialization. Catalan society was already characterized, not only by substantial levels of wealth, but also by a fairly equal distribution of income as a result of the early disintegration of feudal structures there. Feliú de la Peña stated pointedly: "There are certainly no great fortunes in Catalonia, with the result that only medium-sized enterprises can be undertaken."[5]

Economic change was achieved through a process of horizontal growth that occurred between the late seventeenth century and the early nineteenth. Such growth derived from a sustained increase in production without substantial gains in labor productivity and without technological innovations. This growth, however, was accompanied by a steady increase in agricultural productivity, in terms of both labor and income. Both sets of gains can probably be traced to the substitution of cereal crops, which required little labor, by more labor-intensive and remunerative crops, such as grapevines.

Coastal specialization in agro-export products, mainly those of grapevines, favored this internal growth, while the external stimulus came from the rising demand for brandy and wine in European and American markets—and not only in Spanish-American markets as is frequently stated.[6] The effects of the agro-export expansion and of the region's subsequent integration into the Atlantic economy were felt even in areas far from the seaports. The rise in income and the increasing need for foodstuffs and raw materials in the export districts—districts unable to feed themselves because of their increasing specialization—intensified the traditional flow of products (e.g., grain, wool, timber, iron, work animals) from the interior to the coast. Through this trade, the people of the interior were integrated into the export economy and participated in its profits.

This agricultural and commercial prosperity generated, both on the coast and in the interior, a greater demand for light consumer goods. As farmers devoted more of their time and resources to producing foodstuffs for the market (or labored as part-time industrial workers), they were forced to reduce the amount of time traditionally spent in other subsistence activities (e.g., construction and production of hardware, clothes, fabrics). In order to avail themselves of these goods and services, they turned more and more toward the market economy.

The expansion of internal and external trade eventually generated a demand for transportation and other services associated with commercial development. This created even more opportunities for wage labor both in the service sector and in the production of ships, overland transport vehicles, and in the need for work animals. Consequently, income levels rose for large numbers of people and contributed to an expansion in the demand for mass consumer goods.

The rise of the most important industries was linked to this expansion of the home market. Only later, when production reached cost-competitive levels, did the region begin to produce industrial goods for export.[7] Industrial expansion—perhaps one should say protoindustrial—required a favorable investment climate and an acceptable level of efficiency.[8] Both conditions depended on the availability of capital, cheap labor, and adequate trade networks.

Within this fairly egalitarian society, both agricultural prosperity and all the activities associated with the export sector furnished enough of a surplus for investment, or at least for the financial base necessary to obtain capital through mortgages, for example. In addition, agrarian change facilitated a transfer of assets (buildings, irrigation canals transformed into industrial canals, flour mills converted into paper and textile mills) that shifted the potential for growth from the agricultural to the industrial sector.[9] Finally, given that the capital demands for this type of industry (or protoindustry) were very low, a high level of savings was not as necessary as a wide dispersion of savings, the latter being favored by the Catalan social structure.

Two mechanisms—the establishment of industries in rural areas and the population growth that those industries eventually generated—made cheap labor available. Taking advantage of seasonal lulls in the agricultural calendar, especially in less intensive agricultural areas, industrialists were able to recruit large numbers of workers whose opportunity costs were virtually nil and who, consequently, acceded to very low wages.[10] Industries were also located in the countryside because of a need for small waterfalls, since hydraulic energy provided the highest productivity levels possible with preindustrial techniques—a situation that, at the same time, tended to minimize wage costs.[11] All this was facilitated by permanent access to water, under a legal system favoring its individual private property.[12] Another favorable condition was that economies of scale held little significance for this type of industry.

The labor pool grew through a lowering of the marriage age, a decrease in celibacy, and a corresponding increase in the birthrate—all of which were the result of industrial growth itself. Although there is still no quantitative evidence for this, contemporary accounts are highly convincing. Commenting on the trends of recent decades, Barcelona's Junta of Commerce stated in 1814:

> Even in the most remote corners of Catalonia, whole families were busily occupied with the spinning wheel, the loom and the hoe. . . . The rise in the number of children, ordinarily viewed as a burden when there is no means to support or employ them, was now considered a blessing. The number of marriages increased considerably.[13]

The third requirement for the development of an industrial export economy in Spain was the existence of efficient trade networks. Forging commercial links and opening markets for agricultural products, both on the peninsula and abroad, broadened distribution channels for manufactured goods. Whether established by lone venture capitalists or by the agents of family companies or large enterprises, the commercial structures created by the Catalans were characterized by a high concentration within Catalonia and a strong internal cohesion in each of the commercial "colonies."[14] This case clearly illustrates how an ethnic minority, because of its distinctiveness and its linguistic and cultural unity, can incorporate itself into an economy and control trade to a high degree, especially long-distance trade.[15] Catalans were thus compared, in Cuba for example, with Scots and Jews.[16]

Before the industrial revolution, a series of changes took place in Catalan society that, while not implying an agrarian revolution, reinforced the region's most progressive tendencies. The eighteenth century saw a marked increase in both production and productivity as measured by money. These increases were based on a growing specialization in viticulture and a rise in income, in both the export districts and the interior—the interior having participated, directly or indirectly, in the coastal areas' prosperity. In this fairly egalitarian society, a rise in income meant a rise in mass consumption and, in accordance with Engels' law, resulted ultimately in a disproportionate increase in the demand for nonessential goods, especially manufactures. In short, agricultural specialization created a market for industry and ended by creating the conditions needed for an industrial export economy.[17]

The economic mystique—the generalized glorification of values such as hard work and saving—and Catalan self-initiative were symptoms of development, not of its causes. Rather, development was achieved by a process of circular causation through which, according to Myrdal, one change provoked new changes that swept the system's most important variables in the same direction and in a cumulative manner.[18] Growth under conditions of low productivity led almost automatically to economic diffusion.

It is important to emphasize that the key to the whole process lies less in agricultural specialization and viticultural exports than in the relatively egalitarian character of Catalan society. The same combination of push factors in a society with a less even distribution of income—Lower Andalusia, for example—would have produced very different results. They would have generated, instead, a greater demand for luxury goods and probably a tremendous growth of imports.[19]

3. A SINGLE OPTION: THE CONSUMER-GOODS INDUSTRY

The industrial revolution, as W. Arthur Lewis pointed out, did not create industry from scratch; rather, it transformed the industry that already existed. A high level of social mobility, industrialists accustomed to investing and taking risks, a specialized and skilled labor force, a very dynamic agricultural system, and efficient trade networks—all constituted a legacy from the past that prepared Catalonia to take advantage of economic opportunities and to adapt to radical change when necessary.

The loss of the Spanish-American colonies, the economic expansion of the United States, and the resurgence of British exports together disrupted the traditional networks of the export trade in the first third of the nineteenth century. These circumstances led to the destructuralization of the Catalan economy.[20] The region's internal market was, of course, too narrow to trigger an economic expansion by making use of new technologies.

Theoretically, there were two solutions: (1) to turn inward toward the Spanish market and (2) to specialize in manufactures of a particular type or price that would permit the region to create a niche for itself in the world market—the only possibility within the reach of the smaller European economies. In practice, the second option (à la Switzerland) did not really exist because, among other reasons, Catalonia was not an independent country like Switzerland, and its economy was, therefore, subject to external constraints.[21] The first option, then, was the only real possibility, and this was the one undertaken by textile manufacturers. At the end of the eighteenth century and the beginning of the nineteenth, modern methods of production had already been introduced in the region, just as they were being initiated in Great Britain on a larger scale. Between 1833 and 1840, the starting point of Catalonia's modern industrial development, the steam engine was introduced and various textile plants became mechanized in the cotton and wool subsectors. During the next thirty years, a textile factory system was put into place that employed more efficient technical methods and succeeded in increasing production tremendously, improving product quality and reducing prices. Last, the protectionist tariff policy of the period and the construction of railroad lines—a project in which Catalan participation was significant—underlay the region's ability to capture the Spanish market.[22]

The capture of the Spanish market was accomplished in two stages: first, through the absorption of consumer items traditionally supplied by artisans; second, through a process of import substitution. Although illegal, British imports accounted for a substantial part of the internal supply of cotton fabrics for years. At least for the first half of the century, contraband and Catalan production generally supplied two fundamentally different segments of the market: urban demand, with its high income levels, was met by contraband products that consisted of fine, high-priced fabrics, whereas rural demand was met by the Catalan production of coarse cloth for everyday use.[23]

The cotton industry did not forge its own market at the expense of the foreign textile industry; contraband was perhaps more important than ever during the period of Catalan textile expansion (1833–1861). Rather, it forged its own market by displacing rural subsistence production and small traditional industries. This was accomplished through technological transformations that raised productivity and reduced costs.[24] The substitution of fraudulent imports occurred later, after the Spanish internal market was secured. In this way, the Catalan economy came to specialize in textiles.

In comparison with the main continental countries, Catalonia ranked low in the development of its cotton industry in 1861, although if one examines other dates, either before or after 1861, Catalonia would fare better than Switzerland.[25] The figures in the second column of Table 9.5, on the other hand, place Catalonia high in terms of spindlers per inhabitants. It is clear that cotton was critical for the Catalan economy and population. This is further underscored when the relevant data for other textile subsectors are considered. By 1913, Sabadell, Terrassa, and Barcelona together possessed more than 48% of the spindles and 75% of the power-driven looms of the Spanish wool industry.[26]

The Catalan textile industry grew to such an extent, especially the cotton industry, that it looked as a regional monopoly. Three principal factors endowed the Catalan industry with an unusual solvency and with a fiercely competitive edge over manufacturers in the rest of Spain: (1) superiority in terms of business management and specialization and skill of the labor force; (2) important external economies resulting from industrial concentration and interindustrial relations; and (3) the ability to adapt to a Spanish market that was both poor and unstable.

The Catalan cotton industry was not, as had been once written, an aggregation of stagnant lilliputian enterprises against which competition would have been easy, but a well-integrated, hierarchical structure attuned to the size and nature of the market. Medium- and small-sized businesses along with domestic workers (the "putting-out system") formed a few well-articulated groups through which large entrepreneurs exercised very effective decision-making powers and managed to resist, to an incredible degree, sudden fluctuations in

Table 9.5
The Cotton Industry in 1861

	Thousands of Spindles	Spindles/1,000 Inhabitants
France	5,500	147
Germany	2,235	61
Austria-Hungary	1,800	55
Switzerland	1,350	540
Russia	1,000	13
Catalonia	900	529
Belgium	612	136
Italy	450	18

SOURCE: B. R. Mitchell, "Statistical Appendix, 1700–1914," in C. M. Cipolla, ed., *The Fontana Economic History of Europe. The Emergence of Industrial Societies*, vol. 2 (London and Glasgow, 1973), pp. 747–748 and 782. Catalonia: our own estimates.

the larger market. During times of increased demand, it was easy for these large entrepreneurs to mobilize the resources of subordinate producers and thus to increase supply. When crisis threatened, they could eliminate the domestic spinners and weavers and the small producers and thus avoid the negative effects of an industrial downswing.[27]

The development of the whole textile industry was subject to the evolution of the Spanish agricultural sector. The lack of industrial concentration; the lack of specialization in production; and modest-sized family-run businesses were the result of the dimension and nature of the market. This industrial structure has its positive aspects—its plasticity, its innovativeness, and its role as an entrepreneurial training ground—which account for its survival, but it also harbored some fundamental shortcomings that proved insurmountable in international competition.

In discussing the industrial evolution of the period, mention should also be made of other industrial achievements, such as the manufacture of cork stoppers, which was predominant in the area around Gerona and was also one of Catalonia's basic export items. The food industries were also quite important nationwise and included such products as flour; noodles; preserves; chocolate; beer and other alcoholic beverages, especially champagne or "cava"; sugar; sausages; and the like. Last, Catalonia led Spain in the apparel making, furniture, paper, and book industries; the latter industry made Barcelona the most important Spanish language publishing center in the world.

The textile industry was certainly the leading sector of the Catalan economy during this period. Its ability to foster a solid industrial base that would be diverse and competitive in international terms, however, was not that clear. Backward linkages were limited; the chemical and engineering industries, for example, hardly developed.

Less outstanding, but relatively more efficient, was the second leading branch of Catalan industrialization: construction. This industry experienced sustained growth for an entire century. Because of the intense urbanization process that occurred between 1830 and 1930, cities became centers of industrial activity and commercial services. Commerce, in turn, furnished industry with money and initiative. Urban construction also had a dynamic impact on the brick, glass, metal, and gas-lighting industries.

In a second phase, which spanned the years 1890 to 1910, the construction sector contributed to an expansion of the electricity, cement, and engineering industries (e.g., elevators and trolley cars) as urbanization progressed at a rapid pace. In many of the other sectors, Catalonia also maintained a pioneering and hegemonic position vis-à-vis the rest of Spain throughout the entire period. The capital amassed by returning Spanish emigrants who had acquired wealth in Iberoamerica, combined with local capital accumulated in agriculture, especially in wine exports after the destruction of French vineyards by phylloxera, contributed decisively to the industrialization process. Urban investments, as well as investments in such strategic activities as transportation, commerce, and other services were also quite substantial.

4. THE LIMITATIONS AND INADEQUACIES OF INDUSTRIALIZATION

The structural characteristics of Catalan industrialization have determined both its course and its shortcomings. The Catalan economy experienced only modest growth rates, except during the "take-off stage" in the second third of the nineteenth century. This slow increase in industrial output can be explained by the slow growth of Spanish demand.[28]

Industry and the whole Catalan economy failed to meet expectations due to the risks associated with the fluctuations of a poor agrarian-based market. Rural Spain, however, became so backward by the end of the period that the risks were reduced, since the countryside began to represent only a small part of national consumption.

The artificial silk industry serves as a poignant example. In 1935, according to the data of F. Sala Serra, Spanish per capita consumption of rayon textiles was very low. It was 50% of that of France and Japan; 33% of that of Italy and Germany; and only 20% to 30% of that of Belgium, Switzerland, United States, and Great Britain.[29] Neither scarcity nor price were the reasons for such low consumption, since the Spanish product was competitive abroad and was exported in relatively large quantities. The explanations lay, rather, in the regional distribution of consumption: the markets of Catalonia, the Basque Provinces, and Madrid absorbed approximately 75% of domestic consumption, while the inhabitants of these regions represented less than 50% of the total population. Regarding nonagricultural consumer goods, a dichotomy existed between the dynamic industrial and/or urbanized zones with European consumption standards and the stagnant agrarian zones of the south, the central plateau, and the northeast with African consumption levels. This is similar to the Italian case where the southern market also appears to have been quite narrow.[30] Such a dichotomy created an imperfect market, reinforcing archaic structures and backwardness. In this vein, evidence abounds for the lack of specialized and effective distribution mechanisms and for the near impossibility of employing bills of exchange.[31]

Demand does not explain everything, however. The slow growth of the Catalan economy was also determined by the specialization model upon which it embarked. Hoffman stated that, once a certain level of development was reached, the capital goods industry grew faster than the consumer goods industry everywhere.[32] Catalonia's options were limited in this regard, however. The region had no choice but to select the types of industry that required the fewest material inputs. It should be recalled, for example, that Catalan efforts to set up an iron-and-steel industry were pioneering and persevering, though unsuccessful.[33]

The lack of iron and coal seriously hampered the development of an iron-and-steel industry and of several branches of the chemical industry. The shortage of combustible materials also forced Catalonia to import energy on a large scale. From 1841 to 1935 such imports caused a serious strain in the regional balance of both trade and payments.[34]

A basic characteristic of an energy system is its coefficient of external energy dependence, that is, the percentage of primary energy imports in relation to overall gross internal consumption. In the Catalan case, this coefficient was very high—over 70% between 1845 and 1905. It would be difficult to find other economies that reached similar levels of industrial output with such high energy dependence. Nineteenth century Catalan industrialization negates Landes's rule (previously stated by Jean Baptiste Say) that all industrial centers developed in close proximity to coal deposits.[35] As a result of high coal prices, hydraulic energy, derived directly from water or from electricity—always played an important role in Catalonia as well as in Switzerland, Sweden, Norway, Canada, and Japan, where coal was also in all of them missing. Unlike these countries, Catalonia's hydraulic potential was mediocre,[36] even if easily utilizable with primitive techniques. Out of this shortage of natural resources emerged a light industry that was labor-intensive and low-energy-consuming.

Catalonia's lack of energy resources and the need to import fuel resulted in higher costs. This explains, in part, the region's inability to compete in the world market. The rest of the explanation lies in the deficient structures and atomization of Catalan industry and its subsequent failure to reach the technological, organizational, commercial, and financial levels needed for both economies of scale and improved productivity.

Labor costs were also greater for Catalan industrialists than for other European nations (see Table 9.6). This does not mean that real wages were higher for Catalan workers. Because of a tariff protection system that perpetuated agricultural inefficiency,[37] the cost of living in the region was high. The purchasing power of Catalan industrial wages seems, therefore, to have been

Table 9.6
Annual Costs of One Spindle for Cotton Spinning
(in reales)

	Great Britain	Switzerland	France	Catalonia
Premises[a]	9.00	16.77	18.60	23.80
Salaries	13.81	14.52	20.18	27.11
General costs[b]	8.93	10.26	18.81	28.47
Total expenses	31.74	41.55	57.59	79.38

SOURCE: Study conducted by Jose Ferrer Vidal with data for the years 1872 to 1874, reproduced in *Economía i Finances* 11 (November 10): 3–5.
a: Capital interest and amortization of machinery;   b: Fuel, repairs, lighting, insurance, taxes.

below that of the more advanced countries of the continent. In addition, low labor productivity increased wage costs for industrialists.

Regardless of whether the introduction of labor-saving devices in an economy characterized by an unlimited labor supply was socially appropriate or not, the fact is that the Catalan textile industry was slow to adopt technological or organizational innovations because of the workers' strong opposition to any reduction in employment. The struggle against innovation—or, rather, the preservation of a sizable industrial labor market—is one of the most poignant reasons for the rise of strong labor unions in Catalonia and for their radicalism, a fact that historians of social movements have surprisingly overlooked.[38]

When the metal-transforming and engineering industries arose and began to supply equipment to all other industries, material factors became less of a constraint, since labor now represented the highest proportion of the total production costs. Under these circumstances, Catalan industry could have made deep inroads in the world market in the same way that even less developed economies such as that of Sweden and Italy did, exporting, for instance, Husqvarna sewing machines (since 1872), Olivetti typewriters, and Agnelli automobiles. This never materialized in Catalonia for reasons out of control of the region. When the textile industry reached its "take-off stage" in the second third of the nineteenth century, a group of large, well-financed enterprises was established that was able to inject dynamism into the metal-transforming and engineering sector. In other words, private initiative was not lacking. The institutions of Catalonia also supported the industrialization process by providing, among other things, an excellent system of technical education: Barcelona had the only engineering school in all of nineteenth-century Spain.[39]

Rather, it was the economic policies of the government that stifled existing enterprises and sacrificed the future of the sector. Government intervention took two forms: (1) the government temporarily allowed railroad materials to be imported duty-free, depriving the nation's iron-and-steel industry, and especially its engineering industry, of developmental opportunities;[40] and (2) government tariff policies hindered the engineering industry by charging low tariffs on imported machinery, whereas high tariffs were imposed on the industry's material inputs, that is, on iron-and-steel products.[41]

5. CONCLUSION: A NEW SPECIALIZATION STRATEGY

In the 1870s and 1880s, the region's industrial performance deteriorated because of its heavy reliance on a declining textile industry that exhibited only moderate increases in demand. From the following decade on, a new dynamic sector began to take the lead in Catalonia. It was based on the engineering and electrical industries and succeeded in bringing about the revitalization of the entire Catalan economy. This sector's progress became steady in the 1890s, perhaps as a result of the protectionist measures of 1891 and 1906. The most important causes, however, lie elsewhere. First, the devaluation of the peseta in the 1880s, but especially in the 1890s, pushed import prices upward, favoring domestic production. Second, hydroelectricity was introduced in the 1880s, making large quantities of cheap energy available—a development that fostered both industrial diversification and a relative reduction in coal imports. The region's dependence on external energy sources was thus reduced. Later, the tremendous increase in international fuel prices brought on by World War I accelerated this energy-substitution process. How electricity fully replaced steam-energy by the 1920s is shown in Graph 9.1.

The third factor that promoted a shift in Catalonia's industrial specialization was a rise in income. The income elasticity of demand for metal manufactures was much higher than that for nondurable consumer goods such as food and clothing. In addition, the Catalan market for consumer goods had traditionally been more active than that of any other region of Spain. This must have contributed to the location of the new engineering and electrical sector in Catalonia, as opposed to the Basque Provinces, despite some advantages offered by the latter region.[42]

The market enjoyed greater vitality in Catalonia because of the region's former lead in textiles. Wages in this industry were higher than in the rest of Spain.[43] The textile industry also employed large numbers of female workers,

**Graph 9.1   Energy Substitution in the Textile Industry:
The Case of Terrassa**

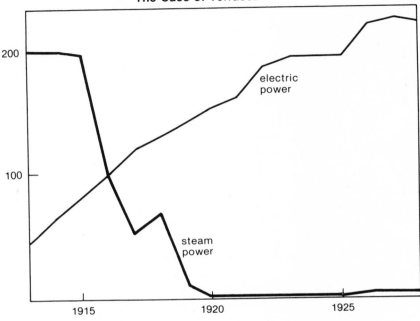

whose wages, in contrast to those in other sectors, were close to those of their male counterparts.[44] This had two important consequences: (1) The overall employment rate was relatively high because of the marked participation of women in the labor force.[45] (2) Since large numbers of women were employed, the average family income in Catalonia must have been substantially greater than elsewhere.

For these reasons, the metal-transforming industry exhibited greater-than-average growth rates in the first decades of the twentieth century and gradually came to rank high in the region's industrial complex. Alongside the old engineering companies, which were unable to compete with large foreign firms because of fluctuations in demand and because of low profits, a small metallurgical industry—composed of small, profitable enterprises specializing in the production of precision instruments; tools; agricultural machinery; and consumer durables from automobiles to sewing machines, stoves, and refrigerators—developed.[46] However, Catalonia lacked the iron-and-steel plants needed to sustain this industry. The region overcame this problem only partially when it built Martin-Siemens furnaces for the sheeting of imported cast iron.[47]

Catalan industrialization, including this late reorientation, fits the description of what Roehl (in a brilliant analysis inspired by Gerschenkron's model of relative underdevelopment) has called a precocious industrialization process.[48] According to Roehl, the pioneer economies of industrialization were probably characterized by:

- a moderate growth rate which, nevertheless, permitted industrialization
- a high proportion of light consumer-goods industries in relation to total industrial production
- an absence of concentration in industrial organization
- a capacity to obtain both technology and capital largely from national sources
- a limited role in the industrialization process on the part of the banking system and the state
- the absence of a militant industrial ideology
- a marked contribution to industrialization on the part of the agricultural sector
- a tendency for the standard of living to parallel global economic growth

The Catalan case conforms with these traits that, in opposition to Gerschenkron's model, lead to the characterization of "pioneer" economies as those in which modern economic growth appears rooted in the distant past and in which development springs from a relatively advanced economy. Modern economic growth began early in Catalonia and, after the introduction of the factory system, followed an industrialization process restricted in scope. Its limitations can be traced to the region's shortage of natural resources, the inadequate size of the Spanish market, and income fluctuations. Industrial growth based, at least in part, on exports was not a viable alternative because, among other things, Catalonia's link to Spain tied the region to the nation's inefficient agrarian sector. For better or worse, the achievements and limitations of Catalan industrialization cannot be explained without taking into account its integration into the Spanish economy.

NOTES

1. For a convincing defense of the advantages of analysis at the national level, especially carried out from a comparative perspective, see S. Kuznets, *Modern Economic Growth: Rate Structure and Spread* (New Haven and London, 1966), pp. 16ff. See also

R. Tilly, "Per Capita Income and Productivity as Indices of Development and Welfare: Some Comments on Kuznetsian Economic History," in R. Fremdling and P. O'Brien, eds., *Productivity in the Economies of Europe,* (Stuttgart, 1983), pp. 30–56.

2. There are some excellent examples of this new approach to the analysis of economic history. See, for example, some of the works collected in S. Pollard, ed., *Region und Industrialisierung* (Göttingen, 1980).

3. L. Cafagna, "Italy, 1830–1914," in C. M. Cipolla, ed., *The Fontana Economic History of Europe,* vol. 4, part 1 (London, 1973), pp. 279–328.

4. Census reports are notoriously unreliable and must be used with caution. Moreover, the employment of diverse compilation methods can alter results substantially in some cases. The application of different formulas to the 1930 data than those used by Gil Ibáñez results in a different distribution but does not fundamentally change his conclusions; using this alternative methodology, the active population in the primary and secondary sectors would fall to 26.2% and 51.6%, respectively, while that of the corresponding tertiary sector would rise to 22.2%. I would like to thank Professor Roser Nicolau of the Department of Economic History, Universidad Autónoma de Barcelona, for revising the census classifications of 1930 and for creating the compilation techniques that produced these figures. In relation to the Spanish totals, see Julio Alcaide Inchausti, "Una revisión urgente de la serie de renta nacional española en el siglo XX," in Instituto de Estudios Fiscales, *Datos básicos de la historia financiera de España, 1850–1975* (Madrid, 1976), pp. 1125–1150. His estimates are similar to those of Gil Ibáñez's for the primary sector (47.3%) but differ for the secondary sector (30.9%) and the tertiary sector (21.7%). Alcaide's projection agrees more with my second estimate for Catalonia. Whatever the case, Catalonia's secondary sector was almost double that of Spain as a whole.

5. N. Feliú de la Peña, *Fénix de Cataluña* (Barcelona, 1683), p. 80.

6. E. Giralt y Raventós, "La agricultura y el comercio catalán del siglo XVIII," *Estudios de Historia Moderna* 2 (1956): 157–176; P. Vilar, *La Catalogne dans l'Espagne moderne. Recherches sur les fondements économiques des structures nationales* (Paris, 1962); J. Torras Elías, "Aguardiente y crisis rural: Sobre la coyuntura vitícola, 1793–1832," *Investigaciones Económicas* 1 (1976): 45–67.

7. Much has been written about colonial trade but very little about Catalan foreign trade. See C. Martínez Shaw, *Cataluña en la Carrera de Indias* (Barcelona, 1981), and J. M. Delgado, "Cataluña y el sistema de libre comercio (1778–1818): una reflexión sobre las raíces del reformismo borbónico" (Ph.D. diss., University of Barcelona, 1981). For a general overview see Vilar, *La Catalogne.*

8. F. Mendels, "Proto-industrialization: The First Phase of the Industrialization Process," *Journal of Economic History* 32 (1972): 241–261. The initial success of his theory is, perhaps, the key to its later rejection after many scholars who read this article did so carelessly. "Proto-industry" did not always lead to industrialization, but wherever the former process took place, the ground was prepared for a vigorous industrial development short of the "factory system."

9. I have developed this thesis more extensively in my "Les relacions entre agricultura i indústria en el desenvolupament capitalista català del vuit-cents. Algunes hipòtesis," in *1er Colloqui d'Història Agrària, Barcelona, 13–15 d'octubre, 1978* (Valencia, 1983), pp. 199–212.

10. On this point my analysis is opposed to that of E. Lluch, *El pensament econòmic a Catalunya, 1760–1840* (Barcelona, 1973), pp. 356–358.

11. The records of the Royal Patrimony (Archives of the Crown of Aragón) contain quantitative data for water concessions for industrial use in the eighteenth century. Between 1735 and 1799, 191 concessions were granted, 59 of which were for fulling mills, 46 for foundries, 40 for calico factories, and 20 for papermills. These figures represent only a fraction of industrial water use, since not all water in the Catalan region was owned by the Crown.

12. See my paper "El Agua en el crecimiento catalán de los siglos XVII y XVIII: derechos de propiedad y utilizaciones energéticas," presented at the Prato meeting of April 1983 held at the Instituto Internazionale di Storia Economica "Francesco Datini." This paper will appear in the forthcoming proceedings of this meeting.

13. Biblioteca de Catalunya. Archivo de la Junta de Comercio de Barcelona. Leg. 92. Esposición al Rey sobre "los males incalculables que irroga a la industria nacional la introducción en el Reyno, de hilados y manufacturas de algodón," August 10, 1814.

14. See the doctoral thesis of Delgado, *Cataluña,* and his "La emigración española a América Latina durante la época del comercio libre (1765–1820). El ejemplo catalán," *Boletín Americanista* 24, no. 32 (1982): 115–137.

15. For further information on the capacity of minority groups to control long-distance trade see P. S. Labrini, *Il sottosviluppo e l'economia contemporanea* (Bari, 1983), pp. 69–70.

16. I have studied this issue in relation to Cuba for the first half of the nineteenth century in "La burguesía catalana y la esclavitud en Cuba: política y producción," *Revista de la Biblioteca Nacional José Martí* 18 (1976): 11–80 (original cat. in *Recerques,* 3, pp. 43–49). They were also called the "Dutchmen of the Mediterranean." See L. Alonso Alvarez, *Industrialización y conflictos sociales en la Galicia del Antiguo Régimen, 1750–1830* (Madrid, 1976).

17. In the opinion of Jovellanos, Catalan wine "is sold more easily" in Asturias than Castilian wine because of the high cost of overland transportation. See "Informe en el expediente de Ley Agraria" in *Obras escogidas,* vol. 2 (Barcelona, 1885), p. 292. In Galicia, Catalan penetration of the salted-fish trade paved the way for cornering the market on wines and calico textiles (L. Alonso Alvarez, *Industrialización*). Despite the author's anticolonial rhetoric, his own data would suggest that Catalan exports to Galicia exceeded imports (p. 82). Even in Lower Andalusia, the competitiveness of Catalan wines and brandies succeeded in opening the market for exports. C. Martínez Shaw, "Las relaciones económicas entre Cataluña y la Baja Andalucía, siglo XVIII: Un intento de interpretación," *Actas del I Congreso de Historia de Andalucía: Andalucía moderna (siglo XVIII),* vol. 1 (Córdoba, 1978), pp. 347–356.

18. G. Myrdal, *Economic Theory and Underdeveloped Regions* (London, 1957).

19. P. Vilar shows that luxury crafts were much more important in that region than in the rest of Castile. See his "Estructuras. Algunas lecciones del catastro de la Ensenada," in *Hidalgos, amotinados y guerrilleros* (Barcelona, 1982), pp. 63–92.

20. It would seem that changes in world trade played a more important role in the destructuralization of the Catalan economy, especially of its export sector, than the loss of the American colonies. The latter development did not seem to have the impact that has been previously alleged, although its immediate effects were, of course, consider-

able. For a reconsideration of this topic see L. Prados de la Escosura, "La independencia hispanoamericana y sus consecuencias económicas en España: una estimación provisional," *Moneda y Crédito* 163 (1982): 49–69.

21. See the works of A. M. Piuz and B. Veyrassat-Herren in *L'industrialisation en Europe au XIXe siècle: cartographie et typologie.* Lyon, 1970 (Paris, 1972); J. F. Bergier, *Naissance et croissance de la Suisse industrielle* (Bern, 1974); and B. Veyrassat, *Négociants et fabricants dans l'industrie cotonnière suisse, 1760–1840* (Lausanne, 1982).

22. For the displacement of traditional fabrics by those of the new fibers see D. R. Ringrose, "Madrid and the Castilian Economy," *Journal of European Economic History* 2 (1981): 481–490. Interesting data are also presented in X. Carmona, "Producción textil rural e actividades marítimo-pesqueiras na Galicia, 1750–1905" (Ph.D. diss., Universidad de Santiago, 1983), and in Ma. T. Pérez Picazo, "El comercio lorquino en la transición del Antiguo al Nuevo régimen, 1780–1850," *Areas* 2 (1982): 43–69.

23. For an estimate of contraband see L. Prados de la Escosura, "El comercio exterior de España, 1790–1830: una reconsideración," *Hacienda Pública Española* 55 (1978): 339–349.

24. J. Nadal, "The Failure of the Industrial Revolution in Spain, 1830–1913," in C. M. Cipolla, ed., *The Fontana Economic History of Europe* vol. 4, 2 (London, 1973), pp. 611–614.

25. According to Mitchell's data for Switzerland, the number of spindles, which had risen from 900,000 to 1,350,000 between 1852 and 1861, declined to 1 million in 1867.

26. For data on the wool industry see J. M. Benaul Berenguer, "Notes sobre la industrialització a Sabadell, 1780–1898," *Arrahona* 12 (1981): 55–78; G. Ranzato, "Industrializzazione spontanea e liberal-democrazia: il caso della 'Manchester catalana,'" *Rivista di Storia Contemporanea* 3 (1982): 399–433, and *Sudditi operosi e cittadini inerti: sopravivenze della società di antico regime nell'industrializzazione di una città catalana* (Milan, 1984).

27. J. Maluquer de Motes, "La estructura del sector algodonero de Cataluña durante la primera etapa de la industrialización, 1832–1861," *Hacienda Pública Española* 38 (1981): 133–148.

28. On the dynamics of demand see N. Sánchez-Albornoz, "El consumo de textiles en España, 1860–1890: primera aproximación," *Hacienda Pública Española* 69 (1981): 229–235; L. Prados de la Escosura, "Producción y consumo de tejidos en España, 1800–1913: primeros resultados," in G. Anes, L. Rojo, and P. Tedde, eds., *Historia económica y pensamiento social* (Madrid, 1983), pp. 455–471.

29. F. Sala Serra, "¿Exceso de producción o consumo deficiente?" *Boletín Oficial del Comité Industrial Sedero* (1936): 369–371.

30. V. Zamagni, *Industrializzazione e squilibri regionali in Italia* (Bologna, 1978), pp. 193–200.

31. C. Sudrià, "Desarrollo industrial y subdesarrollo bancario en Cataluña, 1844–1950," *Investigaciones Económicas* 18 (1981): 137–176.

32. W. G. Hoffman, *The Growth of Industrial Economies* (Manchester, 1958). In reality, Hoffman's assertions derive from a series of gross simplifications. Such industries as paper, graphic arts, and chemical, which chiefly produce consumer goods, are omitted, and the metal-transforming industry, which increasingly produces consumer goods, is

classified as a capital-goods industry. See S. Kuznets, *Modern Economic Growth*, pp. 141–142. In any event, Hoffman's general argument is perfectly valid for the nineteenth century and even for the twentieth, wherever the rise of income has been late and slow and where a systematic expansion of family consumption has not gotten under way.

33. J. Nadal, "Catalunya, la fàbrica de España (1833–1936)," in *Cataluña en la España moderna* (Barcelona, 1983), pp. 28–41.

34. J. Nadal, A. Carreras, C. Sudrià, and I have reconstructed basic energy data sets for Catalonia in the unpublished work "Producció i consum d'energia en el creixement econòmic modern: el cas català." The data presented in Graph 9.2 derive from Mercè Borràs Roca, "La indústria tèxtil llanera de Terrassa, 1900–1930" (Master's thesis, University of Barcelona, 1973), pp. 60–64 and 69–70.

35. J. B. Say, *De la Inglaterra y de los ingleses* (Madrid, 1817), p. 46; D. S. Landes, *The Unbound Prometheus: Technological Change and Industrial Development in Western Europe from 1750 to the Present* (Cambridge, Mass., 1969), pp. 226–230.

36. A. Carreras, "El aprovechamiento de la energía hidráulica en Cataluña, 1840–1920: una aproximación a su estudio," *Revista de Historia Económica* 1, 2 (1983): 31–63. According to my own data, the Catalan electric system had to import hydraulic energy starting in 1919, first from Aragón and then from Andorra.

37. References to this topic are abundant from the end of the eighteenth century on. For a clear assessment of the issue see J. A. Vandellós, "Les nostres indústries: les dificultats de la indústria farinera," *Economía i Finances* 11 (1928): 1–2.

38. The struggle against unemployment is always an important element of labor movements, and Catalonia was no exception. Evidence for worker resistance to labor-saving innovations abounds from the second half of the nineteenth century through the first third of the twentieth century.

39. R. Garrabou, *Enginyers industrials, modernització econòmica i burguesia a Catalunya, 1850 inicis del segle XX* (Barcelona, 1982).

40. This has been the subject of debate and should be argued even more, although for the purposes of this discussion, the engineering industries are as or more important than the iron-and-steel industries. See A. Gómez Mendoza, *Ferrocarriles y cambio económico en España, 1855–1913* (Madrid, 1982), and F. Comín, "Comentarios en torno al ferrocarril y al crecimiento económico español entre 1855 y 1931," *Revista de Historia Económica* 1 (1983)1: 181–196.

41. This situation had its roots in the distant past and brought about the stagnation of the metal-transforming sector. According to the entrepreneur Ferrer y Vidal, "Catalonia is able to produce everything required for industrial production from the steam engine to the last loom, but these goods can be imported from abroad so cheaply that Spanish firms simply cannot compete." See *Información sobre el derecho diferencial de bandera y sobre las aduanas exigibles a los hierros, el carbón de piedra y los algodones . . . por la Comisión nombrada . . . en . . . 1865. IV. Algodones* (Madrid 1867), p. 251.

42. The free trader, Felix de Bona, offered some interesting observations in this regard at the Madrid Society for Economic Policy on December 17, 1857: "Gentlemen, the workers of Catalonia are the most enlightened I have ever seen . . . because vast opportunities exist in Catalonia for both education and wealth. Yes, gentlemen, Catalan workers are rich. Except at their workplaces, they dress like us. On Sundays, they stroll along the Rambla with curled hair and the majority of them wear patent leather boots

and gloves. And there in that enlightened working class is precisely where socialism is dangerous." See *La Tribuna de los Economistas,* vol. 4, 12, pp. 341–343.

43. The wages received by highway workers in a great many provinces in 1859 attests to this. See J. Nadal, *La población española, siglos XVI a XX* (Barcelona, 1973), p. 194. A spinner's wage in 1867 in Vergara was 9 reales compared with 14 in Vilanova i la Geltrú, as cited in *Información sobre el derecho diferencial de bandera,* pp. 255–256. According to an industrialist from Guipúzcoa, named Arbulú, the explanation is that "the skill of Catalan workers is such that they produce more than in our provinces" (ibid).

44. Toward the middle of the nineteenth century there was little difference between the wages of male and female spinners and very little difference between that of male and female weavers. This does not mean, however, that access to higher-paying jobs was equal for both sexes. See I. Cerdà, *Teoría general de la urbanización,* vol. 1, reedited (Barcelona, 1968), pp. 642–644; see also Juan Sallarés y Plá, *El trabajo de las mujeres y de los niños: estudios sobre las condiciones actuales* (Sabadell, 1893), p. 33. According to Sallarés, "the labor of women in large Spanish industries, the cotton industry for example, is equivalent to that of men and in many industries, wages for piece work are the same for both sexes" (p. 33).

45. By 1930 female workers in the textile and apparel industries constituted at least 10% of the total active population of Catalonia.

46. J. Playá, *Estado y estadística de la industria mecánica y eléctrica en la provincia de Barcelona* (Barcelona, 1913).

47. Electrification took place in Catalonia in an atmosphere of fierce competition, as opposed to the monopoly conditions that existed in the rest of Spain. This competition between electric companies encouraged the emergence of new industries and the vigorous expansion of old ones. See J. Maluquer de Motes, "Cataluña y el País Vasco en la industria eléctrica española, 1901–1935," in *Industrialización y nacionalismo: análisis comparativos* (Barcelona, 1984). The low electricity prices that resulted were exceedingly important for new industries of both medium and high energy usage.

48. R. Roehl, "French Industrialization: A Reconsideration," *Explorations in Economic History* 13 (1976): 233–281.

10.

THE BASQUE PROVINCES AND THE WORLD MARKET, 1900–1930*

PEDRO FRAILE
Trinity University

1. INTRODUCTION

THE ROLE OF the Basque Provinces in the industrialization of Spain is one of the most controversial topics in that nation's economic history. An intense political debate surrounds the economic policies of the Restoration (1874–1931)—policies that cut Spain off from the world market and led to an industrial polarization that favored the Basque and Catalonian regions. Many significant studies have also focused on the impact of external trade on the Basque region during the iron-ore export boom, that is, from the end of the last Carlist War (1874) until the turn of the century.[1] Conversely, the international aspects of the Basque economy during the three turbulent decades (1900–1930) have received very little attention.[2]

The extreme protectionist policies of the Restoration, which succeeded in severing Basque links to the world market, were imposed at precisely the time when international trade in steel products and capital goods was reaching a high point. The increase of these imports benefited not only the large suppliers of manufactured goods, such as Great Britain and Germany, but also less industrialized nations. Peripheral regions of Europe such as central Sweden and northern Italy which, like the Basque Provinces, had traditionally exchanged raw materials for British and German manufactures, now took advantage of this new trade. The growing participation of industrial products in the world market contributed substantially to the transformation of the "export

*I would like to thank Professor Juan Hernández Andréu of the Universidad Complutense de Madrid for his critical reading of this essay.

base" in these areas.[3] By 1930, central Sweden and northern Italy had made a transition from being suppliers of raw materials to being important exporters of industrial goods. In these regions, participation in world trade appears to have induced both diversified industrial growth and the adoption and production of advanced technology.

With regard to the economic experience of peripheral European areas—areas similar to the industrialized regions of Spain—this chapter examines the relationship between industrial development and external trade in the Spanish Basque Provinces. The following conclusions will be offered: (1) that the lack of active participation in world trade between 1900 and 1930 deprived the Basque Provinces and the rest of Spain of access to thriving markets for manufactured goods; and (2) that the experience of some regions of the European Periphery points to a relationship between the activities of the "leading export sector" and industrial growth.[4] In addition, the close relationship between external trade and industrial growth in these regions casts serious doubts on the universal validity of the Prebisch-Singer theory, according to which participation in foreign markets with changing technology produces a purely negative effect on underdeveloped countries.

2. THE TRANSFORMATION OF THE BASQUE EXPORT BASE

The mineral export phase of Basque economic growth culminated in 1899. The initial success of the Bessemer converter in British steel mills in the 1850s was followed by the discovery that the new method was viable only with the nonphosphorous ores found in the English region of Cleveland. Consequently, the scarcity of these ores led British manufacturers to make direct worldwide investments in order to assure themselves an adequate supply.[5] The end of the last Carlist War saw a spectacular rise in the export of Basque iron ore to Spain's British markets. Exports increased tenfold during the last decade of the century, reaching a maximum of 5.5 million tons in 1898.[6] From that year on, the ten-year export averages decreased progressively until they became fixed at 1 million tons by the beginning of the Great Depression.[7]

With the contraction of exports, the entire Basque mining economy entered into sudden decline, and the region lost its privileged position as an international supplier of iron ore. The mining labor force fell from 12,000 in 1913 to 4,500 in 1932.[8] As will be seen later, although the Basque link with the British market remained solid, other European and Mediterranean regions began to capture greater shares of the world iron-ore market.

Owing to the capital accumulation generated by mining[9] and the repatriation of colonial capital after 1898,[10] the Basque region was able to reorient its export base toward the internal Spanish market. Participation in the international market—a market in which Basque products had an obvious comparative advantage—was now abandoned in favor of the national market.

Around the turn of the century, and coinciding with the period when protectionist policy was at its peak, the region embarked upon a rapid, though brief and cautious, process of industrialization: the Zorroza Mills were founded in 1890 and the Deusto Mills in 1891; the Basconia and Tubos Forjados associations were established in 1892; in 1900 the Euskalduna Company for the Construction and Repair of Ships was founded, and in 1901 Echevarría Enterprises was established; the merger of Altos Hornos de Bilbao with the Vizcaya and Iberia companies in 1902 gave rise to the firm of Altos Hornos de Vizcaya; the last substantial enterprise to be established, Babcock and Wilson, was founded in 1918.

This group of firms formed the base of the iron-and-steel industry, the most important sector of the entire Basque economy.[11] Other sectors also began to expand, though less conspicuously. In 1901 the Hidroeléctrica Ibérica Company was founded with capital from Bilbao, and in 1907 and 1918, respectively, the Hidroeléctrica Española and Sociedad General de Transportes Eléctricos Saltos del Duero were established.[12] In 1898 and 1901 the Unión Española de Explosivos and the Papelera Española were formed.

During the first thirty years of the century, the industrial growth of the Basque region, although limited, followed a course of high polarization. The concentration of new enterprises in the Basque Provinces absorbed a substantial part of the nation's productive resources. Between 1900 and 1930, more than 3,000 firms worth 2 million pesetas or more were established in Bilbao alone.[13] According to Andoni de Soraluze, of the 23,6 billion pesetas in capital, stocks, and bonds invested in Spanish enterprises : 1929, more than a quarter was Basque.[14] Basque capital accounted for 25% of all financial resources, 38% of all investments in shipbuilding, 60% in mechanical and electrical industries, 68% in shipping, and 62% in iron and steel.

In the latter branches, the most important of the Basque economy, regional concentration was especially pronounced from 1900 to 1930. During these years, the region produced 66.5% of all Spanish pig iron and 68.4% of all Spanish steel.[15] Similarly, 70%, or 355,638 of the 504,784 tons that the Spanish naval industry produced between 1902 and 1940, derived from the shipyards of the Euskalduna Company, the Sociedad Española de Construcción Naval and Beraza.[16]

In short, the rapid industrial development of the Basque Provinces ensured the region a central position in the Spanish economy. At the end of the Civil War, the area contained only 3% of the Spanish population but generated almost 6% of the gross national product.[17] Commenting on the spatial aspects of Spain's economic development during this period, Sidney Pollard states that "Spain showed some of the most clear-cut cases of downward regional multiplier in action."[18]

In spite of a vested interest in presenting Basque industrialization as a local phenomenon, it is by examining the region's international ties that one gains the best perspective on both the internal mechanisms of the region's economic growth and on the industrial development of Spain as a whole. The concentration of industry in the Basque Provinces should be studied within an international context for three reasons. First, international trade policy had, as will be seen later, a decisive effect on the Basque economy. Second, if one wishes to compare Basque economic growth with Spain's general growth by using the evolution of the metallurgical industry as an indicator,[19] an analysis of that sector's total market would be necessary, including that of the world market.[20] Third, at a time when heavy industry and capital goods were undergoing rapid change, Spain's peripheral position in this process would require that the Basque case be approached from a multiregional European perspective.

3. THE INTERNATIONAL MARKET

In his classic article about the relationship between external trade and economic development, K. Berrill states:

> National models of economic growth are unhelpful. They disguise the fact that international trade is often cheaper and easier than internal trade and that specialization between countries is often much easier and earlier than specialization between regions within a country.[21]

In the same vein, Douglass North points out the necessity of framing the analysis of regional growth in an international context and suggests that:

> For economists' purposes the concept of region should be redefined to point out that the unifying cohesion to a region, over and beyond geographic similitudes, is its development around a common export base.[22]

Accordingly, Basque industrialization gains significance when interpreted within the framework of an interrelated network of European regions—a model that I have elaborated on in a previous work.[23] What follows is a description of the model's basic characteristics and its evolution after the transition from British to German hegemony during the decade between 1910 and 1920. From the mid-nineteenth century, the tiny area formed by the southern axis of Wales and northwestern England was transformed into the European Center for the iron-and-steel industry and for the three sectors most closely related to it: coal, the engineering industry, and shipbuilding. This region held the most advanced metallurgical technology and also supplied a disproportionately large share of the world market. Toward the end of the last century, this small area produced half of all British pig iron and coal—a figure that represented one-quarter and one-third of the world total, respectively.[24] Likewise, the majority of the engineering and electrical industries of Great Britain and, for that matter, of the world, were concentrated in this area. The latter's domination of naval construction and technology also led to its almost complete control over half of Britain's external trade and to over one-third of total world trade.[25]

This region functioned as the center in an interrelated regional system that included a vast area of Europe and the Mediterranean. The southern axis of Wales and northwestern England exported technology, capital, and industrial inputs (especially coal) to peripheral European regions. The latter, on the other hand, exported raw materials (especially iron ore) to Britain. As will be seen later, some of these regions, however, were capable of changing the composition of their exports and of making a transition from being suppliers of raw materials to being exporters of industrial goods.

As was mentioned earlier, the British iron-and-steel industry made direct investments abroad in order to assure itself an adequate supply of nonphosphorous ores for its Bessemer converters. The principal suppliers were found on the European and Mediterranean fringe and included the Swedish districts of Orebro and Norbotten, the Spanish Basque Provinces, the Algerian coast, and the Italian island of Elba.

Table 10.1 shows the complementarity between British coal exports to the metallurgical regions of the Periphery on the one hand, and iron-ore exports from the Periphery to the Anglo-Welsh Center on the other. As can be seen, the peripheral regions absorbed between one-third and one-quarter of British coal and coke and, at the same time, satisfied nearly all the English demand for foreign ore.

The role of Spain, particularly of the Basque region, in this international pattern was crucial. Spain was one of the largest consumers of English and Welsh coal. Moreover, 33% of the coal purchased by Spain between 1885 and 1930 was destined for the Basque port of Bilbao.[26] On the other hand, as was

Table 10.1
Trade in Coal and Iron Ore between Great Britain and the Metallurgical Regions of the European and Mediterranean Periphery, 1885–1934 (five-year averages)

	British Exports of Coal and Coke (millions of tons)						British Imports of Iron Ore (millions of tons)					
	A Sweden	B Spain	C Italy	D Algeria	Export Totals	% (A+B+C+D)/E	A Sweden	B Spain	C Italy	D Algeria	Import Totals	% (A+B+C+D)/E
1885–89	1.9	1.3	3.1	—	25.4	24	39	3,129	48	147	3,412	98
1890–94	2.5	1.6	3.9	—	30.7	26	28	3,563	63	159	3,982	95
1895–99	3.5	1.6	3.9	0.5	36.3	26	90	4,897	123	192	5,676	93
1900–04	5.4	2.1	6.0	0.8	45.9	30	167	5,041	90	202	6,140	90
1905–09	5.4	2.5	8.0	1.0	50.9	28	235	5,160	—	407	6,817	85
1910–14	6.3	3.1	9.0	0.6	67.4	28	343	4,109	18	729	6,437	80
1915–19	3.2	1.3	4.8	1.0	39.4	25	249	4,092	7	776	6,099	84
1920–24	4.5	2.3	6.5	1.3	50.9	28	422	2,334	—	810	4,656	76
1925–30	3.1	2.1	6.2	—	47.9	26	491	2,020	—	831	4,293	78
1930–34	—	—	—	—	—	—	345	1,112	—	617	2,995	69

Sources: Great Britain, Annual Statement of the Trade of the United Kingdom with Foreign Countries and British Possessions, 1885–1950; The Economist (1887–1931).

indicated earlier, the Basque region was the main foreign supplier of iron ore to Great Britain.

Spain's predominance as an exporter of iron ore to Great Britain continued even into the 1930s, that is, forty years after the introduction of the Thomas and Siemens converters. The adoption of the latter permitted the use of phosphorous ores from regions like Lorraine in France, Sweden, and Algeria and succeeded in changing the world market for iron ore. By 1913 France (Lorraine) had become the principal exporter of ore, and Sweden was a close third behind Spain (see Table 10.2).

What were the reasons for Britain's long dependence on Spanish ore? The most immediate explanation lies in the slowness with which English industrialists transformed the technical structure of the steel sector. In comparison with other regions, such as the Ruhr, English and Welsh steelmills experienced a delay in technological development. This delay was part of a more general problem, however. The British decadence of the late nineteenth century and the Edwardian Age (1901–1910)—a period that historians call the climacteric of the English economy[27]—was the result of such factors as the caliber of entrepreneurs, the general obsolescence of the production system, and the vast international dimensions of the British economy.

Extensive British investment in foreign raw materials should also be considered when studying this decline. Albert C. Allen, one of the best analysts of the Anglo-German race for iron-and-steel supremacy, underscores the importance of Spanish mines in the rise of relative costs for the British:

Table 10.2
International Iron Ore Market, 1913
(thousands of tons)

Importers			Exporters		
	National			Total	
	Imports	Production		Exports	Production
Germany	14,019	35,940	France	10,066	19,160
United Kingdom	8,028	15,997	Spain	8,907	9,861
Belgium	4,400	149	Sweden	6,440	7,475
United States	2,594	61,980	Germany	2,613	35,940
Canada	2,110	307	Newfoundland	1,605	1,605
France	1,410	19,160	Cuba	1,582	1,582
Austria	940	3,039	Algeria	1,350	1,350

SOURCE: Great Britain, Department of Scientific and Industrial Research, Advisory Council, *Report on the Sources and Production of Iron and Other Metalliferous Ores Used in the Iron and Steel Industry* (London, 1918), p. 18.

After 1895 the cost of Spanish hematites rose sharply in Britain. Britain's commitment to acid steel-making meant that it was becoming more and more dependent on this ore. . . . In contrast, the German steel industry diversified its ore supplies by importing Swedish ore on a large scale. After the mid-1890s, Swedish minette ore mixtures were standard in Westphalia, which meant that German ore costs were slightly lower in 1906–13 than they had been in 1833–89. The divergent movement of British hematite and German basic ore costs put the British steel industry at a serious disadvantage.[28]

The Liga Vizcaína de Productores expressed the same opinion in 1909:

Almost all the iron ore produced in this province is exported to England and Germany with the distinction that the hematites and carbonate of higher quality are exported to the former country, while those of lower quality are sent to the latter. From this it can be deduced that the Germans, having foreseen that iron ore was becoming scarce, have introduced furnaces capable of processing the inferior ores, while England, with the exception of a few forward-looking factories, has continued using the old furnaces.[29]

The high price of Spanish ore and the inelastic British demand confirm both Allen's interpretation and contemporary reports. In spite of the development of "basic" methods, Basque ore prices remained stable throughout the first third of the century. The price list for "best" ore for the years 1906 to 1934 appears in Table 10.3.

In a pioneering study on iron mining in Scandinavia—a study that complements his previous work on Spanish mining—Michael Flinn has demon-

Table 10.3
F.O.B. Price of "Best"
Shipped from Bilbao, 1906–1934
(in British pounds per ton)

Year	Price	Year	Price
1906	17.00	1920	27.00
1909	12.60	1921	16.40
1912	14.00	1922	19.00
1913	14.00	1923	16.00
1914	12.60	1926	14.20
1915	14.60	1928	15.10
1916	14.60	1929	9.60
1917	18.10	1930	11.00
1918	20.00	1933	10.70
1919	29.40	1934	11.10

SOURCE: Centro Industrial de Bilbao.

strated the relative failure of the British to diversify their supply sources through direct investments in Sweden and Norway.[30] Although British companies had invested more than 5 million pounds in the exploitation of Spanish ore before World War I, they subsequently attempted to break their dependence on this ore by establishing in Scandinavia the Magnetic Iron Mountain Smelting, the Swedish Central Railway, the New Gellivara, the Northern of Europe Railway, and the Anglo-Scandinavian Steamship, all enterprises devoted to mining.[31] In spite of these extraordinary efforts, the stated objective was not achieved. *The Economist* expressed its concern over British dependence on Spanish ore in the following terms:

> Failing to find elsewhere the supplies they were in search of, they [Welsh and English steel-makers] have spent enormous sums in developing the rare mineral resources of the North of Spain—perhaps the most revolutionary and unstable country of Europe, and therefore the country of all others where their investments were likely to be unsafe.[32]

Conversely, Spain obtained clearly positive results from this commercial relationship. The opportunity to sell mineral resources at high prices—mineral resources that were being progressively displaced by new technological methods—led to a large capital accumulation in the Basque Provinces. In addition, the region enjoyed a transfer of advanced technology at minimum cost.

Until the beginning of the twentieth century, Basque industry's rapid absorption of foreign technology, especially British, provided the area with an important role in the regional European hierarchy. Acting as a link with the "central" regions, the Basque Provinces channeled the diffusion of late-nineteenth-century British technology. This role—fundamental in a regional interpretation of economic development[33]—was carried out in innumerable personal contacts, direct assessments, inspection trips, and joint projects between Spanish and foreign technicians, all of which is documented in the region's business archives.[34] The experience of the naval and armament industry, presented by C. Trevilock,[35] was repeated successfully in steel and heavy industry. González Portilla has also demonstrated how this technological diffusion resulted in an intensification of iron-and-steel exports at competitive prices.[36]

This absorption of technology was interrupted when the Basque region was cut off from the international market. Technological contacts decreased drastically during the first decade of the century and almost disappeared after World War I. Between 1900 and 1930, however, the diffusion of technological innovations continued throughout the rest of the European Periphery with the exception of the war years. In relation to the international diffusion of steel technology, two of the best specialists in the field have stated:

> In the modern process of technological change, each participant receives from the world at large far more than he gives. Communication, therefore, is the matter of first importance. Throughout the twentieth century—to a large extent even in wartime—the communication network linking Western Europe, Britain, and America has been maintained in a tolerable state of repair. . . . [The] degree of competition and communication between national units has generally been sufficient to join them all to a single international gridwork, with a remarkable resistance to the occasional indolence of industrialists and the recurrent oppressions of politicians.[37]

The rise of protectionism and state intervention that followed the free-trade period of the nineteenth century constitutes the traditional framework for analyzing the European economy between 1900 and 1930. Evidence, nevertheless, shows a growing intra-European commerce during this period, especially in the sectors most fundamental to the Basque economy. Trade in iron, steel, machinery, and capital goods followed an upward trend until the depression.

4. EXPORTS AND INDUSTRIALIZATION

Throughout the first third of the twentieth century, the export sector was an important key to the continued industrial expansion and diversification of the European Periphery, with the exception of the Basque region. The Swedish electric-engineering industry transformed that country into a net exporter of industrial goods before the end of the century,[38] and the industrial products of Liguria and Lombardy were already serious competitors, even in Great Britain, before World War I.[39] Italian shipbuilders, most of whom were located in the coastal regions of Liguria (Genoa, Savona, and Sestri Ponente), ranked seventh in world production and improved that position during the postwar period.[40] Between 1927 and 1940 these shipbuilders exported more than half of their output, that is, an annual average of 40,000 tons.[41] In like manner, Swedish industry achieved a strong position in the international market for naval construction; electric machinery; and basic products like chemicals, iron, and steel.[42] Swedish rolled steel, for example, penetrated all of Europe during this period, as well as markets as far away as Latin America.[43]

At the end of the 1920s, foreign markets were fundamental for these industrial regions that, like the Spanish Basque Provinces, had begun the industrialization process while in the European Periphery. Italy was the fifth exporter of industrial goods in the world and the sixth in chemical products. In the same vein, Sweden occupied twelfth place among exporters of both industrial and chemical goods.[44]

In spite of an increase in customs restrictions on trade,[45] European imports of metallurgical products rose from 4.77 to 7.90 million tons between 1913 and 1929.[46] Germany, for example, increased its steel imports from 300,000 tons in 1913 to between 1.8 and 2.2 million in the 1920s.[47] As is evident in Table 10.4 and Graph 10.1, iron-and-steel sales to Great Britain, far from declining, continued to rise except during the war years. Measured in 1913 prices, the value of British iron-and-steel imports increased from between 10 and 12 million pounds annually before the war to 19 million during the 1920s. In volume, these imports corresponded to more than a million tons before the war and 2.3 million in the 1920s, peaking at 4.4 million tons in 1927.[48]

Table 10.4 also demonstrates that foreign iron-and-steel sales in the North American market—considered by many to be the prototype of twentieth-century industrial protectionism—decreased between 1900 and World War I (see Graph 10.2) but increased considerably during the 1920s, reaching very high levels during the pre–World War II period. Although American imports were low in comparison to the volume of the United States internal market, this additional demand had important effects on certain foreign suppliers.

Table 10.4
British and North American Imports
of Iron-and-Steel Products, 1900–1935
(five-year averages in thousands of tons)

Years	British	North American
1900–04	1,096	—
1905–09	1,161	437
1910–14	1,792	290
1915–19	658	173
1920–24	1,471	390
1925–29	3,312	760
1930–35	1,806	367

SOURCE: Great Britain, *Annual Statement of the Trade of the United Kingdom with Foreign Countries and British Possessions*, London, 1900–1935; United States Department of Commerce, *Foreign Commerce and Navigation of the United States*, Washington, D.C., 1905–1935.

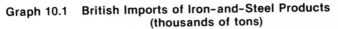

**Graph 10.1   British Imports of Iron–and–Steel Products
(thousands of tons)**

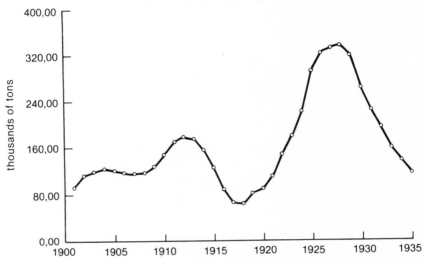

SOURCES: Great Britain, *Annual Statement of the Trade of the United Kingdom with
Foreign Countries and British Possessions, 1900–1935;* United States Department of
Commerce, *Foreign Commerce and Navigation of the United States, 1905–1935;* Project
"Mulhall," Department of Economics, University of Texas, Archives GB and US.

Referring to the impact of the North American market on the Swedish iron-
and-steel industry during this period, E. F. Söderland states:

> Cold-rolled steel was among the most important export items, accounting for 30
> to 50 percent of the aggregate value of American imports of Swedish iron and
> steel, and roughly the same proportion of Sweden's total exports of cold-rolled
> products. American demand must thus have played a large part in stimulating
> the industry's interest in this type of steel processing. Wire rods and drawn wire
> were also important items. For Lancashire iron the U.S.A. remained the largest
> market.[49]

Expansion of international trade in iron-and-steel products, then, was not
limited to Europe. In Latin America, for example, steel imports doubled between 1913 and 1929. In addition, while the market shares of principal
suppliers, like the United States, Great Britain, and Germany, tended to diminish over time, that of the small producers such as Austria, Sweden, Czech-
oslovakia, and Poland increased considerably, especially in the supply of the
larger Latin American countries like Argentina, Brazil, and Mexico.[50]
The expansion of the international market affected not only steel but all

**Graph 10.2   American Imports of Iron-and-Steel Products
(thousands of tons)**

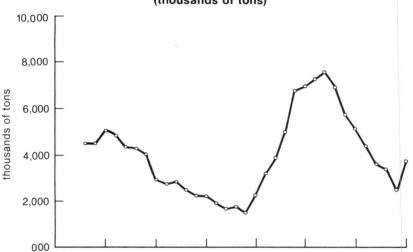

SOURCES: Great Britain, *Annual Statement of the Trade of the United Kingdom with
Foreign Countries and British Possessions, 1900–1935;* United States Department of
Commerce, *Foreign Commerce and Navigation of the United States, 1905–1935;* Project
"Mulhall," Department of Economics, University of Texas, Archives GB and US.

industrial products as well. Measured at 1913 constant prices, world trade
(imports and exports) in manufactured goods rose from an annual average of
$9.6 billion in 1901–1905 to $11.8 billion in 1906–1910 and $14.5 billion in
1911–1913. This volume fell, naturally, during the war and the postwar crisis
but rose again to $15.8 billion during 1926–1930.[51]

The expansion of the European international market for manufactures—a
market to which the Basque region was advantageously related—is presented
in Table 10.5, which shows the imports of each country in 1913 prices. As can
be observed, the high level of industrial imports was interrupted only by
World War I and the postwar crisis.

W. A. Lewis has pointed out that there was no sharp and protracted crisis in
the world market for manufactures until the 1930s.[52] In contrast to raw
materials, the decline of which began in the postwar period, international
prices of industrial goods (and corresponding terms of exchange) remained
firm until 1930–1931.[53] The calculations of Lewis and the League of Nations
tend to corroborate the hypothesis that the peripheral countries of Europe had
an opportunity to develop an export-based industrial strategy until the 1930s.

The case of Great Britain as an importer of industrial products illustrates

Table 10.5
Imports of European Manufactures, 1896–1930
(annual averages in millions of tons)

	Ger.	G.B.	Fr.	Ita.	Belg.	Holl.	Swed.	Switz.	Total
1896–1900	183	386	168	85	—	177	52	81	1,132
1901–1905	215	535	214	120	109	250	58	96	1,597
1906–1910	286	488	282	218	138	312	65	122	1,908
1911–1913	328	578	365	228	159	358	71	135	2,222
1913	338	603	344	226	169	382	76	134	2,272
1921–1925	228	431	187	99	109	172	80	84	1,390
1926–1929	320	676	210	162	131	248	117	131	1,995
1930	293	716	337	175	178	290	151	150	2,290

SOURCE: League of Nations, *Industrialization and Foreign Trade,* Series of League of Nation Publications, II.
Economic and Financial, 1945, II. A. 10 (Geneva, 1945), pp. 160–161.
NOTE: Values are given in 1913 prices.

this situation. As can be seen in Graph 10.3, British imports of machinery, electrical materials, transport equipment, and other capital goods remained constant at an annual average of 18 million pounds (1913 prices) between

Graph 10.3   British Imports of Machinery and Capital Goods
(millions of constant 1913 pounds)

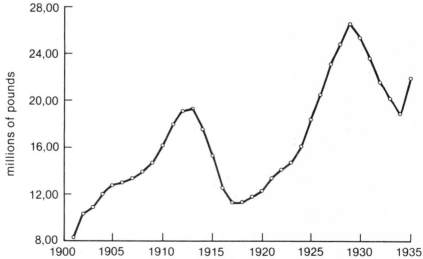

SOURCES: Great Britain, *Annual Statement of the Trade of the United Kingdom with Foreign Countries and British Possessions, 1900-1935;* Project "Mulhall," Department of Economics, University of Texas, Archives GB, Italy, and Sweden.

NOTE: Values of the series have been "smoothed out" by using five-year moving averages.

1900 and 1935, reaching an annual average of 35 million pounds during 1925–1929.[54] In contrast to the traditional characterization of the United Kingdom as an importer of raw materials only, evidence shows that Great Britain was, during the first third of the century, an active market for the industrial products of peripheral countries like Italy and Sweden. Table 10.6 and Graph 10.4 show the rise of Italian and Swedish exports of machinery and capital goods to Great Britain until the depression.

Given this international context, how did Spanish industrial centers react to the expansion of demand for their products? The fact is that Spanish industrial exports never took off. Measured in 1913 dollars, the annual export average of Spanish manufactures rose from $46 million in 1901–1905 to $50 million in 1911–1913, declined to $45 million in 1921–1925, and rose once again to $50 million in 1926–1929.[55] While the industrial regions of Sweden and Italy tripled their total exports between 1900 and 1930, Spanish exports grew by only 8%. Exports of Basque pig iron, which played such an important role in the first stages of the region's industrialization, are evidence of this tendency to lag: an annual average of 35,507 tons of pig iron exported in 1900–1909 declined to 30,153 tons in 1910–1919 and finally to 5,424 tons in 1920–1929.[56] During the period 1926 to 1929, per capita exports of manufactures amounted to $29.00 in Sweden, $10.00 in Italy, and only $3.50 in Spain.[57]

This reorientation of Basque industry toward the home market is tied to the

Table 10.6
Italian and Swedish Exports of Machinery
and Capital Goods to Great Britain,
1900–1935
(thousands of pounds
at constant 1913 prices)

Years	Swedish Exports	Italian Exports
1900–04	250	—
1905–09	204	251
1910–14	244	918
1915–19	352	190
1920–24	340	463
1925–29	544	545
1930–35	591	169

SOURCES: Great Britain, *Annual Statement of the Trade of the United Kingdom with Foreign Countries and British Possessions, 1900–1935*; Project "Mulhall," Department of Economics University of Texas.
NOTE: Figures represent five-year averages.

206   *Pedro Fraile*

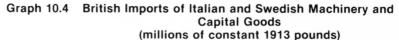

**Graph 10.4   British Imports of Italian and Swedish Machinery and
Capital Goods
(millions of constant 1913 pounds)**

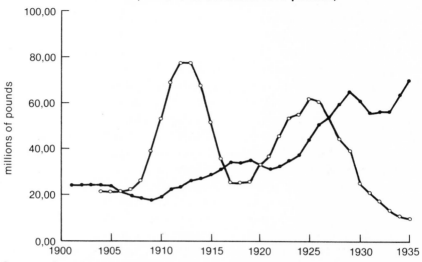

SOURCES: Great Britain, *Annual Statement of the Trade of the United Kingdom with
Foreign Countries and British Possessions, 1900–1935;* Project "Mulhall," Department of
Economics, University of Texas, Archives GB, Italy, and Sweden.

NOTE: Values of the series have been "smoothed out" by using five–year moving averages.

autarchic movement which began during the last years of the nineteenth
century and translated into the growing tariff isolation of Spain's iron-and-
steel market. Spanish protectionism increased progressively with the tariffs of
1891, 1906, 1922, and 1928, and indeed achieved its purpose. While in
Sweden and Italy steel imports during this period reached an annual average
of more than 40% of total internal supply,[58] Spanish iron imports were less
than 4%, and steel imports were only 17%.[59]

   This self-sufficiency led, logically, to a greater and greater divergence between Basque prices and those prevailing in the international market. During
the period 1900 to 1930, for example, Spaniards paid on average more than
twice the international price for pig iron.[60] The difference for rails was over
35%; for T bars, more than 50%; and for steel plates, 80%.[61] These differences
are greater if one considers that the British international prices used for the
above comparison were not the lowest prices on the world market during this
period. A comparison with German prices would produce an even wider
variance.

5. CONCLUSIONS

After World War I, industrial exports did not experience the same crisis as that of raw materials. The term that W. A. Lewis assigned the interwar period—"The Greatest Depression"[62]—refers more to raw materials than to manufactured goods. For Europe, this difference was crucial. Markets for industrial imports remained open until the 1930s, and international demand for manufactured goods had a favorable effect on some of the peripheral regions of Europe.

Within this context, the experience of Basque industrialization suggests that the strategy of economic autarchy implied a serious risk. Although the policy was designed to develop industrial sectors that would otherwise have collapsed when confronted with the lower costs and more advanced technology of foreign competitors, it also deprived the production system of the advantages of specialization and the economies of scale made possible by a larger market. In addition, the traditional objection to the indiscriminate entrance of underdeveloped economies into the international market is based, in part, on the intransmissible nature of the technology of advanced countries.[63] However, this was not the situation of Spain in the first third of the century, when the technology of the Center was accessible and adoptable. On the contrary, it could be argued that, in contrast to the Prebisch-Singer theory, participation in an international market with changing technology not only did not hinder the export position of the Basque region; it also placed British producers at a disadvantage with their German competitors, owing to the inelastic demand (with respect to price) of Spanish ore in the English market.

In view of the above, it is important to ask to what extent the protectionist policy—undertaken in order to foster industrial development in the Basque region—was beneficial for national industrialization. The very mechanisms of regional accumulation, protection, and self-sufficiency not only had adverse effects on other regions—the case of Castile is instructive and is examined later in Chapter 13 of this book by Sánchez-Albornoz—but also brought about the rupture of two very important links: on the one hand, the technological link between innovative European centers and the Spanish metallurgical industry; on the other, the commercial link between Spanish producers and international demand. In conclusion, what one Spanish historian called "the plans of Manchester" to impose a "destructive liberal policy"[64] on Spain could have been responsible for providing the incipient industries of the Basque and Catalan regions with better access to new technology; higher competitive levels; more specialization; and, finally, economies of scale derived from larger markets.

NOTES

1. See esp. Manuel González Portilla, *La formación de la sociedad capitalista en el País Vasco, 1876–1913* (San Sebastián, 1981), and Valerie Shaw, "Exportaciones y despegue económico; el mineral de hierro de Vizcaya, la región de la ría de Bilbao y algunas de sus implicaciones para España," *Moneda y Crédito* 142 (1977): 87–114.

2. Recently, Juan Hernández Andréu, in his *Depresión económica en España* (Madrid, 1980), has investigated the international links of the Spanish economy during the Great Depression and has analyzed the relation of certain sectors—steel, transportation, textiles, and agriculture—to world markets. These sectoral and regional analyses, however, tend to focus on local aspects of the development process. For more information on this topic see Joseph Harrison, "Los orígenes del industrialismo moderno en el País Vasco," *Hacienda Pública Española* 55 (1978): 209–222, and "La industria pesada, el estado y el desarrollo en el País Vasco, 1876–1936," *Información Comercial Española* 598 (1983): 31–32.

3. The concept of the export base is very common in regional analysis and assumes that external demand is crucial to economic development. The export base is made up of those activities that are oriented outside the region and is usually measured according to relative levels of employment in export activities. Geographers and urban planners of the 1950s developed this concept, and today the export base is one of the most widely used instruments in regional economics. See Harry Richardson, *Regional Economics* (Urbana, Ill., 1979), pp. 84–92; for the historical origins of this concept see Richard Andrews, "The Mechanics of the Urban Economic Base: Historical Development of the Base Concept," *Land Economics* 29 (1953): 161–167.

4. Charles P. Kindleberger, *Economic Development* (New York, 1965), pp. 304–305.

5. Only within the British Empire (Ceylon, India, South Africa, Natal, Canada, Saint Lucia, Australia, New Zealand, and Tasmania) did Great Britain continue the direct exploitation of iron-ore mines. Great Britain, Royal Commission on Mining Royalties, *Fourth Report on Mining Royalties* (c. 6977), (London, 1893), pp. 249 and 86–92.

6. Antonio Arregui Mendia, *Orientaciones generales para el desarrollo y prosperidad de la Provincia de Vizcaya* (Bilbao, 1934), p. 73.

7. Ibid.

8. Ibid., p. 74.

9. The accumulation of mining capital under local control between 1901 and 1913 reached 316 million pesetas. See González Portilla, *La formación*, p. 80. In 1892 the British consul in Bilbao estimated that 16 of the 17 million pounds paid for exported minerals remained in the Basque Provinces. Great Britain, Foreign Office, *Diplomatic and Consular Report on Trade and Finance. Spain. Report for the Year 1891 on the Trade of Bilbao* (London, 1892), pp. 11–12.

10. Of the 1.6 million pesetas estimated by Juan Sardá in *La política monetaria y las fluctuaciones de la economía española en el siglo XIX* (Madrid, 1948) as the total amount of repatriated capital, a very large part was invested in the Basque Provinces. See Harrison, "Orígenes del industrialismo," pp. 212–213.

11. References to Basque industrialization during these years abound. In addition to those already cited, see, for example, Julio Lazurtegui, "El comercio, la industria y la navegación en el País Vasco," in *Geografía general del País Vasco-Navarro,* Francisco Carreras y Candi, ed. (Barcelona, 1917), pp. 744–746; Ignacio Olabarri Gortázar, *Relaciones laborales en Vizcaya, 1890–1936* (Durango, 1978), pp. 30–44; Juan Pablo Fusi, *Política obrera en el País Vasco, 1880–1923* (Madrid, 1975), pp. 15–31; and Juan de Begoña, *La Ría que vale millones: Cincuenta años de la Ría de Bilbao, 1901–1951* (Bilbao, 1952).

12. Manuel Aznar, *Un siglo en la vida del Banco de Bilbao* (Bilbao, 1975), pp. 300–302.

13. Julio Lazurtegui, *Plus Ultra Aurrera: Estudio presentado al Concurso de la Caja de Ahorros Vizcaína del 30 de octubre de 1933* (Bilbao, 1934), p. 111.

14. A. de Soraluze, *Riqueza y economía del País Vasco* (Buenos Aires, 1945), pp. 175–180.

15. Alfonso Churruca, *Minería, industria y comercio del País Vasco* (San Sebastián, 1951), pp. 91–102.

16. Summary of naval construction and "Ships launched," *Papeles del Centro Industrial de Bilbao.*

17. The population figure is 3.81% according to Amparo Almarcha et al., *Estadísticas básicas de España, 1900–1970* (Madrid, 1975), p. 4. The figure for the gross national product, on the other hand, is 5.9% as reported in Milagros García Crespo et al., *La economía vasca durante el franquismo: Crecimiento y crisis de la economía vasca, 1936–1980* (Bilbao 1981), vol. 4, p. 100. This figure, however, is undocumented; the authors cite an anonymous source and the figure can be considered only indicative.

18. Sidney Pollard, *Peaceful Conquest: The Industrialization of Europe, 1760–1910* (Oxford, 1981), p. 243.

19. This method of regional analysis is known as shift-share. For a historical application of shift-share see A. P. Thirlwall, "A Measure of the Proper Distribution of Industry," *Oxford Economic Papers* 19 (1967): 46–58, and L. D. Ashby, "Changes in Regional Industry Structure: A Comment," *Urban Studies* 7 (1970): 298–304.

20. This variation of shift-share analysis—the inclusion of the whole international market in a regional/national comparison—has been proposed by David B. Houston, "The Shift and Share Analysis of Regional Growth: A Critique," *Southern Economic Journal* 33 (1967): 576.

21. K. Berrill, "International Trade and the Rate of Economic Growth," *Economic History Review* 12 (1960): 351.

22. Douglas C. North, "Location Theory and Regional Economic Growth," *Journal of Political Economy* 63 (1955): 257.

23. Pedro Fraile, "La periferia siderometalúrgica europea: una nota histórica sobre el País Vasco," *Información Comercial Española* 591 (1982).

24. Ibid., p. 85.

25. Patrick Fitzgerald, *Industrial Combination in England* (London, 1927), pp. 167 and 225–226.

26. *Boletín Minero* (Bilbao) 2 (October 1927): 8; Great Britain, Foreign Office, Annual Series (1884–1904), *Consular Report, Spain, Trade of the District of Bilbao, London*; Churruca, *Minería*, p. 105; and *The Economist* (Commercial History and Review, 1887–1931).

27. The British decline at the end of the nineteenth century is one of the most debated topics in European economics history. There is a substantial bibliography on this topic, and there are always new contributions. See, for example, Sidney Pollard, *The Development of the British Economy, 1914–1950* (London, 1962); D. H. Aldcroft, "The Entrepreneur in the British Economy," *Economic History Review* 17 (1964): 113–134; Harry W. Richardson, "Retardation in Britain's Industrial Growth, 1870–1913," *Scottish Journal of Political Economy* 12 (1965): 125–149; and Donald McCloskey, *Enterprise and Trade in Victorian Britain* (London, 1981).

28. R. C. Allen, "International Competition in Iron and Steel, 1850–1913," *Journal of Economic History* 39 (1979): 929.

29. Memoria de la Liga Vizcaína de Productores, *Papeles del Centro Industrial de Bilbao.*

30. Michael Flinn, "Scandinavian Iron Ore Mining and the British Steel Industry, 1870–1914," *Scandinavian Economic History Review* 2 (1954): 31–46.

31. Ibid., pp. 33–39.

32. *The Economist* (Commercial History and Review, 1880), March 12, 1881, p. 39.

33. See, for example, Brian Berry, "Hierarchical Diffusion: The Basis of Developmental Filtering and Spread in a System of Growth Centers," in *Growth Centers in Regional Economic Development,* N. M. Hansen, ed. (New York, 1972), pp. 103–108, and John Friedmann, "A General Theory of Polarized Development," in *Growth Centers in Regional Economic Development,* N. M. Hansen, ed. (New York, 1972), pp. 82–107.

34. During the last two decades of the nineteenth century alone, the Altos Hornos de Bilbao Company received technical assistance from more than thirty foreign technicians (Altos Hornos de Bilbao, Libros de Actas del Consejo, 1882–1902). Moreover, references to this type of contact are common in the local economic press, such as the *Boletín Minero e Industrial.*

35. Clive Trevilock, "British Armament and European Industrialization, 1890–1914," *Economic History Review* 26 (1973): 254–272.

36. González Portilla, "La formación," p. 101.

37. Norman Pounds and William Parker, *Coal and Steel in Western Europe* (Bloomington, Ind., 1957), p. 257.

38. Lennart Jörberg, *Growth and Fluctuations of Swedish Industry, 1869–1912* (Stockholm, 1961), p. 79.

39. Great Britain, Tariff Commission, *Report on Engineering Industry* (London, 1909), vol. 2, para. 749.

40. League of Nations, *Shipbuilding* (1927), pp. 19–21.

41. Confederazione Generale dell'Industria Italiana, *L'Industria Italiana alla Metà del Secolo XX* (1953), pp. 383–391.

42. League of Nations, Economic and Financial, *Mechanical Engineering* (1927), p. 149.

43. United Nations, Economic Commission for Europe, *Long-term Trends and Problems of the European Steel Industry* (1959), pp. 40–41.

44. League of Nations, *Mechanical Engineering*, p. 149, and League of Nations, Economic and Financial, *Chemical Industry* (1927), p. 41.

45. Using Hienrich Liepmann's data, it can be estimated that the average potential protection—the average ratio between tariffs and international prices—in Germany, France, Italy, Belgium, Austria, and Sweden ranged from 19.6% in 1913 to 23.5% in 1927 and to 27.8% in 1931. See H. Liepmann, *Tariff Levels and the Economic Unity of Europe* (London, 1938).

46. A. Maizels, *Industrial Growth and World Trade* (Cambridge, Mass., 1963), pp. 245–246.

47. D. L. Burn, *The Economic History of Steelmaking* (Cambridge, Mass., 1940), p. 392.

48. Ibid., p. 394; B. R. Mitchell and P. Dean, *Abstract of British Historical Statistics* (Cambridge, 1962), p. 301.

49. E. F. Söderlund, "The Swedish Iron and Steel Industry, 1932–1939," *Scandinavian Economic History Review* 7 (1959): 60.

50. United Nations, *Long-term Trends,* pp. 40–41.

51. League of Nations, Economic and Financial, *Industrialization and Foreign Trade* (1927), p. 1957.

52. W. A. Lewis, "World Production, Prices and Trade, 1870–1960," *Manchester School of Economic and Social Studies* 20 (1952): 105–138.

53. Ibid., pp. 117–118.

54. Great Britain, *Annual Statement of the Trade of the United Kingdom with Foreign Countries and British Possessions, 1885–1950.* London; Mulhall Project, Archive "GB," Department of Economics, University of Texas.

55. League of Nations, *Industrialization and Foreign Trade,* p. 161.

56. *Boletín Minero e Industrial, Estadística Minero-Siderúrgica de España de 1900–1950* (Bilbao, 1953), pp. 424–425.

57. League of Nations, *Industrialization and Foreign Trade,* p. 84.

58. Pedro Fraile, "The Sectoral Role of the Iron and Steel Industry in Spain, 1900–1950" (Ph.D. diss., University of Texas, 1983), table 4.15; Söderlund, "The Swedish Iron and Steel Industry," p. 59.

59. Fraile, "The Sectoral Role," table 4.14.

60. Ibid., table 4.7.

61. Ibid., table 4.8.

62. W. A. Lewis, *Growth and Fluctuations, 1870–1913* (London, 1978), pp. 225–228.

63. This is the situation in many current cases of underdevelopment; contemporary Latin America is a good example. Recommendations for selective economic self-sufficiency accompanied by well-executed planning on a broad industrial front would be more relevant to this situation. See, for example, R. B. Sutcliffe, *Industry and Underdevelopment* (London, 1971), pp. 342–346.

64. Jose María Fontana, *La lucha por la industrialización en España* (Madrid, 1953), pp. 59–61.

FURTHER READINGS

Churruca, Alfonso. *Minería, industria y comercio del País Vasco.* San Sebastián, 1951.

Flinn, Michael W. "British Steel and Spanish Ore, 1871–1914." *Economic History Review* 8 (1955): 84–90.

Fraile, Pedro. *The Sectoral Role of the Iron and Steel Industry in Spain, 1900–1950,* Ph.D. diss. University of Texas, 1983.

———. "Crecimiento económico y demanda de acero: España, 1900–1950," in P. Martín Aceña and L. Prados de la Escosura, eds. *La Nueva Historia Económica en España.* Madrid, 1985, pp. 71–100.

Harrison, Joseph. "Los orígenes del industrialismo moderno en el País Vasco." *Hacienda Pública Española* 55 (1978): 209–222.

———. "La industria pesada, el Estado y el desarrollo en el País Vasco, 1876–1936." *Información Comercial Española* 598 (1980): 31–32.

González Portilla, Manuel. *La formación de la sociedad capitalista en el País Vasco, 1876–1913.* San Sebastián, 1981.

Shaw, Valerie. "Exportaciones y despuegue económico: el mineral de hierro de Vizcaya, la región de la ría de Bilbao y algunas de sus implicaciones para España." *Moneda y Crédito* 142 (1977): 87–114.

11.
EARLY INDUSTRIALIZATION IN ASTURIAS: BOUNDS AND CONSTRAINTS

RAFAEL ANES
Universidad de Oviedo

THE ASTURIAN ECONOMY, predominantly agricultural in the eighteenth century, started to change in the 1830s as coal began to fuel industrialization.[1] This change came in fact late since agriculture was unable to create the broad-based market required for industrial development, in spite of the economic expansion experienced in rural areas. Corn cultivation spread from the second decade of the seventeenth century on; potato cultivation, from the second half of the eighteenth century on, and stockraising and overall farming also expanded. Instead of triggering economic development, however, this expansion served only to increase the population. The subsistence system was thus reinforced, as evidenced by the short list of Asturian imports and exports: fruits such as hazelnuts, chestnuts, walnuts, oranges, and lemons were exported, whereas wine, salt, and grains were imported.[2] Obviously, a demand for industrial products existed outside the region that could have been tapped, but in order to take advantage of it Asturias would have to offer products at competitive prices—a prerequisite that was precluded by inadequate transport and a lack of return cargoes. In fact, the improvement of the transportation system—roads, railroads, and a seaport—was a constant concern during the entire modern period.

The high expectations for industrial development once conceived were not met, and the region then began to focus its initiatives on coal mining. As coal became available in Asturias, new industrialization schemes appeared, but, as always, the lack of transportation facilities halted their realization. Toward the end of the eighteenth century, the following views became widely accepted:

(1) coal should be the basis for industrial development in Asturias; (2) the demand for this natural resource should be found outside the region; and (3) adequate means of transportation must be provided.

In order to be profitable, a coal company had to find customers outside Asturias, since the region's consumption was limited to limestone quarries and to cooking and heating in a few homes.[3] In October 1829 the Dirección General de Minas (National Mining Office) appointed a commission to study Asturian coal mines and make recommendations concerning what commercial ties should be developed with other countries and what should be done to improve output and transportation. This office noted that only an average of 150,000 quintals of coal was exported annually because of the irregularity and expense of transportation to the seaports.[4]

To reduce these high transportation costs, the commission suggested that a road be built to Gijón. The coal road was constructed under contract some years later by Alejandro Aguado, founder of the Aguado, Muriel y Compañía enterprise. He owned mines in Langreo and Siero and was interested in selling coal outside the region in order to make his investments profitable. Construction started on the Langreo-Gijón road in 1838 and continued until 1842. The reduction in transportation costs, however, was not as high as had been anticipated.[5] Still, shipment through Gijón doubled between 1838 and 1842, rising from 9,000 to 18,500 tons.[6]

Local demand would also have had to come from a suitably located iron-and-steel industry. The government tried to attract foreign capital and businessmen to such a venture. In 1828, Gregorio González Azaola was dispatched by the government to France and later to Belgium to contact iron producers.[7] Two Spanish expatriates, Joaquín María Ferrer and Martín de los Heros, introduced him to producers from Liège. When he returned to Spain in 1829, he had chartered a company to study Spanish coal and iron reserves as well as the economic conditions required to establish a steel plant. In the summer of 1829, the Belgian engineer Adolphe Lesoinne toured northern Spain and pointed out the lack of coal in Vizcaya and Santander and the availability of it in Asturias. He felt that Asturias would have been a good place to establish the plant. The government offered various incentives to get the project started; it deferred the levy of mining duties for twenty-five years, and it granted large tracts of iron deposits in Vizcaya. In spite of these incentives, when the famous John Cockerill quit the project in September 1832, the company decided to give up all its mining concessions, except the seaside coalfields of Arnao (Avilés) and the installation of one ironworks plant. Nevertheless, a Royal Decree of November 14, 1833, restated the fiscal incentives granted, and the status of the Asturiana de Minas de Carbón (Asturian Coal Mines) was raised to that of a Royal Company.[8]

The coal from the Langreo Basin, already known as one of the best veins in Asturias, initially found no significant demand in the region. Owing to inadequate communication, not even the Fábrica Nacional de Cañones (National Gun Factory) in Trubia, which the government reestablished in 1846, consumed a substantial amount of coal from that area. Neither did British investors, directed by John Manby, select the Langreo Basin as the location for the Asturian Mining Company in 1844; rather, they undertook to open a coal mine and set up a steel plant in Mieres (the Caudal Basin). The blast furnace for this venture was ignited in 1848, but by the following year it was extinguished. British investors expected the state to build a railroad from Mieres to Avilés. They also thought that another railroad would be built between Mieres and Lena, thus connecting the factories in Mieres with the steelmill of Villallana (owned by the Compañía Lenese Asturiana, established in 1846 by Jacquet and Company and managed by Adrien Paillette). Because no railroad transportation was available, the Compagnie Minière et Métallurgique des Asturies, started in Paris by Grimaldi and Company in 1852, also went bankrupt. In 1861 Numa Guilhou's Société Houillère et Métallurgique des Asturies took over the bankrupt company and also bought the steelmill of Villallana in Bárzana in the township of Lena.[9]

The Langreo Basin finally got a railroad line leading to the port of Gijón. This line was built to facilitate coal transportation from the mining area acquired by Fernando Muñoz, duke of Riánsares, who was married to the queen regent.[10] The duke's money and, above all, his political influence speeded the construction. The construction company initially received a guaranteed yield of 6% on its capital investments and perhaps on capital not even invested. Soon after the railroad was finished, the Sociedad Metalúrgica Duro (Duro Metal Company) was established by the joint partners—Pedro and Julián Duro, Vicente Bayo, and Federico Victoria de Lecea—and by the silent partners Alejandro Mon, marquis of Camposagrado and Pedro José Pidal. The plant put its first blast furnace into operation in 1859. That same year, Casimiro Gil, with the collaboration of Elorza, founded the Sociedad Gil y Compañía in order to start the ironworks located in Vega; in 1864 Duro rented Gil's plant. The factory in La Felguera was erected in 1857, also as a result of the new rail link with the port of Gijón. This railroad brought the iron ore into the plant and shipped iron goods out.[11]

The industrial development of the Langreo Basin was not as extensive as anticipated. Not only was the port of Gijón inadequate; the railroad itself contributed to this lag, since fares and freight costs were high. In addition, the railroad retarded the development of the Asturian iron-and-steel industry by importing duty-free construction materials. Marseville pointed out that "the complete lack of government assistance, as well as the enormous error it committed by allowing all the iron used for the construction of the railroads to be imported, impeded the development of the Spanish iron industry." Pedro Duro, director of the Duro Metal Company, declared:

> since the rails used on our railroads enter the country duty-free and are of inferior quality, we have not tried to make them. There is, however, no doubt that our machinery could produce the rails because we have the required equipment and motor power. If all the imported iron and machine pieces (flywheels and transmission shafts) paid the same duty as iron bars, we could produce yearly 200,000 Castilian quintals of rolled iron with our present production facilities, without an increase in personnel and with a reduction in the amount of fuel per unit of iron produced.[12]

Iron producers asked for protection from the very beginning, but they never received it to the extent desired. The hegemony that Asturias exercised in Spain over iron production from approximately 1860 to 1880 was really La Felguera's, and it ended when the Bessemer process was introduced. The effects of this technical innovation were explained by Francisco Gascué in an 1890 publication: "When a ton of finished iron entailed an expense of 5 to 7 tons of coal, including the coke necessary for the blast furnace, Asturias had the obvious advantage of possessing an abundant supply of high quality coal, as well as a fair amount of ore. However, when approximately 2.5 tons of coal were needed for one ton of finished steel, the circumstances changed radically."[13]

This paralyzed the Asturian siderurgical industry and logically reduced coal demand. Duro's demand, for instance, dropped from 104,000 tons in 1883 to 65,000 tons in 1886.[14] The coal crisis spread throughout the Caudal Basin. It was soon aggravated by the opening in 1884 of the Pajares railroad, which allowed the Aller Basin to compete in coal production.

Asturian industrialists then focused solely on coal mining and requested that the home market be reserved for them through protection, mainly from British coal. In 1890 a pressure group, the Liga de los Intereses Hulleros de Asturias (Asturian Coal Interest League), which later became the Liga General de los Intereses Hulleros de España, was created. The tariff of 1891 doubled the duty on imported coal; from 1.25 pesetas per ton, it went up to 2.5 pesetas.[15] The duty was even raised to 3.5 pesetas for a short while in 1895.

Thanks to this protection, coal mining was extended and increased, not only in the Langreo Basin but also in the Caudal Basin.[16] From 1890 to 1900 coal output doubled, reaching a high point of 1,361,000 tons in 1900.[17] This was achieved through cost reductions resulting from the concentration of production in the most important companies.

In 1886 the companies of the Mosquitera mines, the María Luisa mines, and the La Justa mines were merged in the Sociedad Unión Hullera y Metalúrgica de Asturias (Coal and Metal Union).[18] The purpose of this move was to expand mining, build iron works and communication lines, and bring together persons and companies working in similar fields. In 1888 the Sociedad bought the Sama and Santa Bárbara group of mines. Its capital was expanded from 3.5 million to 5.5 million pesetas; in 1900, additional acquisitions required the issue of capital up to 11 million pesetas. It became 15 million pesetas when, later on, the Unión Hullera and the Sociedad Duro-Felguera merged.

In 1890 the Sociedad Hullera del Turón (Turón Coals) was created by Victor Chavarri and Pedro Gandarias, with the participation of José Tartiere. Basque capitalists entered into Asturian coal mining due to both an increase in the price of British coal and, no doubt, to the Basques' desire to diversify their suppliers while spreading out their investments. This process led to the displacement of foreign capital by Spanish capital, basically Basque capital, in Asturian coal mines.[19]

In 1892 the Sociedad Hullera Española (Spanish Coals) was formed with assets of 20 million pesetas from the mines that Claudio López Bru, marquis de Comillas, had in Aller, the briquette factory in Ujo, and coke ovens and other mines in Lena and Mieres. The Sociedad tried to meet the coal needs of the shipping company Transatlántica Española, whose president was the marquis of Comillas; the railroad firm, Caminos de Hierro del Norte de España, of which the Marquis was a stockholder; and the metallurgical industry.

The increase in coal production also contributed to the opening of ironworks. A division of labor developed: Asturias wrought almost all the pig iron it produced, as well as ingots brought in from Vizcaya. "While the Basque iron and steel industry specialized in a limited number of items that used a small amount of coal and a large amount of pig iron, like iron ingots, rails, girders, bars and levers, the Asturian works shifted to sheeting and wrought-iron and steel products which required more coal per unit produced than the half-finished iron and steel goods made in Vizcaya."[20] Luis Adaro y Magro had anticipated in his writings in 1885 that Asturias and Vizcaya would assist and complement each other in manufacturing, since each region would follow "very different paths yet remain active trading partners in their own products: coal and iron ore."[21]

With these capital investments and initiatives undertaken by the Basques and the investments made by migrants who returned from overseas colonies, the Asturian economy underwent a process of diversification, as evidenced by the creation of banking, transportation, and mercantile enterprises.[22] This economic diversification should have led to a greater modernization of the economy, but it did not; World War I eventually refocused businessmen's attention on coal mining.

In effect, World War I imposed the automatic protection system that coal producers had been seeking for quite a few years. Top prices multiplied the number of mine openings and increased coal production. Although the quality of the coal became worse, this did not worry anyone, because the market absorbed all coal at high prices. Coal production went up from 2.46 million tons and 18,233 workers in 1914 to 3.41 million tons and 33,358 workers in 1918. After the war, the mining industry again began to ask for protection in spite of the fact that the average price of coal continued to rise until 1920; the price reached 70 pesetas per ton, but production costs had also risen. Starting around 1922, mines began to close—especially those that opened up during the war and were located far from railroad lines—and wages began to go down. During the crisis that followed, an eighty-day strike contributed to the overall reduction in coal output, as only 69 firms instead of the 137 that existed in 1917 produced 2.5 million tons.[23]

The request for protection was answered with the tariff of 1922, which raised the duty on imported coal from 3.5 to 7.5 pesetas per ton. Very quickly, in March 1923, the protectionist policies changed, as a premium of 2.50 pesetas per ton was added to the production costs, and a discount of 3.25 pesetas per ton was subtracted from transportation costs. This perhaps explains the production figures given for that year of 3.78 million tons, an increase of 1.28 million tons over the figures for 1922. These figures do not seem accurate, however, in view of an eighty-day strike and other factors. They could represent what was declared for the benefit of the production and transportation premiums. Another type of protection sought for many years and finally offered by the Decree of April 18, 1928, was that railroads be required to use only domestic coal. In spite of all the troubles, coal mining remained the core of Asturian businessmen.

Industrial development altered population distribution in Asturias. Until the mid-nineteenth century the population was widespread and had few important population centers, but during the second half of the century the process of development led to a concentration of population in the central zone of the province. In the six most industrialized municipalities—Langreo, Mieres, Gijón, Avilés, Oviedo, and San Martín del Rey Aurelio—population doubled between 1860 and 1900; the population of these municipalities was 15.6% of the total population of the region in 1860, and it increased to 25% in 1900. From 1877 on, such an increase can be explained only by migrations from other municipalities. This trend continued throughout the first two decades of the twentieth century, letting up only during the 1920s.[24] These changes obviously pressed for the growth of urban centers.

Along with industrial development in Asturias came a specialization in cattle raising.[25] The concentration of population in urban centers led to a reorganization of production in the nearby agricultural zones. The land area used for the cultivation of cereals contracted. Corn was an exception because it could be fed to the livestock, its yield per acre was high, and it was tied into a complex system of crop rotation. Milk production increased steadily, reaching a level of 173 million liters that accounted for 22% of all the milk produced in Spain in 1924. The development of the dairy industry, however, lagged. The first factory that processed cheese and butter from fresh milk did not appear until 1910. This factory, Mantequerías Arias (Arias Butter), ranked for a long time as one of the most important businesses in the sector.

Aside from the specialization in milk production, few other areas of agriculture changed. From July 1, 1892, when the duty on imported sugar from the Antilles and the Philippines rose from 17.6 to 33.5 pesetas per 100 kilograms, beet production increased in Spain as well as in Asturias. In 1893 the Azucarera Asturiana de Verina (Verina Sugar Co. from Asturias) was successfully established and became a model for other refineries in Pravia and Villaviciosa. The demand generated by these refineries led to an increase in the cultivation of sugar beets, especially in the central part of Asturias, to the point where it was thought that beet production would displace that of corn, but this never happened. Refineries proliferated in Spain, and this led to a drop in sugar prices, while increased taxes on sugar put many producers out of business. By 1918, as a result of these conflicting pressures, only one producer remained active in Asturias—the Azucarera de Villaviciosa (Villaviciosa Sugar Co.).

In conclusion, an iron-and-steel industry was developed in Asturias because coal was available. In later years, this industry deteriorated since the region did not have either an abundant or a quality supply of iron ore, yet coal production intensified because of the tariff protection it received. Since coal mining had become such a major activity in the region, Asturias had a hard time trying to diversify its economy. The industrial development in the central area of the region changed the spatial distribution of the population, which tended to concentrate there. With this heavy concentration of people in one zone, a specialization in milk production occurred in nearby rural areas. As cultivated fields were converted to pasturelands, it became impossible for the area to absorb the increase in population; in addition, neither coal nor other industries could offer employment to these people. The result was a massive emigration of people from Asturias to Spanish America during the last two decades of the nineteenth century and the first two decades of the twentieth century.

NOTES

1. Asturias, located on the central coast of the Bay of Biscay, has a land area of 10,564 square kilometers (2.09% of the surface of Spain). The rugged topography of Asturias includes 50% of the area over 400 meters and 38% over 800 meters with large differences of elevation, as 80% of the land area contains gradients of more than 20% and small estuaries with sandbars. The subsoil is very rich in coal, with deposits located principally in the central area of the province in the basins of the Nalón, Aller, Turón, and Caudal rivers; there are also iron-ore deposits as well as deposits of other minerals. Precipitation in Asturias is abundant, and the climate is temperate. Although the soil is relatively poor, the rainfall gives the area a varied and abundant vegetation.

2. Gonzalo Anes, "El Antiguo Régimen: economía y sociedad," in *Historia de Asturias,* vol. 7 (Salinas [Asturias], 1977), chaps. 2 and 3.

3. Gaspar Melchor de Jovellanos, "Informe hecho a S. M. sobre una representación del Director General de Minas," Gijón, 10 de mayo de 1791 in *Biblioteca de Autores Españoles,* vol. 50 (Madrid, 1952), p. 475.

4. *Minas de carbón de piedra de Asturias: Reconocimiento hecho de orden del Rey N. Sr. por una Comisión de Facultativos* (Madrid, 1931).

5. Restituto Alvarez Builla, *Observaciones prácticas sobre la minería carbonera de Asturias* (Oviedo, 1861), p. 10. The mines of Aguado were bought years later by the duke of Riánsares, Fernando Muñoz.

6. *Memoria sobre los productos de la industria española en la exposición pública de 1850* (Madrid, 1851), p. 137.

7. In that year a pamphlet entitled *Hornaguera y hierro: memoria sobre la formación de compañías que beneficiando las ricas minas de carbón de piedra de España establezcan fundiciones de hierro a la inglesa* was published in Paris.

8. The company was established with 450,000 reales by Nicolás-Maximilien and Adolphe Lesoinne, Joaquín María Ferrer Cafranga, and Felipe Riera Roses. In 1849, with incorporation of Jules Heuzer, the company restructured its business activity toward the production of zinc, using calamine from Guipúzcoa and coal from Arnao. In 1853 all interests held by Spaniards were sold, and the company changed its name

to Compagnie Royale Asturienne des Mines. *Compagnie Royale Asturienne des Mines, 1853–1953* (Paris, 1954), pp. 17ff.

9. The Hullera was liquidated in 1868 and sold at public auction on May 5, 1870. Numa Guilhou bought it and established the Sociedad Numa Guilhou, which in 1879 became Fábrica de Mieres.

10. In 1853 these were merged with the mines of Adolphe D'Eichthal, president of the Compagnie Minière et Métallurgique des Asturies.

11. Iron ore came from Vizcaya and from the thirteen mines with forty-two claims that the Sociedad had in the districts of Gozón and Carreño. On the savings provided by this location, see "Información sobre el derecho diferencial de bandera y sobre los de aduanas exigibles a los hierros, el carbón de piedra y los algodones, presentada al Govierno de Su Majestad por la Comisión nombrada al efecto en Real Decreto de 10 de noviembre de 1865," vol. 2 *Hierros* (Madrid, 1867), p. 317.

12. Ibid., p. 58.

13. Francisco Gascué, "La crisis carbonera en Asturias," *Revista Minera* (1887): 7.

14. Ibid., p. 17.

15. In current pesetas these values were much higher, especially from 1894 to 1898, a period during which inflation was greater. For more information on the creation of pressure groups and protectionist tariffs see Germán Ojeda Gutiérrez's unpublished doctoral dissertation, "Transportes e industrialización en Asturias (1833–1907)" (Oviedo, 1983).

16. Rafael Anes and Germán Ojeda, "La minería del carbón en Asturias y los problemas del transporte en las primeras décadas del siglo XX," *Hacienda Pública Española* 69 (1981): 303–313.

17. In that year Spanish coal imports rose to 1.992 million tons. Nadal (1973), appendix 5.

18. Adaro (1983), pp. 167ff. The papers were signed in Paris on May 15, 1884, by the count of Finat, Cahen D'Anvers and León Daguerre Dospital, on behalf of La Justa holding company; by Adolfo D'Eichthal on behalf of the Sociedad D'Eichthal, owner of Mosquitera; and by the marquis de Guadalamina on behalf of the María Luisa company.

19. Manuel González Portilla, *La formación de la sociedad capitalista en el País Vasco (1876–1913)* (San Sebastián, 1981).

20. Ibid., p. 129.

21. Luis Adaro y Magro, "La industria siderúrgica en Asturias," *Revista Minera* (1885): 151.

22. Francisco Erice, *La burguesía industrial asturiana (1885–1920)* (Gijón, 1980); Juan Antonio Vázquez García, "El ciclo económico en Asturias (1886–1972): Un análisis comparativo," *Boletín del Instituto de Estudios Asturianos* 105–106 (1982): 441–466.

23. See José Luis García Delgado, "La industrialización asturiana: de la repatriación de capitales americanos a los beneficios de la Gran Guerra" and "La minería de la hulla entre 1918 y 1936: una larga crisis entre dos guerras," in *Historia General de Asturias* (Gijón, n.d.), vols. 5 and 6.

24. See José Luis San Miguel Cela y Germán Ojeda Gutiérrez, "La población," *Historia de Asturias,* vol. 9 (Salinas [Asturias], 1972), chap. 2.

25. José Luis San Miguel Cela, "La agricultura," *Historia de Asturias,* vol. 9 (Salinas [Asturias], 1977), chap. 3.

FURTHER READINGS

Adaro y Magro, Luis. "La industria siderúrgica en Asturias." *Revista Minera* (1885): 105–177.
Adaro Ruíz-Falco, Luis. *Ciento setenta y cinco años de la sidero-metalurgia asturiana.* Gijón, 1968.
————. "Los comienzos de la minería del carbón de piedra y de los hornos de cok." In Real Instituto Asturiano, ed., *Datos y documentos para una historia minera e industrial de Asturias.* Gijón, 1981.
Anes, Rafael. "La industrialización en Asturias." In *Historia económica y pensamiento social,* pp. 353–369. Madrid, 1983.
Anes, Rafael, and Germán Ojeda. "La minería del carbón en Asturias y los problemas del transporte en las primeras décadas del siglo XX." *Hacienda Pública Española* 69 (1981): 303–313.
————. "La industria asturiana en la segunda mitad del siglo XIX: de la industrialización a la expansión hullera." *Revista de Historia Económica* 1, 2 (1983): 13–29.
Casariego, Jesús Evaristo. *El marqués de Sargadelos o los comienzos del industrialismo capitalista en España.* Oviedo, 1950.
Erice, Francisco. *La burguesía industrial asturiana (1885–1920).* Gijón, 1980.
Gascué, Francisco. *La industria del acero en el Norte de España.* Madrid, 1890.
Historia de Asturias. Economía y sociedad (siglos XIX y XX), vol. 9. Salinas (Asturias), 1981.
Ojeda, Germán. *Asturias en la industrialización española, 1833–1907.* Madrid, 1985.
Vázquez García, Juan Antonio. "El ciclo económico en Asturias, 1886–1935: un análisis comparativo." *Boletín del Instituto de Estudios Asturianos* 105–106 (1982): 141–146.
————. "Creación de sociedades e inversión en Asturias, 1886–1973: El auge de fin de siglo." *Investigaciones Económicas* 12 (1980): 165–185.
————. *La cuestión hullera en Asturias, 1918–1935.* Oviedo, 1985.

12.
ECONOMIC TRANSFORMATIONS IN GALICIA IN THE NINETEENTH AND TWENTIETH CENTURIES

JAIME GARCÍA-LOMBARDERO
Universidad de Santiago de Compostela

IN 1960, Meijide Pardo published an illuminating book on the intrapeninsular migration of Galicians in the eighteenth century. As a result, economic historians began to focus on the "push factors" of Galician emigration and concluded that they derived from an imbalance between the resources of a traditional agrarian production system and a growing population. These findings motivated others to research the region's failure to assimilate the economic changes and transformations that had occurred in other European societies. Moreover, it became necessary to explain the reasons for the slow breakdown of traditional agrarian structures in Galicia, a phenomenon that hindered the formation and integration of articulated markets and that obstructed most attempts at industrialization.

As demonstrated in the recent works of Barreiro Gil (1983), Carmona (1983), and Villares Paz (1982a), there was no general stagnation of the Galician economy, as had previously been thought. Galician society did experience the economic and institutional changes that were occurring in the Western world, but displayed a great capacity for defensive reaction against innovative processes. This capacity for adaptation in defense of the traditional production system succeeded in reinforcing subsistence agriculture. At the same time, the development of certain agrarian and manufacturing activities aimed at production for the market functioned to provide peasants with the money necessary to meet the ongoing "monetization" of the tribute system and to defend their traditional way of life.

In the nineteenth and twentieth centuries, three stages can be distinguished

223

in Galicia's slow and unusual modernization process. Until approximately 1840, the subsistence economy of the Ancien Régime continued to prevail. At mid-nineteenth century, the subsistence economy entered a crisis period and a structural imbalance arose between resources and population, causing emigration to become endemic. At the same time, the area developed a capacity for export-oriented stockraising, and the production of salted meat was transformed into an export industry. Last, during the first third of the twentieth century the coastal centers of industrialization were consolidated, and the agrarian sector turned toward commercial stockraising. In any case, the process of market formation in Galicia was externally oriented and did not lead to an interrelated economy at home as needed for a general and harmonious growth.

1. POPULATION AND EMIGRATION

The demographic growth of the mid-nineteenth century was based on the diffusion of crops that were adaptable to the traditional subsistence system, on the one hand, and on the increased population density that resulted from the labor requirements of this agricultural expansion, on the other. Corn, potatoes, and domestic rural industry explain the steady rise in the population until 1840. Table 12.1 presents figures with respect to Galician population that were compiled from various censuses. In general terms, the population increased by 71% between 1752 and 1930; this represents a cumulative

Table 12.1
The Population of Galicia, 1752–1930

	Total Population	Spanish Population (%)
1752	1,299,312	13.8
1787	1,345,803	12.9
1826	1,585,419	11.2
1860	1,799,224	11.5
1877	1,848,027	11.1
1887	1,894,559	10.8
1900	1,950,515	10.6
1910	2,063,589	10.3
1920	2,124,244	9.9
1930	2,230,281	9.5

SOURCES: 1752 and 1826 estimates; other national censuses.

annual growth rate of 0.30%, much lower than that of Spain as a whole. This lower rate led to a decline in rank of the Galician population compared with that of the rest of Spain.

Estimating the growth rates between censuses, however, one can distinguish three cycles that confirm the previously mentioned periodization of the Galician economy (see Table 12.2). Between mid-eighteenth and the mid-nineteenth century, the population increased in tandem with the consolidation and expansion of subsistence crops—an expansion that created a larger labor force in both agriculture and associated activities, such as rural domestic industry. Around 1840 the subsistence economy, which had favored a rise in population, entered into crisis, and the growth rate slackened until the end of the century. Without social transformations, it was impossible to intensify or expand cultivation; the spread of corn and potatoes into the Galician interior abated, and (as will be seen later) rural industry no longer functioned as a complementary activity. In the absence of an industrial sector, migration became a survival strategy. High rates of emigration, therefore, were directly responsible for the decline in demographic growth rates. Last, the turn of the twentieth century saw important changes in the Spanish economy and society that fostered, once again, an increase in the annual growth rates of the Galician population. This growth, although it did not stem migration, contributed to a new emphasis on stockraising in agriculture and to the consolidation of industrial centers.

Research has been done on the Galician population that clarifies both its structure and its dynamics (Barreiro Gil [1983]: 106–213; López Taboada [1979]: chap. 5). High population density—a characteristic clearly identi-

Table 12.2
Cumulative Annual Growth Rates
of the Galician Population, 1752–1930

Years	Percent	Periods	Percent
1752–1787	0.10		
1787–1826	0.42	1752–1860	0.39
1826–1860	0.37		
1860–1877	0.16		
1877–1887	0.25	1860–1900	0.20
1887–1900	0.22		
1900–1910	0.57		
1910–1920	0.29	1900–1930	0.45
1920–1930	0.49		

SOURCE: Table 12.1.

fied—implies that Galicia's production system was capable of supporting a large number of people. From the eighteenth century on, the highest densities were found along the Atlantic coast rather than inland. Another characteristic is the high degree of the population's dispersion on the land, to the point that by 1920 Galicia contained 40% of the towns and villages in Spain. Hence, there was a preponderance of rural over urban population. In 1857, for example, only 3.48% of the population lived in centers of more than 10,000 inhabitants; in 1920 it had risen to 11%. Galicia's relative lack of urbanization was a symptom of the market's limited development. These demographic features support the general thesis that the economic, industrial, and commercial growth that was centered on the Atlantic coast was an exogenous growth based on trade relations with the exterior—a growth that had little impact on the predominantly agrarian production system of the Galician interior. Between 1830 and 1840 the economic structures that had fostered population growth during the previous century reached a crucial point (Carmona [1983]: chap. 7). The land tenure system had scarcely changed, but the economic activities which complemented agriculture ceased to exist. Migration, therefore, reflected a structural imbalance that derived from a general crisis of the traditional Galician economy, of which periodic subsistence crises were but one aspect. Owing to the failure both of the modernization of agrarian relations and of industrialization experiments, migration was transformed into an escape valve for the rural population of Galicia. Toward the middle of the nineteenth century, the prevailing production system proved itself unable to sustain a growing population.

The surplus population was directed mostly to the new countries of Spanish America, with a net departure of more than 350,000 people during the second half of the nineteenth century and another 300,000 from 1900 to 1930. Approximately one out of every two Galicians left his home either temporarily or permanently. (These statistics were compiled from the works of López Taboada [1979]: 152 and Barreiro Gil [1983]: 156.)

The migratory flow was nourished by a rural population that sought to escape precarious living conditions and was also fostered by the collapse of traditional agrarian structures. As Barreiro (1983: 201–202) points out, migration represented an attempt on the part of the population to adapt to a structural imbalance between the necessities of survival and progress, on the one hand, and the capacity of the prevailing production system to provide them, on the other. In addition, migration played an important role in the formation and articulation of the world market, as it functioned to reallocate human resources to wherever they were needed.

Moreover, migration affected the productive structures of Galician agriculture and accelerated the modernization process. As Barreiro (1983: 208) claims, the massive exodus of the rural population did not prevent agriculture from producing the same volume of goods; in fact, the sector experienced a rise in labor productivity. In addition, the peasantry, being freed of surplus labor, acquired a greater capacity to accumulate capital—a trend that was abetted by remittances from migrants. This capital enabled peasants to become landowners in their own right during the first third of the twentieth century. Last, migrants contributed to the region's progress by encouraging technological improvements, agrarian syndicalism, and specialized production systems. It is clear, then, that migration did not hinder the modernization of agrarian structures in Galicia. However, the very continuation of migration indicates that the region still had a weak agricultural complex and a nonintegrated economy.

In short, the region's demographic history confirms my earlier thesis that the modernization of the Galician economy did not occur in an integrated form but, rather, was a response to external demand on the part of particular sectors.

2. SUBSISTENCE AGRICULTURE AND AGRARIAN CHANGE

Research on nineteenth-century Galician agriculture seems to indicate that the agrarian structures of the Ancien Régime were not substantially altered by the institutional changes and economic transformations of ensuing liberal governments. The changes in land tenure that arose out of the disentailment laws of the 1830s had only a limited impact on Galicia. This was due to the survival of the Ancien Régime's most characteristic institution: the *foro* (a quasi-emphyteutic land-tenure system by which tenants paid a customary quit rent to the owner in return for a long lease that was usually inherited by three subsequent generations). Under such conditions, the sharecroppers and direct cultivators continued to hold ownership in usufruct and were not affected by disentailment. What changed was the nominal owners. The dual property did not disappear, nor was ownership consolidated whether direct or in usufruct. *Foros* and the rents related to them continued to determine land tenure in Galicia until the slow and peculiar transformations of the economy rendered them unviable and unnecessary, dooming them to disappear during the first third of the twentieth century.

During disentailment, the principal purchasers of these rents belonged to the urban bourgeoisie, an uneven group largely devoted to commercial and administrative activities. Large merchants from the urban centers and ports; owners of meat-salting plants; and, in general, people who fell into the category of "commercial bourgeoisie" bought disentailed rents and lands. Carmona demonstrates that disentailment was the historic pitfall in which the commercial bourgeoisie buried any possibility of consolidating itself as a class during a large part of the nineteenth century (Carmona [1982b]: 40). In effect, this was the only group in Galicia that had the capacity to develop economic activities conducive to the formation of industrial capital. Their purchase of *foral* rents, however, diverted capital that could have been invested in industry toward the agrarian sector. More important, this Galician bourgeoisie—consolidated through the transatlantic trade, the meat-salting industry, and the textile trade—became integrated into the complex framework of land tenure and lost its character as a dynamic capitalist class. In order to continue to play its role, now as the agrarian bourgeoisie, it would have to convert the land into a commodity, either by consolidating ownership in the person of the buyer or by selling direct ownership to the peasant cultivator. Neither process was viable. The first was hindered by the legal constraints preventing the expulsion of peasants from their lands; the second, by the peasants' financial inability to purchase those lands. The consequence was that the commercial bourgeoisie was converted into a group of landowners who were unable to modernize agriculture and who became gradually assimilated into the class that lived off rents—a class that appropriated part of the agricultural surplus in a manner characteristic of the Ancien Régime (Carmona [1982b]: 40).

In conclusion, disentailment did not favor the development of capitalist relations in the Galician agrarian sector. On the contrary, it diverted capital from more productive ventures; it condemned the bourgeoisie to non-capitalist endeavors; it reinforced social groups who were interested in maintaining the status quo; and it contributed to the persistence of traditional agrarian structures that would prevent the region from benefiting from any of the bourgeois measures introduced by the Liberal Revolution.

Another proof that the subsistence economy continued to prevail, in spite of disentailment, is that the increase of population until almost mid-century was related to a rise in agricultural output. This rise was achieved through the intensification and expansion of labor-intensive crops. The land under cultivation expanded at the expense of woodlands and public lands, accentuating the imbalance between pastureland, woodland, and cropland. Agricultural intensification through the incorporation of more human labor continued the pattern of the eighteenth century. The cultivation of corn and potatoes also continued to spread throughout the Galician interior and was integrated into the rotation of crops in a manner that required neither a modification of traditional agrarian practices nor an alteration of the land-tenure system. Both products were adapted perfectly to a subsistence economy in which human labor was abundant. Their expansion fostered a rise in population, facilitated the use of fallow lands, and preempted the need for technological advances that would have increased productivity (Carmona [1982b]: 34). During the first half of the nineteenth century, potatoes and corn contributed to the maintenance of a land-tenure system based on *foros* and abetted the process of land fragmentation and the consolidation of the *minifundio* (small holdings). Once again, the needed transformation of the agrarian system was obstructed.

The unusual manner in which disentailment was carried out in Galicia hampered the region's ability to benefit fully from the new Liberal policies, but this does not mean that those policies had no influence there at all. The elimination of tithes and feudal privileges, and their substitution by money contributions to the public treasury, brought about a monetization of peasant obligations that had previously been paid in kind. This allowed commercial relations to penetrate a precapitalist economy, since the farmers now needed to produce a surplus for the market so that they could get cash in order to meet their fiscal obligations. In addition, Galicia experienced increasing fiscal pressure on the small agrarian units because of the tax reform of 1845 that introduced a tax on real estate, crops, and livestock (Villares Paz [1982a]: 224ff.). Peasants, therefore, had to increasingly orient their production toward the market, and this they achieved through a rise in productivity and crop yields. There were, however, many obstacles that hindered the expansion of this process, especially technological stagnation and the inability to undertake the short-term specialization of production.

In short, until the 1840s the behavior of the Galician economy ensured the persistence of a type of agriculture whose dominant traits were production for subsistence and technological stagnation. The abundance of labor in the countryside and the lack of alternative employment opportunities precluded an interest in mechanization on the part of peasants. The rapid elimination of fallow lands during this period does not reflect a modernizing trend. This process of incorporating new lands and eliminating fallow lands through the intensification of labor was not conducive to the introduction of specifically commercial crops. Rather, what it led to was the consolidation of subsistence agriculture in Galicia.

From 1840 on, however, subsistence agriculture in Galicia entered into a period of prolonged crisis. *Foral* rents continued to regulate the land-tenure system and prevented the conversion of land into a commodity, but this period also saw the development of conditions needed to transform the region's traditional agrarian structures. In conclusion, it was not the *foro* redemptions that began in the last third of the nineteenth century that fostered the agrarian transformations; rather, the *foros* became less attractive and later disappeared because transformations in the traditional subsistence system were already under way. Although Galicia continued to exhibit a high degree of local self-sufficiency, a price analysis of typical agricultural products shows a process of economic integration toward the end of the century over which external trade must have had a tremendous influence. The opening of the railroad that linked Madrid and La Coruña and, later, Vigo also facilitated the movement of goods and favored the expansion of commercial agriculture.

A growing need for money and the loss of secondary activities and rural domestic industries (e.g., linen production) led to the revitalization of cattle-raising as a source of money income. This renewed interest in livestock took place from the middle of the nineteenth century on and was especially energized by beef exports to England and Portugal. Galicia had an old cattle-raising tradition, and peasants valued cattle as important possessions that could be used to carry out various agricultural tasks. After 1842 the growing demand for meat on the part of industrialized England made Galician cattle-raising a dynamic export industry. This development accelerated after 1860, when a bovine epidemic spread to the German states that had been traditional suppliers of beef. The statistics presented in Table 12.3, which are aggregated into ten-year periods, trace the evolution of exports.

In addition to the remarkable growth of direct exports to England, cattle were also exported to Portugal, where they were repastured and reexported to England. As Carmona (1982a) has shown, exports to Portugal were needed because Galicia could feed only a limited number of cattle. Therefore, farmers

Table 12.3
Cattle Exports to England, 1842–1900

Periods	Number of Cattle
1842–1850	6,013
1851–1860	22,876
1861–1870	126,515
1871–1880	212,799
1881–1890	174,095
1891–1900	16,523
Total	558,821

SOURCE: Carmona, "Sobre as orixes da orientación exportadura bovina galega," *Grial, Anexo Historia* 1 (1982): 175.

were forced to sell their calves to Portugal for fattening. This favorable spot in the international market, however, did not bring about an immediate and permanent specialization in cattle-raising. Agrarian structures blocked the sector's expansion. The small size of plots, excessive land fragmentation, and the low level of market integration did not favor the formation of farms large enough to specialize in one of the many cattle-related activities. These obstacles also ensured that Galician cattle would be marketed under less-than-competitive conditions in spite of high prices on the world market. Galician farmers were caught in a vicious circle. In order to maintain larger herds, they needed to buy fodder, since they could not produce enough on their small plots. Also, the purchase of more fodder required an initial investment, the capital for which was nearly impossible to accumulate, considering the predominance of subsistence agriculture.

There were, however, some positive developments. External demand for cattle during the second half of the nineteenth century favored the continued expansion of land devoted to pastures and forage crops. This process was accelerated and consolidated during the twentieth century. Exports to England also served to commercially develop certain types of agrarian activities and to create a trade network—developments that later benefited the national market. When England ceased to import beef from Galicia at the end of the nineteenth century, the cattle-raising industry did not collapse. Rather, it began to produce a huge volume of cattle for the Spanish market in the twentieth century. Available data confirm the impact of the rising demand for veal in Spanish cities.

Graph 12.1 includes data on the number of cattle in Galicia. The cattle-raising orientation of the region is highlighted by the Galician cattle industry's ability to produce a commercial surplus with which to supply the inland markets of the peninsula. For example, between 1907 and 1931 the Norte Railroad transported more than 3.7 million heads of cattle from Galicia. The volume of cattle traded (exported and transported by rail) can also be observed in Table 12.4. This rise in exports was paralleled by an increase in the size of herds. According to available data, the number of cattle per hectare increased from 0.44 in 1881 to 1.10 in 1933 (Barreiro Gil [1982]: 355). These figures reflect an increase in cattle-raising and commercial specialization, a trend similar to the one prevailing in the rest of Spain according to Flores de Lemus ("Sobre la dirección fundamental de la producción rural española," rept. in *Hacienda Pública Española* 42–43 (1976): 471–484). It is also clear, however, that forms of organization that pertained to the subsistence system continued to persist during this period. Nevertheless, as Jaime Barreiro (1982:

Graph 12.1   Number of Heads of Cattle in Galicia, 1859–1935

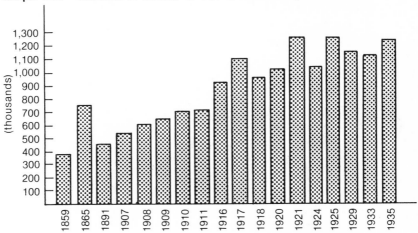

365) has pointed out, it is the growing volume of cattle exports, not the subsistence system, that leads to the conclusion that commercial agriculture and cattle-raising characterized the evolution of the Galician economy during this period.

This commercial orientation of cattle-raising transformed the traditional crop system. As the number of cattle needed to be fed, traditional crops were replaced with pastures and forage crops. At the same time, crops such as

Table 12.4
Number of Cattle Traded, 1842–1931

Periods	Number of Cattle
1842–1851	660.2
1852–1861	3,004.7
1862–1871	20,009.5
1872–1881	34,935.0
1882–1891	38,294.0
1892–1901	46,751.4
1901–1910	97,851.5
1910–1921	196,857.5
1922–1931	226,238.3

Source: M. J. Barreiro Gil, "Notas sobre la evolución histórica de la ganadería," p. 105.
Note: "Cattle traded" here means cattle exported and transported by railway; the figures indicate annual averages according to decades.

potatoes and grapevines, which could be partly commercialized, were expanded. The multicrop subsistence system lost ground, and the cultivation of crops such as wheat and legumes regressed. This is because Galicia's increasing integration into the Spanish market pressured the region into abandoning crops that were cheaply and abundantly available in other regions of the Peninsula.

The expansion of corn fodder, the substitution of barley grain for barley fodder, and the extension of pasturelands confirms, once again, the cattle-raising specialization of the region's agrarian production (see Table 12.5). The growing use of chemical fertilizers and the introduction of agricultural machinery from the second decade of the twentieth century are also indications of the new orientation (Villares Paz [1982a]: 364–371).

The low cost of agricultural labor favored a spatial organization based on the intensive use of human labor that, as indicated earlier, precluded both the introduction of new techniques and a rise in productivity. During this period, however, the cumulative exodus of surplus labor through migration began to favor improved levels of productivity and to facilitate the introduction of new technology in the countryside. No fewer than 500,000 rural workers were displaced from their customary jobs in Galicia during the first third of the twentieth century. This social shift modified the region's productive structures (Barreiro Gil [1982]: 416).

In short, two general conclusions can be drawn. First, it seems clear that the fading away of the *foro* was a consequence of its internal disintegration, not of a process of social action that might have changed the land-tenure system.

Table 12.5
Land Cultivated for Diverse Crops,
1902–1930 (index numbers)

Years	Legumes	Grain	Potatoes	Grapevines
1902	110.0	100.0	100.0	100.0
1905	116.2	91.7	n.a.	113.66
1910	94.6	94.2	125.7	n.a.
1915	128.5	100.0	n.a.	162.9
1920	99.3	86.6	n.a.	166.0
1925	89.5	84.8	175.5	169.0
1930	61.0	79.0	212.4	187.1

SOURCE: M. J. Barreiro Gil, *"Población, propiedad de la tierra y formación del mercado agrario en Galicia, 1900–1930"* (Ph.D. diss., Universidad de Santiago, 1982), p. 389.
NOTE: n.a. = data not available.

Second, the integration and progressive articulation of the agrarian market was carried out independently of the transformations in other productive sectors. This process was the result of external demand for commercial agricultural products. As will be seen later on, the partial modernization of Galicia's agrarian sector was neither carried out alongside, nor went along with, industry and trade. For this reason, surplus labor was not integrated into other sectors when the subsistence system broke down. Instead, emigration continued.

3. THE FAILURE OF INTEGRATED INDUSTRIALIZATION

During the Ancien Régime, rural domestic industry exercised a stabilizing influence on the social relations that governed the traditional agrarian production system. The production of linen for domestic consumption was an essential activity in some districts of Galicia. As Carmona (1983: 13) has shown, however, a part of the cloth was produced for sale in local markets and fairs, providing monetary income for many peasant families. The merchants who purchased these goods usually exported them to Castile or the Basque Provinces. In spite of this commercial aspect of domestic linen production, the industry did not create the momentum for a "putting-out system." The linen and cloth merchants did not belong to the same group, and neither became involved in production. A division of labor per se did not exist; rather, the manufacture of linen was founded upon a barely commercialized agrarian base of low productivity. Within this context, any progress toward regional specialization or technological advancement was very difficult.

Toward the last third of the eighteenth century, the importation of crude linen was authorized. This favored both the growth of textile production and the introduction of commercial relations. A group of import merchants who distributed linen to peasants on credit developed around this trade. This facilitated the peasants' entrance into market relations, since they would now have to conform to a payment schedule for the linen supplies. During this period, there were other factors that favored the commercialization of linen production, such as the liberalization of trade with Spanish America, the prohibition against importing foreign textiles, and the overall growth of the Spanish economy during the eighteenth century.

The rise of textile production, however, neither induced technological advances in the sector nor altered the social relations of production. The modernization of textile production would first require that substantial changes take place in the agrarian sector—changes which were not forthcoming at that time. On the one hand, the manufacture of linen continued to complement agrarian activities; on the other hand, the merchants who imported the raw material failed to initiate the process by which capital accumulated in trade would be converted into industrial capital through merchant participation in production. Consequently, the loss of the colonial market after the struggle for independence, the expansion of Catalan cotton textiles in the Spanish market, and the growing contraband in British textiles hindered a transition toward the industrialization of the textile sector (Carmona [1983]: 19). In short, the persistence of a traditional agrarian structure, the conservatism of a commercial bourgeoisie that became integrated into the traditional landowning class, and the loss of markets constituted the framework in which the crisis and liquidation of Galicia's domestic linen production was set.

Carmona ([1983]: 18ff.) distinguishes three stages in the decline of this activity. (1) During the first third of the nineteenth century, it became impossible for Galician textiles to compete with those of more developed regions, and so the textile trade continually declined. (2) Between 1841 and 1885 there was a total displacement of linen products in urban markets that was fostered by the modernization of transportation and the formation of the Spanish market. The latter developments led to the consolidation of the Catalan textile industry and brought about the regression of domestic manufactures. (3) After 1885, Catalan cotton textiles penetrated Galicia as a result of the opening of railway communications to the interior of the Peninsula, relegating domestic textile production to family consumption. In addition, the disappearance of rural domestic industry constituted an important factor in the complex of elements that led to the nineteenth-century crisis of Galician agriculture.

During this period of uncertain transition, isolated attempts to establish industries of different types (glass, cotton textiles, iron-and-steel products) did not succeed in creating an industrial sector in Galicia both because of the agrarian sector's limited demand for industrial products and because of a lack of external demand that might have created a larger market for these products. While agrarian-related industry disappeared, nonagrarian industry never became viable enough to stand alone. Only one traditional Galician industry, the processing and canning of fish products, became modernized and that was because of the expansion of the world market.

Catalan penetration of the fish-processing industry at the end of the eighteenth century and the closing of the Portuguese market for Galician sardines in 1774 destroyed the industry's traditional organization. As a consequence, new fishing methods and marketing techniques were introduced (Alonso

[1976] and Carmona [1983]: 455–550). From then on, the Catalans held all the cards in the marketing of salted sardines, since they enjoyed a trade network that had already been established on the basis of their maritime commerce. The Catalans became the organizers of production and challenged the prerogatives of the Ancien Régime's privileged groups. This does not mean, however, that the prevailing social order was questioned or that the sector became fully capitalist. There were still many obstacles to the integration of fishing and processing activities. Some of them are as follows: the maintenance of mariners' registers that prohibited nonregistered mariners from fishing and contributed to the rigidity of supply; the salt monopoly that lasted until 1869 and that represented an additional fiscal cost; and several bureaucratic measures that frustrated access to the so-called guaranteed price. With the elimination of these impediments, the sector progressed, and the production of salted fish laid the foundation for a prosperous canning industry.

As will be seen later in this chapter, the canning industry produced effects on the economy that fish salting did not. The first fish cannery was opened in 1842 in La Coruña, though the industry was not firmly established until after the 1880s. This relative delay in the sector's formation was due to a problem with markets. The lack of communication with the interior forced the sector to resort to the coastal trade, where it encountered stiff competition from the fresh fishing industry. And the foreign market was dominated by the French canneries of Brittany until 1870, owing to the latter's ability to overcome the problems of supplying tinplate. Last, the Spanish colonies in the Caribbean represented the Galician canner's sole market, and its limited size permitted the survival of only a small group of enterprises, thereby restricting the sector's development (Carmona [1983]: 466–467).

The first attempts to establish canneries in Galicia were made between 1841 and 1882. Technological problems (packing, manual sealing, very diversified production, and dependence on French technology), as well as problems in the supply of raw materials (tinplate, oil, glass) served to curb the industry's development. The generalized lack of capital in the Spanish economy also affected the progress of the canning industry, especially since this problem was exacerbated in Galicia by a delayed transformation of the land-tenure system. Toward the last third of the nineteenth century, when disentailment ceased to represent a diversion of capital in the rest of Spain, Galician peasants began to redeem their *foros* with money generated by cattle exports and emigrants' remittances, thereby absorbing capital that could have been used for industry (Carmona [1983]: 461–462).

Nevertheless, canneries were rapidly raised during the last two decades of the century: from 6 in 1880 their number rose to 82 in 1905. This jump was also reflected in exports. In 1905 canned fish represented 40% of the total foodstuffs exported from Spain (Carmona [1983]: 473). This growth was motivated by several changes. First, owing to a series of circumstances that favored the transition from fish salting to canning, a new social group arose that was interested in the sector's development. The elimination of the state salt monopoly released funds that were previously tied up in the illegal salt trade. It also meant one step further toward the separation between fishing and processing, since salt smuggling was previously often carried out by fishermen. During this period, the transfer of profits from the fish-salting plants to Catalonia also decreased, with the result that capital accumulation in Galicia was now possible. In addition, remittances from emigrants in Spanish America began to grow to such an extent that some of the returning emigrants invested in the establishment of canning enterprises. Finally, the opening of the railroad line that linked northern seaport of La Coruña with the capital of the nation, Madrid, and the southern part of Vigo inland with Orense broke Galicia's isolation. The canning industry benefited from an easier access to the national market.

Another boon came from the crisis in Brittany's fishing-canning sector in 1882 after sardines disappeared from its coastal waters. This led to an under-supply on the world market. The French responded by penetrating the Galician canning sector through the provision of technology, capital, and a sure market; mixed companies were the vehicle by which they achieved this. In 1882 a commercial treaty was signed with France in which the import duties on Spanish canned goods were reduced by one-third. Exports experienced a spectacular growth and were channeled largely through the port of Vigo, where 43% of the canneries were located in 1907. However, the growth of exports declined at the end of the century owing both to the recuperation of the Brittany's canning industry and to Portuguese competition. At the same time, outdated fishing techniques severely restricted the supply of fish for canning. At the beginning of the twentieth century, the use of dragnets and steamboats in addition to the decline in the peseta's rate of exchange favored the recovery of exports. This was a period in which many canneries were established and in which the introduction of mechanical welding reduced production costs by cutting back on the number of welders needed in the factories. Lastly, with the creation of the Union of Canning Manufacturers, which protected the sector's interests, the Galician canning industry reached maturity and was consolidated.

The canning industry was, therefore, the only industrial sector to become developed and consolidated in Galicia, and it did so independently of developments in the agrarian sector. In other words, the two sectors were separate entities, each with its own market and its own areas of influence. In conclusion, both the limited agrarian transformations and the localized industrialization were oriented toward the exterior, each with its own independent market area, whereas the Galician economy remained loosely interconnected.

FURTHER READINGS

On population and migration see:

Barreiro Gil, M. J. "Población, propiedad de la tierra y formación del mercado agrario en Galicia (1900–1930)." Ph.D. diss., Santiago, 1983.

Beiras, J. M. *Estructura y problemas de la población gallega.* Coruña, 1970.

López Taboada, X. A. *Economía e población en Galicia.* Coruña, 1979.

Meijide Pardo, A. *La emigración gallega intrapeninsular en el siglo XVIII.* Madrid, 1960.

O'Flanagan, P. "The Changing Population Structure of Galicia, 1900–1970." *Iberian Studies* 5 (1976): 61–80.

Rodríguez Galdo, M. X. "A crise agraria de 1853 e a emigración galega a Cuba." *Grial* 57 (1977): 261–272.

———. "Os efectos demográficos da crise de mediados do s. XIX." *Grial, Anexo Historia* 1 (1982): 28–36.

Sánchez López, F. *Los movimientos migratorios en Galicia.* Vigo, 1977.

Vázquez González, A. "Aportación al análisis cuantitativo de la emigración gallega a America (1853–1931)." Master's thesis. Santiago, 1982.

On subsistence agriculture and changes in the agrarian sector see:

Barreiro Gil, M. J. "Notas sobre la evolución histórica de la ganadería gallega (1859–1935)." *Investigaciones Económicas* 19 (1982): 95–112.

———. "La generalización de la producción de mercancías y la modernización productiva de la agricultura en Galicia, 1876–1976," *Revista de Historia Económica* 1, no. 2 (1983): 133–146.

Carmona, X. "Sobre as orixes da orientación exportadora bovina galega." *Grial, Anexo Historia* 1 (1982a): 169–206.

Dopico, F. "Productividade, rendementos e tecnoloxía na agricultura galega de fins do seculo XIX." *Grial, Anexo Historia* 1 (1982): 68–81.

García-Lombardero, J. *La agricultura y el estancamiento económico de Galicia en la España del Antiguo Régimen.* Madrid, 1973.

Rodríguez-Galdo, M. X., and F. Dopico. *Crisis agrarias y crecimiento económico en Galicia en el siglo XIX.* Coruña, 1981.

Villares Paz, R. *La propiedad de la tierra en Galicia, 1500–1936.* Madrid, 1982a.

———. *Foros, Fidalgos e Frades.* Vigo, 1982b.

On the failure of the industrialization process see:

Alonso Alvarez, L. *Industrialización y conflictos sociales en la Galicia del Antiguo Régimen (1750–1830).* Madrid, 1976.

Carmona, X. "La problemática de la industrialización en la Galicia del siglo XIX." In J. Barreiro Somoza, and L. Barrio Murga, eds., *Galicia: rasgos originales y perspectivas de conjunto.* Vigo, 1981.

———. "Producción textil rural e actividades marítimo-pesqueiras na Galicia, 1750–1905." Ph.D. diss., Santiago, 1983.

———. "L'industria rurale domestica in Galizia, secoli XVIII–XIX." *Quaderni Storici* 52 (1982b): 11–24.

Carmona, X., and J. García-Lombardero. "Tradición e modernización nas pescarias galegas: artes de pesca e organización da producción, séculos XVIII–XIX." In *I Coloquio "Santos Graça" de Etnografía Marítima.* Povoa de Varzim, 1982.

Meijide Pardo, A. *Navegantes catalanes y sus fábricas de salazón en la ría de Arosa.* Coruña, 1973.

13.

CASTILE, 1830–1930: THE RISE OF A NEO-ARCHAIC AGRICULTURE

NICOLÁS SÁNCHEZ-ALBORNOZ
New York University

PREVIOUS CHAPTERS have analyzed Spain's industrialization and modernization process between 1830 and 1930—a process whose intensity and success greatly varied. Regions which did not lead those changes were nevertheless part of the general overhaul. The process somehow engulfed the entire nation, making it impossible for the retarded regions to emerge unscathed. Capitalism penetrated these areas also, but instead of fostering industrialization and modernization, it often induced a simplification of old agrarian structures.

This sort of involution toward an economic condition somewhat vestigial occurred especially on the Peninsula's interior plateau, where Old and New Castile occupied the largest area. It also applies, with some variations, to other regions in the interior. Although Madrid lies in the heart of Castile, it is not included in this analysis because, as the nation's capital, it developed independently of the region within which it was located.[1] Castile's regression toward a simpler, more dependent economic condition led it rank lower within Spain's regional scale. The region's growth rate lagged behind that of the more active regions, and its importance in the overall economy declined between 1830 and 1930.

In order to appreciate the extent of Castile's internal change, the economy of the Ancien Régime will be used as a reference point. In his analysis of the modernization process in Catalonia, Maluquer de Motes also described that region on the eve of industrialization. He found that, at the beginning of the eighteenth century, Catalonia already displayed the prerequisites for industrial

240

development, although the process was interrupted by noneconomic events. Consequently, sustained industrial growth was delayed for decades. The Castilian case does not exhibit parallel features. During the Ancien Régime, there certainly were several attempts, both private and official, to establish factories. All failed quickly, however. The idle looms of Segovia, the Cameros Mountains, and the Royal Manufactures attest these frustrated initiatives.[2] Castile did not seem to have the inner dynamism needed for radical change. Neither did its economy—small in scale but relatively diversified—exhibit the kind of gross imbalances that would compel a search for transformation.

At the end of the eighteenth century, the area's economy provided the basic diet of the Castilian population. This consisted of grains and legumes in abundance; some meat and animal fat for cooking; wine; and, occasionally, fruits and vegetables. On the southern plateau, vegetable oil substituted for, or complemented, lard. Here and there, some plant fibers, such as flax, were grown. Large urban centers were not found in Castile. Madrid, of course, was an exception, but when compared with other capitals, such as Paris or London, it becomes clear that it was not such a large outlet for the agriculture and manufactures of the surrounding area.

Cereal production and stockraising were its most suitable and dominant economic activities. In addition, the region extracted a wide range of secondary products—oil, wine, and firewood—with which its inhabitants diversified and supplemented their incomes. Castilians also produced their own clothes, tools, and household goods; there was also a modest manufacturing base that provided a variety of nonagricultural jobs.

While a sizable work force was available, labor was not as abundant in Castile as in other regions, such as the Canaries, Santander, the Basque Provinces or Galicia, where part of the population was forced to emigrate, often overseas. Rather, in Castile there was a seasonal labor shortage. At harvest time, work gangs descended from Galicia and traversed the countryside, reaping the grain fields. Output, income, and employment thus came from a variety of sources. The ordinary man seldom had to look outside Castile for the goods he used to consume frugally. Owing to the economy's simplicity, raw materials and capital goods were not in great demand. At most, some luxury items were brought in from abroad for the consumption of a small privileged class. Such isolation was broken by an outward flow. For the most part, Castile exported one product which has been coveted in Europe since time immemorial—wool. The enormous flocks of sheep that roamed the plateau in search of pasture provided this highly valued product. Because of the volume of these exports, the region earned abroad revenues that, in turn, allowed the accumulation of modest amounts of capital.

Of course, such self-sufficiency did not further close relations either with other areas of the Peninsula or with other countries; nor did it favor an early exposure of Castile to the changes being wrought by industrial capitalism in northern Europe. The diffusion of these changes did not find fertile ground in the region.

Industrialization, at this early stage, was founded on factors and resources with which Castile had never been well endowed. The region had plenty of lands and sufficient labor but had not accumulated large amounts of capital—the factor of production that became the most crucial one after the industrial revolution. Also the region did not possess the rich coal deposits so necessary for the production of energy; nor was it endowed with the most important raw material for new industry—iron. At mid-nineteenth century, Castile was searched intensively by engineers of various nationalities for coal, iron, and other minerals. Their findings were of little substance. The fossils of Barruelo in the province of Palencia fueled the locomotives of the Northern line as well as the gas factories and stoves of Castilians; they could not, however, sustain heavy industry. The same can be said for the coal fields of Puertollano and León, which were exploited later.

The search did not uncover minerals like those found in the Andalusian subsoil—lead or copper pyrites, for example. Iron, which was to play such an important role in the industrialization and capitalization of Spain, was located outside the region. Ore extraction and processing were never significant features of the Castilian economy.

The industrial revolution succeeded in mechanizing textile production. This process was based on the manufacture of a cheap, lightweight plant fiber—cotton. It was brought from overseas and replaced wool, the heavier animal fiber, which had been traditionally imported largely from Castile. The rising cotton industry deprived Castile of its favored position in international trade and contributed to the region's ousting from world market.

The subsequent transformation of Castile was not internally generated; it was, nevertheless, unavoidable. On the national level, the region was part of what could be called an early division of labor. It was a prime area for dry farming in cereals and was to focus on this activity. This specialization was hardly the result of an arduous and dynamic struggle with national and foreign competitors. Rather, it was imposed on the area, and Castile agreed to its assigned role.

Pressured by a series of financial crises—owing, to some extent, to the drop in remittances from the former Spanish-American colonies—the Spanish Parliament prohibited grain imports in 1820. In the short term, the aim of this measure was to halt capital drain; in the long-term, to stimulate domestic production. In spite of the political instability of the period, this prohibition lasted surprisingly—with some minor alterations—almost half a century. When it was finally abrogated, it was replaced by a strong protectionist tariff that remained in force from the last quarter of the nineteenth century until recently, as was mentioned in earlier chapters. In other words, a stop-gap measure was transformed into a systematic policy.[3] A whole network of firmly entrenched interests grew up around this policy and succeeded in distorting the national economy for the entire period.

The prohibition was initially successful, since it relieved the balance of trade from the burden of food imports. The grain-deficient regions, mostly those of the littoral, had to make up for their chronic shortages by trading with the surplus regions of the nation, which they did until the 1870s except when there were poor harvests, shortages, or famines. Producers on the central plateau stopped focusing solely on local or regional consumption and tried to supply the whole country. In this way, the prohibition encouraged the circulation of goods from the interior to the periphery. In short, it promoted national integration.

The growth of trade required a means of communication that would be faster, more punctual, and more suited to bulky cargoes. The railroads, constructed in the second half of the nineteenth century, responded to this new requirement. Favorable prices and improved transportation encouraged a transition to capitalist production for the market. During this period, Castile assumed a dominant position in the national grain market and began to dictate its variations and fluctuations.[4]

The commercialization of Castilian agriculture fostered an alteration of the land tenure system that, in turn, favored further commercialization. During the Ancien Régime, a large proportion of the land was entailed to wealthy families and public corporations, such as the church and the towns. The laws of disentailment promoted the disposal of land, both in large holdings and in individual plots. After the decrees of 1836 and 1855, huge tracts of land were marketed and sold. Many of these holdings, especially communal holdings, consisted of pasturelands and woodlands.[5]

Grain production was, therefore, extended to idle lands. The woodlands and pastures were rapidly plowed over, as Julio Senador bitterly complained still in 1905. In response to a market upheld by protectionist policies, cereal production expanded, though without an increase in productivity. In fact, productivity levels stagnated and even declined, as Gabriel Tortella has mentioned in Chapter 3. This is certainly the reverse of the current situation where such levels have increased, giving rise to an improvement in both the agriculture and the welfare of the region's inhabitants.

In recent years, according to Jesús García Fernández, the area under cultivation has contracted rapidly. Marginal lands have been excluded from cultivation. Because of crop rotation and the greater use of fertilizers, fallow lands have diminished. The adoption of new technology has improved the processes of both planting and harvesting. Consequently, grain yields have increased spectacularly. When the extension of the cultivated area was at its maximum, the average yield was only 6 metric quintals per hectare; today it is about 16. The Castilian population has, therefore, experienced marked improvement in its standard of living. During this transformation, however, agriculture has become less labor-intensive, giving rise to a surplus population that has had to emigrate. Total population has declined, but the urban population has increased. Some of the region's inhabitants have even migrated abroad.

In the past, the expansion of grain cultivation had opposite denotations. Instead of fostering migration, it resulted in the retention of a large rural population. The breaking up of pasture and woodlands required more labor than stockbreeding. There was more work for farm hands, and shepherds had to look for new occupations. A rural-to-urban migration of peasants did not occur. As Pérez Moreda has shown in Chapter 1, cities barely grew during this period; nor did peasants migrate abroad as opposed to their contemporaries in Britain; Scandinavia; Italy; and even in other regions of Spain, most notably Galicia and Asturias. Only later, when the grain expansion slackened and the peasants' impoverishment reached a critical level, did Castilians begin to abandon the land and migrate to the northern mines and other areas of Europe. This migration was especially prevalent in the early years of the twentieth century.

A view which equates a large population with power and prosperity has traditionally prevailed in Castile. This attitude was somehow justified during the Ancien Régime, when economic growth came largely after increases in manpower. Also, the larger the population, the greater general consumption seemed to be. All this was no longer true after the industrial revolution. Growth became a function of capital investment, and the working population was important for its knowhow and consumption standards. Consequently, the retention of large numbers of people in an agriculture of low productivity did not provide them with new skills or raise their standards of living. On the contrary, poor harvests frequently assumed catastrophic dimensions. The subsistence crises of the second third of the nineteenth century were often fatal because an increasing proportion of the population depended on cereal monoculture and thus became subject to its vagaries. Fortuitous food shortages could not be alleviated through imports, since the prohibition hampered grain importation. In such cases, the shortage would spiral until it caused widespread hunger.

During the Ancien Régime, sheep raising provided Castile with substantial wealth. The destruction and sackings that occurred during the Napoleonic War caused the flock to shrink, and the fall in international wool prices left little inducement for its reconstruction. The concurrent expansion of land under cultivation combined with the elimination of the privileges that the Mesta (a traditional association of large sheep breeders) enjoyed succeeded in reducing the amount of land suitable for pastoral migration and even for sheep ranching. All factors combined to provoke a stockraising crisis in the first decades of the nineteenth century. A more intensive type of land exploitation replaced the previous extensive form; small farmers prevailed over the powerful ranchers.[6]

Confronted with the rising importance of cotton, wool textiles were doomed to lose ground. Total wool consumption, however, did not actually decline in the industrial nations. Saxony, for example, was able to prosper as a wool-producing area after importing rams from Castile. At the end of the century, Australian and Argentine sheep raisers also introduced Merino sheep into their new lands. Instead of challenging the cotton supply by offering a higher-quality and higher-priced fiber as their competitors did, Castile permitted its flocks to deteriorate throughout the nineteenth century. Castilian sheep raisers did not select breeder sheep carefully. In the face of a market contraction, they attempted to maintain a high volume of exports at the expense of quality.[7]

In lieu of this capitulation, another alternative was theoretically at hand: to process the raw material (wool) and to export the finished product (cloth). Castile, however, continued to export crude wool. Even the mechanized spinning and weaving of wool for internal consumption was not practiced in Castile (with the exception of Béjar); rather, it was done in Catalonia, along with that of cotton.

Castile missed the opportunity to industrialize through working with its own raw materials. Although wool manufacturing would have reached a crisis later anyway, at least such industry would have created an industrial base and a skilled work force for the region, both of which could have been used for other projects. Thus, Castile failed to generate income, capital, jobs, and labor and management training, and it lost whatever backward linkages any new industry produces. Instead, cheaper cotton fabrics eventually replaced the woolens manufactured by local domestic looms. The Castilian countryside could no longer provide itself with clothing materials and had to purchase cloth either from Catalonia or from abroad. Similarly, the region's inhabitants also ceased to fashion their own wares, tan their own leather, and manufacture their own tools and implements. A wide range of goods turned out in the villages began to come increasingly either from the factories of industrialized Spain or from abroad.

The decline of both sheep raising and crafts left Castile completely dependent on agriculture. For its consumption of manufactured goods, the region had to turn increasingly to outside sources. As Gómez Mendoza has shown in Chapter 5, after the construction of the railroad, Castile was flooded with merchandise from other regions, especially between 1878 and 1913. The region exchanged thereafter its cheap grain and flour for more expensive manufactured goods. The development of monoculture and the failure to adopt new technology led to Castile's subordination to Spain's more developed areas.

At the end of the century, when the virgin soils of the Americas and Oceania were brought under cultivation, their grain flooded the world market. Spain began to import these cereals, cautiously at first, in order to satisfy the increased demand of a growing population. Alarm spread immediately among the local producers of the interior. The prohibition against grain imports, recently lifted was however not reinstated. The new protectionist tariffs could neither stop the entry of cereals nor prevent a relative drop in prices. Instead of reacting vigorously, Castilian producers did nothing but look for palliatives and compromises. Their aim was to preserve a mode of production, some profits, and an outdated social order. Instead of energizing the production system, Castilian farmers attempted to recover control over the market through two strategies: (1) they tried to achieve larger harvests by expanding the land under cultivation, and (2) they cut production costs at the expense of the peasants' standard of living. Strong protectionism permitted the region to retain a high market quota—but at the cost of general impoverishment. In contrast to what was occurring in the rest of Western Europe, Castilian landowners attempted to maintain and even increase agrarian profit margins.[8] At the beginning of the twentieth century, the general feeling in the region's towns and cities was one of atrophy, as portrayed in the literary writings of the Generation of '98.

Opportunities for agricultural diversification first presented themselves on the southern plateau. When the French vineyards were destroyed by phylloxera and wine prices rose, the area of La Mancha became overrun with grapevines. By the time these grapevines achieved full yield, France had rebuilt its vineyards and stopped buying wine in large quantities after 1892. The bonanza had lasted only a short while. La Mancha was forced to turn toward the domestic market. Such mass production of ordinary wine added a new, large-scale activity to the regional economy. Conversely, Old Castile, which also suffered from phylloxera, was slow to reconstruct its vineyards; in some places, like Arévalo and Segovia, they disappeared. Viticulture had never been a prime activity in the region, but it did provide supplementary income to the towns in the Duero Valley. From this time on, Old Castile began to depend on other regions for yet another of its staples.

A similar chain of events occurred with regard to oil. Although lard consumption decreased in the 1880s in La Mancha, it was replaced by olive oil that was produced locally. La Mancha, like Andalusia and the Mediterranean coast, then expanded its olive groves. On the northern plateau, as the use of olive oil spread, pig raising contracted drastically—by more than two-thirds—between 1865 and 1891. Unsuitable for olive cultivation, the region had to import oil from the South.

Cuban independence provided Old Castile with its first opportunity to adopt a new commercial crop. Now that Spain did not have to buy colonial sugar, sugar beets were planted in the irrigable lands of the Duero Valley. This new crop endowed the region with a food industry of national importance. Beets were refined locally, and their sugar was sold throughout the country. Old Castile also increased its potato crop (see Table 13.1).

Table 13.1
Agricultural Gross Product in Old Castile and León,
1860–1931 (in millions of 1910 pesetas)

	1860	*1890*	*1900*	*1910*	*1922*	*1931*
Grain	—	336	425	406	489	482
Legumes	—	40	31	42	72	63
Wine	51	64	52	47	53	52
Potatoes	—	33	33	56	67	115
Sugar Beets	—	2	2	3	4	17
Agriculture	567	519	587	605	753	813
Stockraising	165	130	118	117	164	165

SOURCE: A. García Sanz and J. Sanz, "Evolución económica de Castilla y León en las épocas moderna y contemporánea," *Papeles de Economía* 20 (1984): 345.
NOTE: In 1930 the value (at constant prices) of the regions' output of grain, wine, and stock animals reverted to its 1860 level after recovering from a turn-of-the-century slump. Only the production of potatoes and sugar beets experienced important growth during the post–World War I period. Meanwhile, the population of Old Castile and León slowly increased from 2.1 million in 1860 to 2.5 million in 1931.

This promising note brings to a close a quick review of the changes that occurred in Castile beginning toward the end of the eighteenth century—a time when England and other European regions were on the brink of the industrial revolution. Although Castile remained on the periphery of the industrialization process, it nevertheless did experience change. The Castilian economy did not remain stationary over time, repeating the same monotonous patterns, nor did its landscape remain unaltered. Agrarian capitalism penetrated the region, as grain was produced increasingly for the market and for national consumption. Toward the mid-nineteenth century, some was even exported to Cuba, Puerto Rico, and occasionally to other European nations. With the plowing over of the woodlands, open landscapes became generalized. Last, the region's sheepraising activities contracted, and its crafts virtually disappeared.

The Castilian economy, now capitalist, drifted toward a neo-archaic state. Grain production increased, not through capital inputs, but by expanding the traditional production system—that is, by adding land and labor. In other words, harvests increased in tandem with the expansion of land under cultivation or with population growth. The region's products were neither competitive nor remunerative. Tied to the countryside, the Castilian population remained predominantly rural, and factories and cities did not materialize.

Castilian agriculture was not given over to the cultivation of export fruits, as occurred in Valencia and Andalusia. Nor did Castile specialize in grain production as the result of an active international trade; rather, this came about because of inertia, tariff barriers, and its assigned role within the framework of the national economy.

Cereal monoculture, the contraction of sheep raising, and the loss of crafts led to a gross simplification of the regional economy. Castilians were no longer able to provide their own needs, as they had during the Ancien Régime, and they were increasingly forced to purchase foodstuffs and manufactures from outside. This trade fostered the region's progressive integration into the emerging national economy. Internal barriers diminished while the links between regions became stronger. The integrative process was not carried out on the basis of equality, however, and it resulted in an asymmetrical relationship between regions. The staples of the plateau, which were cultivated with great effort and even at the cost of lowering the peasants' standard of living, were traded for goods with high added value. Economically, Castile remained at the mercy of the nascent industrial regions.

Castilians had no choice but to acquire native manufactures. Apart from protectionist policies that required that the region satisfy its needs from Spanish sources, Castile's shortage of foreign earnings kept it a captive of national producers and precluded trade with more competitive suppliers. Through law and necessity, Castile was transformed into a captive market, especially for Catalan and Basque industries. In this way, the region indirectly subsidized the industrialization of Spain.

The economic evolution of Castile in the nineteenth and early twentieth centuries warrants a comparison with the more recent development patterns of the so-called Third World. At some point, a region with an economy diversified enough to meet its subsistence needs becomes integrated into the world economy. Its soil and climate are especially suited to the production of one or two particular crops. Eventually, the region succumbs to monoculture and begins to depend on imports for all its other needs, especially manufactured goods. In this manner, an economic dependency evolves that is frequently accompanied by political subordination. Like these countries, Castile became integrated into the modern world, not through the development of heavy industry and high finance, but through agricultural underdevelopment. Its integration was, however, different in that it occurred several decades earlier (as in other peripheral areas of Europe) and in that the center on which the region depended was not a foreign power but was located within Spain. Castile was subordinated to the industrializing regions of the nation. Political relations, however, functioned in the reverse; though economically subordinate, the region managed to retain a good deal of its traditional influence. Owing to this disequilibrium between the economic and political systems, vehement disagreements and conflicts arose which would be ventilated during the Civil War.

NOTES

1. For a treatment of the anomalous relationship between Madrid and the surrounding region of Castile see D. Ringrose, *Madrid and the Spanish Economy, 1560–1850* (Berkeley, 1983), and N. Sánchez-Albornoz, *Madrid ante la Castilla agraria en el siglo XIX* (Madrid, 1983).

2. Agustín González Enciso, "La protoindustrialización en Castilla la Vieja en el siglo XVIII," *Revista de Historia Económica* 2 (1984): 51–82.

3. N. Sánchez-Albornoz, *Las crisis de subsistencias de España en el siglo XIX* (Rosario, 1963), pp. 13–45.

4. D. Peña and N. Sánchez-Albornoz, "Wheat Prices in Spain, 1857–1890: An Application of the Box-Jenkins Methodology," *Journal of European Economic History* 13 (1984): 353–373.

5. An important case study of land disentailment in Castile can be found in G. Rueda, *La desamortización de Mendizábal en Valladolid, 1836–1853: Transformaciones y constantes en el mundo rural y urbano de Castilla la Vieja* (Valladolid, 1980).

6. Julius Klein, *The Mesta: A Study in Spanish Economic History, 1273–1836* (Cambridge, Mass., 1920).

7. Grupo de Estudios de Historia Rural, "Contribución al análisis historico de la ganadería española, 1865–1929," *Agricultura y sociedad* 8 (1978): 129–181.

8. R. Robledo, *La renta de la tierra en Castilla la Vieja y León, 1836–1913* (Madrid, 1984).

FURTHER READINGS

An early outline of this chapter can be found in N. Sánchez-Albornoz, "Castilla en el siglo XIX: una involución económica," *Revista de Occidente* 17 (1982): 35–49. For another overview see A. García Sanz and Jesús Sanz, "Evolución económica de Castilla y León en las épocas moderna y contemporánea," *Papeles de Economía* 20 (1984): 333–349. On how the premodern demographic pattern lingered in Castile see V. Pérez Moreda, *Las crisis de mortalidad en la España interior, siglos XVI–XIX* (Madrid, 1980). The odd relationship between Madrid and Castile is discussed briefly in N. Sánchez-Albornoz, *Madrid ante la Castilla agraria en el siglo XIX* (Madrid, 1983); a broader and more elaborate view appears in D. Ringrose, *Madrid and the Spanish Economy, 1560–1850* (Berkeley, 1983). The miserable state of Castilian agriculture at the beginning of the twentieth century was described by J. Senador Gómez, *Castilla en escombros: las leyes, las tierras, el trigo y el hambre* (1915); 2d ed. (Madrid, 1978). R. Robledo has recently studied the evolution of land rents in *La renta de la tierra en Castilla y León, 1836–1913* (Madrid, 1984). For social contrasts in the agrarian world see J. J. Castillo, *Propietarios muy pobres: Sobre la subordinación política del pequeño campesino en España (La Confederación Nacional Católico-Agraria, 1917–1942)* (Madrid, 1984). In F. Manero, *La industria en Castilla y León: dinámica, cáracteres, impacto* (Valladolid, 1983), observations on Castilian manufacturing can be found. J. Muñoz, "Los desequilibrios regionales: El caso de Castilla," in *Castilla como necesidad* (Madrid, 1980), pp. 65–116, refers to a more contemporary period but contains occasional references to earlier events. For recent changes in Castile see J. García Fernández, *Desarrollo y atonía en Castilla* (Barcelona, 1981).

14.

ON THE HISTORICAL ORIGINS OF ANDALUSIAN UNDERDEVELOPMENT

PEDRO TEDDE DE LORCA
Universidad de Málaga

THE SOCIOECONOMIC IMAGE of Andalusia is generally one of underdevelopment and disequilibrium. Although the region generates one of the largest contributions to Spain's Gross National Product, it exhibits one of the nation's lowest per capita incomes. At 103,103 pesetas per year in 1975, it lagged far behind the national average of 144,731 pesetas, and its poverty level was second only to that of Extremadura. There are also noticeable differences in the region's ranking of various economic sectors vis-à-vis the Spanish norm; Andalusian agriculture plays a much more significant role in the region's overall economy than anywhere else in Spain. The uneven distribution of wealth, particularly of land, and the variations in economic capacity from one area of the region to another are enormous. There are glaring inequities in the composition of agricultural and industrial production and of services, as well as in the land tenure system and market relations.

When a general economic crisis occurs (like the ongoing one), regions characterized by long-standing disequilibrium and relative backwardness are more vulnerable, owing to a scarcity of resources and a lack of alternatives. In more positive situations, a rapid reorientation toward other activities or an increase in productivity through technological inputs would mitigate the crisis by permitting greater market penetration. Where this does not take place, as in the case of Andalusia, the crisis leads both to higher unemployment rates than those of other regions and to a decline in investments and economic activity.

The unfavorable economic image of Andalusia does not stem solely from its greater vulnerability to the present crisis. In 1955, when Andalusia began to participate in Spain's industrial revolution, it already ranked low in per capita income, lagging behind both the industrialized areas (e.g., the Basque Provinces, Catalonia, Valencia, and Asturias) and the agrarian regions (e.g., Castile and León). In that year, one-third of the Regional Product was generated by the primary sector.[1]

Regular series of macromagnitudes are lacking for earlier periods, but the impression of an impoverished and unegalitarian Andalusia—that is, a region characterized by many poor people and an unequal distribution of resources— seems quite generalized. Still, there are solid indications that the Andalusian economy was not always inferior to that of the rest of Spain. In this case, one should ask when Andalusian society began to move down vis-à-vis other societies and what the causes of that regression were.

That Andalusia was not always poor and, in fact, was once a prosperous region is borne out in the historical records of the distant past, that is, prior to the nineteenth century. Qualitative evidence reveals, among other things, that the region experienced demographic growth—a noteworthy trend in pre-industrial societies—and engaged in active trade; this, in turn, leads to as-sumptions about the creation of surpluses and the existence of a comparatively efficient economy, perhaps to some degree superior to that of other peninsular regions. The Andalusia of the Lower Middle Ages, which was incorporated into the Crown of Castile, also showed signs of prosperity; Lower Andalusia was home to bankers and merchants, many of them foreigners, even before the discovery of America.[2]

The first quantitative evidence of Andalusia's favorable economic position in relation to the other regions of the Castilian Crown stems from the mid-eighteenth century. According to the Catastro de Ensenada (a general survey ordered by the latter minister), Andalusia made in 1751 the highest contribu-tion to the Gross Product of the Castilian Crown; the region accounted for 577.6 million reales, or 29% of the total, compared with 11.8% for Old Castile and 8.3% for Galicia. Only New Castile approximated Andalusia's contribu-tion, with a figure of 23.2%.

It can certainly be argued that a populated region would logically contribute a considerable share to the Social Product. However, in per capita terms Andalusia's income was still 353.4 reales, ranking third, behind New Castile and Murcia, and almost tied with Extremadura.[3] The high agricultural pro-ductivity of Andalusia, mainly in the Guadalquivir Valley, and its commercial activity, especially that of the transatlantic trade, explain the region's predomi-nance vis-à-vis other regions.

Owing to highly fertile lands—at least in the western part of the region— and the Spanish-American trade, Andalusia's preindustrial economy was rela-tively prosperous within the realm of the Crown of Castile. At the moment, no comparison can be made with the territories of the Crown of Aragón that would include Valencia and Catalonia—a region where important transformations occurred in the eighteenth century. Within the peninsula, both these regions were probably quite advanced economically.

The loss of the Spanish Main was sure to have had a negative impact on the Andalusian economy. Declining shipments of precious metals and a slackening of trade caused a deterioration in the region's economic efficiency, as well as a loss of capital and labor. To what extent were these losses decisive for the future development or stagnation of Andalusia?

The cities that engaged in overseas trade were deeply affected by the loss of the Spanish-American colonies. Ironically, however, the end of the Cádiz monopoly, just before the American trade was cut off, had not resulted in a slump in Andalusia's transatlantic trade, according to Antonio García-Baquero.[4] In the 1820s, however, when the Spanish-American colonies won their independence, exports from Cádiz to Spanish America plummeted to an annual average of 78.5 million reales, as opposed to 265.9 million at the end of the 1780s. Nicolás Sánchez-Albornoz and García-Baquero have collected concrete evidence on the economic decline of Cádiz: the population decreased by one-third in the first quarter of the nineteenth century; out of 600 commercial houses, 227 went bankrupt between 1811 and 1824; and seven-eighths of the foreign merchants abandoned the city. Seville, which might have been able to maintain its colonial trade after the loss of the monopoly, was nevertheless seriously affected by Spanish-American independence. The bankruptcies of 165 commercial houses between 1785 and 1831 attests to this.[5]

Recently, Gonzalo Anes and Leandro Prados have questioned the importance of the Spanish-American trade for Spain's economy and the negative effects of its severance. Prados denies that the loss of the colonies had as dramatic an impact on the Spanish economy as other authors have theorized. He claims that the loss was soon compensated by Spain's closer ties with the industrializing countries of the period.[6] Gonzalo Anes, moreover, postulates that the overall exportation of primary products to Spanish America was only marginally important for the agrarian changes that occurred in Spain from the sixteenth to the eighteenth century; he does, however, acknowledge that these exports may have benefited specific areas linked to the ports of Seville and Cádiz.[7] Citing information from García-Baquero,[8] Anes describes the composition of the agricultural exports destined for Spanish America; wine, brandy, and oil accounted for 90% of the total, and they derived from Cádiz, Jérez de la Frontera, Puerto de Santa María, Sanlucar de Barrameda, Huelva, and Seville. In addition, wines from Benicarló and Catalonia and brandy from Catalonia were also shipped from there; in some cases, the brandy was produced by Catalans living in Andalusia. Almost all the oil exported to Spanish America was Andalusian.

All this confirms that the agriculture of the southern coast, more precisely that of Lower Andalusia, was linked to the Spanish-American market. The volume of transactions, however, seems to indicate that overseas exports in the eighteenth century were not crucial to the agrarian economy of Spain or of Andalusia. Thus, the shift in wine and oil exports from Spanish-American to northern European markets, especially British markets, in the nineteenth century could have kept output high for those Lower Andalusian products, in spite of colonial independence. Leandro Prados has proved elsewhere that sherry and oil exports, mainly to France and Great Britain, expanded. With sherry constituting one-third of wine exports, this rise led to a 27% increase in the land under cultivation between 1818 and 1839 and to an increase of investments in grape growing thanks to the repatriation of Spanish-American capital.[9]

All these considerations lead to a reappraisal of the extent to which the Andalusian economy was affected by Spanish America's loss. Even if the relationship between the region's economy and the Spanish-American market was significant, colonial independence could not have triggered a process of economic decadence. Perhaps the reorientation of Andalusian agriculture and cattle-raising toward the domestic market explains why Seville and Cádiz (and, after 1865, other southern ports) were unable to generate a radical transformation of the region's economy similar to that which occurred in Catalonia, for example. As Vilar has shown, the Catalan economy of the eighteenth century had both foreshadowed and motivated an emerging industrial economy in that region. Expansion of the transatlantic trade played a dynamic role in the formation of Catalonia's market economy, but the region's domestic market (and not only for industrial products) was crucial to Catalan industrialization.[10]

Similar changes in Andalusia's productive economy, or in its internal market, are difficult to observe during the eighteenth century. The majority of manufactures exported to Spanish America from Cádiz were produced outside the region, and a great many merchants who participated in Andalusia's transatlantic trade were foreigners.[11] These facts corroborate the lack of a pivotal relationship between the Spanish-American trade and Andalusia's productive economy. The fundamental sector of the regional economy, agriculture, was probably marginal to that trade.

Moreover, the agrarian sectors most tied to the transatlantic trade were perfectly attuned to the organization of production in Andalusian agriculture. The wine and oil trades were quickly reoriented to other export markets without altering any basic features of the region's primary sector. In the case of Málaga, two studies, one on the eighteenth century by María Aurora Gámez Amián and the other on the nineteenth by José Morilla, demonstrate the steadfast relationship between grape growers, most of whom were *minifundistas* (small landowners), and exporters, many of whom were foreigners. The latter had established themselves in the city in the late eighteenth and early nineteenth centuries. The weakness of the first group and the second group's loss of entrepreneurial efficiency were exposed by the phylloxera crisis at the end of the nineteenth century.[12]

The agrarian structure in the Guadalquivir Valley was different; here the large landed estates predominated, and seasonal wage laborers were employed. There were also others who worked in the preparation, preservation, and transport of the products and who often combined these tasks with purely agricultural labor.

A 1978 study by Miguel Artola, Antonio Miguel Bernal, and J. Contreras shows the persistence of the large landed estates during the nineteenth and twentieth centuries;[13] disentailment did not seem to have altered landownership. Andalusian nobles continued to be the principal landowners in the nineteenth century. A second group originated among eighteenth-century tenant farmers who purchased disentailed and manorial lands during the following century. Around 1850, the aristocrats and this new group constituted between 4% and 7% of the landowners in the province of Seville, while controlling between 60% and 80% of the land. At the end of the eighteenth century, landowners represented 38.4% of the agriculturalists, while tenant farmers represented 61.6%; at mid-nineteenth century, the figures were 78.8% for landowners and 21.2% for tenant farmers. This change in the ratio of landowners to tenant farmers, however, did not affect the ratio between large and small farms.

The income and market value of the land grew steadily between 1700 and 1870. A high point in the value of land was caused by speculation and the search for secure investments. A. M. Bernal has estimated, in a study focusing on three towns, that agricultural profits ranged from 12% to 18% on lands devoted to grain, 20% on those devoted to olives, and more on those devoted to grapes.[14] These exceptional profits help to explain why industrial investments were sluggish and belie the notion of idle farmers who were interested in their lands only as a source of social prestige. They also suggest that there was no lack of interest in economic rationalization that would have prevented new agricultural technology and capital (e.g., irrigation works) from spreading.

Finally, the cost of labor must be considered. Capital and technology usually substitute for labor as soon as the relative cost of labor rises. This cost of labor, in turn, depends on the relationship between its supply and its demand, the labor supply being directly related to population. Vicente Pérez Moreda's recent data show a marked increase in the Andalusian population; between 1797 and 1860, the increase was 55.8%, while in Spain as a whole it was only 48.5%. During the period 1860–1920, the growth rate of the Andalusian population was 41.2%, less than in the previous period just mentioned. It is possible that Málaga's phylloxera crisis reduced the region's growth rate by spurring a fairly large-scale emigration. The total population of the province of Málaga contracted from 519,377 inhabitants in 1887 to 485,229 in 1897 and did not recover its 1887 level until the census of 1910. The rest of Andalusia's population increased continuously until 1920, at a rate above the national average, which was 31.2% for the period from 1860 to 1920.[15]

A substantial population increase combined with large estates, especially in the western and northern parts of the region, resulted in low agricultural wages. A. M. Bernal has collected data on this subject from all the Andalusian provinces. In general, there seems to have been a clear stagnation—or even a depression—in wage levels from 1790 to 1850. At mid-nineteenth century, however, international trends plus the construction of the local railroad brought salaries up to their 1790 levels. Farmhands earned about 6.6 reales, whereas day laborers received 5.5.[16]

Fiscal data show that Andalusia contributed 21.9% of all taxes collected in Spain in 1858. However, within the lower tax brackets (1–10 reales), Andalusian property owners contributed only 11% of all taxes collected in this bracket, while in the higher range Andalusian large landowners paid 50.5% of the total. Many of the property owners who belonged to the 500- to 1,000-reales bracket were from Seville, Cádiz, and Córdoba, provinces noted for their large landed estates; Huelva, Granada and Almería, on the other hand, were characterized by smallholdings and hence by lower tax brackets. In Jaén and Málaga, intermediate tax brackets prevailed.[17] In the province of Jaén and in the district of Antequera in Málaga, large landowners predominated and devoted extensive fields to grain and olives. In the rest of the province of Málaga, especially in the eastern region near Granada, small grape-growers prevailed. The standard of living and income levels of smallholders in the different areas of Andalusia depended, of course, on various circumstances:

quality of soil, farm size, type of crops, existence or lack of irrigation, and the degree of monopoly of demand for agricultural products on the part of merchants and exporters. Although many small family farms produced sufficient income, especially if they were located in vegetable, grain, or olive zones, there were others that frequently experienced great hardship. The case of Málaga's grape growers, mentioned earlier, is an example. In the same vein, a recent study on the sugar industry of Granada illustrates the hardships endured, during the entire nineteenth century, by the medium and small property-owners of the plains, one of the most fertile areas of the province. At the end of the eighteenth century, hemp cultivation became an alternative to that of grain, but the decline of the former during the first few decades of the nineteenth century forced farmers to return to traditional crops; in the absence of new methods or technology that would increase yields and without the possibility of expanding arable land, the plains' economy entered a phase of stagnation until the 1880s, when the first sugar mills for processing beets were established, making this crop prevalent in the area.[18] Subtropical products like cotton and sugar cane in the southern areas and beets on the plains of Granada were among the few crop innovations to appear in Andalusia from the eighteenth to the twentieth century. One change worth mentioning is the expansion of land devoted to olive production; another is the decrease of vineyards during the nineteenth century. Grain continued to be the region's principal crop.

The European cereal crisis of the last quarter of the nineteenth century succeeded in reinforcing the protectionist system of Spanish agriculture, especially Andalusian agriculture. This was counterproductive in the long run, since it prevented the introduction of technology and capital that would have increased yields. At the end of the nineteenth century and the beginning of the twentieth, the relative abundance of labor and a guaranteed national market hindered any modernization of Andalusian agriculture. Andalusia had the potential to modernize earlier than other Spanish regions because of the enormous financial capacity of its wealthy landowners. Modernization did not materialize until the 1950s, however, when alternative employment opportunities for the region's active agrarian population opened up in large Spanish cities and foreign countries. The shortage of workers then led to the replacement of labor with capital. Until 1930 there was some slow progress toward the adoption of technological innovations, such as new fertilizers or agricultural machinery, but still within the traditional economic organization. This slight progress, nevertheless, allowed for a rise in cereal production which reached a high point in the years preceding the Civil War. At the end of the nineteenth century, the statistics of the Andalusian Railroad Company record an advance payment for the transport of farm machinery to the region.[19] François Héran, in an excellent study on the Vázquez family, Sevillian landowners, presents a clear-cut case of the adoption of modern technology in the agricultural areas of western Andalusia in the second half of the nineteenth century. The Portuguese historian, Jaime Reis, has also found evidence of modernization on the part of landholders in southern Portugal during the same period. However, there is contrary evidence that shows a relative regression in technological change during this period. For example, in her book on Carmona (an important village in the area of Seville), Josefina Cruz Villalón concludes that the changes produced during two centuries were insignificant and that qualitative transformations did not occur until as recently as the 1950s.[20]

The replacement of labor with capital depends upon the ratio of prices between one factor and the other. As the rate of population growth diminished in the last third of the nineteenth century and the agrarian crisis of the Mediterranean countries forced increased emigration, labor was partially replaced by capital and technology in order to compensate for declining prices that resulted from increasing yields. This did not generally prevent Andalusia's agricultural entrepreneurs from basing the production of their enterprises on labor until the middle of the present century. This trend was also reinforced by growing protectionist policies that isolated Spanish prices from international trends. During the last decades of the nineteenth century, there was a depression in the entire primary sector, the causes of which were twofold: the phylloxera crisis, which especially affected the coastal vineyards, and a crisis of traditional cattle-raising. The second crisis was fostered by a contraction of pastures that resulted from the disappearance of communal land, on the one hand, and from the cereal crisis in the interior, on the other. The replanting of grapevines and the reorganization of the cattle industry, especially in western Andalusia, contributed to a regeneration of the agricultural economy during the first four decades of the twentieth century.[21]

The agrarian economy defined and conditioned the Andalusian economy from the final years of the Ancien Régime until the Civil War. Phenomena such as the transatlantic trade of the colonial period, or the development of mining in the nineteenth and twentieth centuries, did not alter the basically agrarian structure of the Andalusian economy. During the entire period under consideration, the most characteristic features of the region's agriculture, such as area under cultivation, type of property, and kinds of crops did not undergo any deep changes.

Nor did industry—which transformed the economies of other countries as well as other Spanish regions—develop in Andalusia. According to W. A. Lewis, consumer industries required extensive demand, which was difficult to create in a society where the majority of the population was living at subsistence level. The uneven distribution of wealth and income were serious handicaps that impeded the establishment and development of this type of industry. A few industrial establishments were founded, however, especially in those subsectors which produced essential goods, such as textiles. Jordi Nadal cites many examples, outstanding among them the Industria Malagueña, founded in 1846 by the Larios and Heredia, entrepreneurs from Logroño (in northern Spain), resident in Málaga. After the España Industrial of Barcelona, Industria Malagueña was only the second textile enterprise to be founded as a joint-stock company.

The Industria Malagueña was established with modern technology in a district where the export trade and other industrial activities created a demand for this type of investment. Nevertheless, the phylloxera crisis and the region's general agrarian problems combined to depress demand and launched the enterprise into a prolonged period of stagnation. Other textile factories opened up in Cádiz and Seville, but because of their weak financial structures and small sizes which had a negative impact on operating costs, they could not block English and Catalan textiles from entering the Andalusian market. Nor did they succeed in displacing craft and domestic production; therefore, they had to coexist with the latter, probably until the twentieth century.[22]

An uneven distribution of income may augment investments that result from savings accumulated by a few individuals. In Andalusia, however, the expansion of the consumer goods industry was obstructed by insufficient demand. The development of a capital-goods industry, on the other hand, presupposes other requirements and conditions. Perhaps the most immediate are as follows: first, the proximity to raw materials; second, an adequate supply of capital, both financial and human (entrepreneurs and workers); and third, easy access to markets. In Andalusia the first requirement was abundant, the second scarce, and the third viable by sea transport and later by the railroad.[23]

The subject of foreign investment in Spanish mining, specifically Andalusian mining, has been widely discussed and has been defined as economic colonialism, since part of the market value of the minerals and moreover of the profits escaped the regional and national economies and ended up in the hands of foreign stockholders. In 1913 about 50% of Spanish mineral wealth was indeed the property of foreigners. It has also been argued that the exported mineral had a low added value, since it was processed abroad. Although this did not always happen, it did occur in the very important copper-mining province of Huelva, which accounted for 66% of the world's copper output before World War I. In 1896 the British company, Tharsis, which had a profit margin of more than 18%, owned machinery and foundries in Spain worth 90,495 pounds, while in Great Britain the value of the company's equipment was 122,723 pounds. This seems to corroborate the claim that minerals were processed abroad. In the case of lead, a progression can be seen in Spanish metallurgical activities starting in the 1880s; 441,400 tons were produced in the period 1880–1883, and this increased to 925,800 tons in the period 1910–1914. This was a preeminent period for the mining sectors of Jaén and Córdoba, where there were important mines and foundries in Peñarroya and Linares. The market crisis that followed World War I, however, caused a slump in both metallurgy and lead mining.

Such a critical view of the role of foreign capital should be counterbalanced with some positive observations. First, in 1913, 50% of the capital invested in the sector was Spanish, although the most profitable companies were under the control of foreigners. Second, the balance of payments benefited tremendously from mining development, not only in terms of the balance of capital, but also in terms of the balance of trade. Third, mining stimulated market activity and a monetary economy in Andalusia. It must be considered that part of the value of mineral exports remained in the country, and ultimately a demand for labor in the mining sector had the effect of raising salary levels. Although Andalusian population growth generally affected the agricultural sector in a negative manner, at least in some predominantly mining provinces like Huelva, wages in agriculture and in cattle-raising rose by 50% during the 1880s, according to information provided in 1890 by the Chamber of Commerce and by the Board of Agriculture, Industry, and Commerce of Huelva. Even though this figure of 50% might seem somewhat inflated, it reveals a certain tightness in the labor market. Because of the opportunities for salary advancement, Huelva was the only Andalusian province to experience immigration at the beginning of the twentieth century. Until 1890 the province's population grew by 22%, and its capital grew by 37%.[24] Mining in general could do very little to raise wages in a region with a large population. Mining statistics indicate that, at the start of the twentieth century, about 70,000 people were employed in mining, less than 5% of Andalusia's active population.

It should also be said that there was no alternative to foreign investment. The state had attempted unsuccessfully to develop some excellent deposits, prior to their alienation; and Spanish private interests had refused to invest in some potentially lucrative operations, such as Riotinto. In his recent book on the Riotinto Company, Charles E. Harvey states that the government offered the copper mines for public sale through announcements in newspapers and through representatives in Madrid, London, New York, Paris, and Berlin. The first advertisement in the May 11, 1871, issue of the *Gaceta de Madrid* received little response and was repeated in the July 13, 1872, issue. Four offers were made for Riotinto, and Matheson and Company purchased the deposits for 94 million pesetas.[25] Were there not 94 million pesetas available in Andalusia to invest in an enterprise that would produce enough profits in three years to cover the cost of the operation? The amount was not small, considering that demand deposits in the Banco de España in 1871 did not reach 76 million pesetas, and all bank of issue deposits totaled only 127.5 million. Nevertheless, it would not have been impossible for some ambitious Andalusian capitalists to put up part or all of the 94 million pesetas. The probable reasons why an Andalusian concern did not purchase Riotinto are: a lack of insight into the profitable future of the company, caused in part by the government's losses during previous years; an absence of technical and financial knowhow; and the investment of resources in other profitable sectors, like agriculture.

Manuel Agustín Heredia seems to have been one of the few successful entrepreneurs outside agriculture. In 1832 he established the first iron blast furnace for civil purposes in Spain. The significance of this enterprise was brought to light by Jordi Nadal in a series of works that show that, from 1855 to 1865, Heredia produced between 20% and 25% of all Spanish cast iron. Málaga's iron industry, which was fueled by charcoal, had to convert later to new methods and technology employing coal; the high cost of coal, however, led to the failure of the only industrial experiment that, because of its links with, and effects on, other sectors, could have triggered an important breakthrough for the Andalusian economy. There is a strong possibility that British coal, imported through Málaga and taxed at a lower duty, could have made the iron of the southern foundries competitive.[26] It is clear, then, that the system of protectionism favored the industrialization of regions with abundant natural resources and raw materials and discriminated against those regions in which the most dynamic element of the industrialization process was human capital. The Andalusian iron-and-steel industry was a case in point. Protectionism in this sector, as well as in the agriculture of Andalusia's large landed estates, reaffirmed some profitable but traditional systems by ensuring their survival at the same time that it precluded the transformation of the Andalusian economy.

During the last decades of the nineteenth century and the first decades of the twentieth, industrialization progressed in various Spanish regions, such as Catalonia, the Basque Provinces, Asturias, and Santander. Others, like the agricultural regions of the plateau, maintained their traditional economic structures, but moderate demographic growth permitted a certain stability in the standard of living. In Andalusia and Extremadura (two southern Spanish regions), a rapid rise in population, the persistence of the traditional agrarian system, and the continued uneven distribution of wealth and income condemned the majority of the population to live at the subsistence level, frustrated any possibility of industrialization, and further distanced Andalusia from the rest of Spain in terms of income and economic organization. During the last quarter of the nineteenth century, Andalusia's economic backwardness was apparent in the behavior of its banking system. After the Banco de España was granted the monopoly of issue in 1874, there was no Andalusian credit company until well into the twentieth century. Previously, there were corporate banks in Andalusia that were active mostly in the creation of bank notes. In addition, the region had four banks of issue, in Cádiz, Málaga, Seville, and Jérez, respectively; around 1850, the Banco de Cádiz had accounts on a par with the Banco de Barcelona, and the same could be said for the Banco de Málaga in relation to the Banco de Bilbao ten years later. By mid-nineteenth century, Andalusia's regional banks may have played an important role in the creation of liquid assets. These assets were necessary for the operation of a market economy in which the financing of activities like wine, mineral, oil, and fruit exports, as well as the shipment of foodstuffs to the rest of the country, required adequate means of payment and short-term credit between producers and merchants.

Upon receiving the monopoly of issue, the Banco de España assumed these functions and succeeded in displacing the regional banks in Andalusia as well as in the rest of the nation. Moreover, the Banco de España syphoned off savings, through its branches, and channeled them into credit for the Treasury. Starting in 1900, this flow of resources from the South toward other regions probably became accentuated when large banks, like the Hispano Americano and the Español de Crédito, founded at the turn of the century, opened branches in the cities and towns of Andalusia.[27] In the late nineteenth and early twentieth centuries, there was not enough economic incentive in Andalusia for the establishment of a bank with the purpose of providing medium- and long-term loans. The uneven distribution of wealth and income and the weakness of the economy in extensive areas precluded the emergence of industries that would require these financial services. Mining was financed by foreigners, while the iron and textile industries of Málaga and Seville and the textile industry of Cádiz had been in decline since 1870. It was not a lack of savings that inhibited the establishment of banks—savings certainly existed and in considerable amounts—but rather a lack of insight into what profits could be earned by investing in banking. This should not be surprising, since the principal economic activity of the region, agriculture, was financed by the reinvestment of agricultural profits.

The uneven distribution of wealth and income also implied an uneven distribution of human capital. As was mentioned previously, Málaga's iron industry could survive because the region had a comparative advantage in human capital, as long as protectionist policy did not favor the iron industries of regions endowed with coal and iron deposits. Eventually, tariffs did favor other regions, bringing about the decline of Málaga's iron industry. However, in this case as in many others, managerial skills were brought in from outside the region; the Heredia family was from La Rioja, as were the Larios, merchants and owners of Málaga's textile industry, as well as of the local bank of issue. Also from outside the region came Jorge Loring Oyarzábal, founder of the Andalusian Railroad Company; Manuel Carbonell, one of the biggest Cordovan oil merchants; as well as many of the entrepreneurs who engaged in foreign trade in Cádiz, Jérez, and Málaga from the eighteenth century on.[28] The latter's origins, along with the lack of Andalusian entrepreneurs interested in acquiring the southern copper mines, mentioned earlier, underscore the relative scarcity of human managerial capital within the secondary and tertiary sectors. With regard to human labor capital, there were obviously few skilled workers; the majority of the region's inhabitants had minimal training.

The economic underdevelopment of Andalusia can, therefore, be summarized in the following hypotheses (since there are not enough data to rank them, they appear at random):

1. Nineteenth-century demographic growth depressed wages and impeded the replacement of labor with capital.
2. An uneven distribution of wealth and income discouraged investment in the consumer goods industry.
3. Tariff protectionism precluded an agricultural transformation in methods of cultivation and in the traditional production system, except in the cases of olives, citrus fruits, and other, less important cereal crops. Protectionism also perpetuated an economic system primarily based on extensive agriculture and the use of manual labor.
4. Moreover, the protectionist policy that was forged in the late nineteenth and early twentieth centuries favored the industrialization

of the North and discouraged investment in regions whose comparative advantages lay in the productive capacity of their human capital.

5. In Andalusia, human managerial capital was concentrated in agriculture because of its profitability. Human technical and labor capital in the secondary and tertiary sectors was scarce because of the low income level of the majority of the population. This was translated into an equally low level of training.

6. To these hypotheses, one must add the low yield of traditional agriculture in the majority of eastern provinces, where subsistence plots prevailed.

It is important to emphasize the interdependent nature of these hypotheses. Andalusian underdevelopment was not monocausal; the uneven distribution of wealth and income, for example, does not by itself explain the region's economic dilemma. There are, in fact, historical examples of the coexistence of uneven income distribution and sustained economic growth. According to Eric Jones, for example, the number of large farms increased in eighteenth-century England, and yet the industrial revolution occurred.[29] If, however, an unequal distribution of wealth occurred in conjunction with population growth, a scarcity of human managerial and technical capital, and a protectionist policy that grew more burdensome toward the end of the nineteenth century, the combined result could have been the economic backwardness of Andalusia in relation to other Spanish regions. Economic underdevelopment—a term that is defined in relation to other regions and societies—began in Andalusia around the middle of the nineteenth century. Prior to that period, Andalusia was a traditional agricultural region similar to the rest of Spain. In Gerschenkron's terms, the peculiar economic characteristics of southern Spain conditioned its evolution during the last two centuries and explain its historical process of backwardness.[30]

NOTES

1. Banco de Bilbao, *Renta Nacional de España y su distribución provincial: Serie homogénea, 1955–1975* (Bilbao, 1978).

2. F. Ruíz Martín, "La banca española hasta 1782," in *El Banco de España: una historia económica* (Madrid, 1970).

3. Universidad Autónoma de Madrid, Departamento de Historia Contemporánea, *La economía del Antiguo Régimen: La "Renta Nacional" de la Corona de Castilla* (Madrid, 1977), p. 167.

4. A. García-Baquero, "Independencia colonial americana y pérdida de la primacía andaluza," in *Historia de Andalucía,* vol. 7 (Madrid, 1981), pp. 117–149.

5. N. Sánchez-Albornoz, "Cádiz bajo la ocupación francesa en 1825," in *Mélanges à la mémoire de Jean Sarrailh,* vol. 2 (Paris, 1966), pp. 345–353; A. M. Bernal and A. García-Baquero, *Tres siglos del comercio sevillano (1598–1868): Cuestiones y problemas* (Seville, 1976). Antonio García Baquero, in "Comercio colonial, acumulación primitiva de capital y desindustrialización en la Baja Andalucía: el caso de Cádiz en el siglo XVIII," denies that Spanish-American emancipation frustrated a possible industrialization of Lower Andalusia at the beginning of the nineteenth century. See "Actas del Primer Congreso de Historia de Andalucía," December 1976, *Andalucía Moderna* (siglo XVIII), vol. 1 (Córdoba, 1978), pp. 195–208.

6. L. Prados de la Escosura, "La independencia hispanoamericana y sus consecuencias económicas en España: una estimación provisional," *Moneda y Crédito* 163 (1982): 49–69.

7. G. Anes, "La agricultura española y el mercado americano," in G. Anes, L. A. Rojo, and P. Tedde, eds. *Historia económica y pensamiento social: Estudios en homenaje a Diego Mateo del Peral* (Madrid, 1983), pp. 193–204.

8. A. García-Baquero, *Cádiz y el Atlántico (1717–1778),* 2 vols. (Seville, 1976).

9. L. Prados de la Escosura, "Comercio exterior y cambio económico en España (1792–1849)," in J. Fontana, ed. *La economía española al final del Antiguo Régimen,* vol. 3, *Comercio y colonias* (Madrid, 1982), pp. 171–249.

10. P. Vilar, "La Cataluña industrial: reflexiones acerca de un arranque y de un destino," in Herman Kellebenz et al., eds., *La industrialización europea: Estadios y tipos* (Barcelona, 1980). On the differences between Catalonia and Lower Andalusia in the eighteenth century see J. Fontana, "Comercio colonial e industrialización: una reflexión sobre los orígenes de la industria moderna en Cataluña," in J. Nadal and G. Tortella, eds. *Agricultura, comercio colonial y crecimiento económico en la España contemporánea* (Barcelona, 1974), pp. 358–365.

11. A. García-Baquero, "Independencia colonial americana," pp. 147–148, and Nadal and Tortella, *Agricultura,* pp. 367–368.

12. M. Gámez Amián, *La economía de Málaga en el siglo XVIII: un territorio del Reino de Granada* (Granada, 1983). J. Morilla Critz, *Gran capital y estancamiento en Andalucía: Banca y ferrocarriles en Málaga en el siglo XIX* (Córdoba, 1978).

13. M. Artola, A. M. Bernal, and J. Contreras, *El latifundio: propiedad y explotación* (Madrid, 1978).

14. A. M. Bernal, "Señoritos y jornaleros: la lucha por la tierra," in *Historia de Andalucía,* vol. 7 (Madrid, 1981), pp. 217–295. The purchase of land during the disentailment by former tenant farmers has been confirmed by J. Cruz Villalón in *Propiedad y uso de la tierra en la Baja Andalucía: Carmona, siglos XVIII–XX* (Madrid, 1980), esp. pp. 256–285.

15. V. Pérez Moreda, "La población española en el siglo XIX (1797–1939)," unpublished, 1983. I would like to thank this author for allowing me to quote his figures.

16. A. M. Bernal, "Señoritos y jornaleros," pp. 290–292.

17. Ibid., pp. 278–279.

18. M. Martín Rodríguez, *Azúcar y descolonización* (Granada, 1982).

19. P. Tedde de Lorca, "La Compañía de los Ferrocarriles Andaluces (1878–1920):

una empresa de transportes en la España de la Restauración," *Investigaciones Económicas* 12 (1980): 27–76.

20. F. Héran, *Tierra y parentesco en el campo sevillano: la revolución agrícola del siglo XIX* (Madrid, 1980), esp. pp. 159–195. J. Reis, "Latifúndio e progresso técnico: a diffusâo da debulha mecânica no Alentejo, 1860–1930," *Análise Social* 71 (1982): 371–433. Cruz Villalón, *Propriedad,* pp. 345–346.

21. In addition to the works already cited, the following studies have been published recently on the problems of Spanish agriculture in the second half of the nineteenth century and the beginning of the twentieth. N. Sánchez-Albornoz, *Los precios agrícolas durante la segunda mitad del siglo XIX: El trigo y la cebada* (Madrid, 1975); N. Sánchez-Albornoz and T. Carnero, *Los precios agrícolas durante la segunda mitad del siglo XIX: el vino y el aceite* (Madrid, 1981); R. Garrabou, "La crisis agraria espanyola de finals del segle XIX: una etapa del desenvolupament del capitalisme," *Recerques* 5 (1975): 163–216; Grupo de Estudios de Historia Rural, "Contribución al análisis histórico de la ganadería española, 1865–1929," *Agricultura y Sociedad* 8 and 10 (1978 and 1979): 129–173 and 105–169; *Los precios del trigo y la cebada en España, 1891–1907* (Madrid, 1980); *Los precios del aceite del oliva en España, 1891–1916* (Madrid, 1981); *El vino, 1874–1907: dificultades para reconstruir la serie de sus cotizaciones* (Madrid, 1981); "Notas sobre la producción agraria española, 1891–1931," *Revista de Historia Económica* 1, no. 2 (1984): 185–252, and the unpublished dissertation of F. Zambrana, "La economía oleícola en la España de la Restauración," 2 vols. (Málaga, 1983). On Andalusian agriculture see specifically A. M. Bernal, *La propiedad de la tierra y las luchas agrarias andaluzas* (Barcelona, 1974); *La lucha por la tierra en la crisis del Antiguo Régimen* (Madrid, 1979), and "Economía agraria en la Andalucía contemporánea," *Papeles de Economía Española* 20 (1984): 281–297. On Málaga see the monographic issue of *Gibralfaro,* no. 24 (1972), no. 25 (1973) and no. 26 (1974), directed by J. A. Lacomba. See also J. Guisado, "La crisis filoxérica en España," *Revista de Historia Económica* 1, no. 2 (1984): 165–184, and J. Simpson, "La producción de vinos en Jerez de la Frontera, 1850–1900" in P. Martín Aceña and L. Prados de la Escosura, eds., *La Nueva Historia Económica en España* (Madrid, 1985), pp. 166–191.

22. W. A. Lewis, *Growth and Fluctuations, 1870–1913* (London, 1978); J. Nadal, "The Failure of the Industrial Revolution in Spain," in C. M. Cipolla, ed. *Fontana Economic History of Europe,* vol. 4, pt. 2 (London, 1973), pp. 533–626, and "Industrialización y desindustrialización del Sureste español, 1817–1913," *Moneda y Crédito* 120 (1972): 3–80. A recent work shows that Spanish consumption of textiles in the nineteenth century was considerably lower than that of the United Kingdom or France. See L. Prados de la Escosura, "Producción y consumo de tejidos en España, 1800–1913: primeros resultados," in G. Anes, L. A. Rojo, and P. Tedde, eds., *Historia económica y pensamiento social,* pp. 455–461.

23. P. Tedde de Lorca, "El proceso de formación de la Compañía de los Ferrocarriles Andaluces (1874–1880)," *Hacienda Pública Española* 55 (1978): 367–397, and "La Compañía de los Ferrocarriles Andaluces (1878–1920)," *Investigaciones económicas* 12 (1980): 27–76.

24. *La Reforma arancelaria y los tratados de comercio,* 2 vols. (Madrid, 1890).

25. C. E. Harvey, *The Riotinto Company: An Economic History of a Leading International Mining Concern, 1873–1954* (Penzance, 1981), pp. 16–28. An important work in the

Spanish bibliography is J. Nadal's "Andalucía, paraíso de los metales no ferrosos," *Historia de Andalucía,* vol. 7 (Barcelona, 1984), pp. 366–490.

26. This point is inferred from the cited works of J. Nadal. In *La reforma arancelaria y los tratados de comercio,* vol. 2, p. 661, information provided by the coal and railroad industries demonstrates that in 1890 a ton of English coal (without duties) cost 25.93 pesetas in Málaga while a ton of coal from Belmez cost 29.75 pesetas.

27. P. Tedde de Lorca, "La banca privada durante la Restauración (1874–1914)," in G. Tortella and P. Schwartz, eds. *La banca española en la Restauración,* 2 vols. (Madrid, 1974), vol. 1, pp. 424–430. On the Andalusian banking industry, Manuel Tito has written a series of works. See esp. *Crédito y ahorro en Granada en el siglo XIX,* 2 vols. (Granada, 1978), and *Bancos y banqueros en la historiografía andaluza* (Granada, 1980).

28. R. Castejón, *Génesis y desarrollo de una sociedad mercantil e industrial en Andalucía: la Casa Carbonell de Córdoba, 1866–1918* (Córdoba, 1977); M. Villar, *Los extranjeros en Málaga en el siglo XVIII* (Córdoba, 1982); C. García Montoro, *Málaga en los comienzos de la industrialización: Manuel Agustín Heredia, 1786–1846* (Córdoba, 1978).

29. E. L. Jones, ed. *Agriculture and Economic Growth in England, 1650–1815* (London, 1967).

30. Alexander Gerschenkron, *Economic Backwardness in Historical Perspective* (Cambridge, Mass., 1962).

FURTHER READINGS

Artola, Miguel, et al. *El latifundio: propiedad y explotación.* Madrid, 1978.

Bernal, Antonio Miguel. *La propiedad de la tierra y las luchas agrarias andaluzas.* Barcelona, 1974.

Domínguez Ortiz, Antonio, ed. *Historia de Andalucía.* 8 vols. Madrid, 1981.

Nadal, Jordi, "Industrialización y desindustrialización del Sureste español, 1817–1913." *Moneda y Crédito* 120 (1973): 3–80.

———. *El fracaso de la Revolución industrial en España, 1814–1913.* Barcelona, 1975.

15.

EXPORTS, INTERNAL DEMAND, AND ECONOMIC GROWTH IN VALENCIA*

JORDI PALAFOX
Universidad de Valencia

HOW THE Valencian economy performed during the second half of the nineteenth century and the first third of the twentieth was a source of considerable debate during the 1970s. The attention paid to the industrialization process in Europe and Valencia's linguistic and cultural similarity to Catalonia (one of the few Spanish regions to industrialize in the nineteenth century, as has already been said), combined to rear the impression that an industrial society should have evolved then in the region. In light of this assumption, the lack of industrialization in Valencia was interpreted as an economic failure, and research focused on explaining the causes of this unexpected outcome.[1]

Later research and a new focus have led instead to a substantially different conclusion. The progression of the Valencian economy from 1800 to 1960 is now viewed as a process characterized by both failures and successes. It is currently recognized that the most remarkable achievement of this process was an increasing specialization in the region's most competitive and profitable activities.

Such a "growth without industrialization" was based on agriculture. External demand had induced market-oriented production of staples as early as the late eighteenth century, and the mid-nineteenth-century growth of European demand reinforced this orientation. This demand can be considered the major, but not sole, factor in the region's growth. The rise of the export trade led

*I would like to thank Teresa Carnero for her assistance in the preparation of this chapter. The opinions presented herein are, in fact, in great part shared by both of us—which is, of course, not usually the case. I would also like to express my gratitude to Ernest Lluch and James Simpson for their critical reading of an earlier version of this chapter.

268

to an expansion of the commercialized and competitive sectors of the economy, while the subsistence economy contracted. It also fostered an economic specialization based on comparative advantages and promoted a diversification of supply. Last, sectors that benefited directly from increased demand experienced innovations and a subsequent rise in yields and productivity.

Grapes[2] first, and then oranges,[3] were the crops best suited for this type of growth, a growth quite different from the model of capitalist development followed elsewhere in Spain. Spanish development generally stimulated domestic output through tariff protection and favored internal mechanisms that would reduce competition and expand supply. In addition to these two crops, rice, almonds, and other horticultural products also played a significant role in the expansion of the Valencian economy. Unfortunately, studies on these products are still not available.

Wine and orange exports (through Valencian ports for wine and through Spanish ports in general for oranges) make up an excellent indicator for monitoring trends in supply. By mid-nineteenth century, export statistics suggest a long and spectacular expansion in vine cultivation. From 1848 on the spread of "oidium tuckeri" severely damaged European vineyards. As a result, wine production for export tended to replace brandy distillation in Spain. The expansion of land cultivated to grapevines and the increase in wine output spiraled again after the French phylloxera crisis of the 1870s (see Table 15.1).

Increased French demand, combined with the steady supply of traditional markets, led to an unprecedented rise of the Spanish wine-growing sector.[4] The high alcohol content and strong color of Valencian wine were important factors in the rise of both exports and prices in Valencia. Between 1876 and 1885, the first ten years of the expansion, the average annual growth rate of exports through Valencian ports surpassed 20%. Starting in the period 1891–1895, the French recovery and Algerian competition curbed the export expansion, but a contraction in the total Spanish supply caused by the spread of phylloxera to other areas of the peninsula made Valencia the nation's number one export region. In 1899 exports through Valencian ports accounted for 61% of the national total. Because it is impossible to increase grape production rapidly, the rigidity of short-term supply and the continued external demand for wine brought about a remarkable increase in prices. As shown in Table 15.2 (columns 2 and 5), exports and, to a lesser degree, prices rose tremendously in relation to the 1874–1878 period in almost all markets until the beginning of the 1890s. Closer analysis, however, suggests that the influence of foreign demand on prices did not last long. Columns 3 and 5, which

Table 15.1
Average Annual Growth Rates
of Orange and Wine Exports, 1866–1935
(Over the Previous Five-Year Period)

Periods	Oranges	Wine
1866–1870	9.9	3.2
1871–1875	15.7	13.8
1876–1880	6.7	16.5
1881–1885	2.0	22.1
1886–1890	−0.2	11.6
1891–1895	6.8	−3.0
1896–1900	15.2	−5.1
1901–1905	6.4	−18.7
1906–1910	5.3	−10.7
1911–1915	1.8	20.3
1916–1920	−10.9	8.8*
1921–1925	13.7	−7.2*
1926–1930	0.7	10.4*
1931–1935	1.1	−16.1*

SOURCES: 1866–1915: Luis García Guijarro, *La exportación agrícola española y su importancia en el comercio exterior* (Madrid, n.d.); Wine: Juan Piqueras, *La vid y el vino en el País Valenciano* (Valencia, 1981), p. 107; 1915–1935: *Estadísticas del Comercio Exterior.*
NOTE: It has been assumed that the rate of Valencian orange exports was equal to that of Spain as a whole and that the rate of wine exports was equivalent to that of the total shipped through customs.
*Estimated on the basis of exports shipped through the port of Valencia.

measure the rate of increase or decrease in comparison with the preceding five-year period, show that starting in 1884–1888 exports continued to expand, while prices declined (column 3). During the years from 1889 to 1893, price levels were similar to those of the first period, except for those of the Utiel market, where the decline was even greater. During the last period under consideration, a fall in exports was accompanied by a strong contraction in prices, except for the Utiel market, which once again deviated from the norm.

This and the information provided by Teresa Carnero on the evolution of the French market beginning in 1891 corroborate the view that the expansion of vineyards resulted in a surplus in the medium-term supply.[5] This surplus, rather than the vine disease, seems to have been the fundamental problem that confronted the Spanish, especially the Valencian, grape growers during the industry's apogee. In fact, the land cultivated to grapevines in Valencia rose in the twenty-seven years between 1859 and 1886 at an annual rate of 2.31%. that is, an increase from 124,552 to 230,746 hectares.[6]

Table 15.2
Prices and Volume of Ordinary Wine Exports, 1874–1898

Years	Villena			Requena			Utiel			Benicarló			Alicante			Valencian Total		
	1	2	3	1	2	3	1	2	3	1	2	3	1	2	3	4	5	6
1874–78	18.2	100.0	—	18.8	100.0	—	14.2	100.0	—	21.5	100.0	—	20.6	100.0	—	437,165	100.0	—
1879–83	30.8	169.2	+69.2	29.3	256.1	56.1	26.9	189.4	+89.4	33.5	155.8	+55.8	36.0	177.3	+77.3	1,614,450	369.3	+269.3
1884–88	27.4	150.5	−11.0	24.0	127.9	−18.2	24.6	173.2	−8.5	29.0	134.9	−13.4	29.0	142.8	−19.4	2,752,879	629.7	+170.5
1889–93	19.2	105.5	−29.9	18.8	100.2	−21.7	12.5	88.0	−49.2	22.0	102.3	−24.1	18.7	92.1	−35.5	3,690,312	844.1	+134.0
1894–98	9.2	50.6	−52.1	8.4	44.8	−55.3	14.3	100.7	+14.4	14.0	65.1	−36.4	15.8	77.8	−15.5	2,332,671	533.6	−36.8

SOURCES: Volume and prices in Villena and Requena from J. Piqueras, *La vid y el vino en el País Valenciano* (Valencia, 1981), pp. 107, 138. Prices in Utiel, Benicarló and Alicante from T. Carnero, *Expansión vinícola y atraso agrario, 1870–1900* (Madrid, 1980), p. 229.

NOTES: Columns 1 and 4: pesetas/hectoliters and hectoliters, respectively; columns 2 and 5: 1874–78 index = 100; columns 3 and 6: percent of variation above the previous five-year period.

As wine production entered a downswing, oranges came to prevail, heightening the transformation of the agrarian landscape. Regular shipments abroad, mostly to France and England, started during the 1850s and coincided with the beginning of the viticultural expansion and that of rice cultivation. It was not until the 1870s, however, that the extension of land under cultivation and the increase in exports began to affect the rest of the economy.

Table 15.3 traces the evolution of acreage used for orange production from 1878 to 1936. The average annual growth rate was 4.5%. The 6.5% rate for the period 1878–1904 illustrates how rapidly this crop expanded while traditional agriculture was shrinking.[7] The number of hectares converted into orange groves reflects the intensity of the process of agrarian transformation— a process that, considering its costs, required large investments. Both the expansion of irrigation—possible only through a substantial modernization of the machinery needed to dig new wells and to extract water from continuously greater depths[8]—and the extensive replacement of other crops with orange trees suggest the high profits reaped by the orange growers.

Since Valencian agriculture at the turn of the century was closely linked to the market in the coastal districts, landowners were, of course, aware of the exceptional profits that could be made in the citrus industry. Although the figures given in Table 15.4 present rough approximations, the table presents the most precise data available. The profit rate for oranges is clearly much higher than that derived from any other crop. The lack of data for horticultural products, which experienced the greatest growth rate after citrus fruits in the first third of the twentieth century, does not permit a thorough statistical

Table 15.3
Evolution of Land Area Growing Oranges, 1878–1936
(in hectares)

	1878	1904	1920	1930	1936
Alicante	180	640	500	1,253	4,760
Castellon	1,270	12,847	16,368	18,000	19,232
Valencia	3,400	11,500	20,000	31,500	40,144
Total	4,850	24,837	36,868	50,753	64,136
Annual growth (%)		6.48	2.21	4.08	3.98

SOURCES: 1878: Eduardo Abela, *Crónicas de Agricultura*, cited by Luis García Guijarro in *Hespérides o la riqueza citrícola española* (Madrid, 1957), p. 67; 1904: Ministerio de Agricultura, Industria, Comercio y Obras Públicas, *El regadío en España, 1904*, cited in *La questió agraria del País Valencià* (Barcelona, 1978), p. 21; 1920: Ministerio de Fomento, *Avance estadístico de la producción agrícola en España*, 1922; 1930 and 1936: *Anuario(s) de las producciones agrícolas*, respective years.

Table 15.4
Income Distribution for Some Valencian Crops
(pesetas per hectare and percentages)

	Investment (1)	Gross Earnings (2)	Net Earnings (3)	Income (4)	Income Rate (%) (5)	Profits (6)	Profit Rates (%) (7)	Profit Rates Without Taxes (%) (8)
Oranges (1905)	445	1,320	875	405	91	470	105.6	196.6
Almonds (1909)								
Max.	270	650	380	120	44.4	260	96.3	140.7
Min.	252.6	563	310.4	120	47.5	190.4	75.4	122.9
Rice (1905)								
Ribera del Júcar	813	1,247	433.2	216	26.56	217.2	26.71	53.25
Ribera Alta	837	1,287	450	288	34.40	161.7	19.31	53.37
Olives (1909)								
Max.	187	265	78	n.a.	n.a.	78	n.a.	41.71
Min.	58	104	46	n.a.	n.a.	46	n.a.	55.76
Carob (1909)								
Max.	160	291.2	131.2	n.a.	n.a.	131.2	n.a.	82.0
Min.	70	95.2	25.2	n.a.	n.a.	25.2	n.a.	36.0
Wheat (1909)								
Max.	193.75	280.28	86.53	n.a.	n.a.	86.53	n.a.	44.66
Min.	138.75	140.05	1.30	n.a.	n.a.	1.30	n.a.	0.01

SOURCES: Data for these tentative estimates were taken from the following: for oranges, Antonio Martín, *Manual práctico para el cultivo del naranjo* (Valencia, 1905); for rice, Antonio Martín, *Manual práctico para el cultivo del arroz* (Valencia, n.d. [1905?]). For the remaining crops I have used information provided by Rafael Janini, "Aspecto económico de la reconstitución del viñedo destruido por la filoxera en la región de Levante," included in Cámara Agrícola. *Oficial de Valencia, Congreso de la viña americana. Actas* (Valencia, 1909), pp. 56–95.

NOTE: n.a. = data not available.

comparison. In any event, profit margins for oranges were certainly not low and were probably—except under unusual circumstances—higher than those of any other product.

The transformations in the techniques of production that resulted from this continuous rise in demand were striking. Although the stages in the diffusion curve of these innovations (knowhow, interest, appraisal, test, and adoption) are not known,[9] the overall technical change that took place was nevertheless astounding. In this field, the two most outstanding components of modernization were the general use of fertilizers and the extensive spread of irrigation works. In processing, the most significant innovation was the substantial increase in the number of iron presses for making wine.

The early introduction of guano in 1844 and the attention that its crop yields received from groups who monitored agricultural improvements illustrate how farmers adapted to new conditions of demand.[10] Guano was first used in the expansion of rice cultivation and allowed farmers to overcome the constraints imposed by a rigidity in the supply of traditional fertilizers. As its use spread, guano imports rose from 360,000 metric quintals (100 kg) in 1859 and to 400,000 in 1862.[11] At the end of the nineteenth century, however, chemical fertilizers were introduced, and by the 1930s Valencia became the nation's principal consumer of these products.

Table 15.5 presents the land area under irrigation in the province of Valencia between 1900 and 1928. Columns 1 and 2 show that during the period 1900–1922, the expansion of the irrigated area and the ensuing search for water and investment in irrigation systems were paramount. During the following period (1922–1928), crop substitution was the decisive factor in the evolution of irrigated lands. This change highlights the dynamism of the region's farmers, who shifted crops according to post–World War I price variations. This era coincided with the high point in citrus fruit output. Since contemporary technology was unable to increase the water supply any further, production levels soon met a ceiling.

Column 3, on the other hand, shows that in both periods orange cultivation contributed more to the expansion of irrigated land than did any other group of products and came to absorb nearly 50% of that land by the 1920s. At the same time, the remarkable diversity of horticultural products contributed greatly to the growth of agriculture.

The types of innovation introduced into Valencian agriculture can be considered neutral with respect to the labor force and indicate, although in an impressionistic manner, that there were few problems of labor supply throughout the period under investigation. Only during the Second Republic, when

Table 15.5
Irrigated Area in Valencia, 1900–1928

Year	Total Area		Fruit Trees			Horticultural Products			Meadowlands			Industrial Products			Rice			Cereals and Legumes		
	1	2	1	2	3	1	2	3	1	2	3	1	2	3	1	2	3	1	2	3
1900	144,800	—	11,400	—	—	12,250	—	—	10,300	—	—	6,400	—	—	28,050	—	—	46,409	—	—
1922	135,217	0.7	20,336	2.7	43.77	15,912	1.1	17.94	13,086	1.1	13.64	8,040	1.0	8.03	31,084	10.4	14.86	46,759	0.02	1.71
1928	143,600	1.0	36,590	10.3	48.05	27,760	9.7	35.02	6,000	-12.2	—	11,650	6.4	10.70	33,200	1.1	6.25	24,400	-8.0	—

SOURCE: M. Torres, *Contribución al estudio de la economía valenciana* (Valencia, 1930), pp. 5–6.
NOTE: The contribution to the total growth of the irrigated area has been calculated by estimating the ratio of each crop's increase to that of all other crops that showed an increase rather than by estimating the ratio of each crop's increase in relation to the net increase of the total irrigated area. Columns numbered 1 = hectares; 2 = cumulative annual average rate of increase or decrease; 3 = contribution to the total increase of irrigated lands.

union pressure increased, was there any generalized interest in labor-saving technology in the orange-growing sector.[12]

The distribution and destination of the huge profits generated by the activities of the dynamic sector of Valencia's economy have been the focus of considerable attention. The increasing participation of Valencian merchants in wine exports has been duly recognized; with regard to orange exports, however, the findings of Lucía and Bellver[13] have been unduly extrapolated for the entire export cycle.[14] In the opinion of both authors, the orange trade was organized in such a way that it discriminated against growers and landowners. The trade was controlled by the foreign importers—who secured the purchase of the harvest by making partial advances on its value—and also by the consignees and the shipping companies that took advantage of their ability to provide an unlimited supply of ships for the brief time period when the orange harvest was exported. Josep Picó has written: "The Valencians were only the laborers who grew the crops so that others could take advantage of their hard work; they were exploited by both foreign merchants and regional middle-men."[15]

The situation described in the previous paragraph not only contradicts more reliable accounts, which include references to a "rural aristocracy" of orange grove owners,[16] but is also inconsistent with the magnitude of the crop's expansion and with the few estimates that have been made of its profitability. If Lucía and Bellver's argument were accepted, it would mean that the long-term agricultural expansion in which a substantial part of the population of Valencia's central and northern districts participated was an illusion.

The available information on commercial structure and distribution of income negates the existence of any discrimination against the growers, who in most cases were also landowners. The data collected by the chief agricultural engineer of Castellón toward the end of the 1920s show that profit margins for the various types of oranges were never lower than 200% for groves that had reached full production. This would imply that the large investment required to plant an orange grove was paid off in approximately one year.[17]

While the region's inhabitants participated in the profits of the orange "boom," other situations also arose that were detrimental to the native growers. When demand shrinked because of circumstances, such as World War I, or because of changes in world supply and demand—the Great Depression would be a case in point—the citrus sector failed to develop its own shipping and to control international trade networks. In relation to the first problem, however, the construction or purchase of transportation facilities might not have been an efficient undertaking for the region's growers, considering the volume of orange exports, the seasonal nature of the industry, the level of underdevelopment in the region's shipping tradition, and the insufficient volume of return shipments through Valencian ports.[18] With regard to the second problem, perhaps it should not be expected that the growers could have predicted the future trends of the international market, especially considering that the sector was dominated from its beginnings until the 1930s by a demand that was generally greater than supply, by the atomization of supply, and by inadequate capital for expansion.

The shortage of capital was directly related to the unsuccessful attempt to establish financial institutions that could underwrite the growth of the agro-export sector. The banking institutions that opened around the mid-nineteenth century promoted significant investments in social overhead capital—investments that were indispensable for meeting rising demand—but were swept away by the financial crisis of 1866.[19] Thereafter, Valencians' attempts to form a banking sector were few and shortlived.

The possibility that non-Valencian banking institutions located in Valencia could have drained savings, thereby impairing the region's growth, has also received some attention. Until the end of World War I, there certainly were very few private credit companies.[20] Therefore, such a drain of savings could have occurred only in the 1920s when, as in other Spanish regions, the number of branches opened by the large banks rapidly increased.

The absence of an adequate financial structure and the existence of more profitable alternatives elsewhere have been forwarded as explanations for the limited role of non-Valencian banks in financing the export-oriented expansion.[21] The latter proposition is certainly inaccurate, since Valencia's main crops yielded substantial profits. Instead, outside financing was hampered by several deficiencies in the region's economy, a problem that Clementina Ródenas recently pointed out when she wrote that mixed banking seldom invested in the consumer-goods industry.[22] In the same vein, other issues that should be taken into account are: (1) What volume of credit demand was generated by Valencia's economic activities, characterized as they were by family enterprises? (2) To what extent were the small- and medium-sized rice producers ruined during the agricultural depression at the end of the nineteenth century? At the height of rice production, these producers were heavily indebted to the family banks that operated in Valencia at that time. It would seem risky to suppose a priori the existence of demand unless the concept of "latent demand" were introduced into the historical analysis.

In short, the Valencian economy experienced a rapid process of export-led growth in which the adaptive capacity of producers was notable. The role of European demand in this process must be emphasized, not only because its consequences have not yet received enough attention,[23] but also because, as Ohlin asserts (he refers to industry, but his claims are just as valid for agriculture), "the first step towards such an understanding of the growth process is simply to pay as much attention to the growth of an industry's market as is usually lavished on the growth of its capacity."[24]

The role of exports is more clearly defined in that part of Myint's model of "vent for surplus"[25] which is related to the impact of increased foreign demand on an economy possessing, in Findley's terms, important productive resources that remain idle owing to a lack of alternative uses.[26] Consider as a point of departure a nonindustrialized economy composed of two sectors, crafts (A) and agriculture (B). In the first sector, labor is the dominant factor of production, while in the second, land and labor are dominant, neither of which are used to full capacity. Considering the economy described above, the maximum production level possible will be represented by line pp in Graph 15.1.

Given that an underutilization of resources exists, the economy under consideration, similar to that of Valencia before the expansion cycle, will produce a combination of products determined, for example, by point I located within the production range. In this situation—leaving aside the question of why there was no growth in the past that would have raised production to any point on line pp—a rise in external demand can produce a shift, in that agrarian production rises to E, exports being represented by IE, at the same time that the consumption of artisan goods increases to IC through imports (or through the demand on another economy) resulting in more favorable terms of trade, as reflected by CE.[27]

Trade can thus promote specialization according to comparative advantage if the artisan sector (A), which is less competitive than its foreign counterparts, is progressively eliminated at the same time that a competitive agricultural sector is consolidated that fosters the increased consumption of externally produced manufactured goods—goods that are both cheaper and of equal quality. Complete specialization in agricultural products, for example, would result in the figure formed by TSP', since in this situation the level of production reaches P'. P' corresponds to the level of consumption S, with TS as imports of manufactured goods, TP' as agricultural exports, and OT as the internal consumption of agricultural products.

The preceding model can also be useful in explaining the failure of the traditional artisan sector to transform itself into a modern industrial sector. At

Graph 15.1   Model of the Impact of Increased Foreign Demand on an Economy with Idle Resources

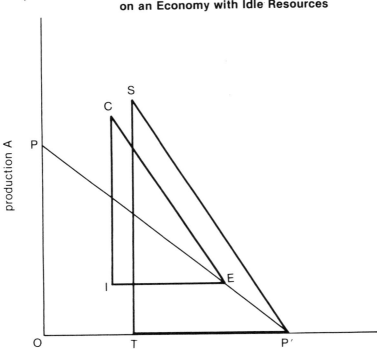

the end of the eighteenth century and the beginning of the nineteenth, these traditional manufacturing sectors were dispersed throughout the region, although three principal centers can be identified: the first, Morella, was in the North and included the districts of L'Alt Maestrat and Els Ports, which concentrated on wool. The second, located in the center of the region, was largely devoted to silk production, although linen, hemp, and matweed products were manufactured a bit farther from the city of Valencia. The third and most important area was centered around Alcoy in the southern part of the region; this area was noted for wool production, although some districts around the city of Alicante specialized in matweed and hemp, both necessary materials for making fiber sandals.[28]

Since the majority of these activities were controlled in the sphere of production and/or commercialization by the dominant social groups of the Ancien Régime, it would not be risky to state that the division of labor was negligible and that the distribution of income was not favorable to producers.

This limited the possibility of expanding supply, since it curbed the flow of profits and investments and prevented the introduction of economies of scale in various sectors. This would imply—taking into account the limited integration of the market during these years—that the high cost of transportation constituted one of the basic factors in the demand structure of these products.[29] The subsequent integration of the market, the social changes that took place in Spain during the first half of the nineteenth century, and the consequences of railroad construction combined to create a type of competition that traditional enterprises could not overcome, given the greater degree of industrial development in other regions, especially Catalonia. Thereafter, the Valencian textile sector was relegated to a marginal position, except for the silk-dyeing industry of Alcoy.[30]

Although market limitations for manufactures prevented traditional industries from benefiting from economies of scale and later caused their collapse, these limitations do not apply to other consumer industries whose rise and development came along with the years of agrarian expansion. The footwear industry of the Vall de Vinalopó, the toy industry of Ibi, the furniture and ceramics industries in Valencia, and the manufacture of tiles in Valencia and Castellón are just a few of the sectors that fostered the industrialization of the 1860s.[31]

During the final decades of the nineteenth century, major technological innovations were introduced into the footwear industry. Moreover, during the first third of the twentieth century, centralization of the various production stages took place that resulted in the sector's first large enterprises.[32] In the capitalist consolidation of the furniture, ceramics, and tile industries, the urban demand of Valencia in the late nineteenth century seems to have played a crucial role; there were also early indications of sales throughout the region and in the rest of Spain, although exact figures for these different markets are not available. All in all, there was a rapid rate of expansion in all three sectors; in the case of the tile industry, this growth was accompanied by a progressive shift toward the northern districts, owing to the existence of superior clay deposits.

The economic activities described in the previous paragraphs originated long before the period under consideration. But there are two issues concerning their subsequent development that must be emphasized. First, the consolidation of these activities as modern industries took place in tandem with the expansion of internal demand, a large part of which was induced by the growth of exports. Second, these manufacturing branches found elsewhere a market that was not heavily supplied as in the case of textiles by products from other regions. Since competitive sectors did not exist, the greater potential size of their market could explain, not only the positive evolution of short-term production related to the expansion of the Valencian market, but also the consolidation of medium- and long-term production. The demand, prompted by the expansion of the market in other regions, led to a decrease in average costs and to a relative specialization that was both horizontal and vertical. The latter trends ensured that Valencian production would have a solid position within the national economy. The development concentrated in these sectors promoted greater growth throughout the entire Valencian economy and reflected an efficient entrepreneurial adaptation to a narrow market—a market that was determined by the uniquely Spanish process of capitalist consolidation.

The economic behavior of the social sectors related to these activities was far from inefficient or backward. The limited industrial investment during this long period was not due to an ignorance of the most profitable investments; rather, the contrary was the case. The powerful stimulus of European demand for agricultural products from the mid-nineteenth century on attracted investments to the agrarian sector. Investments were made in activities that provided a maximum rate of return. These included investments in popular crops, infrastructure, and services, as well as sectors of the consumer-goods industry where comparative advantages existed. Within the context of Spanish economic development, the investment strategy of these social groups cannot be considered backward. When compared with entrepreneurs in other regions, their strategy was far more innovative and more economically progressive. Except for the last few years of the 1920s and the first few of the 1930s, these social sectors lacked the political cohesion to form a united front and to pressure both the administration and rival economic groups to recognize their needs. Had they been able to achieve this, perhaps an attempt could have been made to obtain a change in Spain's extremely protectionist tariff policy.[33]

It was not only agriculture and industry that expanded, however. These two dynamic sectors coexisted with a third, which could be called the traditional sector and in which progress and innovative attitudes were either nil or rare. The modernization of agriculture, the sustained increase in exports, the positive evolution of some industrial sectors, the continued flexibility of producers in the face of variations in demand all occurred in an economy in which methods of production had otherwise advanced very little.[34] Labor specialization had not touched large areas of the region; a notorious shortage of capital precluded necessary transformations (usury was still the main practice of financing at the end of the nineteenth century);[35] and the demand for basic subsistence goods continued to occupy a prominent, if not primary position within aggregate demand. It is presently impossible to measure the importance and evolution of this traditional sector within the total agricultural system, just as it is impossible to quantify what part of the agricultural system was transformed by the stimulus of external demand. Nevertheless, the importance of traditional agriculture is obvious. In addition to abundant qualitative evidence, one must also consider that in the mid-1880s cereals continued to be the primary irrigation crop, according to data collected by property registrars.[36] A few years earlier, in 1878, cereals and seeds absorbed 57% of the irrigated area,[37] and almost half a century later, in 1922, cereals continued to the primary irrigation crop at 53.1% (see Table 15.6).[38] In spite of the advances that took place from the mid-nineteenth century to the early 1920s, the economy still devoted a large part of the most productive land to growing subsistence crops to feed the region's population.

This large traditional sector was the hardest hit by the Great Depression at the end of the nineteenth century. The rise of flour and cereal imports brought a drastic decline in prices and restricted the profitability of domestic production.[39] Although the agricultural crisis was less serious in Valencia than in the monocultural cereal areas of the Spanish interior, the previously cited figures certainly illustrate the problems confronting this still important sector of society.

Rural strife, banditry, and large-scale migration in the southern areas of the region are evidence of the deep crisis that confronted the traditional sector during the last decades of the nineteenth century. The turn toward protectionism in the Spanish tariff policy of 1891, which was supported by Valencia's traditional agrarian sector, permitted the latter to maintain profits by eliminating competition. The enormous profit margins of rice cultivation in the 1930s (28.21% in Valencia as opposed to 13% in Tarragona)[40] shows the validity of Ricardian analysis regarding the extension of cultivation to marginal lands, owing to protectionist tariffs. The stability of wheat cultivation on irrigated lands was also rooted in this process of growth through protectionism.

The limitations imposed on competitive growth by the powerful social groups tied to the traditional sector did not provide the only obstacle confronting Valencia's economic evolution. The limited development of the traditional manufacturing sectors, until their disappearance, and the slow rise of demand for products made by the new manufacturers of the late nineteenth century—who from a global perspective carried on almost marginal operations—demonstrate the basic constriction facing Valencian society: insufficient internal demand resulting from an income distribution that discouraged potential growth.

Table 15.6
Crop Distribution on Irrigated Lands, 1922
(hectares)

	Horticultural Products	Fruit Trees	Industrial Products	Bulbs, Roots, and Tubers	Cereals and Legumes	Artificial Products	Provincial Total
Alicante	825	4,254	3,900	1,567	28,184	5,650	52,280
Castellon	1,275	16,892	987	4,001	14,676	1,446	39,625
Valencia	5,648	20,336	8,040	10,107	77,843	13,086	135,217
Total	7,748	41,482	12,927	15,675	120,703	20,182	227,122

SOURCE: Ministerio de Fomento, *Avance estadístico de la producción agrícola en España* (1922).
NOTE: The totals do not coincide with the sum of the crops because there are other crops that are not included in this table.

Most recent research on the transition from an estate-based to a capitalist society in Valencia does not seem very useful for economic analysis; nor does it lead to any conclusions on the distribution of surplus and its uses at the end of the eighteenth century and the beginning of the nineteenth. Still, as landlords clearly drained much of the surplus, they impeded the diversification of demand for the large majority of the population, limiting both labor specialization and development in manufacturing. Increased commercialization, as has been proved, was compatible with an agricultural expansion, under high seignorial pressure.[41] A rise in the volume of agricultural goods entering the market could have left unaltered the ratio between consumption and investment for the majority of direct cultivators. Or it could even have been unfavorable to investment if the population increased simultaneously and if the positive evolution of average incomes was lower than the demographic expansion. Under such circumstances, the increase of per capita income that probably occurred at the end of the eighteenth century did not give rise to further sustained growth.[42]

It was the spectacular increase in external demand from the mid-nineteenth century on that eliminated the bottleneck that had impeded a higher rate in the rise of surplus. Its impact was limited, however, and did not reach all productive sectors of the economy. Low wage levels due to an abundant labor supply in the expanding sectors, low productivity in the traditional sectors, and the dominant groups' unwillingness to accept any reform that might reduce their privileges[43] were the main obstacles to achieving a higher rate of growth and a more balanced distribution of that growth throughout the entire economy.

What happened during the Second Republic seems instructive. During those years, a rise in wages starting in 1931 that was buoyed by the high rate of exports until 1933 (in spite of the global crisis) resulted in the founding of many new companies—a valid indicator of entrepreneurial expectations.[44] That wage increases—if higher than that of productivity—would ultimately curb expansion does not change the coherence of the previous hypothesis. Meanwhile, the worker's increased consumption certainly had an expansive effect on the consumer-goods sector that formed Valencia's weak industrial base. Since high profits were obtained from the majority of crops, it is reasonable to assume that an increase in real wages before the Second Republic would not have obscured the investment opportunities considered profitable by the capitalists. This also would have induced greater growth of demand for manufacturing activities that, with comparative advantages, could have emerged as competitive manufacturing sectors.

NOTES

1. Ernest Lluch's *La via valenciana* (Valencia, 1976) is an exception to this general rule, in that he analyzes industrial growth independently of the notion of failure.

2. The viticultural expansion has been studied by Teresa Carnero, "La Gran Depressió al País Valencià: crisi i frustració social," in *Raons d'identitat del País Valencià* (Valencia, 1977), pp. 99–128 and 116–125, and by Juan Piqueras, *La vid y el vino en el País Valenciano* (Valencia, 1981), esp. pp. 130–157.

3. In spite of its large role, there are no recent studies on the history of the Spanish citrus industry. The two main works continue to be those of Max Linniger Gaumaz, *L'orange d'Espagne sur les marchés européens: Le problème oranger espagnol* (Geneva, 1962), and of Instituto de Economía, *Economía citrícola* (Madrid, 1950).

4. An analysis of this expansion appears in Teresa Carnero, *Expansión vinícola y atraso agrario, 1870–1900* (Madrid, 1980).

5. Ibid., pp. 219–238.

6. Data on the cultivated area are taken from Piqueras, *La vid y el vino*, p. 140.

7. Ramón Garrabou, "La crisi agrària espanyola de finals del segle XIX: una etapa del desenvolupament del capitalisme," *Recerques* 5 (1975): 163–216.

8. Studies on the agrarian geography of various towns in coastal districts provide some valuable information regarding this process. Two general studies on this topic are Antonio López Gómez, "Nuevos riegos en Valencia en el siglo XIX y comienzos de XX," in Jordi Nadal and Gabriel Tortella, eds. *Agricultura, comercio colonial y crecimiento en la España contemporánea* (Barcelona, 1974), pp. 188–205, and "Los regadíos en Valencia, 1919–1936," *Estudios Geográficos* (1969): 112–113, 397–422.

9. David Metcalf, *La economía de la agricultura* (Madrid, 1974), pp. 65–76.

10. The early use of guano in Valencian agriculture was studied by E. Giralt, "Introducción del guano como fertilizante agrícola en el País Valenciano y en Cataluña," in Emili Giralt, ed. *Dos estudios sobre el País Valenciano,* (Valencia, 1978), pp. 33–66. The new fertilizer generated such interest that in 1846 the Real Sociedad had already published Francisco Polo Bernabé's analysis of the agricultural impact of guano. His study revealed that guano was two-thirds cheaper than traditional fertilizers. See Francisco Polo Bernabé y Borras, *Memoria sobre el guano y su aplicación para varias cosechas en el Reino de Valencia* (Valencia, 1846) (Archivo Real Sociedad Económica de Amigos del País Valencia [henceforth abbreviated to RSEAPV], 1846, C-117, I, no. 7).

11. The year 1859 is taken from Giralt, "Introducción." The year 1862 is from *Varios comerciantes se dirigen a S.M. apoyando la propuesta hecha en el Congreso por D. Antonio Aparici y Guijarro, a fin de conseguir la libre adquisición del guano del Perú* (Archivo RSEAPV, 1862, C-152, I, no. 22).

12. This seems to be demonstrated by the attention given to mechanization in California. A title worth mentioning is Rafael Font de Mora, *Comercio de los agrios españoles* (Valencia, 1938).

13. Luis Lucía, *Problemas regionales: Valencia ante la guerra. Lecciones de educación política y económica* (Valencia, 1917), esp. pp. 57–75; José Bellver Mustieles, *La naranja española en el mundo* (Madrid, n.d. [1927?]), pp. 12–20; and, above all, José Bellver Mustieles, *Esbozo de la futura economía valenciana* (Valencia, 1933), pp. 141–198.

14. Some of the works on this subject are: Emérito Bono, "La base exportadora de la economía del País Valenciano y el modelo de crecimiento hacia afuera" (Ph.D. diss., Facultad de Ciencias Económicas y Empresariales de Valencia, 1974), pp. 301–305; Josep Picó, *Empresario e industrialización. El caso valenciano* (Madrid, 1976), pp. 72ff; Vicent Roselló and Emérito Bono, *La Banca al País Valenciano* (Valencia, 1973), pp. 60ff.

15. Picó, *Empresario e industrialización,* p. 73.

16. de Mora, *Comercio de los agrios,* p. 6.

17. An estimate of income distribution at the end of the 1920s can be found in Jordi Palafox, "Estructura de la exportación y distribución de beneficios. La naranja en el País Valenciano, 1920–1936," *Revista de Historia Económica* 1, 2 (1983): 339–351.

18. This last aspect has already been noted by E. Lluch, *La vía valenciana,* p. 139.

19. Clementina Ródenas, *Banca e industrialització: El cas Valencià* (Valencia, 1978), pp. 199–228.

20. Clementina Ródenas has found that in all Valencia in 1919 there were only three banks and fourteen branches, nine of which were located in provincial capitals. In 1926 these figures increased to four central banks and fifty-seven branches, forty-four of which were outside the capitals. See Clementina Ródenas, *La Banca Valenciana: una aproximación histórica* (Valencia, 1982), p. 78. The banking expansion in Valencia was paralleled by an expansion throughout Spain and is discussed in Juan Muñoz, "La expansión bancaria entre 1919 y 1926: la formación de una banca nacional," *Cuadernos Económicos de I.C.E.* 6 (1978): 48–163.

21. Juan A. Tomás Carpi, *La economía valenciana: modelos de interpretación* (Valencia, 1976), pp. 25–26.

22. Clementina Ródenas, "El sistema financer," in *Historia de la economía valenciana* (Valencia, 1983), p. 111.

23. Emérito Bono's study constitutes an exception in this case. Although precise data on his thesis are not available—the work remains unpublished—he apparently portrays the Valencian economy as sharing certain colonial characteristics. For a synthesis of his conclusions see Tomás Carpi, *La economía valenciana,* pp. 82ff. See also Bono's *La Banca,* pp. 9–28. The thesis presented here opposes the models of both economic colonialism and export-oriented growth.

24. Goran Ohlin, "Balanced Economic Growth in History," *American Economic Review* 2 (May 1959): 353.

25. Hla. Myint, "The 'Classical Theory' of International Trade and the Underdeveloped Countries," *Economic Journal* (1958): 317–337, and "Economic Theory and the Underdeveloped Countries," *Journal of Political Economy* (1965): 477–491. Both articles are reproduced in Hla. Myint, *Economic Theory and the Underdeveloped Countries* (London, 1971). A discussion on development theories in less developed nations can be found in Hla. Myint, *The Economics of the Developing Countries,* 5th ed. (London, 1980), chap. 3, pp. 125–141.

26. R. Findley, *Trade and Specialization* (Harmondsworth, England, 1970). Both models are based on the premise that land is an unlimited resource and that labor is an obstacle to growth. In Valencia this assumption is debatable in both the long- and medium-term, since it was land availability and transformation costs that imposed major restraints on production, not the labor supply. As the model demonstrates, however, the positive effects of increased external trade are incontestable.

27. As can be readily deduced, it is not necessary that the production level be

situated on line *PP'* in order to show an increase through a rise in exports; this is represented by the area of the triangle and defined by line *CE*. Unfavorable terms of trade would position point *C* within the area of *PP'*.

28. Rafael Aracil and Mario García Bonafé, "La no industrialización valenciana: algunos problemas," in *La industrialización valenciana: historia y problemas* (Valencia, 1978), pp. 13–14. An analysis of the last district's evolution can be found in Josep María Bernabé Maestre, *Industria i subdesenvolupament al País Valencià: El calçat a la Vall del Vinalopó* (Mallorca, 1975), esp. pp. 59–72.

29. This is not intended to defend the theory that the limited market integration of the late eighteenth century resulted from the absence of an efficient transport system. On the level of market integration for that period, Josep Fontana's study continues to be useful: see "Formación del mercado nacional y toma de conciencia de la burguesía," in *Cambio económico y actitudes políticas en la España contemporánea* (Barcelona, 1973), esp. pp. 17–31.

30. Rafael Aracil and Mario García Bonafé, *La industrialització al País Valencià: el cas d'Alcoi* (Valencia, 1974). For information on the silk crisis see Vicente Martínez Santos, *Cara y cruz de la sedería valenciana, siglo XVIII–XIX* (Valencia, 1981), esp. pp. 220–256.

31. A synthesis of the evolution of Valencian industry can be found in J. A. Martínez Serrano, Vicent Soler, and Ernest Reig, *Evolución de la economía valenciana, 1878–1978* (Valencia, 1978), esp. pp. 31–68.

32. J. Bernabé Maestre, *Industria i subdesenvolupament*, pp. 74–88.

33. I have tried to trace the process by which the agro-export sector became aware of opposing interest groups in the Introduction to Román Perpiñá Grau's *De economía crítica* (Valencia, 1982), pp. 7–57.

34. This is reflected in the late-nineteenth-century memoirs of Manuel Sanz Bremón, *Memoria sobre el estado de la agricultura en la provincia de Valencia* (1875) and *Contestación al interrogatorio publicado por la Dirección General de Agricultura* (1881), (Barcelona, 1979), pp. 211–288.

35. The vast majority of Valencian responses to the inquiry of *La Crisis Agrícola y Pecuaria* would indicate this. The Consejo Provincial de Agricultura, Industria y Comercio de Castellón provided an excellent synthesis of the situation when it published the following statement: "A year of poor harvests is enough to make one resort to a money-lender—something which the 'landowner' would rather do than sell the land with which he identifies in a certain way," *La Crisis Agrícola y Pecuaria,* vol. 3 (Madrid, 1888), p. 526.

36. Dirección General de los Registros Civil y de la Propiedad y del Notariado, *Memorias y estados formados por los registradores de la propiedad en cumplimiento de lo prevenido en el Real Decreto de 31 de agosto de 1886* (Madrid, 1890), vol. 4. A percentile distribution by municipalities of the irrigated area dedicated to cereal production was estimated from these reports and appears in Jordi Palafox and Teresa Carnero, "La economía del País Valenciano, 1750–1936: Crecimiento sin industrialización," *Información Comercial Española* 586 (1982): 21–22, especially p. 28.

37. The data are based on figures presented in Manuel Márquez Pérez, *Historia de la industria, comercio, navegación y agricultura del Reino de Valencia desde la época de D. Jaime hasta nuestros días* (Valencia, 1910), p. 30.

38. Even discounting the area used to grow rice, the percentage of lands used for

growing cereals and vegetables drops only from 53.1% to 39.46%, while that used for fruit trees is 18.26%; the latter figure does not include scattered trees.

39. The impact of the Great Depression on rice cultivation was studied by Teresa Carnero, "Crisi i burgesia conservadora durant la Gran Depressió: El País Valencià, 1879–1889," *Estudis d'Història Agrària*, no. 1 (Barcelona, 1978), pp. 98–113.

40. Estimates are based on data from "Conferencia de D. Manuel de Torres dentro del cursillo de conferencias sobre el problema arrocero," *El Agrario Levantino* 7 (September and November 1933): 13–16, 21–27.

41. Jones and Woolf define the term "static expansion" in relation to an agricultural system whose increases in output are neutralized by increases in population. See E. L. Jones and J. S. Woolf, eds., *Agrarian Change and Economic Development* (London, 1974), pp. 2ff.

42. This thesis is based on the contributions of Pedro Ruiz, *Señores y propietarios: Cambio social en el sur del País Valenciano, 1650–1850* (Valencia, 1981); María Isabel Morant, *Economía y sociedad en un señorío del País Valenciano: El Ducado de Gandi* (Valencia, 1978); and, above all, Manuel Ardit, *Revolución liberal y revuelta campesina* (Barcelona, 1977), esp. pp. 20–32.

43. Although systematic research is lacking on the workers' standard of living, contemporary accounts abound. The replies to question 21 of the inquiry of *La Crisis Agrícola y Pecuaria*; the numerous medical surveys of the late nineteenth and early twentieth centuries; and Marvaud's testimony, *La cuestión social in España, 1910* (Madrid, 1975), p. 195, all concur that the standard of living was low. The most complete information on this topic, although limited to Alcoy, is provided in Manuel Cerdá, *Lucha de clases e industrialización* (Valencia, 1980), chap. 2, pp. 49–78.

44. The capital of Valencian companies in the consumer goods sector as of January 1 of each year during the 1930s is presented in the accompanying table (1929 = 100).

Year	Wood	Textiles, Clothing & Leather	Foodstuffs	General Commerce	General Index
1930	338.0	103.3	119.1	105.0	121.8
1931	338.1	105.2	118.9	112.2	126.6
1932	339.6	117.5	120.9	124.1	132.3
1933	339.6	174.0	129.0	139.5	149.6
1934	339.6	206.7	128.0	160.0	160.5

SOURCE: Cited by J. A. Martínez Serrano, Ernest Reig i Martínez, and Vicent Soler i Marco in "Análisis de la economía valenciana (1886–1972) a través del indicador de la constitución de sociedades," *Panorama Bursátil*, no. 2 (Valencia, 1976), pp. 62–63.

FURTHER READINGS

Aracil, R., and M. García Bonafé. *Industrialització al País Valencià: Alcoi.* Valencia, 1974.

———— et al. "Els estudis d'història agrària al País Valencià." In *Primer Col.loqui d'història agrària,* pp. 79–117. Valencia, 1983.

Ardit, M., et al. "Estructura i crisi del régim senyorial al País Valencià." *L'Espill* 3 (1978): 59–87.

Historia de la economía valenciana. Valencia, 1983.

Lluch, E. *La vía valenciana.* Valencia, 1976.

Martínez Santos, V. *Cara y cruz de la sedería valenciana: Siglos XVIII–XIX.* Valencia, 1981.

———— et al. *Evolución de la economía valenciana, 1878–1978.* Valencia, 1978.

INDEX

Abela, Eduardo, 272
Adaro y Magro, Luis, 217
Agriculture
  in Andalusia, 257–58
  in Castile, 240–50
  cereal agriculture, 67–68
  disentailment and, 47
  role in economic development, 55–59
  in Galicia, 227–34
  grain imports, 67
  output, 48–50
  productivity, 53–54
  protectionism in, 52
Aguado, Alejandro, 214
Alcaide Inchausti, Julio, 42, 82, 99, 114, 139
Allen, Albert C., 197–98
Alonso Alvarez, L., 235
Andalusia
  agriculture, 257–58
  banking system, 262–63
  foreign investment, 259–60
  iron-and-steel industry, 261
  mining industry, 259–61
André, Eloy, 154–55
Anes Alvarez, Gonzalo, 56, 141, 143, 253
Anes, Rafael, 100, 108, 110, 113
Arango, Joaquín, 35
Armengaud, A., 16
Artificial silk industry, in Catalonia, 180
Artola, Miguel, 255
Asturias
  coal mining industry, 213–18
  industrialization of, 213–22
  population distribution, 218–19
Avery, D., 70

Bairoch, P., 139
Bank of Issue Law (1856), 110
Banking industry
  in Andalusia, 262–63
  in Valencia, 277
Banking laws, 109–11
  Bank of Issue Law (1856), 110

Banking Ordinance (1921), 111
  Credit Company Law (1856), 110
  Joint Stock Company Law (1848), 109–10
  Joint Stock Company Law (1869), 110
Banking Ordinance (1921), 111
Barreiro Gil, M. J., 223, 225, 226, 227, 231, 232, 233
Basque Provinces
  British iron-and-steel industry and, 195–200
  industrialization in, 192–94, 200–206
  international market of, 194–206
Bayo, Vicente, 215
Bellver Mustieles, José, 276
Berend, I. T., 129
Bernal, Antonio Miguel, 255, 256
Bernis, Francisco, 157
Berrill, K., 194
Bertrán y Serra, Eusebio, 68–69
Birth and death rates, seasonal cycle in, 23–26
Bloch, G., 84, 86
Block, Maurice, 83
British iron-and-steel industry, Basque Provinces and, 195–200
Broder, Albert, 70, 103

Cachinero Sánchez, Benito, 28
Cafagna, Luciano, 170
Calvo Sotelo, José, 160, 161
Canosa, Ramón, 108
Carbonell, Manuel, 263
Carmona, Xan, 64, 223, 226, 228, 229, 230, 234, 235, 236, 237
Carnero, Teresa, 270, 271
Carr, Raymond, 154, 157, 160
Carreras, Albert, 77
Castile
  agriculture, 240–50
  industrialization in, 242
  viticulture, 246–47
  wool manufacturing, 245–46

291

Catalonia
  artificial silk industry, 180
  construction industry, 179–80
  consumer-goods industry, 176–80
  cotton industry, 177–79
  energy dependence of, 181
  industrial specialization in, 183–85
  industrialization of, 169–90
  labor costs in, 181–82
Cattle-raising industry, in Galicia, 230–33
Celibacy, 27–29
Cereal agriculture, 67–68
Chavarri, Victor, 217
Checkland, J. G., 70
Chemical industry, 65–66, 72–73
Cipolla, Carlo M., 16, 178
Citrus industry, in Valencia, 272–77
Coal mining industry, in Asturias, 213–18
Cockerill, John, 214
Comín, Francisco, 57
Construction industry, in Catalonia, 179–80
Consumer-goods industry, in Catalonia,
  176–80
Contreras, J., 255
Corporativism, in foreign trade, 155–58
Costa, María Teresa, 75
Cotton industry, 64–65, 68–70
  in Catalonia, 177–79
Credit Company Law (1856), 110
Cros, François, 65
Cruz Villalón, Josefina, 258
Cubillo, Leandro, 154

Demographic trends
  birth and death rates, 23–26
  fertility rates, 21–23
  fluctuations, 13–17
  in Galicia, 224–26
  growth rates in historical regions, 18
  industrialization and, 20–21
  marrige patterns, 26–30
  mortality, 25–26
  occupational structure, 34–37
  in provincial capitals, 31–32
  regional variations, 17–21
  urbanization and, 30–34
Desamortización. See Disentailment
Disentailment, 44–47
  agriculture and, 47
  in Galicia, 228–29

landownership and, 45–46
  Madoz law, 44–45
Dopico Gutiérrez del Arroyo, Fausto, 57
Durán y Ventosa, Luís, 154
Duro, Julián, 215
Duro, Pedro, 215, 216

Economic nationalism. *See* Protectionism
Ellison, Thomas, 69
Emigration, from Galicia, 224–26
Engels, Friedrich, 176
Espartero, Baltomero, 44
European marriage pattern, 26–27
Exports. *See* Foreign trade

Feliú de la Peña, N., 173
Fenoaltea, Stefano, 98
Fernández Díez, Gregorio, 154
Ferrer, Joaquín María, 214
Ferrer Vidal, Jose, 182
Fertility rates, 21–23
Fertilizers, 72–73
Financial structure, 107–8
Financial system
  banking laws, 109–11
  growth rate, 117–21
  intermediation levels, 117–21
  issue ratio, 118–21
  money supply, 121–23
  periodization of, 111–12
  structural changes, 112–17
  structure, 107–8
Findley, R., 278
Finn, Michael, 198
First marriage, age at, 29–30
Fish canning, in Galicia, 236–38
Flores de Lemus, Antonio, 153, 158, 231
Fontana, Josep, 83
Foreign investment, in Andalusia, 259–60
Foreign trade
  corporativism, 155–58
  economic change and, 139–45
  imports, 137–38
  patterns, 135–38
  state intervention, 155–58
  tariff protection, 155–58
  terms of trade, 131–34, 144–45
  trends, 130–35
Foros, 227, 230

Frank André, Gunder, 129
Fuentes Quintana, Enrique, 57

Galicia
    agriculture, 227–34
    cattle-raising industry, 230–33
    demographic trends, 224–26
    disentailment in, 228–29
    emigration from, 224–26
    fish canning, 236–38
    industrialization of, 234–38
    linen industry, 234–35
Gámez Amián, María Aurora, 255
Gandarias, Pedro, 217
García Delgado, José Luis, 108
García Fernández, Jesús, 244
García Guijarro, Luis, 270, 272
García Sanz, Angel, 247
García-Baquero, Antonio, 253
Garrabou, Ramón, 57
Gascué, Francisco, 216
Gay, Vicente, 154
Gerschenkron, Alexander, 185, 264
Gil Ibáñez, Santo Luis, 170
Gil, Casimiro, 215
Godoy, Manuel, 27
Goldsmith, Raymond, 107, 118, 119, 120–21, 124
Gómez Mendoza, Antonio, 101, 141, 143, 246
González Azaola, Gregorio, 214
González Portilla, Manuel, 199
Graell, Guillermo, 154
Grain imports, tariff policies on, 67
Gray, A. N., 73
Gual Villabí, Pedro, 158
Guilhou, Numa, 215

Haines, Michael R., 50
Hajnal, John, 26, 27, 29
Harrison, Joseph, 129
Harvey, Charles E., 70, 261
Héran, François, 258
Heredia, Manuel Agustín, 66, 261
Heros, Martin de los, 214
Herr, Richard, 44, 46, 47
Hirschman, A. O., 95–96
Hoffman, W. G., 79, 181

Imports. *See* Foreign trade
Industrial output
    annual index, 75–89
    fluctuations, 80–81
    method, 75–76
    regional variations, 80
    structural change, 79
    trends, 76–78
Industrialization
    in Asturias, 213–22
    in Basque Provinces, 192–94, 200–206
    in Castile, 242
    in Catalonia, 183–85
    chemical industry, 65–66, 72–73
    cotton industry, 64–65, 68–70
    demographic growth and, 20–21
    in Galicia, 234–38
    iron mining industry, 71–72
    mining industry, 70–72
    periodization of, 83–86
Internal market, railroad construction and, 100–102
Iron mining industry, 71–72
Iron-and-steel industry
    in Andalusia, 261
    British, 195–200
Issue ratio, 118–21

Janini, Rafael, 273
Joint Stock Company Law (1848), 109–10
Joint Stock Company Law (1869), 110
Jones, Eric, 264

Kaldor, Nicholas, 128
Keyder, C., 50
Komlos, J., 84
Kravis, I. B., 139, 146

Labor costs, in Catalonia, 181–82
Landes, D. S., 181
Landownership, disentailment and, 45–46
Lee, W. R., 16
Lesoinne, Adolphe, 214
Lewis, W. Arthur, 130, 176, 203, 207, 259
Linen industry, in Galicia, 64, 234–35
Livi Bacci, Massimo, 13, 14, 16, 22, 27, 29
López Bru, Claudio, 217
López Taboada, A. A., 225, 226

Loring Oyarzábal, Jorge, 263
Lucía, Luis, 276
Luis y Yagüe, R., 56

Madariaga, Salvador de, 155
Madoz law, 44–45
Maluquer de Motes, Jordi, 57, 83, 171, 240
Manby, John, 215
Manufacturing industry, in Valencia, 280–81
Maristany, Eduardo de, 97
Marriage patterns, 26–30
    celibacy, 27–29
    European marriage pattern, 26–27
    first marriage, age at, 29–30
    mayorazgo, 27
Martín Aceña, Pablo, 113, 122, 132, 141
Martín, Antonio, 273
Marvaud, Angel, 153
Massó, Cristóbal, 154
Mathias, P., 169
Mayorazgo, 27
Meijide Pardo, Antonio, 223
Membiela y Salgado, Roque, 56
Mendizábal, Juan Alvarez de, 44
Mining industry, 70–72
    in Andalusia, 259–61
Mitchell, B. R., 16, 69, 71, 73, 84, 178
Mon, Alejandro, 215
Money supply, 121–23
Moreno Villena, Pedro, 48
Mori, G., 169
Morilla Critz, José, 255
Mortality, 25–26
Mortara, G., 171
Mulhall, Michael, 82, 99, 143
Muñoz, Fernando, 215
Muñoz, Juan, 108
Myint, Hla., 278
Myrdal, Gunnar, 128, 176

Nadal, Jordi, 15, 56, 83, 85, 97, 98, 103, 129, 143, 259, 261
North, Douglas C., 194
Nurkse, R., 128, 139

O'Brien, Patrick, 50
Occupational structure, 34–37

Ohlin, Goran, 278
Overland transportation, 93–94

Paillette, Adrien, 215
Palafox, Jordi, 108, 161
Panta, Lorenzo del, 16
Paretti, V., 84, 86
Pérez Moreda, Vicente, 55, 56, 244, 256
Periodization
    of financial system, 111–12
    of industrialization, 83–86
Perpiñá, Román, 154, 157, 158
Picó, Josep, 276
Pidal, Pedro José, 215
Piqueras, Juan, 270, 271
Platt, D. C. M., 97
Population distribution, in Asturias, 218–19
Pounds, Norman, 50
Prados de la Escosura, Leandro, 56, 64, 82, 114, 132, 133, 136, 138, 139, 141, 253, 254
Prebisch, Raúl, 128, 207
Primo de Rivera, Miguel, economic policy of, 158–62
Productivity, in agriculture, 53–54
Protectionism, 152–55
    administrative, 155–58
    in agriculture, 52
Provincial capitals, demographic trends in, 31–32

Railroad construction, 97–99
    internal market and, 100–102
Railroad Law (1855), 96, 103
Ramón y Cajal, Santiago, 153
Ranki, G., 129
Regional variations
    in demographic trends, 17–21
    in fertility rates, 22
    in urbanization, 32–33
Reis, Jaime, 57, 258
Revista Nacional de Economía, 153–54
Ringrose, David R., 56, 93
Ríu, Daniel, 154
Ríu, Emilio, 154
Ródenas, Clementina, 277
Roehl, R., 185
Roldán, Santiago, 108